THE ARDEN SHAKESPEARE
GENERAL EDITOR: RICHARD PROUDFOOT

THE WINTER'S TALE

THE ARDEN SHAKESPEARE

THE ARDEN EDITION OF THE
WORKS OF WILLIAM SHAKESPEARE

THE WINTER'S TALE

Edited by
J. H. P. PAFFORD

METHUEN

LONDON and NEW YORK

The general editors of the Arden Shakespeare have been
W. J. Craig (1899–1906), R. H. Case (1909–44),
Una Ellis-Fermor (1946–58), Harold F. Brooks (1952–82),
Harold Jenkins (1958–82) and Brian Morris (1975–82)

Present general editor: Richard Proudfoot

This edition of *The Winter's Tale*, by J. H. P. Pafford,
first published in 1963 by
Methuen & Co. Ltd
11 New Fetter Lane, London EC4P 4EE
Reprinted twice

First published as a University Paperback in 1966
Reprinted ten times
Reprinted 1982

Published in the USA by
Methuen & Co.
in association with Methuen, Inc.
733 Third Avenue, New York, NY 10017

Editorial matter © 1963 Methuen & Co. Ltd

ISBN (hardbound) 0 416 47470 5
ISBN (paperback) 0 416 47670 8

Printed and bound in Great Britain by
Richard Clay (The Chaucer Press), Ltd
Bungay, Suffolk

To
BETTY

CONTENTS

PREFACE

I AM much indebted to the general editors, first to the late Professor Una Ellis-Fermor, and subsequently to Dr Harold Brooks and Professor Harold Jenkins. Professor Ellis-Fermor, who gave wise guidance at the inception of the work, was particularly anxious that the Commentary should be as full as possible. Dr Brooks has given help of the greatest importance at every stage and in all parts of the edition, particularly in the Commentary: if adequate acknowledgement were to be made of his assistance his name would appear on almost every page. Professor Jenkins became a general editor when the work was in an advanced stage but he also has given extensive and invaluable help. I am most grateful to them all. I am also indebted to Professor Kenneth Muir and to the late Sir Walter Greg for commenting on the Introduction, and to many others who have helped, including editors of some of the other volumes in the series, and members of the staff of the University of London Library. My debt to my wife, to whom the edition is dedicated, is, in this as in all things, greater than I could express.

The list of abbreviations on pp. xi–xiii indicates some of the chief works used: others are noted in the Introduction, Commentary, and Appendices. The edition is not based particularly on any previous edition: of the many used, perhaps reference was most frequently made to *Var.*, *Moorman*, and *N.C. Wint.*

J. H. P. P.

London.
8 June 1962.

ABBREVIATIONS

Abbott	E. A. Abbott, *A Shakespearian Grammar*, 1870.
Alexander	*Shakespeare. The Complete Works*, ed. Peter Alexander, 1951.
A.V.	The authorized version of the Bible, 1611.
Baldwin, *Organization*	T. W. Baldwin, *Organization and Personnel of the Shakespearean Company*, 1927.
Bethell, *Wint. ed.*	*The Winter's Tale*, ed. S. L. Bethell (New Clarendon Shakespeare), 1956.
Bethell, *Wint. Study*	S. L. Bethell, *The Winter's Tale; a Study*, 1947.
Cambridge	Ed. of Shakespeare (W. G. Clark and W. A. Wright), 1863.
Capell	Ed. of Shakespeare, 1767.
Chambers, *Eliz. Stage*	E. K. Chambers, *The Elizabethan Stage*, 4 vols., 1923.
Chambers, *Shakespeare*	E. K. Chambers, *William Shakespeare*, 2 vols., 1930.
Charlton, *Comedy*	H. B. Charlton, *Shakespearian Comedy*, 3rd edn, 1945.
Charlton, *Tragedy*	Charlton, *Shakespearian Tragedy*, 1948.
Charlton, *Wint.*	*The Winter's Tale*, ed. Charlton, 1916.
Comm.	Commentary to the text in the present edition.
Cym. Nosworthy	*Cymbeline*, (New) Arden, ed. J. M. Nosworthy, 1955.
Daniel	P. A. Daniel, 'Time-analysis of the Plots of Shakespere's Plays' (*Trans. N. Sh. S.*, 1877–9, 117–346).
Dyce	Ed. of Shakespeare, 1857.
Evans, *Language*	Sir (B.) Ifor Evans, *The Language of Shakespeare's Plays*, 2nd ed., 1959.
F	The first folio edition of Shakespeare's plays, 1623.
Gerard	John Gerard, *The Herball*, 1597.
Greene, Grosart	R. Greene, *The Life and Complete Works in Prose and Verse*, ed. A. B. Grosart, 15 vols., 1881–6.
Greene, Collins	*The Plays and Poems*, ed. J. C. Collins, 2 vols., 1905.
Greene, *Coosnage*, 1591	*A Notable Discovery of Coosnage*, 1591. *The Second Part of Conny-catching*. 1592. (ed. G. B. Harrison, Bodley Head Quartos I, 1923.)
Greene, *Second Cony-Catching*, 1592	*Ibid.*
Greene, *Third Cony-Catching*, 1592	*The Thirde and Last Part of Conny-catching*, 1592. *A Dispvtation betweene a Hee Conny-catcher and a Shee Conny-catcher*, 1592. (ed. G. B. Harrison, Bodley Head Quartos III, 1923.)

xi

Greene, *He and She Cony-Catcher*, 1592	*Ibid.*
Greene, *Pandosto, Thomas*	*Greene's 'Pandosto' . . . being the Original of Shakespeare's 'Winter's Tale' newly edited by P. G. Thomas*, 1907.
Greg, *First Folio*	W. W. Greg, *The Shakespeare First Folio*, 1955.
Grose	F. Grose, *A Classical Dictionary of the Vulgar Tongue* [1796], ed. E. Partridge, 1931.
Hanmer	Ed. of Shakespeare, 1743.
Harman	Thos. Harman, *Caveat . . . for . . . Cursetors*, 1567 (in *The Rogues and Vagabonds of Shakespeare's Youth*, ed. E. Viles and F. J. Furnivall, 1880, which contains other 'rogue' literature). Harman and other similar books are also in *The Elizabethan Underworld*, ed. A. V. Judges, 1930.
J.E.G.P.	*Journal of English and Germanic Philology.*
Knight	Ed. of Shakespeare, 1840.
Kökeritz	H. Kökeritz, *Shakespeare's Pronunciation*, 1953.
Leavis, *Scrutiny*	F. R. Leavis, 'The criticism of Shakespeare's late plays: a caveat' (*Scrutiny*, x, April 1942, 339–45).
Malone	Ed. of Shakespeare, 1790.
Malone Soc.	Malone Society Reprint.
M.L.N.	*Modern Language Notes.*
M.L.R.	*Modern Language Review.*
Moorman	*The Winter's Tale*, (Old) Arden, ed. F. W. Moorman, 1912 . . . 1933.
N.C.	(The New Cambridge Shakespeare.) Ed. for the Cam. Univ. Press by Sir A. T. Quiller Couch and J. Dover Wilson. Hence *N.C. Wint.* = *The Winter's Tale*, 1931.
N. & Q.	*Notes and Queries.*
Noble, *Biblical Knowledge*	Richmond Noble, *Shakespeare's Biblical Knowledge*, 1935.
Noble, *Song*	——, *Shakespeare's use of Song*, 1923.
O.E.D.	*The Oxford English Dictionary . . . a corrected re-issue . . . of A New English Dictionary*, 13 vols., 1933.
Onions	C. T. Onions, *A Shakespeare Glossary*, 1919.
Ovid	*Shakespeare's Ovid being Arthur Golding's Translation of the Metamorphoses* [1567], ed. W. H. D. Rouse (De La More Press Folios III), 1904, and Centaur Press, 1961.
Phil. Q.	*Philological Quarterly.*
Pope	Ed. of Shakespeare, 1723–5.
Rann	Ed. of Shakespeare, 1787.
R.E.S.	*Review of English Studies.*
Rowe (1)	Ed. of Shakespeare 1709; (2) 2nd ed., 1709; (3) ed. of 1714.
Schmidt	A. Schmidt, *Shakespeare-Lexicon*, 2 vols., 1923.
S.D.	Stage direction(s).
Sh.	Shakespeare. [Abbreviations for Shakespeare's plays and poems follow Onions, p. x.]

Sh.Eng.	*Shakespeare's England*, 2 vols., 1916.
Sh.Jhb.	*Shakespeare-Jahrbuch.*
Sh.Q.	*Shakespeare Quarterly.*
Sh.Sur.	*Shakespeare Survey.*
S.T.C.	A. W. Pollard and G. R. Redgrave, *A Short-title Catalogue of books printed . . . 1475–1640*, 1926.
Sisson	C. J. Sisson, *New Readings in Shakespeare*, 2 vols., 1956.
Sutherland, *Language*	James R. Sutherland, 'The Language of the Last Plays'. *In* J. Garrett, *More Talking of Shakespeare*, 1959, 144–58.
Tannenbaum, Textual notes	S. A. Tannenbaum, 'Textual . . . notes on *The Winter's Tale*' (*Phil. Q.*, vii, 1928, 358–67).
Theobald	Ed. of Shakespeare, 1733.
Tilley	M. P. Tilley, *A Dictionary of the Proverbs in England in the Sixteenth and Seventeenth Centuries*, 1950.
Tillyard, *Last plays*	E. M. W. Tillyard, *Shakespeare's Last Plays*, 1938.
T.L.S.	*Times Literary Supplement.*
Tp. Kermode	*The Tempest*, (New) Arden, ed. F. Kermode, 1954.
Trans.N.Sh.S.	*Transactions of the New Shakespeare Society.*
Traversi, *Approach*	D. A. Traversi, *An Approach to Shakespeare*, 1938, 2nd ed., 1956.
Var.	A New Variorum Ed. of Shakespeare, ed. H. H. Furness, xi, *The Winter's Tale*, 1898.
Walker	W. S. Walker, *A Critical Examination of the Text of Shakespeare*, 3 vols., 1860.
Warburton	Ed. of Shakespeare, 1747.
Wolff	S. L. Wolff, *The Greek Romances in Elizabethan Prose Fiction*, 1912.
Wright	J. Wright, *The English Dialect Dictionary*, 1898–1905.

INTRODUCTION

I. THE TEXT

The only text having authority is that of the First Folio of 1623 (here subsequently referred to as F). This is the earliest text known and all others derive from it. In all probability no quarto was ever printed.[1] The present text is therefore taken from that in F, of which it is, in conformity with the Arden practice, a conservative modernization.[2]

I. THE PRINTING

Any note on the printing of F and the copy which may have been used must open with the warning that these subjects are being intensively studied and that new conclusions may be reached before this introduction (finished in 1961) appears.[3]

The Winter's Tale was apparently printed after some change of plan. It comes at the end of the Comedies, after *Twelfth Night*, but that play ends on the front of a leaf and the back is blank. This is odd because in the comedies several plays have ended on a recto but in each case the next play has begun on the verso: there are no blank pages.[4] It therefore seems that when *Twelfth Night* was

1. The only known reference to an ed. before 1623 is in *The British Theatre*, Dublin, 1750, 16, where a list (by W. R. Chetwood) of Shakespeare's published plays has, as item 29, '*A Winter Nighte Tale*, an Excellente Comedie, 1606'. Malone, in *An Inquiry*, 1796, 350, dismissed many of Chetwood's entries—including this—as fictitious.

2. The facsimile of the F text of *Wint.* ed. by J. Dover Wilson (Faber, 1929) has been used, but points have been checked with *Var.*, the Clarendon Press facs. of 1902 ed. by Sir Sydney Lee, and the Durning-Lawrence and Sterling copies of F in the Univ. of London Library.

3. The chief work used is Greg, *First Folio*, 1955. This refers to studies by A. W. Pollard, E. E. Willoughby, Alice Walker, C. Hinman, P. Williams, and others. Indications of later research are given in F. Bowers, *Textual and Literary Criticism*, 1959. Yet there is little danger in speaking of the F text as if there were no variants, for Hinman, while confirming that there are many, shows that few are important (*Sh.Q.*, July 1953, 279–88, and *Six variant Readings in the First Folio*, Univ. of Kansas Libraries, 1961): he has told me that none are important for *Wint.* His forthcoming *The Printing of the First Folio* will give details.

4. F is a folio made up in sixes, i.e. each gathering consists of three sheets placed

finished the compositor either thought that he had come to the end
of the Comedies section or knew that the copy for *The Winter's Tale*
was not available.

Study of the wear of the type (chiefly by E. E. Willoughby[1]), of
the break in an ornament, known as the satyr ornament, which is
found at the end of twenty-four out of the thirty plays (chiefly by
Greg and Hinman[2]), and of the marginal vertical rules (chiefly by
J. W. Shroeder[3]) seems to prove that at the end, or rather before
the end, of printing *Twelfth Night*, the printers went on to *King
John* and came back to *The Winter's Tale*—and perhaps to finish
Twelfth Night—at some later stage, probably some time after
printing *Richard II*, which follows *King John*. Not only was there
this break in the order of printing but there was also an interval
when the printer Jaggard stopped work on *F* in order to print
A. Vincent's *Discovery of Errors*, 1622, and there may well have been
other breaks in the printing of *F*. Greg tentatively suggests that *The
Winter's Tale* was printed in the latter part of November 1622 and
the whole book finished early in December 1623.[4]

The Winter's Tale is first recorded in the Stationers' Register in
the entry of 8 November 1623 for those plays in *F*—sixteen in all—
'as are not formerly entred to other men'.[5] In 1790, when he was
preparing his edition of Shakespeare, Edmund Malone copied an
entry from the Office Book of Sir Henry Herbert, Master of the
Revels. The book was then in bad condition and is now lost.[6] The
entry, according to Malone, read:

> For the king's players. An olde playe called *Winters Tale*,
> formerly allowed of by Sir George Bucke, and likewyse by mee
> on Mr. Hemmings his worde that there was nothing prophane
> added or reformed, thogh the allowed booke was missinge; and
> therefore I returned itt without a fee, this 19 of August, 1623.

As the date of this licence is presumably nine months after the
play had been printed, Herbert may have seen sheets of the printed

---

one inside the other (see p. xviii, n.2). Until the end of *Tw.N.* the signatures, after
the preliminaries, run evenly in sixes from A to Z, *Tw.N.* ending on Z6r, p. 275.
Z6v is blank and *Wint.* begins with signature Aa, p. 277, ending on Cc2r, p. 303.
Cc2v is blank and unnumbered. The signatures of *Wint.* are normal, i.e. Aa
would be expected after Z, but the blank page at Z6v is abnormal: *Wint.* should
have begun on Z6v. *Wint.* is followed by *John*, the first of the Histories: this begins
with signature a, which is further confirmation of a break in the printing.

1. *The Printing of the First Folio*, 1932.
2. Greg, *First Folio*, 1955; Hinman, *Sh.Q.*, Winter 1956, 100–1.
3. *The Great Folio of 1623*, 1956.   4. *First Folio*, 461.
5. Further evidence that no quarto had been printed.
6. Malone, I. ii. 226; Chambers, *Shakespeare*, ii. 347.

text. It has also been suggested that the old allowed book had been used for the printing and destroyed when that was finished. This is doubted by Dover Wilson (and apparently by Greg) since he believes that the character of the text is such that it could not have been printed from an allowed book.[1] This is disputable since the text of an allowed book might conceivably be a literary transcript; but the point is that Herbert, whose remark is the only recorded mention of the loss of any copy of the text, is speaking some months after it had presumably been printed—he is apparently licensing, or rather, re-licensing, the play for acting[2]—and his words may accordingly have no bearing at all on the apparent delay in printing *The Winter's Tale*.[3] The allowed book may have been lost after the play was printed or as far back as 1619 after the last recorded performance, since the copy for the printed text was certainly not the prompt book.

The apparent oddity about the printing of *The Winter's Tale* could be explained in ways other than by supposing a lost text. There may, for instance, have been doubt as to where the play should go in *F*. *Cymbeline* is placed with the Tragedies, coming at the end of the book. It may be there in error but it is there, and perhaps *The Winter's Tale*, by error or design, was classed with it[4] and re-classed as a comedy in November 1622,[5] and this may explain the peculiarities in the printing of the play.[6] There is little doubt that *The Winter's Tale* was set up by at least two compositors, usually referred to as *A* and *B*, helped, perhaps, by an apprentice[7] called *E*. This can be shown by peculiarities of spelling and other matters. So, for example, on some pages *do* and *go* are always, or almost always, spelt in that way, whereas on others they are usually spelt *doe* and *goe*. These peculiarities were first discussed for *The*

1. *N.C.Wint.*, 112.; Greg, *First Folio*, 415–17.

2. It is, however, possible that the delay was because *Wint.* was not licensed for printing, and even if sheets had been pulled before 19 August 1623, Herbert's licence may be to legalize the printing. The licence of the Master of the Revels seems to have been accepted as authority for printing (Greg, *Some Aspects . . . of London Publishing*, 1956, 103–12, and E. Schwartz in *Sh.Q.*, Aut. 1961, 467–8).

3. Cf. Greg, *First Folio*, 439, n.1.

4. Suggested by J. O. Halliwell in his ed. of Shakespeare (viii, 1859, 46).

5. *Troil.* is called a comedy in the quarto ed. but is a tragedy in *F*.

6. Such a change would be even more satisfactorily explained by postulating an earlier version of the play which was a tragedy—which followed *Pandosto*. It would then be necessary to assume that two vitally different versions existed from some date before April 1616 to 1622. But this is very unlikely. If *Wint.* was, originally, to have been last in *F*, Crane (see p. xviii) may, after all, have been commissioned to produce the text 'on Pollard's principle that the editors placed their best-finished wares in the most prominent positions' (Greg, *First Folio*, 415, n.3).   7. "E"'s contribution is very doubtful.

Winter's Tale by Alice Walker.[1] There is little difference in the quality of the compositors' work but in this play *A* is the more competent of the two.[2]

II. THE COPY

Greg believes that *The Winter's Tale* was printed from an edited transcript made by the scrivener Ralph Crane, possibly from Shakespeare's foul papers.[3] Crane, although apparently not an official member of Shakespeare's company, the King's men, is known to have worked for them[4] and transcripts in his hand exist of several plays.[5] From peculiarities in the use of brackets, apostrophes, hyphens, punctuation, and other matters which are found in these manuscripts and also in certain plays in *F* it is believed that the texts of at least five plays[6] in *F* were printed from transcripts made by Crane.

1. *Textual Problems*, 8–11. The compositors' idiosyncrasies in punctuation are set out by D. F. McKenzie in 'Sh. Punctuation' (*R.E.S.*, Nov. 1959, 361–70).

2. Fuller information on the compositors' work in *Wint.* is in *N. & Q.*, May 1961, 172–8. The pages were set by the compositors almost certainly—except for 293—as shown in the following table. *Page* means the page number in *F* and *A.S.L.* (Act, Scene, Line) means the last line of the *F* page according to line numeration in the present ed. The first gathering of *Wint.* is of 277–88 and the next of 289–300 followed by three odd pages. The conjoint leaves in the first gathering are therefore 277–8 with 287–8, 279–80 with 285–6, 281–2 with 283–4:

Page	A.S.L.	Compositor	Page	A.S.L.	Compositor	Page	A.S.L.	Compositor
277	I. ii. 43	A	286	III. ii. 78	A	295	IV. iv. 546	A
278	I. ii. 153	A	287	III. ii. 200	A	296	IV. iv. 660	A
279	I. ii. 272	A	288	III. iii. 72	B	297	IV. iv. 795	A
280	I. ii. 388	A	289	IV. ii. 22	B	298	V. i. 62	A
281	II. i. 28	A	290	IV. iii. 89	B	299	V. i. 170	A
282	II. i. 142	A	291	IV. iv. 77	B	300	V. ii. 50	A
283	II. ii. 51	B	292	IV. iv. 192	B	301	V. iii. 2	A
284	II. iii. 83	B	293	IV. iv. 327	?B or E	302	V. iii. 110	A
285	II. iii. 199	A	294	IV. IV. 435	B	303	V. iii. 155	B

3. *First Folio*, 415–17, 427.

4. On Crane see F. P. Wilson, 'Ralph Crane, Scrivener to the Kings players' (*Library*, Sept. 1926, 194–215); T. Middleton, *A Game at Chesse*, ed. R. C. Bald, 1929, 27–43; Sir Walter Greg, 'Some Notes on Crane's Manuscript of The Witch' (*Library*, March 1942, 208–22); Middleton, *The Witch*, ed. Greg and Wilson (Malone Soc.), 1950, xiv–xv; J. Fletcher, *Demetrius and Enanthe*, ed. M. M. Cook and Wilson (Malone Soc.), 1951, ix–xi.

5. Including Fletcher's *Demetrius and Enanthe*, Fletcher and Massinger's *Tragedy of Sir John van Olden Barnavelt*, Jonson's *Pleasure Reconciled to Virtue*, Middleton's *Game at Chesse* (three versions), and *The Witch*.

6. *Tp.*, *Gent.*, *Wiv.*, *Meas.*, *Wint.*, and perhaps *2H4* (cf. *N.C.* ed., 116) and part of *Tim.* (New Arden ed., p. xix).

Some of the chief characteristics of Crane's transcripts as summarized by Wilson and Greg are: (1) They are clear and accurate, their punctuation is rather fussy but good, they make lavish use of brackets, hyphens, and apostrophes and some rather peculiar uses of these last. (2) The transcripts are all carefully divided into acts and scenes and in one the names of the characters are massed at the heading for each scene and not usually shown at the point where they actually come in. (3) The stage directions are few and seem to be rather of a literary than theatrical kind.

The Winter's Tale has every appearance of having been printed from a manuscript of just this sort—except that its few stage directions are no more literary than they are theatrical. Its cleanness shows that the compositors had an easily legible text before them. The punctuation is good, there is an extensive use of brackets, hyphens, and apostrophes and some peculiar uses of the apostrophe. The play is carefully divided into acts and scenes, massed entries are used, and there are only forty-three stage directions.[1]

It is therefore probable that *The Winter's Tale* was printed from a transcript made by Crane from a text of good authority. The use of colons after characters' names in scene headings and stage directions which is found in *The Winter's Tale* was a practice of the bookkeeper Edward Knight[2] and offers very slender evidence that he may have revised Crane's transcript for printing in *F*. This in turn may slightly strengthen the case that Knight was the virtual editor of *F*.[3]

Since the *F* text has no sign of having been through the playhouse it is argued that Crane's source was also not a playhouse text. But this does not necessarily follow. Crane was a skilled transcriber and most of his surviving transcripts—all of those mentioned on p. xviii, n.5 except *Barnavelt*—are for private reading, not for the stage; and it is not unreasonable to suppose that sometimes he had to work from prompt copies. That may also have been the case with *The Winter's Tale* and he may have been practised at turning a playhouse text into a literary form. But it is also possible that he had Shakespeare's foul papers or a good transcript of them before him. It has been suggested that he was using a text assembled from players' parts, but the theory is not now widely held.[4] There can

1. For more details see *N. & Q.*, May 1961, 172–8.

2. Cf. his transcripts of *Bonduca* and the *Honest Man's Fortune*.

3. Greg, *First Folio*, 78–9.

4. *N.C. Wint.*, 109–27. The theory in general is put forward by R. C. Rhodes, *Sh. First Folio*, 1923, and Dover Wilson, 'The Task of Heming and Condell' (*Studies in the First Folio, Sh. Assoc.*, 1924). It is attacked by Greg (chiefly in *First Folio*), Chambers (in *Shakespeare*), and R. C. Bald (in ed. of Middleton's *Game at*

be no certainty about the nature of Crane's immediate source except that it was a very good text.

III. THIS EDITION

As with all the Arden texts the punctuation, use of capitals, and spellings have been modernized.[1] Act and scene divisions present no problem, for *The Winter's Tale* is one of the few texts in *F* which are carefully divided and, although these divisions—particularly into acts[2]—probably have no Shakespearian or playhouse authority, no alteration is necessary.

Some alteration with stage directions[3] is, however, unavoidable. Apart from the headings of the fifteen scenes there are only forty-three stage directions in *F*. All the characters appearing in thirteen scenes are massed in the headings to these scenes: in five all the characters do in fact appear at the opening of the scene but in the other eight they do not, and alterations must be made. The *F* directions within the scenes are fairly adequate for entries and exits, and on the whole these are clear from the text even when no directions are given, so that there is little difficulty in inserting them. Few other directions have been added and no indications of place are given. All additions to the *F* text are enclosed in square brackets and indicated in the Collations. The Collations give all unadopted readings from *F* and indicate all readings adopted from later sources, but unadopted readings from later sources, including *F2–4*, are not mentioned unless the adopted version also does not seem wholly satisfactory. There is no attempt to give a general selection of the many alternative readings which have been suggested—not even of those made since the Furness Variorum edition of 1898. In the Commentary references are given chiefly to the other last plays[4] and many references are by indication only: the actual quotation is printed only where it might immediately illuminate something in the play.

Chesse, 1929, 37–43, and in *The Library*, Sept. 1931, 243–8). Possible errors which might have arisen from assembly are at I. ii. 148, IV. iv. 68–70, v. i. 12, v. i. 75, III. ii. 10, but Prof. Dover Wilson tells me (1962) that he would not now support the theory.

1. On peculiarities in the compositors' work see references in notes 1 and 2 on p. xviii.

2. That Shakespeare's plays were originally written without act divisions and performed without act pauses is the opinion of H. L. Snuggs (*Sh. and Five Acts*, 1960, 117).

3. On S.D. and scene headings in *F* see *N. & Q.*, May 1961, 172–8. This also lists printers' errors, which are not recorded in this ed.

4. *Per., Cym., Tp., H8*. And, naturally, references have come more from these plays than from others.

Unless otherwise specified, references to other plays of Shakespeare are to *The Complete Works* edited by P. Alexander. References are frequently given only to the first or to the key line, not to the whole passage. Abbreviations of titles of Shakespeare's plays are those used by Onions, *A Shakespeare Glossary*, x.

2. DATE AND AUTHORSHIP

I. DATE

The most important evidence concerning the date is the note by Simon Forman that he had seen the play at the Globe on Wednesday, 15 May 1611. This is contained in a manuscript in the Bodleian[1] which includes seven leaves headed *The Bocke of Plaies and Notes thereof per formans for Common Pollicie.*

Forman was a notorious quack doctor and astrologer and it is presumed that these memoranda are for his general guidance to be prudent in the affairs of life. He notes performances of four plays he had seen in 1611—*Richard II* (not Shakespeare's play), *Cymbeline*, *Macbeth*, and *The Winter's Tale*—giving a short account of each and, except for *Cymbeline*, the date on which and the theatre (the Globe) at which he had seen them. The entry on ff. 201v and 202r reads:[2]

In the Winters Talle at the glob 1611 the 15 of maye ☿[3]
Obserue ther howe Lyontes the kinge of Cicillia was overcom wt Jelosy of his wife with the kinge of Bohemia his frind that came to see him. and howe he Contriued his death and wold haue had his cup berer to haue poisoned. who gaue the king of bohemia warning therof & fled with him to bohemia / Remēber also howe he sent to the Orakell of appollo & the Aunswer of apollo. that she was giltles. and that the king was Jelouse &c and howe Except the Child was found Again that was loste the kinge should die wthout yssue. for the Child was caried into bohemia & ther laid in a forrest & brought vp by a sheppard[4] And the kinge of bohemiā his sonn maried that wentch & howe they fled into Cicillia to Leontes . and the sheppard hauing showed the letter of the nobleman by whom Leontes sent a was[5] that child

1. Ashmole, 208, ff. 200–13. The notes were first printed by J. P. Collier in *New Particulars regarding the Works of Sh.*, 1836. An easily accessible modern printing is by E. K. Chambers in *Shakespeare*, ii. 337–41. The notes have been condemned as a Collier forgery but they are genuine. Further details and references to the dispute are in *R.E.S.*, Aug. 1959, 289–91.

2. The transcript is made from the manuscript.

3. This sign is the symbol for Mercury and therefore for Wednesday. 15 May 1611 was a Wednesday.

4. *sheppard*] this is the last word on f. 201v.

5. *a was*] away *or perhaps* it was.

and the Jewells found about her. she was knowen to be Leontes
daughter and was then 16 yers old

Remember also the Rog that cam in all tottered like coll pixci/.[1]
and howe he feyned him sicke & to haue bin Robbed of all that
he had and howe he cosoned the por man of all his money. and
after cam to the shep sher with a pedlers packe & ther cosoned
them Again of all their money And howe he changed apparrell
w^t the kinge of bomia his sonn . and then howe he turned
Courtiar &c / beware of trustinge feined beggars or fawninge
fellouss

This proves that the play was written before 15 May 1611. The
earlier limit of date cannot be fixed with equal certainty, but there
is reason to suppose that it was written after 1 January 1611, the
date of the first performance at Court of Jonson's *Masque of Oberon*
in which there is a dance of ten or twelve satyrs. In *The Winter's
Tale* there is a dance of twelve satyrs and the servant announcing
them says, 'One three of them, by their own report sir, hath danced
before the king' (IV. iv. 337–8). Although this does not necessarily
refer to anything outside the world of the play, it may be a topical
allusion to the performance of the masque.[2] There is even a theory
that Shakespeare's Company had a monopoly of masque dancers
which co-operated regularly with Jonson in his work.[3] It has been
argued that the dance is an integral part of the masque but rather
like an addition to the play and so the play could have been written
before the masque and the dance inserted later. But the argument
is unconvincing, for the dance is an integral part of the play, coming
in naturally and appropriately. When W. Sorell says that 'Dances
in Shakespearian plays come necessarily out of the plot, are carefully planned and prepared for' he mentions the satyrs' dance in
The Winter's Tale.[4]

Such other signs as there are fit well with a date early in 1611.
Herbert's statement[5] that *The Winter's Tale* had been formerly
licensed by Sir George Buck is of little value for dating the play
because, although Buck officially succeeded Edmund Tilney on

1. *coll pixci*] Colle- or Colt-pixie = hobgoblin, particularly in the form of a
ragged (tattered) colt which leads horses astray into bogs, etc. (*O.E.D.*). Cf.
'to colt me thus' = 'to lead me astray' (*1H4*, II. ii. 36).

2. This evidence was first put forward by A. H. Thorndike in *P.M.L.A.* xv,
1900, pp. 114–20, and repeated in his *Influence of Beaumont and Fletcher on Sh.*, 1901.
The suggestion seems eminently plausible, although not to J. C. Maxwell (*N.C.
Cym.* xi–xii), who would place *Wint.* after *Cym.* but in 1609–10. Cf. *Wint.* IV. iv.
132n.

3. W. J. Lawrence, 'The date of "The Duchess of Malfi"', *Athenaeum*, 21 Nov.
1919, 1235–6.

4. 'Sh. and the Dance' (*Sh.Q.*, Summer 1957, 380).   5. See p. xvi.

20 August 1610, it is known that during Tilney's illness Buck acted for him and was licensing plays from 1606 onwards. But the language, style, and spirit of the play all point to a late date. The tangled speech, the packed sentences, speeches which begin and end in the middle of a line, and the high percentage of light and weak endings are all marks of Shakespeare's writing at the end of his career.[1] But of more importance than verse tests is the similarity of the last plays in spirit and themes.[2] *The Winter's Tale* is beyond doubt one of the group which also includes *Pericles*, *Cymbeline*, *The Tempest*, and *Henry VIII*, and practically all authorities now consider that these are very late plays and accept, with minor variations, the approximate dates given by Chambers.[3] The nature and use of the songs also provide strong evidence for a late date. In tracing the sequence of Shakespeare's songs R. Noble says that the songs of *The Winter's Tale* are essentially of Shakespeare's last period, and the view is also held by J. M. Nosworthy.[4]

Shakespeare may have begun to write *The Winter's Tale* before the end of 1610 but may not have started it until after the performance of *Oberon* on 1 January 1611: in any case he had certainly finished the play in time for it to be performed on 15 May 1611.

There are records of other performances and possible allusions to the play in Shakespeare's lifetime. In 1842 P. Cunningham published documents[5] containing an entry for the year ended 31 October 1612, 'The Kings players: The 5th of nouember A play Called ye winters nightes Tayle'; and Jonson's gibes (perhaps in 1612) at dramatists who keep no unity of time or place, and in 1614 at those who 'beget *Tales*' may refer to *The Winter's Tale*.[6] The play

---

1. On metrical and other verse tests see Chambers, *Shakespeare*, ii. 397–408. Further details are given in G. König, *Der Vers in Shakespeares Dramen*, 1888, 134 and by F. G. Fleay and J. K. Ingram, both in the *Trans. (Publications) of the New Sh. Soc.*, 1874.

2. See pp. xliv–l.

3. *Per.* (1608–9), *Cym.* (1609–10), *Wint.* (1610–11), *Tp.* (1611–12), *H8* (1612–13), in *Shakespeare*, i. 271; cf. *Sh.Sur.* iii, 1950, 30. One or two critics have hazarded opinions on earlier dates, e.g. J. Hunter, *A Disquisition on the Tempest*, 1839, 72, and *New Illustrations of Sh.*, 1845, i. 416 (*Wint.* not later than 1602. Hunter cites Chalmers and Malone in support, but Malone subsequently changed to the generally accepted 1611); Janet Spens, *Elizabethan Drama*, 1922, 92, and F. Mathew, *An Image of Sh.*, 1922, 41, suggest a first version of *Wint.* written before 1600 and revised 1611.

4. 'Music and its function in the Romances of Sh.' (*Sh.Sur.* xi, 1958, 60–9).

5. *Extracts from the Accounts of the Revels at Court* (Sh. Soc.), 210. The authenticity of this has been challenged but was established by A. E. Stamp in *The Disputed Revels Accounts reproduced in Collotype Facsimile* (Sh. Assoc.), 1930. (Plate XIII).

6. *Every Man in his Humour*, Prol. 7–9, 15, and *Bart. Fair*, Induction, 130.

was acted again at about the time of the wedding of the Princess Elizabeth on 14 February 1613, for on 20 May 1613 John Hemmings was paid for fourteen plays, including *The Winter's Tale*, which had been performed during the wedding festivities.[1]

II. INTEGRITY

Just as there is no real challenge to the 1610–11 period for the date of composition, so there has been no serious suggestion that the play is not by Shakespeare, although, of course, it has been said for this, as for all Shakespeare's plays, that others had a hand in its composition. Pope was perhaps the first to express doubts:

> If I may judge from all the distinguishing marks of his style, and his manner of thinking and writing, I make no doubt to declare that those wretched plays, *Pericles, Locrine, Sir John Oldcastle . . .* cannot be admitted as his. And I should conjecture of some of the others, (particularly *Love's Labour Lost, The Winter's Tale*, and *Titus Andronicus*) that only some characters, single scenes, or perhaps a few particular passages, were of his hand.[2]

Many since have thought *The Winter's Tale* a poor play but few have considered that any major part of it is not by Shakespeare. In the present century J. M. Robertson, R. Flatter, and T. A. Dunn have seen the hands of Chapman, Fletcher, and Massinger respectively in the play, but none has given reasons which are at all convincing.[3] Then there is the school of thought which believes in disintegration throughout Shakespeare and particularly that members of his Company may have been responsible for odd lines or even scenes.[4] But this is all guesswork. Certainly no one can say that actors may not have suggested odd lines or even scenes, but no one must underestimate Shakespeare's skill in varying his style to accord with special situations and characters[5] and in writing doggerel when it was required. There are no convincing arguments that any part of *The Winter's Tale* is not by Shakespeare.

III. EVIDENCE FOR EARLIER VERSIONS

It has been noted that no text is known earlier than 1623 either of the play or any version of it.[6] One or two critics have guessed

1. Chambers, *Shakespeare*, ii. 343.

2. *Works of Sh. . . . ed. Pope*, 1723–5, I. xx.

3. Robertson, *The Genius of Sh.*, 1930, 132–6; Flatter, *T.L.S.*, 4 Apr. 1952, 237, and *Sh.: neu übersetzt von R. Flatter*, 1954, iv. 489–90; Dunn, *Philip Massinger*, 1957, 269, n.5.

4. E.g. Baldwin, *Organization*, 303. See also Dover Wilson in *N.C. Wint.*, 127.

5. Cf. H. Craig, 'Sh.'s Bad Poetry', *Sh.Sur.* i, 1948, 51–6.

6. See p. xv, n.1. There are also entries in the Stationers' Registers for 22 May

that there was an early version which Shakespeare revised in 1611 but their suppositions carry no conviction.[1] The suggestion that Herbert's reference to a missing allowed book may be to a play different from the one before him has no foundation and is rightly refuted by Greg.[2] It has been said that the appearance of Hermione's spirit to Antigonus is proof that when the play was first written Hermione did actually die, as in *Pandosto*, because in Shakespeare's day it would not have been thought possible to see the spirit of a living person.[3] But this is not so: Donne describes his vision of his wife in February 1612, he being in Paris and she, alive, in London,[4] and Romeo dreams that he sees Juliet come and find him dead (*Rom.*, v. i. 6). Donne's wife appeared rather like a spirit but he did not assume that she was dead and Antigonus need not have assumed that Hermione was dead, but Shakespeare wished both to strengthen the audience in their belief that she was dead and to give Antigonus a reason for landing the babe in Bohemia.[5] There is nothing in the dream of Antigonus to indicate that there was ever a version of the play in which Hermione actually died. There is indeed no evidence for this of any kind[6]: Hermione's survival is certainly the most drastic and fundamental of the changes from *Pandosto*; but the play seems based on her survival, and with reconciliation so obviously in Shakespeare's mind the change seems one which must naturally and inevitably have been made.

Other reasons which are sometimes advanced for suspecting that the play has been altered from an earlier version are that Leontes' jealousy comes on too suddenly, that Paulina's reconciliation with Leontes in III. ii is too sudden, that Autolycus does not fit into the play properly, that the recognition scene (v. ii) should have been shown and not recounted, and that Simon Forman makes no reference to the statue scene. Much of this could simply be discounted as due to mistaken standards of consistency or taste in the propounders, but counter-arguments can easily be offered.

Many believe that Leontes' jealousy is indicated before I. ii. 108

1594 and 29 June 1624 for Edward White of a 'booke entituled a Wynters nightes pastime' (Arber, *Transcript of the Registers*, 1875, ii. 307b; 1877, iv. 82). No copy is known. 'Night' is in the title of the play performed on 5 Nov. 1612 (see p. xxiii), and was used by Chetwood (see p. xv, n.1).

1. See p. xxiii, n.3. There is little evidence even of current re-drafting. There is a doubtful verse-fossil at IV. iv. 162–7.

2. *T.L.S.*, 25 Apr. 1952, 281.

3. J. E. Bullard and W. M. Fox, letter in *T.L.S.*, 14 Mar. 1952, 189.

4. I. Walton, *Lives of John Donne*, etc., Saintsbury, 1927, 40. The episode first appeared in the 1675 ed. (*v.* Oxf. Bib. Soc. ii, 1930, 337).

5. Antigonus assumes that Hermione was found guilty and executed and hence Polixenes is the babe's father. Cf. p. lix, n.4.   6. But cf. p. xvii, n. 6.

and is not unrealistically sudden.[1] But even those who hold it to be unduly sudden must agree that Shakespeare is full of sudden-nesses[2]: things have to happen quickly on the stage where the whole traffic is ended in two hours or so. The Elizabethans were used to suddenness in the drama; and when Shakespeare wrote his plays, which cover much time and space, some developments had to be abrupt. Greene, although he says that Pandosto's jealousy is cause-less, does give some cause, but he brings it about as quickly as Shakespeare does: the difference is that in Greene it is undramatic while in Shakespeare it is dramatic and startling. This demand for speed can also explain Paulina's reconciliation with Leontes at the end of III. ii, though there are slight signs of hurried composition or alteration in this scene.[3] Yet even if the text were altered it can hardly now be known whether the original version ever got beyond the author's desk. It is, at the end of III. ii, impossible to see when or by whom the plan to conceal Hermione could have been made, but this is merely extra-theatrical matter which cannot trouble an audience. Autolycus is to some extent developed from Capnio in *Pandosto* and influences the action exactly as Capnio does. It is true that Autolycus is a vivid character who has little to do with the plot, but he has something to do with it and much to do with the spirit of the play in which he is organic. The fact that he had been Florizel's servant but that there is no recognition when they meet (IV. iv. 625) is purely conventional. On the recognition scene there are many views: perhaps the most loudly voiced is that the episode should have been shown and that in its present form it is one of the weakest parts of the play,[4] but some editors, critics, and actors

1. *N.C. Wint.*, 131, and N. Coghill in *Sh.Sur.* xi, 1958, 31–3. Cf. pp. lvi–lviii.

2. E.g. Lear's sudden decision to abdicate and sudden fury at Goneril (I. iv. 252ff.); Claudio's immediate willingness to believe Don John (*Ado*, III. ii. 110); Malcolm's and Donalbain's immediate suspicion of Macbeth (II. iii. 119); the fallings in love in *Tw.N.*, and Sir Toby's marriage to Maria; Duke Frederick's sudden murderous hatred for Rosalind in *ATL.* and decision to banish her; the sudden love of Proteus for Silvia and sudden forgiveness of Proteus by Valentine and Julia (*Gent.*, II. iv. 190, v. iv. 78, 116); and many others.

3. There is at least one loose end (III. ii. 189n.; and cf. v. iii. 126n.). This is the only scene (except for omission of reference to the babe in II. iii) where entrances of characters are not fully recorded. Paulina enters twice but there is no record of her entry or of that of the Messenger. But although Paulina's *volte-face* is a little strange it is not un-Shakespearian and suddenness here and with Leontes (cf. pp. lvi–lviii) can be paralleled in *Oth.* and elsewhere (cf. *N.C. Oth.*, xlvii–l). These matters may also be seen as examples of Shakespeare's fascination 'by the very difficulty of making the psychologically improbable . . . appear possible' and it must be remembered that 'ideas about what is psychologically possible change from age to age' (*Mac.*, New Arden, ed. Muir, lv).

4. E.g. *N.C. Wint.*, xxiii.

hold that it had to be recounted.[1] At all events nothing about the scene indicates a changed version of the play. That Forman does not mention the statue scene is no argument that he did not see it. His notes were for 'common pollicie'. He was recording things which could be useful to him: one third of his notice is devoted to the roguery of Autolycus and the lesson to be learnt.

The only conclusion to be drawn is that there is no evidence for an earlier version of the play.

3. SOURCES[2]

The main source is Greene's *Pandosto*.[3] Shakespeare read widely, as is shown particularly by his vocabulary, and there are echoes of a little of his reading in the play: he even made some slight deliberate use of a few books other than *Pandosto*; but as sources for *The Winter's Tale* all these put together are insignificant in importance compared with Greene's romance. Shakespeare took *Pandosto* and worked at it carefully,[4] quarrying material from it for a play just as he had worked with Lodge's *Rosalynde*, Plutarch, Holinshed, and other sources.

I. PANDOSTO

Greene's prose romance was apparently first published in 1588. In modern spelling its title reads:

> Pandosto. The Triumph of Time. Wherein is discovered by a pleasant History, that although by the means of sinister fortune Truth may be concealed, yet by Time, in spite of fortune, it is most manifestly revealed. Pleasant for age to avoid drowsy thoughts, profitable for youth to eschew other wanton pastimes, and bringing both to a desired content. *Temporis filia veritas*. By Robert Greene, Master of Arts in Cambridge. *Omne tulit punctum qui miscuit utile dulci*.

The title reveals something of the author's purpose but it is a typical Greene title.[5] The running title—'The history of Dorastus

1. E.g. A. J. F. Collins ed. of *Wint.* (Tutorial Sh.), xix–xx; G. G. Gervinus, *Sh. Commentaries*, 6 ed., 1903, 815; Sir John Gielgud (privately to the editor). See also pp. lxi–lxii, lxxxviii.

2. For sources of characters' names see pp. 163–5.

3. A text is given on pp. 181–225.

4. It is coming to be seen with what care Shakespeare used his sources. Cf. *N.C.Rom.*, xi, *N.C.Cæs.*, xiii–xix, and R. A. Foakes in *H8* (New Arden ed.), xxxv. But see p. xxx, n. 1.

5. *Omne tulit* is from Horace, *Ars Poetica*: 'He has won every vote who has blended profit and pleasure, at once delighting and instructing the reader' (Loeb ed., ll. 343–4). It was a common motto of the day and a favourite with Greene, who uses it at the end of *Friar Bacon and Friar Bungay*, in *Greene's Vision*

and Fawnia'—became the main title in most of the seventeenth-century editions. There were editions in 1592, 1595, 1607, and 1614, and at least thirteen more later in the century.[1] In the editions before 1607 the Oracle says 'the king shall live without an heir' and so does the play,[2] but all editions from 1607 onwards say 'the king shall die without an heir'. It is therefore probable that Shakespeare was here copying from an edition before that of 1607.[3]

The text, given on pp. 181–225, has frequently been reprinted.[4] Most editions of *The Winter's Tale* summarize the romance and compare it with the play, and this has also been done by K. Muir.[5] A comparison may be opened with parallel lists of characters:

Pandosto   *The Winter's Tale*

1. *Corresponding characters*

Pandosto	*The Winter's Tale*
Pandosto, King of Bohemia	Leontes, King of Sicilia
Bellaria, Queen of Bohemia	Hermione, Queen of Sicilia
Garinter, their son	Mamillius, their son
Fawnia, their daughter	Perdita, their daughter
Egistus, King of Sicilia	Polixenes, King of Bohemia
Dorastus, his son	Florizel, his son
Franion, Cup-bearer to Pandosto	Camillo, Adviser to Leontes and Cup-bearer to Polixenes (also partly derived from Capnio)
Porrus, an old shepherd, reputed father of Fawnia	Old shepherd, reputed father of Perdita
Gaoler	Gaoler
Capnio, servant to Dorastus	[Autolycus, as the former servant to Florizel] [See also Camillo]

(Grosart, xii. 224) and in the titles of at least nine of his works besides *Pandosto*. He was also fond of *Temporis Filia Veritas* and in most of his titles claims that his work is for young and old and for pleasure and profit.

1. There were also abridged, chap-book, and ballad versions (see J. O. Halliwell's ed. of Shakespeare, viii, 1859, 3–5). The first version printed and discussed as a Shakespeare source is apparently that given by Charlotte Lennox in her *Sh. Illustrated*, 1753, ii. 1–87.

2. III. ii. 135. And the sense 'live' is confirmed by Paulina at v. i. 38–40.

3. Particularly so since it seems rather more natural to say 'die' here than 'live'. Forman reported 'die' and the actor may well have said 'die'. The wording of the play often follows that of the romance so closely that Shakespeare was at times almost certainly copying from the latter (see p. xxx) just as he copied from sources in other plays (cf. p. xxvii, n.4; *Tim.*, ed. H. J. Oliver, New Arden, v. iv. 70–3; and *N.C.Cæs.*, xvii).

4. Collier, *Sh.'s Library*, i, 1843 (2nd ed. iv, 1875); J. O. Halliwell ed. of Shakespeare, 1859, viii. 8–36; ed. by P. G. Thomas, 1907; ed. by J. Winny in *The Descent of Euphues*, 1957. Nearly complete texts are in *Var.* and in the ed. of *Wint.* by Henry Morley published by Cassell. A text will be given by G. Bullough in a later volume of *Narrative and Dramatic Sources of Sh.* (i–iv, 1957–62).

5. *Sh.'s Sources*, i, 1957, 240–51, 253–4, 257.

2. *Characters without correspondence*

———	Paulina (has very slight correspondence with Gaoler of *Pandosto*)
———	Antigonus
Mopsa, wife to Porrus	———
———	Emilia, Hermione's attendant
———	Clown, the Old Shepherd's son
———	Autolycus, as the singing rogue [But see Capnio above]
———	Mopsa & Dorcas, Shepherdesses
———	Lords, Gentlemen, Ladies, Servants, Shepherds, Shepherdesses, Satyrs
———	Time, the chorus.

It will be seen that the play enriches the story by adding characters and using all those in the original except one. The king and queen of Bohemia become monarchs of Sicilia and Greene's king of Sicilia becomes king of Bohemia. Accordingly, events which take place in Sicilia in Greene occur in Bohemia in Shakespeare and vice versa, and so the famous Arcadian scene leaves the traditional Arcadia of Sicily for Bohemia.

For the rest, Shakespeare followed the story closely except in two vitally important incidents. Whereas in the romance Bellaria dies after her trial and Pandosto commits suicide at the end of the story, in *The Winter's Tale* Hermione is preserved and finally she, Leontes, and Perdita are reunited and reconciled. In Greene it is Bellaria who asks that the Oracle be consulted but in the play this is Leontes' own idea (although Hermione appeals to the Oracle at III. ii. 115).

The one character in *Pandosto* not used by Shakespeare is Mopsa the Shepherd's wife: she is the typical shrewish but shrewd peasant wife of folklore who is ready to belabour her good man with tongue or cudgel but equally quick to see which side her bread is buttered. Although not prominent she has at least as much life as anyone in *Pandosto*, but Shakespeare chose only to use her name for a shepherdess.

Camillo is a much stronger and more prominent character than Franion and is also partly derived from Capnio: Porrus is not much developed by Shakespeare, but in Autolycus Shakespeare creates a character very different from Capnio. The latter serves his prince; Autolycus says that he once served Florizel (IV. iii. 13–14) and takes a chance to do so again (IV. iv. 833–43) but only for his own ends. Yet his one part in the plot is exactly the same as Capnio's— he prevents the shepherd telling the king the truth about Perdita, and enables the lovers to elope. Autolycus is mainly Shakespeare's invention but is to some extent built from Capnio with the aid of coney-catching rogues Greene had described elsewhere. The idea of softening the king by a sight of the babe is developed from the action of the gaoler in Greene who tells the king of the expected birth; but Greene has no Paulina. Greene has nothing like the curiously impressive brief description of the Oracle in III. i. Antigonus and his dream have no counterpart in Greene. The shepherd is not much more substantial in Shakespeare than he is in Greene. The sheep-shearing scene in IV. iv is developed from a hint in *Pandosto* that there was a meeting of farmers' daughters and Fawnia was mistress of the feast. Fawnia has a little more character than most of the personages in Greene but she lacks Perdita's magic beauty. The preliminary wooing of Fawnia by Dorastus, long-drawn-out and tedious in Greene, is omitted by Shakespeare; the two are already sworn lovers when they first appear. The visit of Polixenes and Camillo disguised to the sheep-shearing is Shakespeare's invention. In Greene it is Dorastus, helped by Capnio, who plans the elopement and the lovers reach Bohemia by chance: in Shakespeare Camillo organizes the voyage to Sicilia. But the most striking difference is in the dénouement. The recognition of Fawnia/Perdita is told in Greene almost as effectively as it is recounted in the play, but in Greene, after festival games, the marriage of the lovers and the suicide of Pandosto, the story fades out in an ambiguous conclusion where it is not clear whether Fawnia has died.

Comparison of the romance with the play will show how closely Shakespeare used his source. 'There are more verbal echoes from *Pandosto* than from any other novel used by Shakespeare as a source'.[1] To see how close the sense and phrasing often are, comparison at least of the following passages[2] should be made:

Pandosto	*The Winter's Tale*
191, 14–15	II. iii. 4–6, 20–1
193, 14–15	II. iii. 154–5
193, 19–20	II. iii. 178–82
194, 28–33	III. ii. 12–21
195, 1–3	III. ii. 54–7

1. K. Muir, *Sh.'s Sources*, i. 247. The close verbal parallels have long been noted, e.g. by W. Harvey in his ed. of Shakespeare, 1825, xx. Shakespeare's plays are, of course, something utterly different from their sources however carefully these may have been used. He does not simply 'turn' *Rosalynde* or *Pandosto* into a play.

2. References to *Pandosto* are to the text in App. IV. Some of the many other references to corresponding parts of the play are given in that text.

Pandosto	*The Winter's Tale*
195, 11–13	III. ii. 109–14
196, 23–8	III. ii. 132–6
197, 17–32	III. ii. 28–33, 45–8, 73–6, 115
199, 30–3	III. iii. 65–8
202, 13–15	IV. iv. 1–3
210, 34–5	IV. iv. 25–30
215, 13–15	IV. iv. 761–4
221, 28–9	IV. iv. 576–8

To anyone reading romance and play consecutively, or even comparing the above passages, the picture is inescapable of a Shakespeare who, having closely studied the story and made his plot, had
Pandosto at his elbow as he wrote, and as he wrote from time to time
turned to the book to refresh his memory, using it sometimes almost
verbatim, sometimes with little change, and sometimes with much,
and sometimes departing from it altogether, but finding there the
constant source for most of his material.

Apart from the tedious self-communings of Pandosto, Bellaria,
Fawnia, and Dorastus, Greene's story is told with artistic economy
—'by its speed, economy and clarity it achieves admirably what it
sets out to do. The lively eventfulness of the story alone would
assure it a hearing',[1] and it is rather surprising that Greene did not
make a play of it.

Since he is turning a story into a play Shakespeare naturally
concentrates on action, cutting out monologues and descriptions.
He gives life to characters and does everything possible to give
credibility to the plot. His greatest technical difficulty was to indicate the passage of time and to show something of its effect. Both
can be done more neatly, with more even development, in a
romance than in a single play—it is rather different with the English historical plays—and the former is perhaps more convincingly
done, to a reader of both works, in *Pandosto* than in *The Winter's
Tale*. But neither problem causes difficulty on the stage[2] and the
effect of the passage of time is more convincing in *The Winter's Tale*
than it is in *Pandosto* or even than it is in the other last plays where
it is important—in *Pericles* and in *Henry VIII*.

In *Pandosto* there is no pronounced break in the story or change
in its atmosphere. When the scene shifts from one country to
another there is no need of Father Time, for Greene skilfully and
economically shows the child growing up: on one page (201) it is
said that the babe has learned to speak, that she has become seven
years of age, then ten, and then sixteen. This simple account of the

1. J. Winny, *The Descent of Euphues*, 1957, xvii–xxi.   2. Cf. pp. lii, lx.

passage of time was not possible in the play. A faint indication of comedy coming into *Pandosto* may be seen in Mopsa the Shepherd's wife. But there is no happiness in the first part of *Pandosto* whereas *The Winter's Tale* has the two happy episodes of Hermione persuading Polixenes and of Mamillius.

Greene gives important clues to the chief moral of his story—that time will tell—in his title and in the opening paragraph on jealousy.[1] He makes Pandosto's jealousy understandable and he does so with economy for he leads up to its outbreak as quickly as Shakespeare does—in about 120 lines of prose where Shakespeare uses about 150 lines of verse and prose.

Greene's title announces that Time is to triumph over evil chance and bring truth to light. The evil is that of jealousy, but truth will out, given time. All this is to be shown in a pleasant tale that will at any rate keep youth out of mischief and old men awake. Pandosto is killed at the end just 'to close up the comedy with a tragical stratagem' but no doubt also to give moral satisfaction to young and old in showing that justice is done. The kingdoms and persons long estranged by his crime are re-united[2] in friendship but his jealousy has caused death and he must suffer: his spiteful distrust must bring bloody revenge.[3] Even so, in the pleasant history, his death jars and does indeed seem to have been caused simply for a 'stratagem'. At Garinter's death Pandosto thinks that Apollo has made a mistake and has taken vengeance on the wrong person. Shakespeare expands this hint, and in the death of Mamillius Leontes sees that Apollo has taken vengeance on him, on Leontes himself.

1. In the Epistle Dedicatory Greene says simply: 'So I present unto your honour the triumph of time' and does not refer to his book by any other title. Authors of the day—Greene among them—liked to refer to their works as showing the results of time. *Menaphon* also claims to decipher 'the triumphs of inconstant Time' and to show that virtue will triumph 'maugre the wrath of Envy, or the resolution of Fortune'. The themes of Fortune and Time occur constantly in Greene's prose writings, which are analysed by Wolff (367–458).

2. This reconciliation, so important also in *Wint.*, is emphasized in *Pandosto*, p. 224, ll. 29–31.

3. For Greene as for Raleigh confession and penitence are not enough and violence must be punished: 'the bloud that is vniustly spilt, is not againe gathered vp from the ground by repentance' (*Hist. of the World*, 1614, B3). And for Shakespeare too 'Time's glory' is not only 'to calm contending kings, / To unmask falsehood, and bring truth to light' but also 'To wrong the wronger till he render right' (*Lucr.*, 938–43). But Leontes is not guilty of blood. Greene shows in his *Mirror for Modesty* (1584) 'how the Lord . . . plagueth the bloudthirsty hypocrites with deserved punishments' but Shakespeare clears Leontes of any death by intention. Nevertheless freedom from blood guilt, or even intention of it, does not always save. In *Per.* Cleon suffers, but is far less guilty than Leontes.

In Greene the treatment of jealousy is very short and the story soon moves to Dorastus and Fawnia, which is its main part. Shakespeare, however, makes the story of Leontes' jealousy a large part —about half—of the play.

In *Pandosto* it is indeed Time which achieves results. That is to say there is little in the characters which shows the working of strength, loyalty, self-sacrifice, love, or other virtue. Although Pandosto is 'furiously incensed by causeless jealousy' some cause is shown for his suspicion; nevertheless the jealousy and its results in Greene are mechanical whereas in Shakespeare the passion is human and evil. *Pandosto* is a rather pedestrian story with some grace but without jollity and happiness, without the vigour, beauty, and humanity of *The Winter's Tale* and the authority which comes from 'a mature and practised philosophy'.[1] At the same time it would be unjust to Greene to compare his story with the play. If it is said that *Pandosto* is undramatic, it must also be said that it is not a play; it is a prose romance in style somewhat in the tradition of *Euphues* but with more life and charm than there is either in Lyly's work or in Greene's own Euphuistic stories of *Mamillia*.

II. MINOR SOURCES

Shakespeare may have read the four known works of Francis Sabie—none of which has been edited since the sixteenth century— and particularly *The Fissher-mans Tale*, 1595 and *Flora's Fortune. The second part and finishing of the Fisher-mans Tale*, 1595. These were based on Greene's *Pandosto*[2] but E. A. J. Honigmann[3] believes that Shakespeare had read them because a very few parallels in *The Winter's Tale* seem slightly more like Sabie than Greene.[4]

1. J. F. Danby, *Poets on Fortune's Hill*, 1952, 48.

2. M. Dorothy Maudsley, *The Use of Latin Sources in . . . Francis Sabie* (Chicago Univ. thesis), 1936, 43.

3. Secondary sources of *Wint.* (*Phil.Q.* xxxiv, Jan. 1955, 27–38).

4. E.g. IV. iv. 26–7, 30, 'taken . . . shapes of beasts . . . humble swain'. The words *take, shape, swain* occur in the corresponding passage in Sabie (1 *F. T.*, sig. C4) but are not in the corresponding passage in *Pandosto* (p. 210). The dream of Antigonus and the storm are not in *Pandosto* but there is a dream in Sabie and the distracted mother has similarities in appearance and speech with Hermione in the dream of Antigonus. Another minor coincidence is that in *Pandosto* six messengers go to the Oracle but two in Sabie and in *Wint.* Honigmann also suggests, but on slender evidence, that Shakespeare may have used the French version of *Amadis de Gaule* for the names Florizel and Perdita, 'la Perduë', 'la bella Perdida' in the original *Amadis*, and perhaps for the episode of a statue brought to life. Honigmann notes that the Proserpine myth is treated by Bacon in *De Sapientia Veterum*, 1609 (116–22 Proserpina sive Epintus) and that Claudian's *Rape of Proserpine*, 1617, was translated by Leonard Digges, who may have been known to Shakespeare.

Many have noted Shakespeare's indebtedness to Ovid's *Meta-morphoses*, which he knew well, probably in Latin as well as in Golding's translation.[1] One relationship is in the story of the rape of Proserpine:

> While in this garden *Proserpine* was taking hir pastime,
> In gathering eyther Violets blew, or Lillies white as Lime . . .
> *Dis* spide hir: lovde hir: caught hir up: and all at once well
> neere . . .
> The Ladie with a wailing voyce afright did often call . . .
> By chaunce she let her lap slip downe, and out the flowres went.[2]

Another is in Autolycus[3] and yet another is in the story of the ivory statue of a woman made by Pygmalion and at Pygmalion's prayer given life by Venus, from which Shakespeare probably took the idea of Hermione as a statue.[4] But in the revealing of the statue there are several striking parallels with the *Alcestis*.[5]

Shakespeare almost certainly used Greene's Cony-catching Pamphlets[6] and may have known Harman and some of the other rogue literature. No doubt the tricks of London rogues were common topics of conversation and were also well known from literature going back at least to the account of sharpers in Ascham's *Toxophilus*, 1545; but Shakespeare's descriptions seem so close to Greene's that they are probably drawn from him. Greene's pamphlets tell many tales of how 'every shop, church, session, hanging, yields a careful man work'. He gives accounts of pickpockets attracting crowds by singing ballads[7] and describes in detail the trick by which a rogue pretends to be ill and picks the pocket of the

1. Early in his dramatic career Shakespeare shows his knowledge of the *Meta-morphoses* (*Tit.*, IV. i. 42ff.).

2. *Ovid*, v. 491–500 (p. 111). Cf. *Wint.*, IV. iv. 116–18.   3. See p. 165.

4. A. R. Fairchild, *Sh. and the Arts of Design* (Univ. of Missouri Studies, xii, 1, Jan. 1937). The passage is *Metam.* ll. 247–97 (Loeb), 265–324 (Golding, ed. Rowse, 1904, pp. 206–7). Shakespeare may also have known Lyly's *Woman in the Moon* or La Caze's *L'Incest Supposé*. The Pygmalion story was well known and was used before in Shakespeare's day, e.g. J. Marston, *The Metamorphosis of Pig-malions Image*, 1598, and in Pettie's *Petite Pallace of Pleasure*, 1576; 1608. For reference to Chettle's *Patient Grissil* see p. lxiii, n.4.

5. Esp. ll. 1121–50 (Loeb). Although apparently no English version, there were several editions in Latin before 1611. The parallels were noted by I. Gollancz in his ed. of *Wint.*, 1894. There is a possible hint for Hermione's self-sacrifice in Pettie's conclusion to his version of the *Alcestis*: 'This seemeth strange unto you, Gentlewomen, that a woman should die and then live again, but the meaning of it is this, that you should die to yourselves and live to your husbands' (*Petite Pallace of Pleasure*, 1576; 1608. Ed. Gollancz, 1908, 1, 196, or H. Hartman, 1938, 145).

6. Especially *Second Cony-Catching*. Cf. IV. iii. 76, 99; IV. iv. 258–9nn.

7. *Third Cony-Catching*, 27.

good Samaritan who comes to his aid: 'one of the crue . . . went to the farmer and walkt directly before him and . . . cried alas honest man helpe me, I am not well, & with that sunck downe suddenly in a sown, the pore Farmer seeing a proper yong Gentleman (as hee thought) fall dead afore him, stept to him, helde him in his armes, rubd him & chaft him . . . the whilest the Foiste drewe the farmers purse and away'.[1] This is close enough to Autolycus's trick (iv. iii. 50–80), and Shakespeare may have had the passage in mind. The name *Mamillius* (and perhaps other things) may have come from Greene's *Mamillia*. *Greene's Vision*, 1592, almost certainly by Greene, contains accounts of jealousy and may have been known to Shakespeare. The extent of Shakespeare's knowledge and use of Greene has not been fully explored. Resemblance between the plots of *The Winter's Tale* and *The Thracian Wonder* has been noticed[2] and whoever wrote that play probably took the plot from Greene's prose romance *Menaphon*, 1589. *Menaphon* refers to Apollo's oracle at Delphos and so does *The Thracian Wonder* (ii. i end, iii. i. 1, 6), which also introduces Time in the Chorus (i. iii). Its resemblance to Greene's own play *Orlando Furioso* is noted by O. L. Hatcher,[3] who considers that *The Thracian Wonder* was written between 1600 and 1610 although not printed until 1661.

It can hardly be by chance that so many names in the play come from Plutarch, and it is a reasonable assumption that Shakespeare used North and glanced through the stories, at any rate of Camillus and of Agis and Cleomenes, choosing names for his characters.[4] Perhaps a little of Merrythought from *The Knight of the Burning Pestle*[5] was at the back of Shakespeare's mind when he was creating Autolycus.[6] He certainly knew the popular comedy *Mucedorus*, which includes a jealousy theme, which shows Segasto and Amedine chased by a bear, and which has the line 'My mind is grafted on an humbler stock.'[7] That *The Pedlers Prophecie*, 1595 (by Robert Wilson), may have contributed to Autolycus was noted in the *New Shakespeare Society's Trans.*, 1877–9. Pt. i, 108,[8] and Shake-

1. *Second Cony-Catching*, 41.

2. E.g. J. Marks, *English Pastoral Drama*, 1908, 49 (where the resemblance is exaggerated).

3. *M.L.N.*, xxiii, Jan. 1908, 16–20.   4. See pp. 163–5.

5. *The Faithful Shepherdess* and probably *Philaster* and *The Maid's Tragedy* also preceded *Wint.*

6. See p. lxxx, n.7.

7. *Muc.*, i. i. 48; *Wint.*, iv. iv. 93. J. M. Nosworthy holds that Shakespeare took a few suggestions from *Muc.* for *Wint.* and *Tp.* (*Cym.*, New Arden ed., 1955, xxv).

8. *The Pedlers Prophecie*, D3r–v (Brit. Museum copy):

    Ped. Conyskins maydes, conyskins for old pastes,

        What lacke you, what buy you, any good pinnes, . . .

speare may have known the pedlar's song in Mundy's *The Downfall of Robert, Earl of Huntingdon*, 1601.[1] But these pedlar, cony-skin songs were popular (cf. Gerrard's song in Fletcher's *Beggar's Bush*, III. i. 101–18, not earlier than 1615), and could be read or heard in many places. No doubt echoes from contemporary prose romances can be found in all the last plays. One example is Emanuel Forde's *Parismus: the Renowned Prince of Bohemia*,[2] which, although not a source, may have made some contribution to *The Winter's Tale* and these other plays, although it may itself merely be another work indebted to Greene. There is also slight evidence that Shakespeare may have made some direct use of Angel Day's version of *Daphnis and Chloe* (1587), which is one of the sources of *Pandosto*.[3]

Some of the extensive literature on Shakespeare's reading refers to *The Winter's Tale*,[4] and echoes from many books which would be known to an educated person of Shakespeare's day are found in the play,[5] which also contains echoes from his own writings. The

---

Of wares for each of you, I have a very great heape . . .

Ped. And it will please you to help to sing a ballet before you go,
    I wil teach you cunningly to make the water.

Arti[ficer]. I know the Pedler can sing pleasantly,
    Both upon the booke, and also without.

Tra.[veller]. I will sing, seeing he desireth me so instantly,
    But to sing by heart, to agree I stand in doubt.

Ped. Behold I have ballet books here,
    Truly pricked, with your rests, and where you shall come in.

Mar[iner]. Then we foure wil make an honest quere,
    I will follow, if the Pedler will begin.

                    Hic can[tant].

1. See *Wint.*, IV. iv. 220n.

2. Part 1, 1598 (repr. 1608), Part 2, 1599 (repr. 1609). It contains accounts of attempted murder by a jealous lover, storms, shipwrecks, life in caves and on a desert island. In Part 1, Sig. F1r, Parismus, seeking a lost hawk, is captured by outlaws and thereby saved from murder. On R2v is the passage, 'The King of Bohemia had not sailed above two daies space, in great hope soone to recouer the Coaste of *Bohemia*.' In the epistle dedicatory (A3r) Forde says, 'I . . . have presumed to present your Honour with this Fancie, intituled *Honours Triumphe*.' The work is not so entitled but the words could also be applied to *Wint*. Perhaps Forde, like Shakespeare, used *Pandosto*: the dedications in *Pandosto* and *Parismus* both mention that Apollo gives oracles to rich and poor and that Philip of Macedon accepted grapes from a peasant.

3. See p. lxv.

4. E.g. Selma Guttmann, *The Foreign Sources of Sh.'s Works*, 1947 (a bibliography); Percy Simpson, *Studies in Elizabethan Drama*, 1955 (for Latin sources. See also reviews in *R.E.S.*, 1956, 424–7, and *T.L.S.*, 6 May 1955, 237); V. K. Whitaker, *Sh.'s Use of Learning*, 1953; A. Thaler, 'Sh. and Spenser' (*Sh. Ass. Bull.*, 1935, 192–211).

5. E.g. *The Bible*, *A Mirror for Magistrates*, Sidney's *Arcadia*, Spenser's poems, Puttenham's *Arte of English Poesie*, Florio's Montaigne, Bacon's *Essays*, and Sylvester's trans. of Du Bartas's *Divine Weeks*.

influence of the Greek romances on Elizabethan writers has had extended discussion,[1] and E. C. Pettet has analysed four other streams feeding the romantic literature of about 1600, although, as he points out, it is unnecessary to explore these streams in detail because they are epitomized in Spenser's poetry and Sidney's *Arcadia*[2]: certainly Greene was indebted to these, as well as to *Euphues*. But it is obviously wrong to hunt too closely for minor 'sources' in the work of such a mind as Shakespeare's.[3] In its pastoral elements Shakespeare's creative power transcends tradition and sources. Greg has commented[4] on what happens

> whenever a great creative artist adopts . . . and takes into his work any merely outward and formal convention. It was rarely that in his plays Shakespeare showed any inclination to connect himself even remotely with pastoral tradition. *The Two Gentlemen of Verona* traces its origin, indeed, to the *Diana* of Montemayor; but all vestige of pastoral colouring has vanished. . . A more apparent element of pastoral found its way many years later into *The Winter's Tale*; but it is characteristic of the shepherd scenes of that play, written in the full maturity of Shakespeare's genius, that, in spite of their origin in Greene's romance of *Pandosto*, they owe nothing of their treatment to pastoral tradition, nothing to convention, nothing to aught save life as it mirrored itself in the magic glass of the poet's imagination. They represent solely the idealisation of Shakespeare's own observation, and in spite of the marvellous and subtle glamour of golden sunlight that overspreads the whole, we may yet recognize in them the consummation towards which many sketches of natural man and woman, as he found them in the English fields and lanes, seem in a less certain and conscious manner to be striving in plays of an earlier date.

This is wise and sensitive comment not only on Shakespeare's use of tradition and sources and on the pastoral element in *The Winter's Tale* but on the realism and on the wonder of the whole play.

4. THE LAST PLAYS

I. SURVEY OF CRITICISM

Pericles, Cymbeline, The Winter's Tale, and *The Tempest* were writ-

1. E.g. by Wolff and Moorman (esp. pp. xix–xxv).

2. *Sh. and the Romance Tradition*, 1949, esp. p. 12.

3. Among many who have emphasized the futility of overdoing this sort of source-hunting is Sir Henry Thomas in *Sh. and Spain*, 1922, 10, 22—a lecture which suggests another slender link between the last plays in showing that there are possible Spanish 'sources' for them all.

4. *Pastoral Poetry and Pastoral Drama*, 1906, 411. (For the English pastoral drama and its origins see chaps. IV ff.)

ten at the end of Shakespeare's career[1] and are notable for distinguishing characteristics common in varying degrees to them all. With the exception of *The Tempest* they are roomy plays in that they have scenes in many places and countries and they all show or recount events taking place over a lengthy period of time[2]: they are often called romances and they are romantic in true Elizabethan senses of the word,[3] dealing with love in people of high estate, events controlled by supernatural agency and by chance, and heroic adventure in both courtly and arcadian settings. They are written in similar style and have similar peculiarities of language and versification. Virtue, beauty, and happiness are in them all; but they contain evil, ugliness, and misery too, and at times they all come near tragedy: yet they all end happily. Their story is of the evil caused by jealousy, hatred, or treachery and of the conquest of this evil in the course of time by integrity, constancy, and courageous love aided by good fortune. It has even been said that they are so closely connected that 'the prospect of understanding *Cymbeline* without *The Winter's Tale* and *The Tempest* is poor indeed',[4] and whether this is accepted or not, it must certainly be agreed that these plays are of a kind.[5]

Among surveys of criticism of the last plays may be mentioned those by F. Kermode,[6] J. M. Nosworthy[7] and, for the period 1900–57, P. Edwards.[8] Although *The Tempest* has always been popular, the others have received much adverse comment[9]: but in the nine-

1. Cf. p. xxiii, n.3. P. Cruttwell in *The Shakespearean Moment*, 1954, 94, points out that it may be dangerous to assume that Shakespeare himself regarded these plays as his last.

2. In *Cym.* there is a feeling that much more time has gone by than that taken up by the action. This is partly because we know that the journeys between Italy and England would take time, but mainly because of the pre-play story, as in *Tp.*, and because Cymbeline's boys, now young men, were last seen by him as babes. According to Daniel the times represented on the stage, followed by the actual times for the plots, are approximately: *Per.*, 14 days–16 years; *Cym.*, 12 days–6 months]; *Wint.*, 8 days–16 years; *Tp.*, 3 or 4 hours for both. Cf. also pp. xliv–l.

3. Cf. E. C. Pettet, *Sh. and the Romance Tradition*, 1949.

4. Tillyard, *Last Plays*, p. 1.

5. This is further emphasized by the note on similarities in plot, structure, and themes on pp. xliv–l.

6. *Tp.* (New Arden), 1954, lxxxi–lxxxviii.

7. *Cym.* (New Arden), 1955, xl–xlviii.   8. *Sh.Sur.* xi, 1958, 1–18.

9. Dryden, 1672, included *Wint.* and *Per.* among those plays 'made up of some ridiculous and incoherent story . . . [and] either grounded on impossibilities, or at least so meanly written, that the comedy neither caused your mirth, nor the serious part your concernment' (*Defence of the Epilogue*, in *Essays*, ed. W. P. Ker, 1900, i. 165). Pope, 1725, thought *Per.* 'wretched' and that much of *Wint.* could not have been written by Shakespeare (*Works of Sh.*, 1, xx). Charlotte Lennox, in

teenth century was developed the well-known view that the plays exhibited the serene and mellow tranquillity of Shakespeare in retirement. This is foreshadowed by Derwent Coleridge in 1852[1]; it is best known as expressed by Dowden in 1874[2]; it was, more or less, also the view of Swinburne, David Masson, F. J. Furnivall, B. ten Brink, Sir I. Gollancz, Sir Sidney Lee, and others. But many considered that the last plays showed a falling off; Shakespeare was ageing and tired,[3] and in 1904 Lytton Strachey reacted strongly and denounced the plays as poor and careless work of a Shakespeare 'bored with people, bored with real life, bored with drama, bored, in fact with everything except poetry and poetical dreams.'[4] Strachey also showed that there was tension and ugliness in these plays, but, in dismissing the Dowden view as uncritical sentimentality and describing the plays as 'grotesque', Strachey himself overstated his case and gave an uncritically biased picture. At all events Dowden's view, or something like it, has continued and is widespread in popular criticism even today: but the reaction against it has also continued to be strong, although on lines different from those followed by Strachey.

Perhaps the keynote of modern criticism is that the plays are experiments.[5] So, for example, it is held that Shakespeare, like Beaumont and Fletcher,[6] was trying to cater for a new taste which the Court masque[7] may have helped to develop and also to write

---

Sh. Illustrated, 1753, ii. 75, said of *Wint.*, 'if we compare the ... Play with the paltry Story on which it is founded, we shall find the Original much less absurd and ridiculous' (cited in *Var.* 352). For Warburton, *Wint.* is 'a monstrous composition' (see p. 177).

1. In his ed. of the dramatic works of S. T. Coleridge, p. vii, he describes *Zapolya*—his father's imitation of *Wint.*—as being 'distinguished by a diffused and tender grace—a mellow tint, as of commencing autumn', which is precisely the kind of language used by Dowden.

2. *Sh. . . . his Mind and Art*. But it is in *Shakespere* (Literature Primers), 1877, 60 that Dowden first classifies the last plays as 'on the heights'.

3. E.g. Barrett Wendell, *Wm. Shakespeare*, 1894.

4. 'Sh.'s Final Period' (*Independent Rev.* iii, Aug. 1904, 405–18. Repr. in Strachey's *Books and Characters*, 1922, 47–64, and *Literary Essays*, 1948, 1–15).

5. This view had been expressed by T. R. Price in 'The construction of "A Winter's Tale"' (*Shakespeariana*, Oct. 1890, 195–207). This may be the first examination of the structure. Price describes the play as a diptych—a tragic followed by a comic element, fused into a whole, a romantic play.

6. The questions whether *Per.* preceded Beaumont and Fletcher's plays and the extent of Shakespeare's part in *Per.* are disputed. J. M. Nosworthy suggests that *Per.* preceded *Philaster* (*Cym.*, New Arden, 1955, xxxvii–xl) but A. H. Thorndike's view that *The Faithfull Shepherdess* and *Philaster* may have preceded *Per.* (*Influence of Beaumont and Fletcher on Sh.*, 1901, 92) is still tenable.

7. Influence of the masque may be shown in *Wint.* by the songs and music, the two dances, the dressing up for the feast, and the statue scene.

plays suitable for the Blackfriars,[1] the indoor theatre where finer points could be emphasized by artificial light. Shakespeare and his Company would have been interested in the possibilities of the indoor theatre, and its acquisition has even been given as the simple reason for the last plays—they are Shakespeare's experiments in writing for such a theatre and a courtly audience.[2] The audiences in the private theatres were on the whole more cultivated and better educated than those of the public theatres[3] but they were far from being entirely courtly, and, whoever they were, they also attended the public theatres. The last plays appeal to all tastes: they are not written especially for the moral world of a coterie theatre.[4]

Most critics feel that there was much more in Shakespeare's mind when he wrote these plays, and there is almost general agreement that at this time he was particularly interested in the theme of reconciliation.[5] Quiller-Couch discussed this in several works[6]: he considered that, because reconciliation needs space and time, Shakespeare was for a while baffled and 'simply did not know how to do it'. His view was that *Pericles*, *Cymbeline*, and *The Winter's Tale*, although they show progress, are diffuse and clumsy and, on the whole, are failures, but that triumphant success was achieved in *The Tempest*.[7] This view of the playwright experimenting with new material is ably developed by J. M. Nosworthy in his discussion of *Cymbeline* as an experimental romance, but Nosworthy holds that full success is reached both in *The Winter's Tale* and in *The Tempest*.[8]

Alongside opinions that the plays are mainly experiments in dramatic art are those which regard them as having profound philosophical significance which is largely expressed through

1. Acquired by the King's men in 1608 although, because of the plague, probably not used until late in 1609. See J. Isaacs, *Production and Stage Management at the Blackfriars Theatre*, 1933. But A. M. Nagler in *Sh.'s Stage*, 1958, 102, considers that performances at the Blackfriars probably differed little from those at the Globe.

2. G. E. Bentley, 'Sh. and the Blackfriars Theatre' (*Sh.Sur.*, i, 1948, 38–50).

3. W. A. Armstrong, 'The Audience of the Elizabethan Private Theatres', *R.E.S.*, Aug. 1959, 234–49.

4. A. Harbage, *Sh. and the Rival Traditions*, 1952, esp. 53–6.

5. Not, of course, a new interest for Shakespeare: but even in the Comedies reconciliation is achieved not without suffering—as with Malvolio.

6. *Sh.'s Workmanship*, 1918; *Studies in Literature*, 3rd ser., 1929, 114–15; *N.C. Wint.*, xviii–xxvi.

7. 'beaten thrice—in *Pericles*, in *Cymbeline*, in *The Winter's Tale*—with a fourth and last shot, in *The Tempest* bringing down his quarry from the sky' (*N.C. Tp.*, 1921, xxvii).

8. *Cym.*, esp. xlviii–lxii. Indeed there is a current tendency to class *Wint.* with, or even above, *Tp.*

imagery and symbolism in word and structure; and to many the plays are myths or allegories. Interpretations range from simple analyses of *The Tempest* as an allegory of Shakespeare's dramatic life and *The Winter's Tale* of his personal life—a scarcely concealed autobiography[1]—up to much profounder studies. E. M. W. Tillyard,[2] F. C. Tinkler,[3] and F. R. Leavis[4] regard the last plays as developments from the tragedies, showing not only destruction but also, what is only suggested in the tragedies, reconstruction and rebirth brought about by virtue and time. For D. A. Traversi the plot of *The Winter's Tale* is 'a perfect example' of Shakespeare's 'symbolic technique'. The play is on the virtue of Grace: when Perdita mentions carnations and streaked gillyflowers it is obvious to Traversi that 'the *carn*-stem has a clear connection with the flesh, and "streak'd gillyvors", "bastards" between crude nature and the realm of "grace" '.[5]

H. Oppel[6] and D. G. James[7] also write on the plays as developments from the tragedies. James discusses them as non-Christian myths on the theme of finding something, both material and spiritual, which had been lost, set in stories of an originally perfect life suffering a sudden loss of innocence from an irruption of necessary tragedy and evil but by its virtue recovering the lost perfection. James considers that the plays are not altogether satisfactory, from the surely mistaken view that they 'are comparatively formless (with the exception of the *Tempest* . . .) and thereby show a failure of expressiveness'.

G. Wilson Knight in several works[8] writes on the last plays as allegories of 'great creating nature' and 'myths of immortality' and considers that the argument on grafting in *The Winter's Tale* (IV. iv. 82–103) is 'a microcosm of the whole play'. Indeed he believes that the whole of Shakespeare's work offers nothing greater than *The Winter's Tale* 'in tragic psychology, humour, pastoral, romance' and in this allegory of creating nature. F. J. D. Hoeniger[9] agrees

1. L. Dobbs, *Sh. Revealed* [1948], 192–3.   2. *Last Plays.*

3. 'The Winter's Tale' (*Scrutiny*, Mar. 1937, 344–64) and 'Cymbeline' (*ibid.*, June 1938, 5–19). Attacked by Fr. A. A. Stephenson in *Scrutiny*, Apr. 1942, 329–38.

4. *Scrutiny.*

5. *Approach*, 1956, 261, 274. But *carn*- here has nothing to do with *flesh*: its connection is with *crown*.

6. *Sh.'s Tragödien und Romanzen: Kontinuität oder Umbruch?* 1954.

7. *Scepticism and Poetry*, 1937, 205–41.

8. Particularly in *The Crown of Life*, 1947, 76–128, 'Great creating Nature: an essay on *The Winter's Tale*'.

9. 'The meaning of The Winter's Tale' (*Univ. of Toronto Quar.* xx, 1950, 11–26); *The Function of Structure and Imagery in Sh.'s Last Plays* (Ph.D. thesis, Univ. of

with Knight's comment on the grafting argument and holds that the symbolism of *The Winter's Tale* revolves round the life–death–life pattern of nature and of human existence. The views that the plays—particularly *The Winter's Tale*—deal with the theme of the strife between art and nature and express allegorically a vital philosophy of creation and growth are held by Traversi, Tinkler, Tillyard, E. A. J. Honigmann,[1] and others.

In the allegory and myth school are several critics who believe that these plays, and particularly *The Winter's Tale*, are symbolic of growth based on classical myths of the seasons or that they are allegorical expositions of Christianity. Apparently the earliest of the classical myth group was the Baconian W. F. C. Wigston, who elaborated the 'extraordinary parallel presented between Perdita and Persephonê (or Proserpine), and between Hermione and Demêtêr (or Ceres)' and said that since, with the recovery of Persephonê, the spring comes again to the earth, the 'myth of Demêtêr *is therefore a Winter's Tale*' which Shakespeare had in mind when choosing the title for a play which, like the others, contains 'a planned spiritual Rebirth or Revelation through time'.[2] In the other group perhaps the ablest exponent was S. L. Bethell[3] who believed that Shakespeare in most of his work, but chiefly in these plays, was expounding Christian doctrine, especially that of redemption. The last plays, except *Pericles*, do indeed deal with forgiveness and reconciliation, which are certainly Christian virtues,[4] but Bethell's views are extravagant and meet with little support.[5]

Although few critics entirely accepted Lytton Strachey's condemnation of the last plays, nevertheless there have been[6] and still

---

London, 1954, unpublished); 'Prospero's Storm and Miracle', *Sh.Q.*, Winter 1956, 33–8).

1. 'Secondary Sources of The Winter's Tale' (*Phil.Q.* xxxiv, Jan. 1955, 27–38).

2. *A New Study of Sh.*, 1884 [Anon.], and *Bacon, Sh. and the Rosicrucians*, 1888. Cf. also *H8* (New Arden ed. R. A. Foakes, xli and lxi).

3. *Sh. and the Popular Tradition*, 1944, *Wint. study*, *Wint. ed.*

4. As they are virtues of other religions before and since Christ. Cf. F. Neilson, *Sh. and The Tempest*, 1956, 103–4.

5. Cf. Bonamy Dobrée, 'On (not) enjoying Sh.' (*Essays and Stud. . . . English Assoc.*, 1956, 39–55). Bethell takes any opportunity, however fanciful, to refer incidents or words in *Wint.* to Christian scriptures or doctrine. An example is given in the Comm. to III. iii. 112–15. An extreme example of interpretation as Christian allegory is 'Sh.'s Allegory: The Winter's Tale' by J. A. Bryant, Jr. (*Sewanee Rev.* lxiii, 1955, 202-22). Here Leontes is the Jew, Mamillius 'suggests the Jewish Church', Perdita 'the true Church', Polixenes the Gentile, and Paulina (apparently) St Paul. 'Hermione the redeemer is St Paul's Christ'. Perhaps this inspired 'Mrs Bennet and the Dark Gods' by D. Bush (*Sewanee Rev.*, 1956, 591–6). See also Bryant's *Hippolyta's View*, 1961, 207–25.

6. Since the 17th century. Cf. p. xxxviii, n.9.

are many, besides Quiller-Couch and D. G. James, who regard them—except *The Tempest*—as being rather ineffective, the work of a Shakespeare whose powers are failing. H. B. Charlton considers that 'Shakespeare the dramatist is declining in dramatic power' and that the plays are no more than 'afterthoughts to the tragedies'.[1] V. K. Whitaker asserts that there is 'an actual falling off in the last plays' and that, 'except perhaps *The Tempest*', they lack power in their dramatic impact. He considers that only a few are worth discussing, *The Winter's Tale* not being one of them,[2] and James Sutherland, although not decrying the plays, detects a tiredness in their language.[3] In uncritical asides it is easy to meet such comment as that *The Winter's Tale* is nothing more than 'the expression of a poet's rather wayward mood'[4] or even 'It may strike us as strange that Shakespeare could have been so careless of his reputation as to lend his name, at the very summit of his powers, to that absurd pot-boiler, *The Winter's Tale*'.[5] Yet these are in the minority and the tendency is rather to read too much into the last plays, particularly in treating them as allegories—almost as cabbalistic documents—containing, according to various interpretations, a variety of hidden meanings and even doctrines. A healthy warning that this has been overdone is given by P. Edwards, who suggests that 'We can probably afford some fallow years in discussions concerning the seriousness of the Romances'.[6]

Nevertheless, with all these conflicting views there seems to be a growing appreciation of the quality and power of the plays and of their unity of design and structure: their poetry has always been appreciated. There is, especially, agreement that the plays have a certain elusive quality which is peculiar to them and it is probably this that many have in mind when they speak of the serenity of the plays. They are quieter and less 'gestured'[7] than earlier plays and their ultimate effect is one of happiness and satisfaction. It may be said that this last is so simply because the plays are made to end happily; but the reason is deeper. The gods, good fortune, and even magic play their part, yet the plays end happily also as a result of the struggle and suffering, the virtue, in the widest sense of

1. *Comedy*, and *Tragedy*.   2. *Sh.'s Use of Learning*, 1953, 314.
3. Sutherland, *Language*.
4. Review of Granville Barker's production, *The Times*, 23 Sept. 1912, 7, d.
5. Harold Nicolson, *Good Behaviour*, 1955, 160.
6. 'Sh.'s Romances: 1900–57' (*Sh.Sur.* xi, 1958, 17). Critics in any age must naturally be confident of progress ('We have left Bradley fairly behind', Leavis, *Scrutiny*, 340).
7. Noted by A. Gerstner-Hirzel in 'Stagecraft and Poetry' (*Sh.Jhb.* xci, 1955, 208) and *The Economy of Action and Word in Sh.'s Plays* (The Cooper Monographs, 2), 1957.

that word, of several characters.[1] They win their reward and we rejoice with them; and it is chiefly this combination of fine human quality and the good fortune which comes to its aid which gives the plays an atmosphere of happiness and vitality.

Yet some part of the essential quality of the plays must always be elusive. When T. S. Eliot[2] attempted to give what he called a 'dim outline' of the ideal towards which poetic drama should strive, he said:

> It is a function of all art to give us some perception of an order in life, by imposing an order upon it. . . Beyond the nameable, classifiable emotions and motives of our conscious life . . . there is a fringe of indefinite extent, of feeling which we can only detect, so to speak, out of the corner of the eye and can never completely focus; of feeling of which we are only aware in a kind of temporary detachment from action. . . This peculiar range of sensibility can be expressed by dramatic poetry, at its moments of greatest intensity. At such moments, we touch the border of those feelings which only music can express. . . Nevertheless, I have before my eyes a kind of mirage of the perfection of verse drama, which would be a design of human action and of words, such as to present at once the two aspects of dramatic and of musical order. It seems to me that Shakespeare achieved this at least in certain scenes . . . and that this was what he was striving towards in his late plays.

This perhaps describes what many have had in mind in speaking of the 'dream-like' quality of the last plays.

Nevertheless, any survey of the criticism and general nature of the last plays must close by emphasizing their high dramatic quality. Whatever Shakespeare may have had in his mind, whatever other use of the plays he may have foreseen, he wrote them for the stage. This is shown not only by the fact that they act well but by the remarkable way in which most 'difficulties'—of structure, of plot credibility, of tangled speech, or anything else—are immediately resolved by the simple expedient of mentally putting the plays on the stage; and of them all this is perhaps most strikingly true of *The Winter's Tale*.

II. RELATIONSHIP IN PLOT, STRUCTURE, AND THEMES

In basic plot *The Winter's Tale* and *Pericles* have close similarities, and those two plays and *Cymbeline* are close in echoes of thought and word. In *The Winter's Tale* and in *Pericles* there is a wide gap of time in which infants grow up, and there are scenes in different

1. Human effort, suffering, and self-sacrifice are least evident in *Tp.*
2. *Poetry and Drama*, 1951, 33–4. Repr. in *On Poetry and Poets*, 1957, 86–7.

countries.[1] In each a king stays nearly a year away from his realm and believes his wife to be dead though in fact she is in a form of religious retreat. In each the royal couple have one daughter who is separated from them both immediately after birth, endangered at sea, and later believed—at least by the king—to be dead. In each a king, his life in danger, escapes on the advice of a counsellor, and a queen's daughter is mistress of a feast. In the final act the daughter is first restored to the king and then all three are reunited and the daughter kneels to her mother. Each play contains the theme of jealousy although this is much more prominent in *The Winter's Tale* than in *Pericles*. An essential difference between the plays is that in *Pericles* the king does not sin or cause the separations and therefore the question of final forgiveness and reconciliation does not arise.

Cymbeline is also close to *The Winter's Tale* in plot and language, but the plots of *Cymbeline* and *The Tempest* do not have a time-gap; they depend on a pre-play story. The plot of *The Tempest* is unlike other plots in the group, yet in *The Tempest*, as in the other plays, a central character is sinned against and there is forgiveness and reconciliation at the close.

In all the plays there are parents and children. In each there is one of the normal dramatic conclusions of comedy—in three there is the immediate prospect of marriage of a central young couple and in the other the re-uniting of a young couple who were recently married when the play opened. But there is also ahead a re-established life for the older central characters. A vital characteristic is that in varying degrees both these main groups of characters suffer and have to win their reward by hard struggle against adversity. Here again the comparison is closest between *Pericles* and *The Winter's Tale*. In each the old suffer severely, in each the young woman is put to great physical danger and subsequent hardships. The young men are not called upon to suffer: Florizel has his resolution tested but Lysimachus has no test after

1. 'Truely . . . quoth the Curate . . . what greater absurditie can be . . . then to see a child . . . in the first *Scene* . . . in his swadling cloutes, and issue in the seconde already growne a man . . . and . . . Comedies, whose first Act began in *Europe*, the second in *Asia*, and the third ended in *Africa* . . . and the Comedie being grounded on a fiction, to attribute unto it the verities of a Historie, and . . . some guls are found to affirme, that all perfection consists herein, and that they are too daintie that looke for any other' (*Don Quixote* (1st Span. ed., 1605), trans. Shelton, 1612 (ent. at Sta. Hall, Jan. 1611) Book 1, Part 4, Chap. 21, pp. 556–7). This 'parallel' with the well-known passage in Sidney's *Defence*, 1595 (*Works*, ed. Feuillerat, iii, 1923, 38) is noted by W. P. Ker (*A Book of Homage to Sh.*, ed. I. Gollancz, 1916, 49–51, 'Sidney and Cervantes are subdued, as Shakespeare is not, in presence of the great authorities'—i.e. in respect for classical idols).

his conversion. In *Cymbeline* the young suffer, the woman having incomparably the harsher test. As for the old, there is not, in the same way as in *Pericles* and *The Winter's Tale*, a couple at all, and the future is faced by the man alone. *The Tempest* again shows differences from the others. The young have no real suffering; they do not, in any comparable way, win their ultimate happiness by suffering and struggle; their significance is mainly symbolic. But, although only for a short time, the man undergoes the labour and dishonour of log-bearing[1] and, as a babe, the woman has been exposed to mortal danger at sea, which was also the first hazard of the young women in *Pericles* and *The Winter's Tale*. Indeed in each play except *Cymbeline* the sea offers dangers to most of the young and in *Pericles* and *The Tempest* also to the old.

Dangers of 'the parallels game' are well known, but just as there is a structure of action and plot and of character relationships, so also is there a structure of themes, and the same themes recur throughout the last plays. They are of course not always of similar importance in each play but even the following list[2] will show that in composing these plays the same ideas were constantly in Shakespeare's mind.

First there is Jealousy, of a murderous nature, as so often in Shakespeare even outside the tragedies.[3] In *The Winter's Tale* jealousy is the motive power which starts the play off and carries it along for some time. It is also found in *Pericles* (Dionyza, of Marina) and in *Cymbeline* (the Queen, of Imogen). In *The Winter's Tale* jealousy leads to belief that a wife is unfaithful and to a desire to have her killed and this belief and desire are paralleled in *Cymbeline*. Reconciliation, Forgiveness, and Mercy constitute major themes in *The Winter's Tale*, *Cymbeline*, *The Tempest*, and *Henry VIII*. Loss and Finding, Restoration and Reunion are major and related themes in all the last plays, first of persons, particularly of daughter and heir (but of son and daughter in *Cymbeline* and of son alone in *The Tempest*) and of husband and wife (in *Pericles*, *Cymbeline*, and *The Winter's Tale*); but also, in each play, of kingdoms, possessions, and rank, of innocence, honour, good name,

1. A formal test of his love imposed by Prospero (*Tp.*, I. ii. 451–2, IV. i. 5–6). Yet Ferdinand receives dire threats (I. ii. 460–4), his labour is heavy (III. i. 10), and his predicament is described as austere (IV. i. 1). We are clearly meant to think that he suffers, and he is shown to be honourable.

2. The list is of the chief themes found both in *Wint.* and in one or more of the other last plays. It could be greatly extended and much could be written on many of the themes. Such expansion would not only have its dangers but be out of place in this introduction, where the object is simply to indicate thematic relationship between the plays.

3. E.g. *AYL.*, *Wiv.*, *MND.*

self-esteem, self-knowledge,[1] and happiness. In *Pericles* and *The Winter's Tale* there is, or is promise of, a new union of kingdoms; in *Cymbeline* and *The Tempest* a renewed friendship between states.

Time, Growth, Decay, and Regeneration are related themes important in all the plays. They all, in various ways, show the effect of the passage of time. In *The Winter's Tale* and in *Pericles* this is done in a similar way. In *Cymbeline*, although the action covers only a few months, there is the effect of the passage of considerable time—see p. xxxviii, n.2; and even in *The Tempest*, where the time of the action is short, the same effect is present, due largely, as in *Cymbeline*, to the pre-play history of events and to the fact that at the end of the play an older generation sees grown up those who were last seen as babes.[2] Growth is not only physical but is also in the development of character and moral nature, and in the winning of self-knowledge. In *The Winter's Tale* it occurs in Hermione, Antigonus, Florizel, Leontes, and Autolycus. In *Pericles* it is seen in Pericles, Marina, and Thaisa; in *Cymbeline* in Posthumus, in the king and the princes, and in Imogen; and in *Henry VIII* in Wolsey, Henry, and Katharine. With Growth there is in the lives of the old in all the plays the unmistakable theme of Decay. Regeneration in the old is shown in *Pericles* and *Cymbeline*, where they are helped by the young: in *The Winter's Tale* and in *The Tempest* the old achieve promise of a new life largely by their own efforts aided by other adults; the young play little active part in the struggle. The young men in *Cymbeline*, *Pericles*, *The Winter's Tale*, and *The Tempest*, and particularly in the first three, achieve a new spirit largely by the influence of the young women: indeed the influence, with a power almost divine, of Feminine Beauty and Purity, particularly of the young, is strong in all the plays. In *Cymbeline* and in *Pericles* the young women have to undergo the harshest trials and suffering, comparable with that of the older woman in *The Winter's Tale*, whereas the young women in that play and *The Tempest* have no comparable trials and dangers in their adult lives: but Resolute Womanhood, the trials and fortitude of women of noble character accused unjustly and made to suffer unjustly, is a marked theme in every play except *The Tempest*. Constancy to an ideal or a person, in adversity and suffering, is of fundamental importance in *The Winter's Tale* (Hermione, Paulina, Camillo, Florizel) and of high importance in *Cymbeline* (Imogen, Belarius, Pisanio), *Pericles* (Marina, Helicanus), and *Henry VIII* (Katharine, Cranmer); and

1. As a normal part of a dénouement characters are shown, or discover themselves, in their true light: 'all of us [find] ourselves' (*Tp.*, v. i. 212).

2. And, as noted by Daniel (119), in such touches as ''tis fresh morning with me / When you are by at night' (*Tp.*, III. i. 33).

Personal Self-Sacrifice is strongest in *The Winter's Tale* (Antigonus, Camillo, Hermione, Florizel—in the first two it is without hope of reward).

After a certain point assessment of the importance of themes is difficult, partly because opinions will vary with the varying natures, and even varying moods, of individual spectators or readers[1]; but it is obvious that the above list could be greatly extended.[2] And in addition there is a recurrence in the plays of characters, incidents, patterns, settings, and phraseology[3] which are equally striking in showing relationships between the plays. Sufficient has already been said about certain major characters, particularly the wife and daughter, but another example is the king or noble who does evil.[4] In all except *Pericles* the evil-doer is forgiven, and in all, except perhaps *The Winter's Tale*, the end has greater promise of happiness than the beginning. Another recurrent character is the Bosom Counsellor to a King.[5]

In pattern there is fluctuating light and shadow in all the plays; and although it is not quite true to say that in all the action moves from a dark past to a bright future, yet the plays show striking similarities in the turns of Fortune's wheel. There are marked similarities also of scenes and incidents within this pattern—for example, the *storms* and *shipwrecks* in *Pericles*, *The Winter's Tale*, and *The Tempest*, which bring immediate evil, or appearance of evil, but, except in *The Winter's Tale*, have good developing from them.[6] They also extend the sense of violence and disruption into

1. A simple but important fact. For example, even if Autolycus is presented as plain rogue some people will still laugh at him while others will take a serious view.

2. E.g. Justice and Injustice are important chiefly in *Wint.*, *Tp.*, and *H8*. Honour, with special concern for the personal Good Name, is vitally important in *Cym.* and *Wint.*—for Leontes as well as for Hermione—and only slightly less so in *Per.* Integrity, Steadfastness, and Courage are important in all the plays, particularly in *Per.*, *Cym.*, and *Wint.*, and notably in the women, as in Katharine in *H8*; and Patience, especially in the women, is evident in *Per.* (Marina and Thaisa), *Cym.*, *Wint.*, and *H8*. Constant Love in adversity and trial is exhibited in *Cym.*, *Wint.*, and *H8*, and Loyal Friendship and Service in all the plays, whereas the opposites, Treachery and Conspiracy, are found in *Per.* (Dionyza), *Cym.*, *Wint.* (Leontes concerning Polixenes), *Tp.* (pre-play and Sebastian and Antonio) and *H8* (Wolsey concerning Buckingham).

3. This is especially noticeable between *Wint.*, *Per.*, and *Cym.* Examples are cited frequently in this Introduction and the Comm. Cf. also p. 164 (Leontes/Posthumus).

4. *Per.*, *Cym.* (the Queen), *Wint.*, *Tp.*, *H8*.

5. *Per.* (Thaliard and Helicanus), *Wint.*, *H8*.

6. In immediate post-storm events comparison is again closest between *Wint.* (befriending of babe by shepherds) and *Per.* (befriending of Pericles by fishermen).

a wider context: the passions of men are felt to be a part of the natural order. Quite apart from this they are, of course, dramatic devices achieving immediate ends in the progress of each play.[1] The *rural scenes* have for some critics a fertility significance; they are regarded as symbolic of the re-birth which is a theme in the plays. It has even been suggested that the restoration of summer in the Proserpine myth is exhibited in Perdita—presumably the early Perdita—and that there is actually a pointer to this in Perdita's one reference to Proserpine.[2] Other incidents are the *ceremonial or elaborated revelation at the conclusion* of all the plays,[3] the *recovery of the believed dead* which is found in all except *Henry VIII*, and the attempt of a jealous king or queen to murder by *poisoning*.[4]

And then there are those elements and episodes which give a rather diffused but yet characteristic atmosphere to these plays. In the first place there is the *fairy tale and other folklore*. All the plays, except *Henry VIII*, not only found their plot on a fable but contain much traditional folk-lore and episodes which are the stock-in-trade of the fairy tale.[5] There is also the *supernatural and the dream*: in *Pericles* and *The Tempest* there are magicians, and although magic and chance are more important in those plays than they are in *Cymbeline* and *The Winter's Tale*, yet *Cymbeline* has its Jupiter and Soothsayer and *The Winter's Tale* its Oracle and the apparent magic of the statue; and *Pericles*, *Cymbeline*, *The Winter's Tale*, and *Henry VIII* all have dreams containing supernatural manifestations. Finally there are the *masque, dancing, music, and songs* which play their part in varying degree in all the plays. Although *Pericles* has no formal masque, Gower, like Time in *The Winter's Tale*, has something of the function of a presenter of a masque, there are dumb-show episodes and the appearance of Diana in a vision, and there are dances and music. *Cymbeline* has a form of masque in the dream of Posthumus, and *The Winter's Tale* has the sheep-shearing feast and dances as well as the statue scene. *The*

1. There is also the thunder and lightning in which Jupiter descends in *Cym.*; the Oracle speaks in a voice of thunder in *Wint.*; and thunder accompanies Ariel as a Harpy in *Tp*. But thunder with a theophany is conventional.

2. See p. xlii. Even the Shepherd's simple statement of fact, 'thou met'st with things dying, I with things new-born' (III. iii. 112), is sometimes considered to be a reference to the Proserpine myth.

3. *Per.* (revelation), *Cym.* (intricate dénouement), *Wint.* (statue scene), *Tp.* (revelation and chess-playing), *H8* (Christening ceremony).

4. In *Per.* and *Wint.* a jealous king asks his counsellor to poison another king and in *Cym.* a jealous queen attempts to poison a princess.

5. E.g. the identification of recovered children by clothing, jewellery, or special marks (*Per.*, *Cym.*, *Wint.*). This is common also in classical comedy. See p. lxiii.

Tempest has the dancing of the strange shapes at the banquet in
III. iii and the masque of Ceres. *Henry VIII* has the masquers' dance
at Wolsey's banquet, the dancing of the Spirits of Peace in IV. ii,
and the pageantry of Coronation and Christening. Music and songs
grow in importance from *Pericles* to *The Tempest*. Music is used, as
normally in Shakespeare, on both solemn and formal occasions
and, to mark happiness and jollity, particularly for the dance.[1]

These elements all combine to create a rhythmic development
which is similar in all the plays. Harmony is broken by evil in
human character, and is righted by human virtue aided by the
gods: yet this virtue acts in conjunction with the natural processes
of continuing life working silently through time; and so, together,
man and nature finally succeed in re-creating peaceful harmony.

5. THE WINTER'S TALE

1. THE NATURE OF THE PLAY

It is not easy to give a precise definition of the last plays: they are
a curious genre and, with their marked similarities, there are perhaps also more differences between them than is generally allowed.
'Romance' and 'Realism' are dangerous terms, but if one is not too
particular they are useful in speaking of elements in these plays.
The plays are all to some extent romances, but they all contain realism[2] in plot and character, a picture and interpretation of life which
is deeper than mere verisimilitude. Like the others, *The Winter's
Tale* can be called a romantic tragi-comedy, but it has a strong element of realism in plot, incident, character, and language; stronger,
perhaps, than in any of the others.[3] The situations involve true
human feelings and the characters are much more than conventional symbolic characters of romance. Some of the plot is of the
world of fantasy, but that can be said of the plots of all Shakespeare's non-historical plays: they are all romantic in this sense.
Hence, although no better term than romantic tragi-comedy can
be suggested, it must be emphasized that the elements of realism in
the play are strong: by no means everything is merely conventional or symbolic, there is much in the play of which the most
important meaning is that meaning which is the most obvious and
literal. The opinion that as Iachimo and Leontes are slighter than
Iago and Lear it is easy to see that the villainy of the one and rage

1. On the music and songs in *Wint.* see relevant Comm. and pp. 172–4, and on
the mysterious power of music v. iii. 98n.

2. The term is used in the sense of 'illusion of actuality'.

3. But Leavis, *Scrutiny*, 344, holds that *Tp.* differs from *Wint.* in being 'much
closer to the novelist's "reality"'.

of the other will come to nothing, is a view which is now difficult to evaluate; but it is one which might also be held on the grounds that strong common sense is more evident on the side of virtue in *Cymbeline* and *The Winter's Tale* than in *Othello* and *Lear*.[1] And this practical, realistic, element in *The Winter's Tale*, woven so closely into the fantasy, is one reason why the play is difficult to analyse. It would be dangerous to yield to the temptation to search too closely for 'realism' simply because most critics ignore it. It would indeed be dangerous to have any single line of approach to a play which may well be 'a supreme instance of Shakespeare's poetic complexity'.[2]

The Winter's Tale is a work of art composed to give pleasure from the stage, and must be appreciated as a stage play. This applies to the whole and to its parts: the sense of any particular passage means its dramatic sense. *The Winter's Tale* has more qualities as a narrative than many plays but must not here be considered as a story, and still less as a study of something or other, or as an allegory. Concern must be with the text and the action on the stage, and the normal Elizabethan stage conventions must be understood and accepted. The play must be judged as by a spectator who is allowing himself to be caught up by it in performance and to be carried away into its illusion. Many 'difficulties' only come into existence because this is forgotten. When and by whom was the plan to conceal Hermione made? How could Hermione have been concealed? These and similar matters cannot occur to an audience. They cannot exist when the play is performed and therefore do not arise in an appreciation of it. The same is true of anachronisms and other errors of fact and minor loose ends. The play is in a pre-Christian era and should therefore not refer to an Emperor of Russia, the betrayal of Christ, Whitsun pastorals, a puritan singing psalms to hornpipes, a Christian burial custom or Giulio Romano.[3] As for the loose ends which analysis may easily discover—Paulina could

1. And this may be why there is never the same feeling in *Wint.* as there is in *Lr.* that 'Oppress'd Nature sleeps', that nature opposes or at least will not help the good. Of course, by the time in *Wint.* roughly corresponding to that where the above comment occurs in *Lr.* (III. vi. 97), it is known that nature will awake and that there will also be rest to heal what has been broken. In *Wint.* virtue is in the supernatural as well as in man. The prophecies in *Mac.* come from an evil source and are at once sensed as certain to lead to evil, whereas in *Wint.* the Oracle is immediately recognized as benign.

2. Leavis, *Scrutiny*, 341.

3. Where all characters wore contemporary or conventional dress, other anachronisms would also be accepted. These trivial matters must be ignored. They have nothing to do with the play on the stage. One might as well ask how the shepherd and his wife knew Perdita's name or where she learned reading, writing, and a little classical mythology.

not have known of Leontes' plot to have Polixenes poisoned; the shepherd should not say that Antigonus is an old man because he can know nothing about him; the Shepherd and Clown ought to have recognized Autolycus and the clothes he wore; Hermione says that she knew by Paulina that the Oracle gave hope that Perdita might survive, but she herself heard the Oracle; and finally, Bohemia is given a coast. But these things do not worry an audience; they cannot indeed be noticed in the quick movement of the play. In dramatic analysis it is easy to make too much of motivation. Why did Leontes become jealous? Why did Paulina have such a sudden change in her attitude to Leontes? Certainly these events have to appear dramatically possible, but by far the most important thing about them is that they are on the stage as they are. If they are accepted by an audience, nothing is wrong; they can contain no problem. Camillo did not know how or why Leontes' suspicions had grown, but he very sensibly says that it is better to 'Avoid what's grown than question how 'tis born' (I. ii. 433). And so with the audience—their minds are engaged with what is happening, what is coming, not with searching for reasons to account for what has happened.[1]

Even the 'difficulty' about the sixteen-years gap is theoretical only. There is no difficulty when the play is seen or read. Coleridge, when he wrote *Zapolya* (1814–16) 'in humble imitation of the Winter's Tale',[2] noted in the Advertisement that the 'effect does not, in reality, at all depend on the time of the interval; but on a very different principle. There are cases in which an interval of twenty hours between the acts would have a worse effect (i.e. render the imagination less disposed to take the position required) than twenty years in other cases'.[3] Furthermore a work of art is entitled—almost required—to make use of conventions.[4] However improbable any convention may be it is, in a sense, a piece of

1. Shakespeare 'was often careless, and often perfunctory . . . and his artistic conscience did not impel him to be scrupulous in avoiding inconsistencies of time, action, and characterization. No doubt he was aware how very easily dropped threads pass unnoticed on the stage' (Chambers, *Shakespeare*, i. 228).

2. Not to mention *Cym.* Incidentally, Coleridge tried to prevent any search for hidden meanings in *Zapolya*: 'I shall be well content if my readers . . . judge it as a Christmas tale.'

3. A similar point is made by Mrs Inchbald (see p. 176, n.6).

4. And most of those found in *Wint.*—for example, non-recognition and the complete efficiency of the most transparent disguise—are among the commonest of stage conventions. Portia and Nerissa are completely unrecognizable to their husbands in Venice, but in Belmont Lorenzo immediately recognizes Portia in the dark by her voice alone. There is great difference, however, between the use of this convention in such plays as *Mer.V.* and *AYL.* and its almost unnoticeable use in *Wint.*

realism, if it is generally accepted. Such a work is also entitled to direct us, chiefly by the sort of thing it is, to raise or not to raise certain questions. In *The Winter's Tale* much of the background of the story is conventional, although strongly threaded with realities of human vices and virtues; and certain episodes are, so to speak, deflected away from the audience.

II. THE TITLE

Many see important meaning in the title, particularly a suggestion that the play is an allegory of the seasons[1] or even, in the hint that the fable is a fantasy, an invitation to seek for profundity in the play.[2] In the first place it can be agreed that the title is a good one as a catch-phrase which is easily said and remembered. 'A winter's tale', or similar expression, meant an old trivial tale of some length suitable for nothing better than to while away a winter evening. There are many examples of contemporary use, of which the most apposite are perhaps those cited from Peele and Jenkinson.[3] Yet although the phrase was common it may not be altogether a coincidence that it appears in print at least twice in 1610—in *A Mirror for Magistrates* (which Shakespeare may have been rereading at that time[4]) and in Campion. The play itself speaks of sad tales being best for winter and of old tales.[5] Elsewhere Shakespeare refers to these old tales as trivial pieces of fiction,[6] and the very word 'tale' could mean then, as now, something untrue, not to be taken seriously.[7] This is the obvious meaning which the title would have had to Shakespeare's audiences, but the use of the definite article may be intended to suggest that the play contains

1. E.g. W. F. C. Wigston. See p. xlii above.   2. Bethell, *Wint. ed.*, 9, 12-15.

3. E.g. Marlowe, *Dido*, II. iii. 59; *Jew of Malta*, II. i. 25; Greene, *Perimedes the Blacksmith* (title); Peele, *Old Wives Tale* 1595 (Malone Soc., 1908), 104, 119, 'a merry winters tale would driue away the time trimly', 'content to drive away the time with an old wives winters tale'; T. Campion, *Two Bookes of Ayres*, 1610, ed. Vivian, 1909, 126; *A Mirror for Magistrates*, 1610 ed. by J. Higgins (title); D. Jenkinson, *Triumph of Faith*, 1613 (D4v), 'Let our mirth be . . . spirituall mirth, not foolish laughter, which is madnesse or worse, not iesting and iybing . . . not vnclean speeches . . . not winter tales, and foolish stories, the diuels chronicles, which neuer need printing we can so well remember them'. [This reference—which could be an allusion to the play—I owe to Mr John Crow.] Other examples of the phrase in contemporary use are given by J. O. Halliwell in his ed. of Shakespeare, viii, 1859, 45-6.

4. *Cym.*, Nosworthy, xviii.   5. II. i. 25-6, v. ii. 27-9, 62-3, v. iii. 116-17.

6. E.g. *Ado*, I. i. 186; *AYL.*, I. ii. 105; *Mac.*, III. iv. 65; *R2*, v. i. 41; *3H6*, v. v. 25.

7. 'as light as tales' (*MND.*, III. ii. 133), 'Truths would be tales, / Where now half tales be truths' (*Ant.*, II. ii. 138), 'the tale is notorious, and as notorious that it was a tale' (Sidney, *Apologie*, 27).

much of the hardness and bitterness of the season.[1] The first part of the play takes place in winter (II. i. 25) and even in the pastoral scene the season approaches winter (IV. iv. 80 and p. lxix, n.6).

But to say that the title may have no particular depth and that the fable is simply an old tale, is by no means to say that the play itself lacks profundity. Nor does it follow, because the fable is a fantasy, that the play is also an incredible fantasy. Indeed it is necessary to consider the relationship of play to fable with this matter of credibility in mind.[2]

III. DRAMATIC STRUCTURE

Some notes on the structure of the play are given on pp. xxxvii–liii: what may be called structural mares' nests—some of the non-existent 'problems'—are mentioned on pp. li–liii, the plot 'realism' on pp. lxiv–lxvii, and the main themes, with the importance of Time,[3] on pages xliv–l, lxvii–lxx.

It has long been noted that the play, rather like *Pericles*, could be divided into two parts, and references to its 'first' and 'second' parts are common—the first usually taken as ending with the close of III. ii and the second consisting of all the rest of the play or at any rate of everything from the opening of IV. ii.[4] There used to be almost general agreement that the structure was clumsy, the play loosely, even carelessly, put together, and the opinion is still held,[5] although the quite contrary, and surely correct view, that the play is a masterpiece of skilful construction, is gaining ground.

If the play is to be divided it is better to give it three parts—the first period at Leontes' Court, the second in Bohemia, and the third at Leontes' Court again. But *The Winter's Tale* is not a

---

1. Cf. 'sap-consuming winter' (*Err.*, v. i. 311), 'he is flint; / As humorous as winter' (*2H4*, IV. iv. 33), 'churlish winter's tyranny' (*ibid.*, I. iii. 62), 'winter tames man, woman and beast (*Shr.*, IV. i. 19), 'death, that winter' (*H8*, III. ii. 179), 'furious winter's rages' (*Cym.*, IV. ii. 260), and *Wint.*, II. i. 25.

2. See pp. lxiii–lxvii.   3. On Time see IV. In. and pp. 167–9.

4. So T. R. Price in 1890 (see p. xxxix, n.5). When Granville Barker printed the play for his production in 1912 he put the words 'End of Part I' at the close of III. iii, where he had the single interval.

5. So Quiller-Couch: 'its first and second halves are disparate...the carpentry gapes ... so that this play never fits into our mind as a whole' (*N.C. Wint.*, xxv). Even Greg can speak of the play's 'sprawling structure' (*First Folio*, 421, n.4) and F. Kermode, writing on structure, can say 'by common admission that play [*Wint.*] already staggers under the weight of diffuse but necessary incident' (*Tp.*, 1954, lxxvi). But some early critics recognized its unity—e.g. Davies in 1780, Cole in 1859 (see pp. 177–9), and Price in 1890 (see p. xxxix, n.5). And among early moderns, Agnes M. Mackenzie says, 'it is written both carefully and beautifully . . . it is lucid, shapely, in its way even compact' (*The Women in Sh.'s Plays*, 1924, 428–9).

dramatic curiosity consisting of separate parts;[1] it is a whole, and its unity has the rhythm and vitality of a great work of art. In spite of the fact that it is spread over a wide area and many years, the plot is perfectly clear. It is true that the first period, at Court, is almost wholly an unhappy time where mad jealousy threatens absolute disaster; that the second, coming after sixteen years in another country and different milieu and largely with different people, is, for its first half, extremely happy; and that the last period, again at Court, is chiefly one of mellow happiness and reconciliation.[2] But all these parts belong to and complete each other. Some events occur by chance and some by design, as in life; well-ordered life is broken into chaos, which is resolved only by deep and prolonged effort and divine aid. But it *is* resolved, and the whole plot shows a pattern of life which has meaning and a clear unity in design—that essential unity which Hurd distinguished from the classic unity in 1762 when discussing the *Faerie Queene*[3]—and this meaning and unity give the play constant impetus.

Timon has been described as a play with all-embracing love as its first part and all-annihilating hatred as its other part with an empty gap between.[4] *The Winter's Tale* has hatred in the first part and love, where there was hatred, in the last, but no empty gap. Not only does the middle part stir the mind and heart of itself, but by the contrast of its beauty, love, youth, confidence, happiness, country life, and venial roguery, it intensifies the dramatic effect of the ugliness, the oppressive adult madness, hatred, and murderous crime at court in the first part and the sober serenity of the last. It is so essential to the plot that, if it were removed, the last part also could not exist.

Of course, the sheep-shearing scene has been acted by itself, and it has often been noticed that III. ii has a Miltonic close fitting for the end of a tragedy—certainly the first part could be acted alone. But this sort of thing is true of most plays: pieces can be acted separately. Yet these pieces are not the plays, and neither the sheep-shearing nor any other part is *The Winter's Tale*—that, made up of three main 'parts', is an indivisible whole, a true dramatic unit.[5]

1. It has even been described as consisting of two 'plays'.
2. More or less the old formula that a comedy should begin in trouble, be centred in love, and end in joy.
3. *Letters on Chivalry*, ed. Edith J. Morley, 1911, 122.
4. Muriel St Clare Byrne in *Sh.Q.*, Autumn 1957, 468.
5. I have once or twice been told by critics who regarded the play primarily as a fantasy that, on seeing it performed, they were impressed and rather puzzled by the logic, vitality, and coherence of the plot.

The play has been fairly popular on the stage.[1] Criticism of it comes largely from the study,[2] but from the study too come many appreciations of its fine, and evident, dramatic qualities. In original performance, at any rate at the Globe, it was probably played through almost continuously[3] and in modern times the tendency is to play it rapidly.[4]

The development of the plot must be discussed briefly with reference only to matters of special dramatic interest. The first scene is a short quiet introduction where two speakers tell each other things they already know, giving the audience necessary information and emphasizing the general happiness in order to heighten the effect of the unsuspected blow which is imminent.[5] The friendship of the kings is clearly of the traditional kind, which, it must be remembered, is one of deep passion[6] and the opening of the play is as quiet as its close. Then, giving a picture of intense dramatic irony in the happy and confident Queen, the play moves quickly to Leontes' jealous outburst at I. ii. 108, which brings up a problem of practical importance for every producer. When is this jealousy first clearly shown? There is much conflict of opinion[7]: apparently the older school assumed that there is no indication of Leontes' jealousy until I. ii. 108,[8] whereas in modern times there is a belief that Leontes should show that he is jealous from his first appearance.[9]

1. See pp. 175–81.

2. Perhaps this is overstated. The prevalence of adaptations up to c. 1850 is itself criticism from the stage. And cf. Mrs Inchbald, p. 176, n.6 below.

3. See p. xx, n.2. C. Leech holds the less probable view that the five-act structure, presumably with four main pauses in performance, had become established by the beginning of the seventeenth century ('The Structure of the Last Plays', *Sh.Sur.* xi, 1958, 19–30, esp. 21, 24–5). Leech believes that the structure of *Wint.* 'is firmly made and in the traditional mode'.

4. Cf. Granville Barker. See p. liv, n.4.

5. In *Pandosto* a warning is given, and some critics hold that in the play the early emphasis on happiness is intended as a covert warning. The opening scene of *Cym.* is similar to that of *Wint.* except that it is in verse. In each there is extravagant praise of a character who is soon to suffer.

6. L. J. Mills, *One Soul in Bodies Twain. Friendship in Tudor Literature*, 1937, 202, 258–9. Cf. v. iii. 54n.

7. There are two opinions in *N.C.Wint.* Quiller-Couch obviously thinks that the jealousy is first shown at I. ii. 108 and it provokes one of his many outbursts against the play: 'it strikes us as merely frantic . . . a piece of impossible improbability' (xvi). But in the same book Dover Wilson states that Leontes should show his jealousy from the outset (p. 131, n.9–10; p. 133, n.62–75, 83–6).

8. There seems to be no evidence that actors have shown Leontes to be jealous before I. ii. 108 until recent times. Hazlitt's account of Kemble's display of growing jealousy almost certainly refers to Leontes in the play after I. ii. 108 (see p. 178).

9. R. J. Trienens in 'The inception of Leontes' jealousy' (*Sh.Q.* iv, 1953, 321–6)

In *Pandosto* the onset of jealousy was slow. The 'melancholy passion' which was 'a long time smothering in his stomach, began at last to kindle in his mind a secret mistrust, which, increased by suspicion, grew at last to a flaming jealousy that so tormented him as he could take no rest'.[1] It is natural to assume that a dramatist will take as his point of departure the moment when the 'kindling' begins: Shakespeare was concerned to show jealousy in action, not to make a study of its causes or development. In *Pandosto* the visit of Egistus is recounted from the beginning; but the play opens with Polixenes' visit almost at its end and things have begun to move rapidly. In the text there is no apparent indication that Leontes says or does anything to show jealousy before I. ii. 108 or that any one on the stage is aware or even suspicious of anything of the kind.[2] The arguments that this is not so are unconvincing and can at any rate be answered.[3]

---

surveys the literature and supports the view that Leontes shows jealousy from the start, and so does N. Coghill (*Sh.Sur.* xi, 1958, 31–3).

1. P. 186. Leontes' diseased imaginings, as at I. ii. 115–17, 125–6, 183–5, 284–96, do give the impression that he had been thinking about his injury for a long time (W. W. Lawrence, *Sh.'s Problem Comedies*, 1931, 199–200).

2. Hermione herself is not aware of it until II. i. 62. Since Camillo was unaware of Leontes' jealousy it is reasonably certain that no one else in the play could have suspected it. See I. ii. 213–16n.

3. Briefly, the arguments for 'Jealousy from the start' are: (1) Until I. ii. 108 Leo. is taciturn. This is true: his ten speeches have only nineteen lines in all. Subsequently he is rather verbose. (2) Herm. says that Leontes' persuasions are cold (I. ii. 30). (3) Leo. notes pointedly that Herm. can persuade Polix. but he cannot (I. ii. 87). (4) Leo. is preoccupied and apparently does not hear the talk between Polix. and Herm., for at I. ii. 56 Polix. yields and agrees to stay, yet at 86 Leo. asks whether he has been won yet. (5) There must be action between Herm. and Polix. that can be misinterpreted as is indicated by I. ii. 115–17, 125–6, 183–5, 284–96. (6) Some conversation before I. ii. 108 may be equivocal. N. Coghill (*Sh.Sur.* xi, 1958, 33) holds that Polixenes' reference to nine months and description of himself as 'like a cipher, / Yet standing in rich place' mean that the audience cannot 'fail to wonder' whether Polix. may not be the father of the expected child. Answers are: (1) Leo. is obviously concluding a talk with Polix.; he has used up his arguments and his few speeches are little to go on. Furthermore, abruptness lies more in manner and tone than in length and Leontes' words could all be said in a warm and friendly way. Othello is a man of few words early in *Oth.* but is not then jealous. (2) and (3) Hermione's comment on Leontes' lack of warmth could be just the belittling of a husband in company which is the accepted privilege of a loving, confident wife. Leontes' speeches just before I. ii. 108 are those of a devoted and appreciative husband: 'At my request he would not' itself could be just that—an echo of 'Well said, Hermione' (I. ii. 33). It could be an ominous half-aside, but it could also be the loving husband's admiration for his able wife's success. And that the latter is so is supported by Leontes' following lines, which are happy, loving memories of their early courting days. (4) Leo. may not be pre-occupied. For a character not to hear is normal stage convention. Herm. and Polix. do not hear Leo. from 108 to 127. In the happy passage II. i.

Since no other character shows awareness of jealousy in Leontes before I. ii. 108 and since nothing in the text warrants the assumption that he himself is conscious of it, he should clearly not be represented on the stage as a man in the grip of jealousy. The most we can assume from his taciturnity is that although apparently happy he is a little uneasy, somewhat puzzled and hesitant. He lacks the confident serenity which radiates from Hermione. And his worry grows: he is probably meant to hear the equivocal lines I. ii. 83–6. If he is represented in this way the audience will have some preparation for the shock, which will nevertheless not lose its dramatic effect, because, although the audience should sense that something may be wrong, they will not know what it is.[1]

The play then passes through the tense fast-moving career of Leontes' mad jealousy, which apparently defeats the good in Hermione supported by Paulina and others. It moves quickly to a dénouement which comes too late, after the evil has triumphed: the pronouncement of the Oracle is the pivot on which the play turns. The proof of innocence indeed arrives in time for the accused to hear it, but she 'dies' under the second stroke of fate[2] before Leontes repents. The intensely dramatic episode closes with the remorse of the king for the fatal damage his madness has caused. The storm has blown itself out and there is a calm and reconciliation which is like the ending of a tragedy.

But this movement has been broken by the short Oracle scene (III. i), which has a spiritual significance, bringing health again into the life of the play not only by what is said and how it is said but by the animation which is the essence of the scene. The earlier part of the play is static. It is all in or near Leontes' palace—a setting which has become impregnated with his jealousy, the atmosphere oppressive and tense. But the speed of the messengers described at

---

2–20 Herm. is out of earshot although she has no one except the speakers to engage her attention. (5) These passages after I. ii. 108 are the forgeries of jealousy. *Oth.*, II. i. 250, speaks of 'paddling palms' and it is there clear that this can be normal behaviour to the normal mind. After all, 'Trifles light as air / Are to the jealous confirmations strong / As proofs of holy writ' (*Oth.*, III. iii. 326. But cf. v. iii. 54n.). (6) The conversation seems to be quite unambiguous. It must be made clear that Polix. has been there nine months to make it possible that he is the child's father. In 'like a cipher' Polix. is referring to himself, not to Herm., and his meaning is clear (I. ii. 1–2n., 3–9n.).

1. But see p. lvii, n.1.

2. The death of Mamillius is the heaviest mortal tragedy in the play. Good cannot triumph over evil without loss and this is a part of the price paid in the struggle for victory. Antigonus and the mariners are also to die and their deaths are also part of the price; but they are more remote and more obviously to be ascribed to natural causes outside the protagonists in the struggle.

the end of II. iii and again in III. i, and the language of III. i—'The climate's delicate, the air most sweet, / Fertile the isle'—create an entirely different atmosphere which has for some time contained little that was delicate or sweet. There is also the reminder that man is not in sole control of his fate, that the gods are powerful and benevolent and are intervening.[1] The change shown in this scene brings a sense of relief and hope.[2]

This hope is confirmed in III. iii, the scene which links[3] the first and second 'parts' of the play; for any doubts about the outcome are removed when the babe is saved. Again there are vigorous action, fresh air, the country, and elements of nature in contrast to the atmosphere of Leontes' court. Here too are a dream with a supernatural manifestation and a storm from which evil arises, and each is a dramatic device achieving important ends in the development of the play.[4] But it is reasonable to see, even here, the heavens behaving 'as troubled with man's act',[5] the storm and savage beast showing and symbolizing in nature the evil which is being done by human agency in exposing the child, even though storm and beast are also agents in the development of the plot. It is only to be expected that the actual and symbolic force of nature in *Lear* and *Macbeth* should be here only in muted form, since the experience of *The Winter's Tale* is not to be tragic, ending in catastrophe,

1. The account of the Oracle has some similarities with the descent of Jupiter in *Cym.* (v. iv. 93ff.), but Apollo's words are more explicit than Jupiter's Merlinesque message.

2. Nevertheless even here it is also possible to sense the tragic precipice. The opening lines of this short scene echo those of the short I. vi of *Mac.*: 'the air / Nimbly and sweetly recommends itself / Unto our gentle senses . . . The air is delicate'; and those lines can never be recalled without a sense of impending tragedy.

3. This linking scene is discussed by Tillyard, *Last Plays*, 76–8.

4. The dream of Antigonus convinces the audience that Hermione is dead. They know she was innocent. But it convinces Antigonus that she was guilty and has been executed; and her spirit orders him to take the child to its father's country and warns him of his own fate. (Charlton, *Wint.*, 1916, xviii, says, 'Antigonus, despite . . . his vision of Hermione, believes in the Queen's guilt.' But it is precisely because of his vision that he believes it.) The death of Antigonus has been criticized as morally and dramatically unnecessary (e.g. *N.C.Wint.*, xx; Raleigh, *Shakespeare*, 1907, 137). But dramatically it is necessary to remove Antigonus, for a living Antigonus would return to Leontes with his news and spoil the play; and the ship's crew might do likewise. In performance their deaths hardly evoke pity or terror. That of Antigonus is blurred by a semi-comic account, and no death is on stage, where other matters absorb the interest. *N.C.Wint.*, xx, also asks, 'why, in the name of economy, not engulf Antigonus with the rest—or, better still, as he tries to row aboard?' The answer is that it was essential economy to dispose of him on land, for only so can the Clown get his name (III. iii. 96) and his handkerchief and rings, and so prove that he is dead (v. ii. 66–7). These deaths are also a moral retribution. Cf. v. ii. 70–2.　　5. *Mac.*, II. iv. 5.

but one of disaster resolving to tranquillity and a restored order.

That, from the structural point of view, the gap of time is a purely theoretical difficulty has been shown above and the nature and function of Time and his speech are discussed elsewhere.[1] Unlike other Shakespearian Choruses[2] this in *The Winter's Tale* is limited to a single appearance, but its function is similar to the others. In *Henry V* the Chorus craves for indulgence for the passage of time and for inability to show numbers and space[3]: in *The Winter's Tale* Time asks to slip over sixteen years but also gives information in the manner of a combined epilogue to the earlier part of the play and prologue to the next. The appearance of Time has been criticized as a clumsy device and even held to be an interpolation not by Shakespeare.[4] This criticism is still encountered but there is also a reaction which perhaps attaches too much importance to the character and his speech. Time's speech acts valuably as a programme explanation,[5] and like a programme it is read, so to speak, in an interval. Time himself and the speech are, and are surely meant to be, quite outside the play,[6] so that the listener can assimilate the information without being distracted by the action. The speech has a perfectly obvious and important purpose and is almost certainly an original part of the text written by Shakespeare.

With Autolycus come for the first time the singing voice, cheerfulness, and light-hearted irresponsibility, a dramatic relief leading to the famous sheep-shearing scene. In this, the short debate between Perdita and Polixenes has, by modern critics, been given extraordinary and surely excessive importance. The passage is

1. Pp. xlvii, lii, iv. i n., and pp. 167–9.   2. See p. lxxxvi, n.7.

3. *N.C. Wint.*, xxvn. wrongly implies that the *H5* Chorus does not ask excuse for time but only for space. (Cf. *H5*, Choruses to i and v.)

4. Quiller-Couch calls it an admission of incompetence by the dramatist, who cannot compress and concentrate time save by 'the indulgence of our kind friends in front' (*N.C. Wint.*, xxv); Dover Wilson considers it not to be by Shakespeare (*ibid.*, 127), and even Greg (*First Folio*, 417) holds that it is 'no essential or integral part of the play' and 'might easily have been provided in the playhouse' although it may contain 'some Shakespearian turns of phrase'. See n.1 above and p. 179, n.3.

5. Noted by G. L. Kittredge in his ed. of Shakespeare, 1936, 432.

6. In stage adaptations, like those of Garrick, Morgan, and Kemble, Time and his speech are omitted; and in many complete editions, Time's speech is not counted as a scene. This is but natural. In a narrative it is the author's business to tell of time gaps: he fulfils the function of Time in the play. And so when this story is told as a story—as by Greene and the Lambs—no such character as Time is needed. But in a play the characters present the story: they cannot 'show' a gap of sixteen years; a piece of narrative must be introduced and a narrator is needed. That is precisely what Time is. In *Per.* it is Gower. In *Cym.* and *Tp.* the time gap is pre-play and the narrators are Belarius and Prospero. On the distinguishing language of Time see pp. lxxxviii, 168.

held to show gentle, but powerful and fertile, nature the creator, and to be symbolic of the growth, love, and promise of fertility in Florizel and Perdita, just as the storm and the bear may be considered as symbols in destructive nature for evil in man. Obviously much could be written on such a theme, and much indeed has been.[1] It is curious that so many critics who see profundity in the passage assert that it is strange in its context, that it has obviously been brought in, and this, to them, is additional proof of its intentional special significance. But the passage is not intrusive and is not in the least strange. The topic was a common one of the day and arises naturally in the conversation, focusing attention on, and showing something of the character of, a new and important person in the play, a country girl of unusual charm and beauty.[2] It is chiefly from this short passage that comparisons of the play are made with the Proserpine myth and the theme of the seasons 'interwoven with that of youth and age, of death and resurrection'.[3] The passage does indeed also associate Perdita with nature's flowering time and with a distrust of that which sophisticates nature; but even in its associations it is not so important as the flower-passage which follows (103–29) and Florizel's praise of Perdita (135–46), for these bring out the goodness and the power of beauty which is a main theme in the play. Concentration on 'the great debate' has perhaps deflected attention from the important passages which follow.

The realistic idyll goes on happily for the first half of the scene but, after the blow falls when Polixenes declares himself, the spirit changes. It is true that the serious threat of disaster does not last long, since Florizel's constancy and Camillo's help are sufficient assurances that all will be well. Nevertheless life becomes rather grim and earnest: Florizel and Camillo are not without confidence but there are no more flowers, feasting, dance, or song. The last act returns to Leontes' court. The scene in which the meeting of the kings and the recognition of Perdita is recounted is often criticized as ludicrous or comic,[4] but N. Coghill considers it to be 'among the most gripping and memorable of the entire play . . . a

1. E.g. G. Wilson Knight (in several works but particularly in *The Crown of Life*, 1947), E. M. W. Tillyard, F. C. Tinkler, F. R Leavis, D. A. Traversi, E. A. J. Honigmann, S. L. Bethell, and F. J. D. Hoeniger. See above, pp. xli–xliv.

2. Cf. pp. xli–xlii, lxxvii, and iv. iv. 83, 88–92, 104, v. ii. 98nn. It must be difficult for those who have read so much on the passage not to regard it as being especially memorable and important, and as standing out from its context.

3. F. D. Hoeniger, 'The meaning of *The Winter's Tale*' (*Univ. of Toronto Quar.*, Oct. 1950, 23).

4. E.g. G. R. Foss, *What the Author meant*, 1932, 143, and Bethell, *Wint. ed.*, 224 (although Bethell naturally thinks that the phrases have deep significance for the 'inner meaning' of the play). See also pp. xxvi–xxvii, lxxxviii.

masterpiece'.[1] Probably few would go as far as this, but there is no
doubt that the incident must be recounted. If staged it would
lengthen excessively an already long play, it would be tedious because much would have to be said which was well known to the
audience, and it would weaken the final scene.

Much has been said about the final scene: it is, and—although
with dissentient voices—has always been held to be, a scene of
great power and beauty[2] and is pre-eminently one which can only
be fully appreciated when performed. It completes the dénouement begun in the previous scene and, whatever symbolic meaning
may be read into it, the scene is primarily a straightforward eluci-
dation of the mystery: 'the whole climax, or "miracle" (if miracle
it be) does not . . . necessarily involve any mystic flight beyond the
boundaries of human life and a distinctly human situation'.[3] The
dénouement is a surprise. There is no warning[4] and the long period
of the statue's stillness is consummate stagecraft to make the
audience be 'reconvinced against hope that she is a statue'.[5] As
in the *Alcestis*, the wife who has come back to life does not speak to
her husband[6]: it is Paulina and Leontes who speak freely. Paulina
has achieved her triumph: husband, wife, and child are reunited in
complete reconciliation and, of those three, the chief agent in

1. *Sh.Sur.* xi, 1958, 39.
2. There are numerous expressions of appreciation. 'In delicacy and tenderness there are few finer scenes in the whole range of the Shakespearean drama'
(W. H. Hudson ed. of *Wint.*, 1909, xlvii); 'affecting and of such extreme beauty'
(A. J. G. Collins ed. of *Wint.* [?1950], xviii); 'Of all Shakespeare's *coups de théâtre*,
the descent of Hermione from her pedestal is perhaps the most spectacular and
affecting' (N. Coghill in *Sh.Sur.* xi, 1958, 39). On the other hand Mrs Lennox in
1753 considered the scene 'low and improbable'—a view hotly opposed by Mrs
Inchbald in 1822 and T. Campbell in 1838 (see *Var.*, 352–5). For Hartley Coleridge the scene goes 'beyond all dramatic credibility'; and even Bethell (*Wint.
Study*, 103) speaks of the 'staginess' of the scene.
3. Convincingly argued by A. H. R. Fairchild, *Sh. and the Art of Design* (Univ.
of Missouri Stud. xii, No. 1, Jan. 1937) and A. Bonjour, 'The final scene of *The
Winter's Tale*' (English Stud. xxxiii, Oct. 1952, 193–208) from which this quotation is taken.
4. As there is in *Cym.*, where Jupiter tells at v. iv. 107 that all will be well.
5. N. Coghill in *Sh.Sur.* xi, 1958, 40.
6. In *Wint.* this may exemplify the doctrine that 'true love cannot speak—
For truth hath better deeds than words to grace it' (*Gent.*, ii. ii. 18) and 'Silence
is the perfectest herald of joy: I were but little happy if I could say how much'
(*Ado*, ii. i. 275): but it is clear from the fact that Hermione's one speech is to her
daughter, and from her words, that her heart and mind are primarily on her
daughter. Because Perdita has only two short speeches in the scene and Hermione
one, it has been suggested that these two parts elsewhere in the play were
originally doubled. But feeling is deepest in these two: others speak more freely.
That 'Great joys, like griefs, are silent' (S. Marmion, *Holland's Leaguer*, v. i. 38),
is probably proverbial.

achieving this happiness, and the one who has suffered most in so doing, is Hermione.

IV. THE FABLE AND THE PLOT

The fable is important because there never can be complete escape from it. What some feel to be the dream quality of the play largely arises from the fact that a drama of emotional and spiritual strife of characters who are very much of this world and who are frequently in domestic settings, is superimposed on, or rather inextricably mingled with, a fairy story.[1] The fable is indeed of that kind, and it is also a traveller's tale of many peoples and places,[2] a romance, to be taken as Chaucer took such a book 'to rede and dryve the night away'. The story, in common with the fables of many contemporary plays, contains much commonplace folklore. The story of the babe of noble origin who is either cast adrift at sea or left in deserted country but who is saved, brought up by humble foster parents, and eventually recognized by clothing, jewels, or some personal mark and restored to fortunate estate is widespread from early times and in many languages. The lover-prince disguised as a country swain is similarly common; so is the opposition of a royal parent to an apparently imprudent match, and so is the constancy of the lovers. The accused Queen, the story of the faithful wife charged with adultery but cleared and restored to her husband's favour, is old and widespread.[3] It is also typical of these stories, as well as those with the 'patient Grissel' motif,[4] that the harsh trials and sufferings of the wife or maid are not shared at all by the man, or at least not in any comparable way. Yet the man always shares to the full in the final blessings, and, however guilty and responsible for the sufferings of others, he is ultimately absolved by facile excuse,[5] if any is needed at all. The fable also

1. Something similar is seen in *All's W.* and *Meas.*, and indeed the mixture of popular romance with realism of the actual world is shown in all the earlier romantic plays, especially in *AYL.* Even in *Lr.* another kind of realism is woven through a folk-tale.

2. So Stevenson, perhaps taking it from *Wint.*, gives as a sub-title to *The Master of Ballantrae*: 'A winter's tale', 'a tale . . . which extends over many years and travels into many countries.'

3. Cf. S. Trenkner, *The Greek Novella in the Classical Period*, 1958, 61.

4. The last novel of the *Decameron* tells of Grizelda's loving endurance; there is passage of time long enough for a baby boy and girl to reach marriageable age when they are restored to Grizelda their mother, who had been led to believe that they were dead. Grizelda's husband, the Marquess, had meanwhile lived without a wife. The story, popular since the *Clerk's Tale*, has points for comparison with that of *Wint.* and was used for the *Patient Grissel* plays of John Phillip (?1565) and Chettle and others (1600).

5. So, following the convention, for the scoundrel Proteus it was his 'penance

tells of a sheep-shearing feast—an old and widespread custom—
and there is folklore embodied in the talk of flowers and of customs
of one kind and another, particularly in that famous scene.

As to the plot itself, the first thing to be noticed is that Shakespeare has taken pains to turn improbabilities, even impossibilities,
in the fable, into possibilities; and the changes to make the plot
credible are striking. In *Pandosto* the babe is abandoned in an open
boat.[1] Its survival and guidance by the elements from Bohemia to
Sicilia is so impossible that credibility does not arise. Similarly
when Fawnia leaves Sicilia with her lover, although they do not set
out for Bohemia, we do not need to be told that the fates will get
them safely there. But in the play none of this is left to miraculous
chance. No doubt 'Fortune brings in some boats that are not
steer'd',[2] but this one is not of that kind: it has a professional at the
helm. The babe is sent off in charge of Antigonus in a ship: there
is no reason why it should not survive, and Antigonus is specifically
directed to take the ship and babe to Bohemia.[3] In Greene there is
no Antigonus: Shakespeare introduces him largely to make plausible the deposit of the babe, and then has to dispose of him on shore.[4]
The return journey is an equally striking instance of Shakespeare's
deliberate changes to give credibility. In *Pandosto* the young couple
reach Bohemia by fortunate mishap; but in the play the whole
operation is carefully planned with Camillo preserved to plan it.
There are many instances of this kind even in smaller points. Greene
does not say how long Egistus has stayed, but the play specifically

---

but to hear, / The story of your loves discovered' (*Gent.*, v. iv. 170); it is enough
for Claudio to say, 'yet sinn'd I not, / But in mistaking' (*Ado*, v. i. 260); the treble-
dyed Angelo is merely told that his evil quits him well (*Meas.*, v. i. 494); and
Bertram, deceitful, lying, and slanderous to the end, is forgiven without semblance of excuse (*All's W.*). But these plays are comedies and are to be judged
as such.

1. In *Tp.* survival is almost entirely providential. But there is attempt to give
faint plausibility, for although the boat is 'A rotten carcass of a butt', food,
water, and 'necessaries' are provided (1. ii. 146, 160–5). Miraculous voyages are
also common in legends of Saints.

2. *Cym.*, IV. iii. 46.

3. Some critics seem to have a perverse determination to ignore the planning
in the play. So Quiller-Couch can say, 'Old Antigonus on shipboard just bumps
on the first coast he comes to and deposits Perdita' (*Sh.'s Workmanship*, 1918, 324).
Even J. M. Nosworthy in his excellent *Cym.* (New Arden, 1955, xxxvii) says dis-
order can be remedied 'only . . . as in *The Winter's Tale*, by an extraordinary
series of coincidences'. There is no extraordinary series of coincidences. The
dénouement is naturally overwhelming to Leontes, Hermione, and the court, but
it has not come about mainly by chance; although, of course, chance has not been
entirely eliminated—it brings Florizel and Perdita together and the Shepherd to
the shore at the right time.

4. See p. lix, n.4.

states that Polixenes had been nine months in Sicilia to make it plausible that he could be the father of Hermione's child. That a healthy boy should die of grief in a day or two on hearing of his mother's disgrace may seem unlikely. But the case is not presented so crudely. The audience learns that the boy is ill, a sense of time is given to his illness by the deftly realistic touch that he is making some progress and that he has a physical sickness (II. iii. 9–11). It is not until the next act, 300 lines on, that his death is announced, so that the shock comes as a perfectly credible event, a death from physical illness accentuated by grief. In *Pandosto* Garinter is simply struck dead by Apollo. Autolycus, the Shepherd and Clown, Mopsa and Dorcas, with the songs and tunes, introduce everyday realism from contemporary life. The straying of sheep hardly needs rationalization but even here Shakespeare adds a reason. Wolff notes that Shakespeare could have taken details directly from Angel Day's version of *Daphnis and Chloe* (1587) or have borrowed them from *Pandosto*. But one detail, that of the hunt, is in Day but not in *Pandosto*, and so Wolff considers

> that Day's 'Daphnis and Chloe' is not only a secondary but a primary source of 'The Winter's Tale'. . . Shakespeare seems to have desired to employ, in 'The Winter's Tale', normal causation and human motive wherever possible, instead of chance . . . What more consonant with dramatic economy than that Shakespeare should have borrowed this hunt . . . to send the bear that devours Antigonus, and at the same time to frighten the sheep away from the hills so that the shepherd must seek them along the shore and there find the child?[1]

There is at least as high a degree of realism in *The Winter's Tale* as there is in most of Shakespeare's non-historical plays[2] and Shakespeare has deliberately re-fashioned the tale to give it this illusion of actuality.[3] It is interesting that the major improbabilities in the play—such as Hermione's concealment and the planning of it—are all entirely extra-dramatic. A plot of the *Pandosto* fable kind would require an atmosphere of fantasy. But the passions, virtues, and conflicts in which Shakespeare was interested could not survive in an atmosphere which was entirely one of fantasy; and so Shakespeare did much to make the play realistic too. *The Winter's Tale* has the intensity of actuality along with the imaginative stimu-

---

1. Wolff, 452–5. Greene mentions 'wolves or eagles' as reasons for the lost sheep and the attractions of 'sea ivy' (p. 199). Ivy, by the sea, is introduced in *Wint.*

2. There is no comparison, for example, with the impossibilities of *Err.*, *Gent.*, *Tw.N.*, *MND.*, or *AYL.*, not to mention *Per.*, *Tp.*, or even *Cym.*

3. Even the flight of Polixenes is rationalized, more, for example, than that of Macduff (*Mac.*, IV. ii).

lus which pure realism inhibits. There is a strong web of realism running through the warp of romance.

Not only did Shakespeare carefully bring credibility to the fable whenever it was important to do so, but most of the characters and staged episodes are intensely credible. Henry Morley[1] held that Leontes' passion is not a crime but an outbreak of insanity, of which it is a common form. Morley believed that 'it is hard for any man to have lived long in a wide circle of . . . acquaintances, and never to have seen Leontes', and he also believed that the madness is depicted so faithfully to life that Shakespeare must have seen it. The essential points of Leontes' jealousy and of the misery it causes are indeed a picture of something which can be met in ordinary life. Just as the Elizabethan court was not remote from the people but in many ways domestic, so is that of Leontes.[2] The episode has the air of being a family matter—as indeed it is. The community is small and intimate. Leontes knows Paulina so well that he knew that she would come and plague him (II. iii. 44). Everyone knows that Antigonus is not master in his own house but that he admires his wife, as henpecked men often do. Leontes, when crazed, becomes violent and abusive and intolerable to everyone including himself, as would be expected in a weak man accustomed to power. His courtiers and Paulina regard him with some contempt, as is shown by the aside of Antigonus at II. i. 198 saying that Leontes will be a laughing-stock and his retort at II. iii. 109 telling Leontes that he would leave himself with hardly one subject.

But the dramatic quality of this part of the play is high. The weakness of Leontes and the domestic atmosphere of the court give all the more dramatic force to the vigour and downrightness of Paulina and to the noble dignity and gracious strength of Hermione. It is indeed a moving dramatic story of defeat, of courageous fighting against the horrible and incomprehensible power of madness. When the scene moves to Bohemia and to Autolycus and the sheep-shearing, the milieu is indeed different but the scene and characters are very much of the Elizabethan world. Though Florizel and Perdita have something of the traditional artificiality of Arcadia, the sheep-shearing is not a conventional idyll but largely a realistic picture of a well-known popular festivity: 'The

---

1. Ed. of *Wint.*, 1905, 10–11. Cf. A. Symons on Leontes' jealousy: 'For sheer realism, for absolute insight into the most cobwebbed corners of our nature, Shakespeare has rarely surpassed this brief study' (*The Henry Irving Sh.*, vii, 1890, 320).

2. One of the first pieces of realism in the play is the nature of Leontes' court, which is remote indeed from any romantic world of make-believe, of fine conventional courtesy, or other fantasy.

country life is given the fullest force of actuality'.[1] Even the recounting scene (v. ii), so often particularly condemned as artificial,
is, on the contrary, a piece of almost precise Jacobean realism. The
gentlemen and their language would be seen and heard in court
circles every day.[2] *The Winter's Tale* has a much stronger element
of realism than most critics[3] seem to believe.

V. EVIL AND GOOD, TIME, GROWTH AND DECAY

The force which starts the play into action is 'that great foe to
faith, foul jealousy'[4]: the play demonstrates the harm which this
may do not only to persons other than the one overcome by the
evil but to that person himself, and it shows the triumph of resolute
noble womanhood. The play is also concerned with the passion for
justice and personal honour and with the virtues of integrity,
loyalty, courage, love, patience, and self-sacrifice.[5] It shows how
their power, aided by the gods and good luck, in time helps to
defeat the evil caused by jealous hatred, to restore most of the good
which had been destroyed and to bring about forgiveness and
reconciliation among all, or nearly all, concerned. There is dramatic tension, ugliness, and incipient tragedy, there is beauty
and charm which equal anything of the kind in Shakespeare, and
there is humour, roguery, and great happiness. Especially is it
shown that although uncontrolled violent human passion can

1. Tillyard, *Last Plays*, 43. See also IV. iii. 37n. and cf. *AYL.*, Arden ed. by J.
W. Holme, 1940, xx–xxi.

2. See p. lxxxviii. The intention in the above paragraphs is simply to illustrate
that Shakespeare's creative imagination was making accurate use of what he had
seen.

3. Critics who otherwise diverge widely in their views of the play—e.g.
Dryden, Pope, Warburton, Johnson, and in modern times Strachey, Quiller-
Couch, Wilson Knight, Bethell, Cruttwell, Leavis. The play is constantly but
wrongly referred to as if it were simply pure fantasy. Quiller-Couch can say, 'in
play after play he gets his people into a woodland, or a wooded isle, where all
are ringed around with enchantment, and escape the better for it. It is so in
A Midsummer-Night's Dream, in *A Winter's Tale*, in *The Tempest*. Men and women
are lost to the world for a time, to indulge their own happy proclivities and go
back somehow regenerated' (*N.C. AYL.*, 1926, x). The truth of this might be
debated for the other plays: for *Wint.* it is quite untrue. There is no woodland,
wood-magic, or island. There is countryside, but it is no land of make-believe,
no wood near Athens or Forest of Arden: nor do all the people enter it; and those
who do certainly do not all indulge their own happy proclivities or return
regenerated. Leavis (*Scrutiny*, 344) can speak of unreality 'penetrating and trans-
muting everything' in *Wint.* P. Edwards notes with approval that 'Bethell shows
how important is the avoidance of realism' in *Wint.* (*Sh.Sur.* xi, 1958, 13).

4. J. Fletcher, *The Faithful Shepherdess*, I. ii. 83. Jealousy is also the moving force
in *Pandosto* (see Wolff, 424–5).

5. The main themes are discussed on pp. xliv–l.

bring disaster to the sufferer and those around him, the gods can be benevolent and will aid those who understand affliction in others and who are strong and will not be shaken in their integrity. Lives and years which have gone cannot be recalled, evil cannot be conquered quickly or without some suffering and loss, but all the leading characters survive and these are reunited and reconciled with understanding, forgiveness, and love in as nearly complete happiness as the trials of life are ever likely to allow. It is not a Beaumont-and-Fletcherian facile reconciliation[1] but one which has been won and earned by human effort aided by the gods, and the play is the dramatic story of that fortunate struggle.

Leontes is overcome with the passion of jealous hatred. His murderous passion is the only real evil in the play. There is no spiritual sin, hardly anything indeed which an Elizabethan audience would have called evil, in the kingly wrath of Polixenes or the roguery of Autolycus.[2]

Hermione on the other hand is a woman not only of deep virtue but of divine strength in the power of her unconquerable love, which is love for her husband, her daughter, her friends, and her own honour and good name. Her nature is open and her love is generous. She is outstanding in the forces which fight against evil, but she is not alone; she is supported by good in other human beings and by good fortune.

The evil spirit which possesses Leontes does great harm, some irreparable but some which is to prove capable of repair. When the destruction is at its height Apollo shocks and terrifies Leontes. He is brought suddenly to see his sinful weakness for what it is, and he immediately repents. There is no prolonged soul-searching and inward struggle: Fate bludgeons him to his senses. But there can be no quick cure for such disease and no quick repair of the disaster it has caused. Cure and healing must take time: strength can only be built up slowly. The evil has so permeated his mind and spirit that these have to be re-formed, to some extent re-created. Solitude, long spiritual strife, repentance, and prayer are necessary. It must also not be forgotten that time, healing time, is equally necessary for Hermione. She has been wounded almost to death: she herself knew that there could be no easy remedy[3] just as Iago knew that

1. Cf. 'Merrythought: Methinks all we, thus kindly and unexpectedly reconciled, should not depart without a song' (*K. of B.P.*, v. iii. 181–3).

2. But see p. lxxx, n.7.

3. 'When you shall come to clearer knowledge . . . / You scarce can right me throughly, then, to say / You did mistake' (II. i. 97). Time was not necessary for Imogen or Posthumus, for he had simply been tricked. The case is quite different in *Cym.*

healing must take time and patience.[1] No immediate reconciliation could have healed Hermione because a major part of any cure for her must consist of the knowledge that Leontes had been purified and healed by expiation for his sin. It was necessary for her soul that she should be able to forgive fully and completely, and such forgiveness must be won: it cannot be given where there is any suspicion of unworthiness. That the gods will demand a long time of expiation is also emphasized in Paulina's bitter outcry.[2]

The struggle between good and evil, then, makes the basic conflict of the play. For evil to spend itself and good come to triumph, for estranged men and women to be reconciled, time has to pass.[3] Evil may destroy suddenly but healing must be slow. In *The Winter's Tale* time is a necessity, and the passage of time must show growth or decay or both.

It is however also dramatically necessary for the young to grow up; yet the arcadian scene is not to be regarded as a period of relaxation for the dramatist. Actions arising from happiness and virtue are as important as those which spring from unhappiness and evil, and are at least as likely to be the outcome of a responsible attitude to life. There is no deeper significance in violence than there is in gentleness, and this famous scene is as much an integral part of the play as any other. After the misery in the hate, strife, death, and decay at the court in the first part of the play, it is with masterly rhythm that the play moves on to happiness in the love, life, youth, growth, and power of beauty[4] in the floral countryside in the second part. Here the young are shown as having grown by nature, and their growth is emphasized by reference to great creating nature.[5] Some critics describe the scene as one of sap springing in the tree, symbolic of regeneration. But this is not really so. The gaiety is confined to the first half of the scene and even here there are already autumnal tones. There are the forebodings of Perdita, and the season of the year is late summer or even autumn[6]: it is

1. 'How poor are they that have not patience. / What wound did ever heal but by degrees?' (*Oth.*, II. iii. 358). And cf. 'Those wounds heal ill that men do give themselves' (*Troil.*, III. iii. 229).   2. III. ii. 210–14.

3. The necessity for time is emphasized in the title of *Pandosto* (see p. xxvii).

4. This power is a most important part of the virtue in the play. See pp. lxi, lxxvi–lxxviii. It has somewhat similar force in *Pandosto*.

5. IV. iv. 88. But see IV. iv. 88–92n.

6. The considerable evidence on the time of year is rather conflicting. Sheep-shearing should take place in mid-June (see IV. iii. 37n.). Perdita says 'the year growing ancient, / Not yet on summer's death, nor on the birth / Of trembling winter', which seems to indicate autumn. She gives some 'flowers / Of middle summer', but Polixenes calls others 'flowers of winter', suitable to his age. Perdita laments that she cannot give spring flowers (IV. iv. 79–82, 106, 113).

certainly not the time of the springing sap. Nevertheless it is Flori-zel's constancy in love which makes the last act possible.

Growth, as by nature, is also seen in the old, and it is here—in Leontes—that some find a weakness in the play, for he shows little sign of spiritual or moral growth. In so far as Shakespeare intends to give him personality Leontes is really a picture of a rather ordinary man all the time and at the end of the play an ageing man,[1] who indeed ought to be even older than his years. This leads to the question of decay. There are seeds of decay earlier in the play but they are most noticeable at the close. There is great happiness, but for the old it is a mellowed autumnal happiness,[2] which is all as by nature. Autolycus has sobered down, the widowed Paulina is sadder and, even though she is swept again into matrimony, her last words express much of the tone of the closing scene. The wrinkled Hermione[3] and her husband move on towards what must be the closing period of their lives, and even though that may last many years there is, right to the end of the play, the sense of the constant progress of time, 'Th' inaudible and noiseless foot of Time' which 'steals'[4] and which must show both growth and decay.

VI. CHARACTERS[5]

It is difficult to discuss characters in any play and particularly so in one which is a complex mixture of realism and fantasy. It is a commonplace of criticism to say that characters cannot be dis-entangled from a play but must be considered as parts of it, and as

1. Like Pandosto (p. 218, l. 11) he is about fifty (see i. ii. 153–60n.), which would be old age in 1611.

2. Some critics hold that there is greater happiness and greater prospect of hap-piness at the close of the play than at its opening. E.g. 'the play issues into a fairer prosperity than had first existed' (Tillyard, quoted approvingly by Edwards in *Sh.Sur.* xi, 1958, 13). Opinion must depend on the view taken about the onset of Leontes' jealousy. If there is no sign of this before i. ii. 108, then there is greater happiness, and prospect of it, at the beginning of the play than at the end; but the opposite is true if Leontes is jealous from the start. If—as it seems to me—there is initially only a small, vague cloud on the horizon, then the happiness is greater at the beginning. But it is difficult to compare two states of happiness which are so different. Initially, except perhaps for Leontes, it is a free, joyous, youthful, and sparkling happiness. At the end it is not of that kind, since the people have changed. We hear no 'Apprehend nothing but jollity' from Florizel: indeed, he is mute. Nevertheless there is promise of a new completeness in life 'not in spite of the old sorrow but because of it' (A. M. Mackenzie, *The Women in Sh.'s Plays*, 1924, 429), as there is not in the tragedies, e.g. *Lear*.

3. Yet Hermione's was not Donne's *Winter-face* but that *Autumnall* face com-pared with which 'No *Spring*, nor *Summer* Beauty hath such grace' (Elegy ix). Beauty, and the virtue in beauty, must be seen here too.

4. *All's W.*, v. iii. 41. Time is the thief that 'comes stealing on by night and day' (*Err.*, iv. ii. 60). 5. For the sources of characters' names see pp. 163–5.

parts of it, moreover, only when the play is on the stage where 'the
very persons' of the story may be seen 'as they were living'.[1]
Furthermore, characters must not be regarded wholly as individuals but largely as vehicles carrying ideas and themes and so acting as pointers to indicate the direction of interest that a play com-
pels.[2] *The Winter's Tale* is not the story of one person or even of a
group of persons but rather of passions, virtues, and actions. Nevertheless throughout Shakespeare the virtues, vices, and themes are
real and human and, vehicular though they may be, characters
must also have individuality; and the Victorians, however unjustifiably they treated characters as individuals detachable from
a play and even with extra-play lives,[3] yet were understandably
fascinated by the profound interest of personalities created by
Shakespeare's vast imagination, detached sympathy, and understanding of people. 'Preoccupation with "character" ' certainly
may be 'disastrous to disciplined attention',[4] but so may preoccupation with any one aspect of a play. It is naturally impossible to dis-
entangle the personal from the carrier element in most characters
but it is important to realize that both are usually there. In *The
Winter's Tale* characters are sometimes stage figures and often carry
various themes: nevertheless, as in all Shakespeare's plays, the
personality of each character has importance whatever its other
functions may be.

Leontes

Realistic treatment could make a harsh estimate of Leontes; but
he is primarily an agent to bring an evil force rapidly into play.
We must accept that he is lovable since he inspires affection in
Hermione, Paulina, Mamillius, Polixenes, and Camillo. But he is
not a great man: what greatness he has comes from his royal
position, his mad fury, the magnitude of the disaster he causes
and, by reflection, from the greatness and dignity of Hermione: he
has none of the kingly graces listed by Malcolm.[5] Little estimate
can, however, be made of him before he easily gives way to causeless jealousy and thereby arouses astonishment, anger, and ridi-

---

1. *H8*, Prol., 26–7. Cf. 'Commedies . . . fram'd to the life', *Troil.* (Epistle to 4⁰,
1609).

2. L. C. Knights, 'The Question of Character in Sh.' (in J. Garrett, *More
Talking of Sh.*, 1959, 68).

3. The dangers in laying too much stress on personality and in pseudo-critical
investigations of irrelevant matters are brought out by L. C. Knights in *How
many children had Lady Macbeth?*, 1933, and by (W). A. Sewell in *Character and
Society in Sh.*, 1951, *passim*, pp. 6–8 on Leontes.

4. J. Lawlor, 'On Historical Scholarship and the Interpretation of Sh.'
(*Sewanee Rev.*, 1956, 193).   5. *Mac.*, IV. iii. 91–4.

cule in those around him, and then, as he himself is made beast-like by his wild fury,[1] inspires terror by violence coupled with royal power. Weakness is also shown in his vacillation, his blustering abusive language, and his anxiety to stand well in public opinion.[2] A man of normal quality and susceptibility would be far more appalled than he is with the realization (as he believes) that he has wantonly murdered a noble and lovely wife, an only and most promising son, and—with particularly vindictive cruelty—an infant daughter. He is not to be examined closely as a man; he is more important as a vehicle, and it is better to concentrate on his jealousy than on his character, for Shakespeare uses him to show mad jealousy, and this picture is real enough.[3] At first he suffers the double torment of one 'Who dotes, yet doubts, suspects, yet strongly loves.'[4] Then his love becomes hate as his passion destroys all peace of mind[5] and he suffers loss of sleep, which some critics hold to be almost sufficient excuse for his crimes. Like Amintor[6] he has been brought '. . . to that dull calamity, / To that strange misbelief of all the world / And all things that are in it.' But Amintor was brought to that state by someone else, with true and terrible cause: Leontes reaches it without cause; mistrusting himself he mistrusts everyone. He deceives himself, and, like the deceived Lysander, is convinced that 'The will of man is by his reason swayed', and since his reason tells him that Hermione is unfaithful, anyone who cannot see this must be 'most ignorant by age, Or . . . born a fool' (II. i. 173). His jealousy is at once overwhelming and murderous, and the main theme of the first part of the play is often described as Leontes' 'hatred' of Hermione. The crazed madman is eventually shocked, frightened, and sobered into repentance. We must assume that he had a noble heart, which, as Paulina says, is touched (III. ii. 221), and that he is then truly repentant. That is what the quick movement of the play demands. We must also

1. '. . . there is not in nature / A thing, that makes man so deform'd, so beastly, / As doth intemperate anger' (Webster, *D. of Malfi*, II. v. 74–6). When Othello's mind becomes diseased he too is bestial in his language and treatment of Desdemona (*Oth.*, IV. ii). Like Thersites, Leontes is lost in the labyrinth of his fury (*Troil.*, II. iii. 1).

2. He fears being called a tyrant (II. iii. 121). He sends to the Oracle—an action on which the play turns—but this is only for confirmation to show others that he is right (II. i. 180, 191). For him Hermione is already condemned (III. ii. 90).

3. Cf. p. lxvi. Causes of the jealousy are no concern of ours: 'jealous souls / . . . are not ever jealous for the cause, / But jealous for they are jealous' (*Oth.*, III. iv. 160) is more fitting for Leontes than for Othello.   4. *Oth.*, III. iii. 174.

5. Jealousy is usually described in Shakespeare as mad (*Err.*, II. i. 116) and self-harming (*Err.*, II. i. 102).

6. Beaumont and Fletcher, *The Maid's Tragedy*, IV. i. 216.

think of him as carrying out his vow of daily penance (III. ii. 238) during sixteen years and agree with Cleomenes that Leontes has 'perform'd / A saint-like sorrow' (v. i. 1–2). But from the text it is difficult to see that he is changed: there is no evidence that he has, like Wolsey, come to know himself and to be aware of his littleness and still less of its blessedness.[1] Anyone who has come to have a sense of his sin and to be sorry for it must be said to have grown to some extent. Leontes had no choice: he was bludgeoned to his senses and to sorrow, but he is not shown as achieving humility, and his 'growth' seems to be what may be described as an unavoidable minimum in the circumstances. He is not meant to show greatness, in either storm or calm, but as a stage figure he must be accepted, as he apparently is by Hermione, at least as a reformed and con-trite man.

Hermione

Hermione is one of many Shakespearian characters in whom qualities, sometimes unexpected, are revealed by changes of cir-cumstance. She is beautiful, spirited and witty, frank and friendly; she is confident and successful in her position and happy and secure in her husband's love right to the moment when his jealousy is first made known to her (II. i. 56). After that she can never be gay and vivacious again. It is a vivid piece of dramatic irony and a vivid picture of a personality. When Leontes' madness puts her to the test, then the deeper quality of her character is shown, the strength and spirit, the dignity and deep generosity which have been partly hidden, and Hermione magnificently faces the ap-palling, sinister evil of Leontes' sudden mad jealousy. At first she naturally thinks that he jokes or has been deceived, then she is sorry for him but spirited enough to rebuke him sensibly and with kindness (II. i. 58, 78, 95). Then, when ordered to prison, she sees that something has happened beyond her control and she accepts

---

1. *H8*, III. ii. 378, IV. ii. 66. But of course Wolsey had fallen: Leontes was handi-capped by remaining a king. Yet he has no sovereign shame and shows little evidence of spiritual growth: he is chiefly conscious of the wrong he did to him-self (cf. Bertram, *All's W.*, v. iii. 14). A true penitent for wife-murder should not say that if he re-married he would murder his wife if Hermione's ghost appeared, or tell Florizel that his mother was obviously a faithful wife—a stock phrase, but one which should not so readily have come to Leontes. Worst of all is his desire for Perdita (v. i. 62, 123, 222). Yet it is essential to suppose that some revelation comes to Leontes, that the years have for him not been wasted, and that, if not quite like Richard II and Wolsey, he has come to see something of what he truly is. It must be remembered that, for Leontes, his personal honour had been out-raged. The main characters throughout Shakespeare naturally show human weaknesses and those of Leontes are plain throughout the play.

the position with a courageous dignity which affects everyone except Leontes. What Antigonus, Paulina, Emilia, and others say about her shows the honour and affection in which she is held.[1] Her nobility in iii. ii, the power of her integrity and courage, the clearness of her mind and speech, in contrast with those of Leontes, make one of Shakespeare's loveliest pictures of resolute womanhood. Hermione has a steadfast passion for justice, for the right; she would vindicate her honour not for herself but for her family (iii. ii. 43, 110),[2] but above all she will be true in her love and to her ideals. Her retreat is not merely a necessary stratagem required by the plot for other reasons but deliberated action prompted and sustained by her character. She has an utter honesty of soul and her love guides her to take responsibility for those she loves, but the main object of her self-sacrificing devotion is her daughter. This is shown not only by the fact that in the final scene she speaks only to her but because the only reason she gives to explain why she has remained apart from her husband is that the Oracle gave hope that Perdita lived (v. iii. 125–8).

Paulina

The gaoler knows Paulina 'for a worthy lady/And one who much I honour' (ii. ii. 5), and she is immediately shown to be loyal, resourceful, spirited, and resolute. She thinks, and acts quickly. She commands respect by her courage, ability, and goodness, not because she is feared,[3] and the essence of her character is brought out within a few lines of her first appearance. In the next scene even in her fury she is a very woman, especially in displaying likenesses between father and child. She is brave like Iago's wife[4] and in this and other qualities she has affinities with Hermione and with Katharine (*Henry VIII*). Her frank, outspoken sanity acts as a foil to the introverted morbid madness of Leontes just as does her robust courage to the more refined strength of Hermione. She may again show tenderness in her apology to Leontes (iii. ii. 218–32), but perhaps she is already opening her campaign for keeping him repentant since this is so like her speeches in Act V and exhibits the

1. Yet one of the most memorable tributes comes later from Leontes when he says that Hermione 'was as tender as infancy and grace' (v. iii. 26). This is perhaps the chief sign of his spiritual growth.

2. Hermione shows the conventional fear of dishonour but not of death. The importance of social order is repeatedly emphasized in Shakespeare's plays and there is Iago's famous speech on good name (*Oth.*, iii. iii. 159). Cf. *R2*, i. i. 167, 177.

3. The passage ii. ii. 39–42 shows tenderness and even poetry in her nature.

4. Cf. *Oth.*, iv. ii. 11–18, v. ii. 158–70.

calculated tactlessness[1] which is her favourite weapon. Yet her words here and later show deep human understanding: she can sympathetically appreciate Leontes' weakness and the nature of his disease.

In Act V it is learnt that Paulina has throughout the time-gap stage-managed everything for the dénouement.[2] Paulina was convinced of her husband's death sixteen years ago (III. ii. 231) and so the confirmation is no great shock, especially as it is accompanied by Perdita's return and the fulfilment of the great purpose in Paulina's life. She skilfully 'produces' the final scene and then, with tenderness and the right touch of pathos, announces retirement to end her days lamenting her husband. But, in the tradition of great actresses, retirement is deferred, for she is swept into the arms of Camillo and, while registering grief for Antigonus with one eye, Paulina, with the other, no doubt records appropriate joy at the bliss newly thrust upon her. And Camillo has acquired a wife beyond price.

Polixenes

Polixenes is obviously a necessary stage figure and in the first part of the play is little more. In IV. iv he is much more important in bringing out the character and beauty of Perdita and, in the rhythmic parallel, as a force for evil, although on a minor and softened scale, to Leontes in the early part. Although chaos threatens again only for a fleeting spell, Polixenes' blustering threats and vacillation are reminiscent of Leontes' behaviour.[3] He is much more a personal character in this scene as the heavy father a little in the manner of old Capulet, but even here he mainly serves to emphasize the social outrage which lay in the prospect of a prince marrying a peasant.[4] In Polixenes Shakespeare was able to use his source with little alteration.

1. She says that she ought to be punished for reminding the king of what he should forget (III. ii. 225) but immediately reminds him thrice, and continues to do so.

2. A heavy task, but obviously one that we are not meant to scrutinize. She has kept Hermione hidden a short distance from the Court. She has caused it to be believed that she has a statue of Hermione, she has (we can be sure) cared for her family (II. i. 144), and she has helped to keep Leontes penitent and firm in his resolve not to re-marry. An audience will not dwell on these details but will have more than a general sense that Paulina has been wonderful. She is the planner, like the Friar in *Ado*. There the pretended death of an injured woman is openly planned, but Shakespeare gives an earlier sketch of Paulina's thought in the Friar's words at IV. i. 212–42.   3. And cf. v. i. 200–1.

4. Even Ophelia was not socially good enough for a prince 'for on his choice depends / The sanity and health of this whole state' (*Ham.*, I. iii. 20). 'It would be very difficult to consider sixteenth-century outlook apart from its deeply in-

Camillo

In the first part of the play Camillo is closely modelled on
Franion: in the second he is mainly Shakespeare's creation but is
to some extent developed from Capnio. He is important structur-
ally in the play as a link between the three 'parts'.[1] Like Paulina he
is brave and loyal, but his loyalty is first of all to the right, not to a
person; and for the sake of honour and justice he deserts his master[2]
and sacrifices everything dear to him, with no thought of gain.[3] He
is straightforward, intelligent, and of sympathetic understanding:
an able administrator, good friend, and resolute man of action: he
works to resolve the chaos and plans and achieves the re-uniting in
Sicilia. Like Helicanus he is 'A figure of truth, of faith, of loyalty'[4];
vital as a link in the play and as an agent working for happy
reconciliation.

Perdita

Like Autolycus, Perdita has a brief period of great prominence
and then, as a person, becomes little more than an important
mute[5]: but when she is prominent—in the first part of Act IV—she
is at least as much a striking personality as a conventional character. She is chiefly important in her personification of virtuous
charm, grace, and beauty. The audience are prepared by Time and
Camillo for a shepherd girl wonderfully 'grown in grace' and 'of
most rare note'[6] and that is what she must be seen and heard to be.
These attributes influence everyone[7] and that influence remains
important when her character—even as a stage figure—has faded.
Her very appearance captivates young and old, and throughout the
play her grace and loveliness are felt to be a remarkable power.

---

grained concern with order and degree' (J. Winny, *The Frame of Order*, 1957, 17).
Although Autolycus is enjoying himself at IV. iv. 770–82, he probably does not
greatly exaggerate popular feeling at any attempt to 'draw our throne into a
sheepcote'. Cf. E. M. W. Tillyard, *The Elizabethan World Picture*, 1958, Ch. 2,
'Order'.

1. Cf. A. Bonjour, 'The final scene of *The Winter's Tale*' (*English Stud.* xxxiii,
Oct. 1952, 196–7).

2. In extreme distress, when Camillo's flight can be treated as evidence against
her, Hermione says that all she knows of it 'Is that Camillo was an honest man'
(III. ii. 74).

3. He loves his native land (IV. ii. 5). In IV. iv he again sacrifices his interest—
this time with Polixenes—in order to help to resolve the chaos.

4. *Per.*, v. iii. 93.

5. For the last third of Act IV and all of Act V. In this there is a marked difference from *Pandosto*, where Fawnia is at her strongest after she and Dorastus
reach Pandosto's court.

6. IV. i. 24, IV. ii. 43.

7. Except Autolycus. Cf. p. lxxx.

Like Pastorella in *The Faerie Queene*,[1] and as convention requires, her innate quality, her royal strain, is shown in her natural grace and authority. This very attribute makes it difficult for her to assume the homely duties of the mistress of the feast. She is, the Shepherd complains, retired as if she were simply one of those bidden to the feast. But for all this her country breeding is also evident. Unlike Florizel she is ill at ease in festive attire: she dislikes being so 'goddess-like prank'd up,' it makes her feel that she is playacting and it is not natural. She does not like flowers produced by cross-breeding, and even if this is spontaneous, still such flowers are bastards.[2] Perdita, like many country people, has a general and rooted dislike for artificiality in all forms, including make-up (IV. iv. 101).

Perdita is a shepherdess and her speech is frank and outspoken like that of all Shakespeare's women. There is little spiritual and nothing sentimental in the expression of her love for Florizel. She is womanly, as in the realistic pattern simile at IV. iv. 383, but unlike Fawnia does not sigh; she speaks little of her love; she is no Juliet or Sylvia: 'I cannot speak so well', she says of Florizel's protestations of his love, to which she refers in language of the folds, as his 'desire to breed by me'. But she also personifies beauty, and breath-taking beauty and grace are in everything about her, not only in her appearance and actions[3] but in her language. Her lovely speech of flowers combines these qualities with the freshness and vitality of someone who really knows the flowers: it is not simply a formalized poem.[4] There is a deep reality in that Perdita's speech is charged with human experience, in contrast, for example, with the purely descriptive quality of Oberon's famous passage.[5] Many have commented on Perdita's verse, which has the strange sweetness, without the tragic grief, of Ophelia's or Marina's lines,[6] but yet something too of the indefinable sadness of the

1. For a comparison of Perdita with Pastorella see A. Thaler, 'Sh. and Spenser' (*Bull. of Sh. Assoc.*, Oct. 1935, 192–211).

2. The popular mind has deep-rooted aversion from unnatural cross-breeding and even from bastardy in general. 'Bastard' has the sense not only of 'illegitimate' but also of 'inferior'. In England it is the most offensive term of opprobrium. 'Bastard slips shall not take root' (*Bk of Wisdom* iv. 3) was R. Shaw's text at Paul's Cross in 1483 (J. Gairdner, *Hist. of Rich. III*, 1898, 79). Shaw knew that there could be no deeper discredit in the popular mind than to be branded a bastard. (Cf. *R3*, III. v. 75; III. vii. 122, 127, 200; and *Wint.*, IV. iv. 83n.)

3. This is continually emphasized, e.g. IV. i. 24; IV. ii. 43; IV. iv. 32, 109–10, 135–46, 156–61, 176–7; v. i. 94, 130, 213; v. ii. 36.

4. Cf. F. E. Halliday, *The Poetry of Sh.'s Plays*, 1954, 172.

5. *MND.*, II. i. 249–52 ('I know a bank'). Cf. H. Fluchère, *Shakespeare*, 1953, 182–4.

6. *Ham.*, IV. v. 172; *Per.*, IV. i. 14–16.

ballads and much else of the magic of great romantic verse.[1]

Criticism is sometimes heard that the part of Perdita is often given to 'some pretty little fool'.[2] If this implies that Perdita herself has deep intelligence it is surely wrong[3] and concentration on virtuous beauty and grace[4] is right. She is also peasant, matter-of-fact, and down-to-earth with certain peasant views held with peasant obstinacy. And so the 'debate' with Polixenes shows her the peasant, not really understanding the argument, but obstinate, leading to the more important passage[5] where her main attributes, her loveliness and grace in person, in movement, poetry, and dance, charm all who see her and constitute a powerful and abiding force in the play.

Perdita carries on the theme of resolute womanhood and constancy which Hermione had shown, but this is secondary to the importance of her beauty.[6]

Florizel

Florizel carries the themes of resolution, constancy, and self-

1. Hazlitt (*Works*, ed. Howe, iv, 35; xx, 209–11) compares with the flower passage in *Lycidas* and 'dare not give the preference'.

2. Cf. Tillyard, *Last Plays*, 43.

3. Qualities required to play a part are of course not necessarily those of the actual character, although they may overlap, as they must with Perdita. We are nowhere directed to think that Perdita is particularly intelligent. In her talk with Polixenes she cannot grasp distinctions between art and artificiality. Her most impressive remark is made to Camillo at iv. iv. 576 and even this primarily shows resolution. His comment that 'she seems a mistress / To most that teach' clearly refers to resolution and moral worth. Like Lucetta she has 'no other but a woman's reason'. She thinks so because she thinks so (*Gent.*, i. ii. 23. Cf. *Troil.*, i. i. 105). But of course Perdita has plenty of natural good sense; she is by no means stupid or vacant, for there can be no true charm where there is no understanding vitality in the eyes. Cf. Browning, *Fra Lippo Lippi*, 215–18.

4. Virtue and purity are shown in Marina, Imogen, Perdita, and Miranda and seem to signify that they also possess all other womanly virtues, including beauty. This virtuous beauty may be a convention but it is also a vital power in *Wint.* Cf. 'beauty must be obeyed because it is beauty' (*Pandosto*, 205, last l.).

5. iv. iv. 103–80.

6. Perdita considers Florizel before herself and is self-denying, but not in the greater manner or degree of Hermione, Antigonus, Camillo, Florizel, or Imogen. She wishes to release Florizel for his own good, not for hers. She is fearful from the outset about their betrothal not because she is timorous for herself but for him. She must also regard the alliance as not being 'right' and she is loyal to the right. As with Leontes, a realistic interpretation—which would be quite unreal—could make a rather lowly estimate of Perdita. She lacks the sparkle, humour, and intelligence of Beatrice, Viola, or Rosalind. Autolycus' reference to her as a 'clog' could be defended from her forebodings and dejection. She has often to be told to cheer up and, in what she says, brings little strength to Florizel. But she brings him invincible strength by her beauty, grace, and virtue.

sacrifice. Superficially he is the conventional figure of the disguised lover-prince, but his character also has marked individuality. By nature he is happy, brave, and resolute: almost his first words, 'Apprehend / Nothing but jollity' and 'let's be red with mirth' (IV. iv. 24, 54), typify his irrepressible confidence and happiness, but he can be arrogant, headstrong, and unduly brusque.[1] His love-making has been unjustly described as pretty and sentimental,[2] for it is in fact ardent, manly, and animated. Yet his love is also full of loveliness and grace; and it is interesting to see how, inspired by these qualities in Perdita,[3] love brings them out also in one who, apart from his love, lacks them. There are few differences in treatment between the play and its source which are more striking than the love-making of Dorastus and Fawnia and that of Florizel and Perdita.

But it is his resolution and courage which are of vital importance in the play. He has to 'carry' Perdita, for she, in true womanly fashion, is practical and aware of all the difficulties and dangers which, for Florizel, do not exist. She would have broken away,[4] but there are no anxieties for Florizel: inspired, not by the practical encouragement and help, but by the grace and beauty of Perdita, he will sacrifice everything for his love and can see no obstacle as insuperable: and this is of fundamental importance in the resolution of the chaos.

Autolycus[5]

Autolycus is to some extent modelled on Capnio, who is an old servant of Dorastus described as being 'a wily fellow'.[6] He influences the action first in compulsorily providing Florizel's disguise to assist him to reach the ship, and next in deflecting the Shepherd and Clown from their proposed visit to the king and

1. To an Elizabethan this side of his character would be the natural realism of princely authority, which would also excuse the effrontery with which he lies to Leontes in v. i, although there is also much of the conventional in this: it only asks a little generosity to include his lies among those lovers' perjuries at which Jove laughs. At worst they are mere dramatic conventions: Paulina acts a lie for sixteen years; Portia lies easily when she says that she is going into a monastery (*Mer.V.*, III. iv. 31).

2. A. H. Thorndike, *Influence of Beaumont and Fletcher on Sh.*, 1901, 134.

3. And of course, as convention requires, 'as they say base men being in love have then a nobility in their natures' (*Oth.*, II. i. 213).

4. And has obvious defence. See p. lxxvii, n.6. This is traditional behaviour in such couples, and there is also the traditional protestation of honourable love by Florizel (IV. iv. 33, 150–3), which was also made by Dorastus (*Pandosto*, 211): it is frequent in Shakespeare (e.g. *Rom.*, II. ii. 143; *Tp.*, IV. i. 15ff., 95) and is a main theme of Fletcher's *Faithful Shepherdess*.

5. Perhaps played by Armin.   6. *Pandosto*, p. 215, l. 1. See also p. 165.

getting them on board. His part in the plot accordingly has some importance: he is not one of the 'uninterested persons' having no part in the story, like many of Shakespeare's fools; but he is not usually regarded as a fool at all.[1] It is difficult to place him but he has something in common with Feste. A. C. Bradley[2] has shown that Feste, beloved of no one, cares for no one, but is a natural singer and is gay.[3] He lives in a world of his own: his main task is to look out for himself and so he has an eye for the main chance and is not susceptible to charm, female or other. All this could be said of Autolycus, who certainly has an important artistic function in the play apart from his share in the plot. His worldliness and wit bring relaxation and relief of high dramatic value. He is also a delicate foil to Florizel. Both are arrogant[4] but Florizel is willing to sacrifice all for love. Autolycus would sacrifice nothing: his philosophy is to look out for number one. Florizel is susceptible to Perdita's beauty: Autolycus is susceptible to nothing of the kind. He also serves as a faint rhythmic parallel to the evil in Leontes in the first part of the play.[5] In so far as Autolycus is a thief, a pickpocket, and a cheat, he could, in the study, be unpleasant. But his crimes are understandable, and in a sense, even healthy, and, felony or not, they are venial in comparison with those of Leontes. On the stage the crimes of Autolycus are hardly felony at all; they are primarily tricks: that the Clown should be robbed is almost as if he had slipped on a piece of orange peel or as if Autolycus, with appropriate patter, had performed a conjuring trick.[6] For Autolycus has the great overriding virtue of being merry-hearted[7]: and

1. So, for example, he is not mentioned even by R. H. Goldsmith in *Wise Fools in Sh.*, 1958.

2. 'Feste the jester' (in *A Book of Homage to Sh.*, ed. I. Gollancz, 1916, 1649–69. Reprinted in Bradley's *A Miscellany*, 1929, 207–17).

3. The Jolly Miller is the popular exemplar.

4. Like Feste, Touchstone, and other 'fools', Autolycus airs his arrogant superiority with the delightful self-deceiving conceit of true comedy. Cf. IV. iv. 606–7, 746–8.

5. Leontes, centred on himself, acts from irresponsibility to life, and so does Autolycus. But the one is enveloped in black madness and is incompetent while the other has a sunny, roguish competence. Yet Autolycus presents a producer with a problem, for the scene is sensibly affected by the degree of unpleasantness which the character shows. It would seem that there should be just enough of the sinister in Autolycus to make the audience aware that it is there, but no more. Autolycus should be mainly a happy rogue. But see following two notes.

6. Nevertheless it is plain theft: it is not to be interpreted—as Jessica's theft could be—as virtuous action. But the play certainly does not lead the audience to sympathize with the Clown.

7. 'For a light heart lives long' (*LLL.*, v. ii. 18). He is a youthful Merrythought with the morals of a Figaro. Autolycus often echoes Merrythought (*K. of B. Pestle*) 'A merry heart lives long-a" (I. iv. 9); 'To what end should any man be sad

he is an intelligent rogue, a schemer of ability: he excites admiration and provokes laughter at the same time, and like Feste he is a natural singer.[1]

The realism in his character is emphasized by its weakness, not only the moral weakness which he takes no pains to conceal, but weakness which allows his spirits to be depressed by changed circumstances. He is at his best up to the end of IV. iv. After that he is not quite so cocksure, a little deflated, and he does not sing. As Bassanio advised elsewhere, Autolycus too has been forced to allay his skipping spirit with some cold drops of modesty. Life has become more serious for everyone, Autolycus included. Earlier he is so central that it can almost be said—as surely he would have said—that it is he, Autolycus, who is compassing the motion of the play, so to speak: later, as events change, he becomes merely one of the puppets and a minor puppet, and he senses the change. Unlike Falstaff he has no disastrous fall, but his position, and with it his panache, have indeed deteriorated.[2] But in his ups and downs Autolycus is a vital, vivid, and unforgettable character.[3] Johnson mentions no other character in his brief note on the play and his comment 'The character of *Autolycus* is very naturally conceived, and strongly represented'[4] is, accordingly, high praise indeed.

---

in this world' (II. viii. 10); 'Who can sing a merrier note / Than he that cannot change a groat' (IV. v. 3); 'I would not be a serving man . . . and no work would I do. . . This is it that keeps life and soul together, mirth' (IV. v. 14–20); 'Care . . . I defy thee . . . though I want drink to whet my whistle, I can sing' (v. iii. 3). Yet Merrythought lacks guile and roguery whereas Autolycus is enough of a Panurge to be whipped out of court for such 'virtues'. And there is enough of the undesirable in Autolycus for the audience to be reminded, humorously though it be, of thievish tricks and untrustworthy individuals—Forman supplies contemporary proof of this (see p. xxii), and even though he was seeking personal guidance, Forman's evidence here is important. It must also be remembered that in 'The Names of the Actors' in *F* Autolycus is 'a Rogue' and a rogue as described by Harman (36–41) is not a pleasant person.

1. 'I can bear my part—you must know 'tis my occupation' (IV. iv. 296). There are six songs in the play: five are by Autolycus solo and in the sixth he leads a trio. See pp. 172–4.

2. Witness his feeble attempt to call attention to his importance in the action (v. ii. 114–25).

3. There is an obvious picaresque element in Autolycus. But although he may be in the tradition of *Lazarillo de Tormes* (First English ed., 1586) and Nashe's Jack Wilton (*Unfortunate Traveller*, 1594), and may even be said to have affinities with Merrygreek (*Ralph Roister Doister*) and Diccon the Bedlam (*Gammer Gurton's Needle*), yet Autolycus is emphatically of Shakespeare. Just as the robust personality of Jacke of Newberie (in print before 1611) is created by Deloney from knowledge of such characters and of peasant life, so Autolycus derives from Shakespeare's knowledge of contemporary life.

4. *General Observations on Sh.'s Plays* (in *Works*, ed. Murphy, 1792, ii. 148).

Of the other characters *Mamillius* has attracted most critical attention. A boy of about seven,[1] he is one of Shakespeare's small group of children who have similarities in character and function.[2] To some Mamillius is a symbol of innocence slain by evil; a tragic recognition that the innocent do suffer with the guilty. To others he symbolizes frustrated youth and growth, the young plant nipped in the bud. But he does not need to be symbolic to have importance. He helps to bring out the characters of Leontes and Hermione and to give a human, domestic atmosphere to the court: his open goodness acts as a foil to the introverted evil in Leontes and his charm and vitality add to those qualities in the total effect of the play.[3] It has been suggested that Mamillius is 'something of a child-Hamlet' since one explanation of his sickening to death is his shame at the supposed sin of his mother and consequent taint upon himself.[4] This shame is taken by Leontes to be another sign of his son's noble character. But whatever importance is attached to Mamillius it must be remembered that his episode follows fairly closely that of Garinter in *Pandosto*.

VII. STYLE AND LANGUAGE

The play is mostly in blank verse with some prose, the only rhyme being in the speech of Time and the songs. *The Winter's Tale* is one of ten plays of Shakespeare which open with prose: prose is next used at the first appearance of Shepherd and Clown, half-way through III. iii. Polixenes and Camillo use it when they plan their visit to the Shepherd and so, briefly, do Camillo and Florizel when the prince changes clothes with Autolycus. A different prose, but rather like that of the opening scene, is used for re-

1. This seems the right age for one who is a child yet already something of a public figure, known to the whole nation as 'a gentleman of the greatest promise', a page, kissed by ladies, who can yet offer to fight and can argue with wit.

2. That Mamillius is the culmination of a short series of 'delicate, charming and intelligent' boys (*R3*, *Tit.*, *John*, *Cor.*) is suggested by the Countess de Chambrun (*Shakespeare*, 1957, 198). *Mac.* should be added: the glimpse of Macduff's son, also so soon to die, strongly recalls Mamillius.

3. A memorable comment on the death of Mamillius—sometimes criticized as being over-sentimental—is Swinburne's in *A Study of Sh.*, 1880, 222 (cited in *Var.*, 129n.). Like Perdita's beauty, although in a less striking way, the charm of Mamillius has a lasting effect in the play. Even after sixteen years Paulina remembers him as 'jewel of children' (v. i. 116)—although, of course, Paulina is then making every effort to keep Leontes grieving and patient.

4. A. Harbage, *Sh. and the Rival Traditions*, 1952, 250. Cf. *Wint.*, I. ii. 330; II. iii. 12–17; III. ii. 144–5, 195–8. This is not a comparison to be elaborated; but a rather curious likeness between Ophelia's description of Hamlet (*Ham.*, III.i. 152–4) and some of the references to Mamillius (*Wint.*, I. i. 35–45; III. ii. 195–6) may be noted. (Cf. C. B. Watson, *Sh. and the Renaissance Concept of Honour*, 1960, 412.)

counting the recognition of Perdita and the meeting of the kings. Of the common folk (Perdita never being of these) blank verse is used only by the Shepherd: the others, including Autolycus,[1] always use prose except when singing.

It has already been noted that in *The Winter's Tale* the language has all the marks of that of Shakespeare's late period: the play could be given an approximate date from its language alone.[2] The characteristics of language in the early and late periods, 'the mellifluous facility of the one and the compressed, often cloudy, pregnancy of the other',[3] have often been discussed, but perhaps little has been added to Bradley's comments on the language of the later tragedies and the last plays:

> the style, in the more emotional passages, is heightened. It becomes grander, sometimes wilder, sometimes more swelling, even tumid. It is also more concentrated, rapid, varied, and, in construction, less regular, not seldom twisted or elliptical. It is, therefore, not so easy and lucid, and in the more ordinary dialogue it is sometimes involved and obscure. . . On the other hand, it is always full of life and movement, and in great passages produces sudden, strange, electrifying effects. . . But readers who . . . object to passages where . . . the sense has rather to be discerned beyond the words than found in them . . . will admit that, in traversing the impatient throng of thoughts not always completely embodied, their minds move through an astonishing variety of ideas and experiences, and that a style less generally poetic than that of *Hamlet* is also a style more invariably dramatic.[4]

The unity of *The Winter's Tale* in style and language is not simply

1. Except when he speaks as *grand seigneur* at IV. iv. 746–8.

2. P. xxiii. For the songs, see pp. 172–4.

3. Gladys D. Willcock, *Sh. as a Critic of Language*, 1934, 3. The 'pregnancy' is sometimes sparkling, e.g. IV. iv. 135–46.

4. *Shakespearean Tragedy*, 1904, 88–9 (cf. also 85–7, 332, 336, 357). In this, as in other matters, perhaps we should not be too sure that 'We have left Bradley fairly behind' (cf. p. xliii, n.6). Many edd. of *Wint.* naturally have sections on the language, e.g. Charlton's, 1916, 170–8. Bethell, in *Wint. ed.*, 18–22, expounds a theory of metaphysical wit in the play which he had given less specifically in *Wint. Study*, 1947, 20–8. Other studies include F. C. Tinkler, 'The Winter's Tale' (*Scrutiny*, Mar. 1937, 344–64); Sister Miriam Joseph, *Sh.'s Use of the Art of Language*, 1947; H. Craig, 'Sh.'s Bad Poetry' (*Sh.Sur.* i, 1948, 51–6); *R3* (*N.C.* ed. D. Wilson, 1954, xxxiii–xxxvi, discusses tangle speech in the early as well as late Shakespeare); *Tp.* (New Arden ed. Kermode, 1954, lxxvii–lxxxi); *Cym.* (New Arden, ed. Nosworthy, 1955, lxii–lxiv); Elizabeth Tschopp, 'Zur Verteilung von Vers und Prosa in Sh.'s Dramen' (*Schweizer Anglistische Arbeiten*, 41, 1956 [Zurich Univ. thesis, 1953]); Evans, *Language*; Sutherland, *Language*; M. M. Mahood, *Sh.'s Wordplay*, 1957; T. R. Price, 'Word-play and puns in Wint.' (*Shakespeariana*, 1889, 221–7).

that of a play mainly in blank verse: it is a profound and rhythmic unity in which the language not only accords with plot, theme, character, and incident, but also characterizes, helps to fix, all these; and it also accords with and helps to produce general and particular dramatic effect.[1] Language is subtle enough in ordinary usage: with Shakespeare its subtlety is profound, and much of the virtue of *The Winter's Tale* derives from the power, beauty,[2] and decorum of the language. In her pioneer work on imagery Caroline F. E. Spurgeon noted that although no dominant symbol seemed to occur, *The Winter's Tale* gave her a sense of waves of imagery: she felt that the idea in Shakespeare's imagination seems 'to be the common flow of life through all things, in nature and man alike . . . the oneness of rhythm, of law of movement, in the human body and human emotions with the great fundamental rhythmical movements of nature herself',[3] but W. H. Clemen,[4] although attaching great importance to the imagery in the last plays, considers that there is 'less density and continuity of imagery' in them than there is in the tragedies.

The opening conversational prose is a kindly, courtly language, in marked contrast with the poetry which it immediately precedes and in strong dramatic ironical contrast with the tangled, involved speech which is soon to follow.[5] This speech, chiefly of Leontes after the onset of his madness, is frequently cited as the classic example of this kind of language in the late Shakespeare. Many comments on it have been made in addition to those of Bradley[6] but two simple points are perhaps not sufficiently emphasized. The first is that characters must speak in character, and that Leontes from I. ii. 108 to III. ii. 141 is a man crazed with jealousy.[7] He is at times

1. This aspect of the play is discussed in detail in Traversi, *Approach*, 1938, 11–15, 127–45.

2. Including the music of the language itself. Cf. Una Ellis-Fermor, 'Some Functions of Verbal Music in Drama' (*Sh.Jhb.*, xc, 1954, 37–48).

3. *Sh.'s Imagery*, 1935, 305.

4. *The Development of Sh.'s Imagery*, 1953, 180, 195–213.

5. The speeches of Hermione before I. ii. 108 spring naturally from a light and merry heart and so are filled with dramatic irony; e.g. her play with Polixenes' effeminate oath 'Verily' and the speech beginning 'What! have I twice said well?' (I. ii. 46–108).

6. P. lxxxiii above. So Dover Wilson ascribes such tangled and incoherent speech to carelessness or lack of 'finish' on Shakespeare's part or to 'logical breakdown or syntactical incoherence' because images and ideas came so thick and fast into his mind that he was 'unable to create a logical or syntactical framework quick enough to carry them' (*N.C. R3*, 1954, xxv–xxvi).

7. Just as Paulina—who also has her incoherencies—is from II. iii. 27 to III. ii. 214 an angry, excited woman. The speech of Polixenes also becomes tangled and somewhat incoherent when he is shocked and frightened.

incoherent as a jealous man in a state of mad uncertainty must be. His speech is tangled because his mind and emotions are tangled. The second point is only a reminder that a play must be studied as a play in action. Shakespeare's words are material always for the stage: they are used and complemented by the actor's art which Shakespeare so perfectly understood. There is sometimes little point in analysing his sentences grammatically, but there is always point in analysing them with the actors in mind. As with anachronisms and loose ends, grammatical shortcomings are of no importance so long as the sense—which often means an attitude of mind or an emotion—is transmitted to the audience. And so the incoherent language of Leontes, Paulina, and Polixenes is fitting in that, in sense, emotion, and verbal music, it accords with, and indeed materially helps to fix, their characters, the themes they convey, and the incidents in which they take part. It is worth noting, too, that the incoherence of this language can be exaggerated. There are only one or two passages which are difficult to understand[1] when heard or read quickly. The general sense is clear, and the full sense and force are perfectly clear when the passages are given with appropriate expression, tone and emphasis, movement and gesture by all on the stage. And since this is so it is as much an error to treat this language as a 'difficulty' as it is to bother about anachronisms and loose ends. On the stage there is no difficulty. All plays must be written in 'dramatic language' and the phrase more truly describes the language of the last than that of the early plays.[2] When Leontes is shocked and sobered into repentance his language is sobered too.

1. Notably i. ii. 136–46.

2. The accepted view is that Shakespeare was experimenting with language, as with other matters, in the last plays. Shakespeare expressed complex thought in early plays with normal grammatical language (cf. *All's W.*, New Arden ed., G. K. Hunter, 1959, lviii) and he also occasionally wrote tangled speech in early plays (cf. *N.C. R3*, ed. D. Wilson, 1954, xxxiii–xxxvi). He may have been experimenting with 'loose parenthetical syntax' in the last plays; but it is natural that as he became more thoroughly a man of the theatre he should develop a technique of writing which was mainly for the stage, and should more and more see and hear primarily the actor as he wrote. It may be Shakespeare's reliance on the actor which makes Evans (*Language*, 206) sense 'some imaginative exhaustion' though great technical skill in the language of *Wint.* Sutherland (*Language*, 152) detects a tiredness in the language of the last plays and says that at times 'Shakespeare is *not* writing correctly: he is writing at speed' and, in speaking of 'helter-skelter' speech also in early plays, Sutherland says that 'the meaning comes through; but . . . has to some extent been *pushed* through by the vigour and determination of the writer' (*Language*, 147, 153). But the abundance and rapidity of thought is a distinguishing mark of the last plays and the style depends much on this. It may be noted that parentheses are not peculiar to Leontes' speech. Parenthetical remarks are fairly evenly distributed throughout the play: lavish use of brackets was probably a habit of the scrivener Crane. (See p. xix.)

Until that time the tempo is fast, there is indeed a 'fevered quick-ness'[1] and his utterances are often twisted; but subsequently, as in the last speech in III. ii, his speech is deliberate, steady, and straight-forward and it remains so throughout the last act[2]: it is the speech of a man restored to sanity, and the language, more than anything, tells of Leontes' recovery.

The unevenness, the irresponsibility, of Leontes and his speech in the first part of the play are brought into emphasis by the strong precision of Hermione's dignified language, and both, and indeed all characters, use language which gives a strong illusion of reality.[3] And the reality of Leontes' mental agony[4] is as harsh and bitter as the language. In this part of the play the language, to a large extent, is the very play. *Macbeth* in its action as well as in its language is full of tumult and storm; but in *The Winter's Tale* the tumult is mainly in the words; there is, especially in the first part, comparatively little action. There are rhythmic and musical changes in the taut bareness of Camillo's disclosure to Polixenes, in the happy scene with Mamillius, in the healthy vigour of Paulina's robust and downright speech, and notably in the messengers' account of the Oracle.[5]

Hermione's speech in which she says that she has no wish to live may be compared with Imogen's,[6] but Imogen's is gentler, simpler, the speech of a younger woman. Hermione's is more fitted for a court of justice, Imogen's for the countryside. The language char-acterizes both speaker and scene as it does throughout the play: so the language of Time befits the character in its rather naïve sim-plicity and befits the 'scene' as being an episode quite distinct from the course of the play. It is verse, but different verse from any found elsewhere. This stilted language of Time is conventional formal speech used also for choruses elsewhere in Shakespeare,[7] and

1. Evans, *Language*, 206.

2. The difficulty at v. i. 59 is probably due to corruption of the text.

3. Evans, *Language*, 206, holds that the 'rough and abrupt phrases' in the first part of the play have an effect which is even 'more subtle than a direct realism.' Bethell asserts that the characters, although they use realistic vocabulary, do not speak in character and that 'The style represents Shakespeare's mind, not the character's; indeed, it draws our attention *away from* the speaker to what is spoken about' (*Wint. ed.* 22, 205, n.6). This latter can only be recorded as a point of view which I do not share.

4. Cf. I. ii. 108–20, 137–46, 284–96, 324–33; II. i. 36–52, 64–78, 100–5; II. iii. 1–9. There is complexity in the language of other characters (cf. p. lxxxiv, n.7) and even—of a different sort—in the last four lines of Time's speech.

5. I. ii. 412–13, II. i. 1–32, II. iii. 32–129, III. i.

6. *Wint.*, III. ii. 91–116; *Cym.*, III. iv. 44–129.

7. Chorus (*Rom.*), Rumour (*2H4*), Chorus (*H5*), Gower (*Per.*), Chorus (*H8*). But there are also many differences here. One must not, for example, equate the

sometimes for the speech of apparitions.[1] Here it provides essential information, but it has to be, as it is, in some way like the old-fashioned rustic Father Time.[2] The heroic couplet is also used in Gower's Epilogue to *Pericles* and for the 'chorus' in *Henry VIII* (Prologue and Epilogue) and rhymed couplets are at the end of some of the 'chorus' passages in *Henry V* and *Romeo and Juliet*, and in all these there are affinities with the language and spirit of Time's speech. This pageant language was probably as convention-al as stage dialect and is precisely the language which an audience would expect from old Father Time. Gower specifically states[3] that modern wits will find an old man's rhymes rather simple and antiquated and that they are lame. The purpose of this language is not simply to characterize the speaker but to differentiate him from 'normal' characters in the play and to emphasize that he is in one sense outside the play.[4]

The language also characterizes speakers and episode in the dream of Antigonus. The bluff Antigonus of II. i and II. iii has sacri-ficed self-interest and put his life in peril; he has taken charge of a babe and he has, in a dream, a spiritual visitation. His experiences have changed his character, and his language has changed. There is something finer, even a nobility, in his last speech which char-acterizes the new Antigonus and lightly foreshadows his death.

In great contrast this is immediately followed by the homely, rustic prose of Shepherd and Clown. Later on there is remarkable dramatization of incident and character through language in the

---

almost epic language and style of the Choruses in *H5* with the stage archaic style, in short couplets, of Gower in *Per*. Yet they all differ from the other language in their particular plays. Cf. p. 168.

1. E.g. *R3* (v. iii. 118–76), *Cym.* (v. iv).

2. 'If the speech were better it would not be so good' (Shakespeare, *Works*, ed. G. L. Kittredge, 1936, 432).

3. *Per.*, I, Prol. 11–14; IV, Prol. 48.

4. This use of language for separating characters from the main stream of a play seems to warrant further study. A good example is the language used for the play in *Ham*. There are, of course, affinities with all language which is used parenthetically to give an audience necessary information. Some of Shake-speare's earlier blank verse when used for this purpose (e.g. *All's W.*, IV. iv. 1–14) has stylistic affinity with Time's speech. But rustic characters who are within a play, even in such a marginal way as the gardeners in *R2* (III. iv), do not use this distinguishing language. J. C. Maxwell has suggested that Shakespeare always used a commonplace style for pageants (*N.C. R3*, ed. Dover Wilson, 1954, xxxiv). (See also p. 168.) The language used for the masque in *Tp.* (IV. i) differs in tone from, and is more formal than, that used elsewhere. Prospero, as magician, uses language which is rather different from that used by Prospero the normal man and even in one speech the language changes from that of the one to that of the other, e.g. v. i. 33–87, at l. 50).

changed speech of the Shepherd, first, as noted above, in the
authority of the Shepherd as a landowner and then in the verse of
the doomed old man.[1] There is throughout a nice distinction between the language of the Shepherd and that of the Clown: there
is always something more of age and responsibility in the Shepherd's speech than in that of his son.[2]

Prose is used instead of verse to characterize incidents as well
as persons, and differences in kind of prose and kind of verse have
the same purpose. The prose used by the Gentlemen in v. ii to
recount the meeting of the kings and the recognition of Perdita is
a good example. The language is at first sight ornate and artificial, but it is courtly language of the time which accurately char-
acterizes the Gentlemen. Its very 'artificiality', which has caused
some, including Bethell, to reject it as a burlesque, is in fact nothing
of the kind, but precisely the opposite—a piece of contemporary
reality.[3] Elsewhere the slower tempo of the prose is a stylistic and
dramatic contrast to the quicker verse, acting in a normal way, and
as described by Bonamy Dobrée, as a 'rhythmic brake',[4] but the
language of the Gentlemen is a fast, tumbling, breathless speech
characterizing the speakers by its kind,[5] and the situation by its
tempo. There are probably few passages in Shakespeare which
more intensely demand an Elizabethan ear and attitude of mind
for their proper appreciation. This applies both to the whole and
to individual words and phrases: a modern interpretation, for
example, of the description of Paulina with, simultaneously, 'one
eye declined' and 'another elevated' could easily treat the account
as ludicrous and might even lead to jocular comment on Paulina's
ocular gymnastics. But this would be wrong interpretation of a
phrase which simply meant 'with a mixture of grief and happiness'.[6]
This scene then moves back into the comedy prose of the rustics
which had ended the previous act. The last scene is in the same
verse of measured seriousness found at the beginning of the act

1. For a detailed analysis of the Shepherd's verse see F. E. Tinkler, 'The
Winter's Tale' (*Scrutiny*, Mar. 1937, 349–51).

2. Not only in iv. iv. but also in v. ii.

3. Even the tears are at least conventional reality. For although tears are
womanish, a man may, off-stage, weep for joy. Cf. the recounting in *Ado* (i. i.
19–25).

4. *Histriophone*, 1925, 27.

5. It is 'a messenger-speech scene for several voices' in 'the same dialect of
early seventeenth-century refinement and wit as is used by Archidamus and
Camillo' in i. i (N. Coghill, 'Six points of Stage-craft in The Winter's Tale' in
Sh.Sur. xi, 1958, 39). It is a rather heightened form of the speech in i. i in a faster
tempo.

6. See v. ii. 74–5n.

until Paulina invokes the 'statue' to move. The tenseness of the situation is then characterized by the language, particularly by Paulina's short phrases with marked pauses between each: the excitement comes briefly into the general speech and the play moves quietly to its close.

THE WINTER'S TALE

CHARACTERS IN THE PLAY[1]

LEONTES, King of Sicilia.
MAMILLIUS, young Prince of Sicilia.
CAMILLO,
ANTIGONUS,
CLEOMENES, } Four Lords of Sicilia.
DION,
POLIXENES, King of Bohemia.
FLORIZEL, Prince of Bohemia.
ARCHIDAMUS, a Lord of Bohemia.
OLD SHEPHERD, reputed father of Perdita.
CLOWN, his son.
AUTOLYCUS, a rogue.
A Mariner.
A Gaoler.

HERMIONE, Queen to Leontes.
PERDITA, daughter to Leontes and Hermione.
PAULINA, wife to Antigonus.
EMILIA, a lady attending on Hermione.
MOPSA,
DORCAS, } Shepherdesses.

Other Lords and Gentlemen, Ladies, Officers, and
Servants, Shepherds, and Shepherdesses.

Time, as Chorus.

SCENE: Partly in Sicilia and partly in Bohemia.

---

1. In *F* the list is given as 'The Names of the Actors' on p. 303 at the end of the play and concludes with the word FINIS. Like those in *F* for *Gent.*, *Meas.*, and *Oth.*, it was probably drawn up and put in at the printing house to fill a page which would otherwise be largely blank. It does not include the Mariner, the Gaoler, Mopsa, Dorcas, or Time: Emilia is described simply as 'a Lady': otherwise the descriptions are as given above. There is no mention of 'Ladies, Officers' among the extras. Mamillius is Mamillus in the list but Mamillius elsewhere in *F*; Cleomenes is Cleomines and Autolycus is Autolicus throughout *F*. A babe and a bear are also required, and carters, neat-herds, and swine-herds (three of each) for the satyrs' dance at IV. iv. 343. In 1709 Rowe (1) added Mopsa and Dorcas and made the list of extras to read 'Goaler, Shepherds, Shepherdesses, and Attendants'. For the names of characters see pp. 163–5.

THE WINTER'S TALE

ACT I

SCENE I

Enter CAMILLO *and* ARCHIDAMUS.

Arch. If you shall chance, Camillo, to visit Bohemia, on
the like occasion whereon my services are now on
foot, you shall see, as I have said, great difference
betwixt our Bohemia and your Sicilia.

Cam. I think, this coming summer, the King of Sicilia   5
means to pay Bohemia the visitation which he justly
owes him.

Arch. Wherein our entertainment shall shame us: we will
be justified in our loves: for indeed—

Cam. Beseech you—   10

Arch. Verily I speak it in the freedom of my knowledge:
we cannot with such magnificence—in so rare—I
know not what to say—We will give you sleepy
drinks, that your senses (unintelligent of our insuf-
ficience) may, though they cannot praise us, as little   15
accuse us.

Cam. You pay a great deal too dear for what's given
freely.

Arch. Believe me, I speak as my understanding instructs
me, and as mine honesty puts it to utterance.   20

ACT I

Scene I

Act I] *Actus Primus. F.*   Scene I] *Scœna Prima. F.*   10. Beseech] 'Beseech *F.*
19. Believe] 'Beleeue *F.*

Scene i] Sicilia: in or near Leontes'
palace.
8–9. *Wherein . . . loves*] 'In that visit
our [inadequate means] to entertain

you will make us feel ashamed, but we
will be vindicated by our affection,
which shall make up for it.' This courtly language is similar to that of v. ii.

3

Cam. Sicilia cannot show himself over-kind to Bohemia.
They were trained together in their childhoods, and
there rooted betwixt them then such an affection
which cannot choose but branch now. Since their
more mature dignities and royal necessities made   25
separation of their society, their encounters, though
not personal, have been royally attorneyed with in-
terchange of gifts, letters, loving embassies, that they
have seemed to be together, though absent; shook
hands, as over a vast; and embraced, as it were, from   30
the ends of opposed winds. The heavens continue
their loves!

Arch. I think there is not in the world either malice or
matter to alter it. You have an unspeakable comfort
of your young prince Mamillius: it is a gentleman of   35
the greatest promise that ever came into my note.

Cam. I very well agree with you in the hopes of him: it is
a gallant child; one that, indeed, physics the subject,
makes old hearts fresh: they that went on crutches

27. have] *F2;* hath *F.*   30. vast] *F;* Vast Sea *F2.*

23. *affection*] This friendship is of
a deeply emotional kind. Cf. v. iii.
54n.

26. *encounters*] intercourse, meetings.
Cf. III. ii. 49.

27. *have*] For 'hath' as third person
plural see Abbott, §334, and cf. I. ii. 1.

attorneyed] performed by proxy. An
attorney is a substitute or deputy.

30. *vast*] a waste, a wide expanse of
country, sea or time. Cf. 'Thou god of
this great vast' (the sea) (*Per.*, III. i. 1);
Tp., I. ii. 327; *Ham.*, I. ii. 198; and
'all the world's vastidity' (*Meas.*, III.
i. 70).

31. *ends ... winds*] as from the sources
of winds blowing from opposite points
of the compass; i.e. from points
separated by a great distance—a
world apart. In contemporary maps
and emblem books it is common to
find faces of cherubs representing
winds blowing from the four corners,
and there are frequent references to
these ends and winds, e.g. *Cym.*, II. iv.

28, III. iv. 34–5; *Per.*, III. Prol. 17;
Matthew, xxiv. 31; *Philaster*, III. i. 121;
Donne, *Divine Poems*, VII.

31–4. *The heavens ... alter it*] The
irony is marked. The heavens do not
continue their loves and there is soon
found to be malice and matter (even
though imagined) to alter it.

35. *Mamillius*] See p. lxxxii. From
this reference to Mamillius to the end
of the scene the hyperbole is no longer
expressed in courtly idiom but in
simple and direct speech. The high
dramatic quality of the passage lies in
the irony of the promised brilliant
future of Mamillius, in the emphasis
on the necessity for a king to have an
heir, and in looking forward to the
Oracle and to the long time of waiting
until the king has an heir who is also
a son-in-law. *Cym.*, I. i, echoes this
scene, and the extravagant praise
there given to Posthumus (I. i. 19–22)
recalls that here given to Mamillius.

38. *physics the subject*] acts as a cor-

ere he was born desire yet their life to see him a man.   40
Arch. Would they else be content to die?
Cam. Yes; if there were no other excuse why they should
    desire to live.
Arch. If the king had no son, they would desire to live on
    crutches till he had one.   *Exeunt.*   45

SCENE II

Enter LEONTES, HERMIONE, MAMILLIUS, POLIXENES,
        CAMILLO, [*and Attendants*].

Pol. Nine changes of the watery star hath been
    The shepherd's note since we have left our throne
    Without a burden. Time as long again
    Would be fill'd up, my brother, with our thanks;
    And yet we should, for perpetuity,   5

Scene ii
Scene ii] *Scœna Secunda. F.*   S.D. *and Attendants*] *Theobald; not in F.*

dial, reinvigorates the whole nation.
'The subject' is plural, standing for
'all the king's subjects'. Cf. *Lr.*, iv.
vi. 108; *Ham.*, i. i. 72; *Meas.*, iii. ii.
129.

Scene ii
Scene ii] In Leontes' palace.
1–2. *Nine . . . note*] The shepherd has
recorded the passage of nine months.
This period is a minimum to make it
possible that Polixenes could be the
father of Hermione's child. It can also
be regarded as a maximum for reasonable holiday absence from a throne
and family. The moon is 'the moist
star' (*Ham.*, i. i. 118) and 'the gover-
ness of floods' (*MND.*, ii. i. 103).
Although associated with Diana and
therefore with chastity, the moon is
also associated with fertility and with
growth and decay (Frazer, *Golden
Bough*, vi, Adonis, etc.; ii, 1936, 129–
39).
    1. *hath*] perhaps another example of
the old plural (cf. i. i. 27) after

changes but possibly a normal singular
after *note*.
    3–9. *Time . . . before it*] 'I could spend
another nine months thanking you and
yet leave for ever in your debt; and so,
like the figure 0, which can greatly
increase value when put in the right
place, I must with one "thank you"
multiply the many thousands of others
that would stand before this 0.' Cf.
H5, Prol. 15–16, and the note in New
Arden ed. by J. H. Walter, 1954, who
cites from J. Baret, *An Alvearie or . . .
Dictionarie*, 1580, Sig. A8r (A briefe
Instruction of Arythmetike): 'a called
a ciphre, which is no Significatiue
figure of it selfe, but maketh the other
figures wherewith it is ioined, to
increase more in value by their place
. . . in euerie Compound, or Digit
number the first place is from the right
hand to the left, and there you must
first begin to count the value of your
number'. By itself O is worthless: 'thou
art an O without a figure . . . thou art
nothing' (*Lr.*, i. iv. 192–4).

Go hence in debt: and therefore, like a cipher
(Yet standing in rich place) I multiply
With one 'We thank you' many thousands moe
That go before it.

Leon.   Stay your thanks a while,
And pay them when you part.

Pol.   Sir, that's to-morrow.   10
I am question'd by my fears, of what may chance
Or breed upon our absence; that may blow
No sneaping winds at home, to make us say
'This is put forth too truly'. Besides, I have stay'd
To tire your royalty.

Leon.   We are tougher, brother,   15
Than you can put us to 't.

Pol.   No longer stay.

Leon. One seve'night longer.

Pol.   Very sooth, to-morrow.

Leon. We'll part the time between 's then: and in that
I'll no gainsaying.

Pol.   Press me not, beseech you, so.
There is no tongue that moves, none, none i' th' world,
So soon as yours, could win me: so it should now,   21
Were there necessity in your request, although
'Twere needful I denied it. My affairs
Do even drag me homeward: which to hinder

---

19. beseech] 'beseech *F*.

8. *moe*] more. This form is often used for the comparative of *many*. *O.E.D.* mo C2. Cf. IV. iv. 274; V. ii. 127.

11–14. *I am question'd . . . truly*] The passage is much discussed but the general sense is clear. Polixenes is merely saying here and at 24–5 that because of affairs of state he must go home. This was perfectly understood by Camillo who remembers Polixenes' reason and cites it at 216. The passage may be paraphrased: 'I am tormented by my fears concerning what may happen by chance or develop because of my absence. [I am tormented in this way in order] that no biting winds may [indeed] blast [affairs] at home,

and make me say that there were only too good grounds for this [anxiety].' Cf. *Lr*, IV. iii. 1–6.

13. *sneaping*] biting. Cf. *LLL.*, I. i. 100; *Lucr.*, 333.

15–16. *We are . . . to 't*] 'I can stand any test of that kind which you could put on me.'

19. *so*] 'in such a manner', 'to such an extent' (Schmidt 3).

21–3. *So soon . . . denied it*] 'If what you are asking were really essential to you, your request should prevail this time also, even though [for my own sake] it were important for me to refuse.'

24–5. *which to hinder . . . to me*] 'To

Were (in your love) a whip to me; my stay,   25
To you a charge and trouble: to save both,
Farewell, our brother.
Leon.   Tongue-tied our queen? speak you.
Her. I had thought, sir, to have held my peace until
You had drawn oaths from him not to stay. You, sir,
Charge him too coldly. Tell him, you are sure   30
All in Bohemia's well: this satisfaction
The by-gone day proclaim'd: say this to him,
He 's beat from his best ward.
Leon.   Well said, Hermione.
Her. To tell, he longs to see his son, were strong:
But let him say so then, and let him go;   35
But let him swear so, and he shall not stay,
We'll thwack him hence with distaffs.
Yet of your royal presence I'll adventure
The borrow of a week. When at Bohemia
You take my lord, I'll give him my commission   40
To let him there a month behind the gest
Prefix'd for's parting: yet, good deed, Leontes
I love thee not a jar o' th' clock behind

oppose this call would (if you will excuse me saying so) be grievous to me.'

31–2. *this . . . proclaim'd*] 'the pleasure of this news we had yesterday'.

34–7. *To tell . . . distaffs*] 'To say that he longs to see his son would be a strong reason, but [if that is what he feels] let him out with it [—you see he has never said this—] and let him go. And if he would go so far as to swear on oath that this is his reason we would then not only allow him to go but would use every effort to pack him off home at once.' She refers to this in 28–9, but in 48–9 appears to contradict the view expressed here. For the difference between *saying* and *swearing* see II. i. 62–4 and v. ii. 158nn.

38–9. *Yet . . . week*] 'Yet I will risk the loan of your royal presence here a week longer.' *Adventure = risk*, since a loan must be repaid.

38–42. *Yet . . . parting*] Rowe (1) noted that this part of the speech is addressed to Polixenes.

39–42. *When . . . parting*] 'When you are delighting my lord in Bohemia I will give him permission in advance to stay there a month beyond the allotted time.' And so Hermione will repay the 'borrowing' of Polixenes for a week. For *take = charm*, delight, cf. III. ii. 37; IV. iv. 119.

40. *give . . . commission*] authorize.

41. *let him*] allow him (to stay).

gest] the stage or halt in a journey, especially a royal progress: hence, as here, the time allotted for such a stage or halt. *O.E.D.* †gest *sb.4*.

42. *good deed*] in very truth, indeed.

43–4. *not a jar . . . lord*] 'not a tick of the clock less than any other lady—whoever she may be—loves her husband'. We must assume these two ellipses but it is not clear what part of speech *she* is. Shakespeare often uses

What lady she her lord. You'll stay?
Pol.   No, madam.
Her. Nay, but you will?
Pol.   I may not, verily.   45
Her. Verily!
You put me off with limber vows; but I,
Though you would seek t' unsphere the stars with oaths,
Should yet say 'Sir, no going'. Verily,
You shall not go: a lady's Verily's   50
As potent as a lord's. Will you go yet?
Force me to keep you as a prisoner,
Not like a guest: so you shall pay your fees
When you depart, and save your thanks? How say you?
My prisoner? or my guest? By your dread 'Verily',   55
One of them you shall be.
Pol.   Your guest then, madam:
To be your prisoner should import offending;
Which is for me less easy to commit
Than you to punish.
Her.   Not your gaoler then,

50. lady's Verily's] Ladyes Verely'is *F*.

the pronoun as a noun. Cf. iv. iv. 350.

47. *limber*] limp, flabby. Verily is a feeble expression; one of the 'pretty oaths that are not dangerous' (*AYL.*, iv. i. 169); the sort of oath one would expect from 'a comfit-maker's wife' (*1H4*, iii. i. 248).

48. *unsphere the stars*] reference to the Ptolemaic theory that the stars moved in spheres round the earth. Hence 'put the stars out of their normal course'.

50. *Verily's*] an instance in *F* of the use of an apostrophe to indicate an elided vowel; a practice which later became more common.

53. *fees*] In addition to fees charged for special quarters, food, bedding, release from irons, etc., it was customary—at least from the time of Henry VI, and perhaps of Henry III, until 1774—to make prisoners pay a fee on release even if they were innocent. The fees were sometimes paid to the Clerk of the Assize, or of the Peace,

or the Sheriff, but they were also claimed by gaolers. The legality of these fees and the precise officer to whom they should be paid are obscure, but they were certainly claimed by different officers, and particularly by gaolers, as common practice from the 15th to 18th centuries. Another contemporary reference is in Heywood, *A Woman killed with Kindness*, 1607 (*Dramatic Works*, 1874, ii. 106, 128; *A Woman*, etc., ii. ii. 10, iv. ii. 26—in McIlwraith, *Five Elizabethan Tragedies*, 1938). The best treatment seems to be in the unpublished Oxford B.Litt. thesis, 1952, *Life and Conditions in London Prisons, 1553–1643*, by Clifford Dobb, especially 240–7. See also John, Baron Campbell, *Shakespeare's Legal Acquirements*, 1859, 59–60, and A. Crew, *London Prisons*, 1933, 30, 47, 62, 69.

57. *import offending*] 'imply that I had committed some offence against you'.

But your kind hostess. Come, I'll question you   60
Of my lord's tricks, and yours, when you were boys.
You were pretty lordings then?

Pol.   We were, fair queen,
Two lads that thought there was no more behind,
But such a day to-morrow as to-day,
And to be boy eternal.

Her.   Was not my lord   65
The verier wag o' th' two?

Pol. We were as twinn'd lambs that did frisk i' th' sun,
And bleat the one at th' other: what we chang'd
Was innocence for innocence: we knew not
The doctrine of ill-doing, nor dream'd   70
That any did. Had we pursu'd that life,
And our weak spirits ne'er been higher rear'd
With stronger blood, we should have answer'd heaven
Boldly 'not guilty', the imposition clear'd
Hereditary ours.

Her.   By this we gather   75
You have tripp'd since.

Pol.   O my most sacred lady,
Temptations have since then been born to 's: for
In those unfledg'd days was my wife a girl;
Your precious self had then not cross'd the eyes
Of my young play-fellow.

Her.   Grace to boot!   80

65–6. And . . . two?] *As F;* And . . . eternal. / *Her.* Was . . . two? *Hanmer.*
70. nor dream'd] *F;* no, nor dream'd *F2.*   80. Grace] Oh! Grace *Hanmer.*

67. *twinn'd lambs*] lambs which were
exactly alike. Cf. 'twinn'd stones'
(*Cym.*, I. vi. 34), 'twind cherries'
(*Philaster*, II. ii. 87).

70. *The doctrine . . . dream'd*] The line
is a syllable short. Perhaps 'doctrine'
was pronounced as three syllables. But
F2's guess 'no, nor' may be right; the
'no' might easily have been omitted
(by haplography) in *F*.

72–3. *weak spirits . . . blood*] 'youthful
natures never been made more
aggressive by our physical development and passions'.

74–5. *the imposition . . . ours*] The con-

struction seems to be a Latinism and
may be paraphrased: '[assuming] the
penalty imposed on us, [original sin,]
which is ours by heredity, to have
been removed'. Polixenes is saying
that if he and Leontes had continued
in their state of youthful innocence
they would have been able, when
called to their final account, to plead
themselves guiltless of all personally-
committed sin, that is, of all sin except
original sin.

80. *Grace to boot*] Grace in addition!
i.e. 'What next indeed!' Cf. 'Saint
George to boot' (*R3*, v. iii. 301). For

Of this make no conclusion, lest you say
Your queen and I are devils. Yet go on;
Th' offences we have made you do, we'll answer,
If you first sinn'd with us, and that with us
You did continue fault, and that you slipp'd not   85
With any but with us.

Leon.   Is he won yet?

Her. He'll stay, my lord.

Leon.   At my request he would not.
Hermione, my dearest, thou never spok'st
To better purpose.

Her.   Never?

Leon.   Never but once.

Her. What! have I twice said well? when was't before?   90
I prithee tell me: cram 's with praise, and make 's
As fat as tame things: one good deed, dying tongueless,
Slaughters a thousand, waiting upon that.
Our praises are our wages. You may ride 's
With one soft kiss a thousand furlongs ere   95
With spur we heat an acre. But to th' goal:
My last good deed was to entreat his stay:
What was my first? It has an elder sister,
Or I mistake you: O, would her name were Grace!

'boot' = 'something extra' cf. *Wint.*, iv. iv. 638, 675, 833; *Troil.*, iv. v. 40, I'll give you boot; I'll give you three for one'; *1H4*, iii. ii. 97; *Lr.*, v. iii. 301.

83–6. *Th' offences . . . us*] Leontes must come back within hearing at this point and *N.C.Wint.* suggests that he is meant to overhear and misinterpret 'these equivocal words' and to show the audience that he does so. This is probably so.

84–5. *that . . . that*] if . . . if.

88. *dearest*] spoken as one syllable, as frequently with superlatives. Cf. Kökeritz, 266.

91, 94. *cram's . . . make's . . . ride's*] This use of the apostrophe for the *u* of *us* is unusual. For a note on the use of the apostrophe in the *F* text see *N. & Q.*, May 1961, 175–6.

92–3. *one . . . upon that*] 'A good deed

which is not praised means that a thousand others, which would have been inspired by that praise, are never done.'

94–6. *You may ride 's . . . acre*] 'You will get far more out of us by kindness than by harsh treatment.' 'Heat' = race at full speed; cf. 'hot-foot', 'dead-heat'.

96. *goal*] point.

98. *elder sister*] sounds proverbial but no usage of the kind can be traced. It is apparently an appositive use in the sense of 'fellow', of which the earliest record in *O.E.D.* (sister 10b) is 1641.

99. *would . . . Grace*] 'Grace' is used extensively by Shakespeare with varied meanings. In 80 it is little more than an exclamation. Here it refers to the 'elder sister' or the former of

But once before I spoke to th' purpose? when?   100
Nay, let me have't: I long!
Leon.   Why, that was when
Three crabbed months had sour'd themselves to death,
Ere I could make thee open thy white hand,
And clap thyself my love; then didst thou utter
'I am yours for ever.'
Her.   'Tis Grace indeed.   105
Why lo you now; I have spoke to th' purpose twice:
The one, for ever earn'd a royal husband;
Th' other, for some while a friend. [*Giving her hand to Pol.*]
Leon.   [*Aside*] Too hot, too hot!
To mingle friendship far, is mingling bloods.
I have *tremor cordis* on me: my heart dances,   110
But not for joy—not joy. This entertainment
May a free face put on, derive a liberty

---

104. And clap] *F2; A* clap *F*.   108. S.D. *Giving . . . Pol.*] *Capell; no S.D. in F.*
S.D. *Aside*] *Rowe (1); no S.D. in F.*

Hermione's two good deeds. She has playfully accused Polixenes of being about to say that there was devilry in her influence on Leontes, and in the same vein she now hopes that there will be something of the opposite, of grace, found in her other good deed when she learns what that was; and at 105 she expresses relief to find that it is so.

101. *I long*] so Katharine in *LLL.*, v. ii. 244, where the ladies' speech and bantering tone are much like those of Hermione here.

104. *And*] Perhaps a manuscript ampersand was mistaken for *A* in *F.* Cf. ii. iii. 99.

clap] The custom still exists of clapping or shaking hands to 'strike' a bargain; the hands are struck together and then clasped. Formerly —at least in Ireland—it was customary to strike hands while bargaining and to clasp them only when agreement was reached (*Folk-Lore Record*, iv, 1881, 103). Cf. *O.E.D.* clap V7; *H5,* v. ii. 129, 'and so clap hands, and

a bargain'; *John*, III. i. 235; Heywood, *A Woman killed with Kindness*, I. i. 106; J. Aubry. *Remaines of Gentilisme*, 1881, 56; *The Countryman*, Summer 1959, 230; *The Dalesman*, May 1961, 122.

109. *far*] *farre F.* Perhaps the comparative. Cf. IV. iv. 432n.

110–11. *dances . . . for joy*] Noble, *Biblical Knowledge*, 79–80, 247, considers this passage proof that Shakespeare used the Psalter (*Ps.* xxviii. 8) since the Bishops' and Genevan Bibles do not use 'dance'. The audience would expect 'for joy' after 'my heart dances' and the text carefully indicates the opposite. However, although the phrase is not in Tilley it is probable that to speak of the heart dancing for joy was common usage. Cf. 'Anon for joye his herte gan to daunce' (Chaucer, *Franklin's Tale*, 1136).

111–14. *This entertainment . . . agent*] 'This cordial treatment may be justified in being quite open, may take its liberty from sincerity, generosity, or warm-heartedness, and be a credit to the doer.'

From heartiness, from bounty, fertile bosom,
And well become the agent: 't may, I grant:
But to be paddling palms, and pinching fingers,   115
As now they are, and making practis'd smiles
As in a looking-glass; and then to sigh, as 'twere
The mort o' th' deer—O, that is entertainment
My bosom likes not, nor my brows. Mamillius,
Art thou my boy?

Mam.   Ay, my good lord.

Leon.   I' fecks: 120
Why that's my bawcock. What! hast smutch'd thy nose?
They say it is a copy out of mine. Come, captain,
We must be neat; not neat, but cleanly, captain:
And yet the steer, the heifer and the calf
Are all call'd neat.—Still virginalling   125
Upon his palm!—How now, you wanton calf!
Art thou my calf?

Mam.   Yes, if you will, my lord.

Leon. Thou want'st a rough pash and the shoots that I have
To be full like me: yet they say we are
Almost as like as eggs; women say so,   130
(That will say any thing): but were they false
As o'er-dy'd blacks, as wind, as waters; false

---

124. heifer] Heycfer *F.*

115. *paddling*] amorous hand-clasping. *Oth.*, II. i. 249, 'Didst thou not see her paddle with the palm of his hand?'; *Ham.*, III. iv. 185, and cf. p. lvii, n.3 and I. ii. 125.

117.] The line has two extra syllables. A common suggestion is to omit *looking* since *glass* = looking-glass (IV. iv. 14).

117–18. *to sigh . . . deer*] to sigh like the call of the hunting-horn announcing the death of the deer. Perhaps there is also a quibble upon 'dear' and Hermione's sigh indicates—to Leontes' diseased mind—complete surrender to Polixenes (*N.C. Wint.*).

119. *brows*] reference to the cuckold's horns.

120. *Ay*] The spelling for this word here and throughout *F* is 'I'.

I' fecks] in faith.

121. *bawcock*] fine fellow. Fr. *beau coq.*

123. *neat*] Leontes 'recollecting that "neat" is the ancient term for horned cattle' adds 'not neat, but cleanly' (Johnson).

124. *heifer*] With the *F Heycfer* cf. *2H4* (Q), II. ii. 155, *Heicfors.* The word is from M.E. *hekfere.*

125. *virginalling*] playing as if upon the virginals—paddling. Cf. I. ii. 115 and *Sonn.* cxxviii. There is also ironic association with 'virgin'.

128–9. *a rough . . . like me*] a bull's shaggy head and horns to be fully like me. *O.E.D.* and *Wright* record *pash* in dialect use meaning *head.*

130. *as like as eggs*] Tilley, E66.

132. *o'er-dy'd blacks*] black clothes

As dice are to be wish'd by one that fixes
No bourn 'twixt his and mine, yet were it true
To say this boy were like me. Come, sir page,   135
Look on me with your welkin eye: sweet villain!
Most dear'st, my collop! Can thy dam?—may't be?—
Affection! thy intention stabs the centre:
Thou dost make possible things not so held,
Communicat'st with dreams;—how can this be?—   140
With what's unreal thou coactive art,
And fellow'st nothing: then 'tis very credent
Thou may'st co-join with something; and thou dost,
(And that beyond commission) and I find it,
(And that to the infection of my brains   145
And hard'ning of my brows).

Pol.   What means Sicilia?

Her. He something seems unsettled.

Pol.   How, my lord?
What cheer? how is't with you, best brother?

Her.   You look
As if you held a brow of much distraction:
Are you mov'd, my lord?

---

148. What] *Hanmer; Leo.* What F.
line in F.

148-9. You look . . . distraction] *One*

---

made weak and unwearable—because
vitriol was used in black dye—by over-
dyeing. Cf. Lyly, *Euphues, The Anatomy
of Wit*, 1581 ed., 'To . . . the Gentlemen
Schollers of Oxford': 'the foolish
Dyar, who neuer thought his cloth
blacke vntill it was burned' (Arber,
English Reprints, 1868, 207).

as wind, as waters] Tilley, W86. Cf.
'false as water', *Oth.*, v. ii. 137, and
Troil., III. ii. 190; *Ham.*, III. iv. 45.

134. *bourn*] F borne. Boundary.

136. *welkin*] blue as the sky.

137. *collop*] 'a small piece of meat'.
Hence 'flesh of my flesh', 'my own
flesh and blood'. The only other use in
Shakespeare is *1H6*, v. iv. 18, 'God
knows thou art a collop of my flesh'.
Cf. Tilley, C517.

137-46. *Can thy dam . . . brows*] See
pp. 165-7.

147-8. *How . . . brother?*] Hanmer
and many since give the whole passage
to Polixenes, as here. Some, including
N.C.Wint. and Bethell, *Wint. ed.*,
follow *F*, believing that Leontes is trying to dissemble. But the speech seems
to belong wholly to Polixenes. In 146
Polixenes apparently addresses Hermione and she replies to him in 147.
Then they both turn to Leontes, and
Polixenes asks him, with concern, how
he is feeling, for the phrase 'how is't
with you?' almost always carries the
sense of 'are you feeling well?' (cf. *Tw.
N.*, III. iv. 82-3; *Oth.*, III. iv. 30; *Ham.*,
III. iv. 116-17; *Mac.* II. ii. 58). Then
Hermione adds her anxious inquiry.
This is surely how it would be pre-
ferred on the stage.

150. *mov'd*] made angry, exasper-
ated. Cf. 'Do as I bid you, or you'll

Leon.   No, in good earnest.   150
How sometimes nature will betray its folly,
Its tenderness, and make itself a pastime
To harder bosoms! Looking on the lines
Of my boy's face, methoughts I did recoil
Twenty-three years, and saw myself unbreech'd,   155
In my green velvet coat; my dagger muzzl'd
Lest it should bite its master, and so prove,
As ornaments oft do, too dangerous:
How like, methought, I then was to this kernel,
This squash, this gentleman. Mine honest friend,   160
Will you take eggs for money?
Mam. No, my lord, I'll fight.

158. do] *Rowe* (*1*); do's F.   162. my lord] *F; Hanmer omits.*

move me else' (*Per.*, II. iii. 72) and
H8, v. i. 46.

151. *its*] also in 152, 157, 266, and
III. iii. 46—in each case printed *it's* in
F. The possessive pronoun *its* is found
10 times in *F* of which 6 are in *Wint.*
The old possessive *it* is found 14 times
in *F* of which 2 are in *Wint.*—II. iii.
177; III. ii. 100 (*Var.*, 32).

153–60.] Mamillius is probably
about 7 (see p. lxxxii) and so this passage indicates that Leontes is about 30;
roughly the same age as Pandosto, who
is about 50 when Fawnia is 16 (*Pandosto*, p. 218, l. 11).

154. *methoughts*] a 17th-cent. variant
of *methought* perhaps by analogy with
methinks.

156. *dagger muzzl'd*] Perhaps the
dagger was in some way locked into
the sheath so that it could not be used
but served only as an ornament. However, books on arms and costume show
no evidence of such a practice; and it
is unknown to those living authorities
I have consulted. Knives, often unsheathed, were carried for use at
meals, as general tools, and as weapons
—as they are by some in Italy and elsewhere today. The meaning may simply
be that the knife was sheathed; but this
is unlikely, as unsheathed knives would
hardly be worn by royalty.

160. *squash*] unripe pea-pod; here =
youngster. Cf. *Tw. N.*, I. v. 148: 'Not
yet old enough for a man, nor young
enough for a boy; as a squash is before
'tis a peascod'.

honest] Leontes may use this term,
here and at 211, to emphasize to himself that Mamillius is both honourable
and legitimate.

161. *eggs for money*] Proverbial
expression meaning 'to be put off with
something of inferior value' (not
'worthless' as in *O.E.D.* egg 4), as to
accept payment with eggs instead of
with money. The proverb probably
arises from the practice, which still
existed in the west country early in this
century, of paying children with eggs,
when they were plentiful and cheap,
for such services as running errands,
gathering blackberries, mushrooms,
etc. Cf. *O.E.D.* egg 4, and Campion,
Hist. of Ireland, Bk 2, Ch. 9, 1571
(printed 1633): 'notwithstanding his
high promises . . . is glad to take eggs
for his money'. Eggs were cheap in
Shakespeare's day and the word was
used to signify anything of little value
(cf. *All's W.*, IV. iii. 233). Cf. G. B.
Harrison and H. Granville Barker,
Comp. to Sh. Studies, 386; B. Stevenson,
Book of Proverbs, 1949, 671, and Tilley,
E90.

Leon. You will? Why, happy man be's dole! My brother,
　　　Are you so fond of your young prince, as we
　　　Do seem to be of ours?
Pol.   If at home, sir,   165
　　　He's all my exercise, my mirth, my matter:
　　　Now my sworn friend, and then mine enemy;
　　　My parasite, my soldier, statesman, all.
　　　He makes a July's day short as December;
　　　And with his varying childness cures in me   170
　　　Thoughts that would thick my blood.
Leon.   So stands this squire
　　　Offic'd with me: we two will walk, my lord,
　　　And leave you to your graver steps. Hermione,
　　　How thou lov'st us, show in our brother's welcome;
　　　Let what is dear in Sicily be cheap: 175
　　　Next to thyself, and my young rover, he's
　　　Apparent to my heart.
Her.   If you would seek us,
　　　We are yours i' th' garden: shall 's attend you there?
Leon. To your own bents dispose you: you'll be found,
　　　Be you beneath the sky. [*Aside*] I am angling now,   180
　　　Though you perceive me not how I give line.
　　　Go to, go to!
　　　How she holds up the neb, the bill to him!

179. you'll] you'le *F*.

163. *happy . . . dole!*] proverbial
expression meaning 'Good luck to
you', 'May his fortune be that of a
happy man' (cf. *Wiv.*, III. iv. 64;
Shrew, I. i. 134; *1H4*, II. ii. 73, and
Tilley, M158).

166. *exercise*] habitual employment
or activity. Conveys the sense of 'I
spend all my time with him'. Cf. *3H6*,
IV. vi. 85, 'his daily exercise'; *Tp.*, I. ii.
328, 'All exercise on thee'.

171–2. *So stands . . . me*] 'This youngster performs the same office with
me.'

172. *we two*] i.e. Leontes and
Mamillius.

my lord] Polixenes.

173. *graver*] The adjective means
'worthy', 'venerable' and is used to

contrast with Leontes' walk with his
boy, but also in bitter irony.

177. *Apparent*] 'heir apparent to my
affections'.

179. *you'll*] *F* version may be an *e* for
d misprint but is probably normal
phonetic spelling of 'you'll' as 'I'll' is
normally printed *Ile* (e.g. 162). 'You'd'
is normally printed 'you'ld', e.g. II. i.
18; IV. iv. 111. Compositor A in *F*
usually printed *you'le* or *you'll*, *wee'le* or
wee'll where B printed *you'l* or *wee'l*.
This page was set by A. Cf. p. xviii,
n.2.

183. *neb*] originally meaning 'beak',
later 'nose' and 'mouth' (*O.E.D.* neb
1b). Grose gives: 'the face and mouth
of a woman; as, She holds up her neb;
she holds up her mouth to be kissed'.

And arms her with the boldness of a wife
To her allowing husband!
        [*Exeunt Polixenes, Hermione, and Attendants.*]
                Gone already!   185
Inch-thick, knee-deep; o'er head and ears a fork'd one.
Go, play, boy, play: thy mother plays, and I
Play too; but so disgrac'd a part, whose issue
Will hiss me to my grave: contempt and clamour
Will be my knell. Go, play, boy, play. There have been,
(Or I am much deceiv'd) cuckolds ere now,   191
And many a man there is (even at this present,
Now, while I speak this) holds his wife by th' arm,
That little thinks she has been sluic'd in 's absence
And his pond fish'd by his next neighbour, by   195
Sir Smile, his neighbour: nay, there's comfort in't,

185. S.D. *Exeunt . . . Attendants*] Rowe (*1*) *after 184; no S.D. in F.*

185. *allowing*] authorizing, complaisant. Cf. I. ii. 263 and *Tim.*, v. i. 160.

Gone] possible triple senses—'left Leontes' presence', 'lost to Leontes as a wife', 'departed from virtue and abandoned in sin'.

186. *Inch-thick*] probably refers to the inch board, the thickest normal plank. To see or swear through an inch board was proverbial (Tilley, I61). The sense is 'solid, and so beyond all doubt'.

fork'd one] Leontes may be referring to himself in this line, and 'fork'd' may mean the cuckold's horns. But the whole line may refer to Hermione, describing her as deeply involved, deceitful, and double-dealing (fork'd). Yet in either case the horns were probably in Leontes' mind.

187–9. *Go, play . . . grave*] 'Go and amuse yourself boy: your mother is amorously disporting herself and I am performing a part too [i.e. of an honoured husband whereas in fact I am a cuckold], and when the nature of my part is disclosed to the world I shall be taunted and derided for the rest of my life.' The word 'play' has

first the sense of 'boy's play', next that of 'amorous play' with secondary meaning of 'playing a part, deceiving', which leads to the third meaning of the playing of the actor, purporting to be something which he is not. Cf. M. M. Mahood, 'The fatal Cleopatra: Shakespeare and the pun' (*Essays in Criticism*, I, July 1951, 206–7) and *H8*, I. iii. 45; I. iv. 46; *Tp.*, v. i. 185.

188. *disgrac'd*] Miss Mahood notices the double sense of *ungraceful* and *shameful* and J. C. Maxwell suggests to me that the word here also has the sense of *unpopular* and compares 'well-graced' (*R2*, v. ii. 24).

191–207.] With Leontes' outburst here and elsewhere on the faithlessness of women cf. the similarly mistaken Posthumus in *Cym.*, II. iv and v.

195. *his pond fish'd*] Cf. 'strange fowl light upon neighbouring ponds' (*Cym.*, I. iv. 85).

196. *Sir Smile*] Polixenes may be smiling at this point: Shakespeare frequently speaks of villainy and deceit concealed by a smile, e.g. 'smiling, damnèd villain' (*Ham.*, I. v. 106); 'villain with a smiling cheek' (*Mer. V.*, I. iii. 95); and cf. *2H4*, Prol. 9–10;

Whiles other men have gates, and those gates open'd,
As mine, against their will. Should all despair
That have revolted wives, the tenth of mankind
Would hang themselves. Physic for't there's none;   200
It is a bawdy planet, that will strike
Where 'tis predominant; and 'tis powerful, think it,
From east, west, north, and south; be it concluded,
No barricado for a belly. Know 't,
It will let in and out the enemy,   205
With bag and baggage: many thousand on 's
Have the disease, and feel 't not. How now, boy?
Mam. I am like you, they say.
Leon.   Why, that's some comfort.
What, Camillo there?
Cam. Ay, my good lord.   210
Leon. Go play, Mamillius; thou'rt an honest man.
                                    [*Exit Mamillius.*]
Camillo, this great Sir will yet stay longer.
Cam. You had much ado to make his anchor hold:
When you cast out, it still came home.

---

208. they] *F2; not in F.*   211. S.D. *Exit Mamillius] Rowe (1); no S.D. in F.*

3H6, III. ii. 182; *Mac.*, II. iii. 139; *Tit.*, II. iii. 267; *Cæs.*, II. i. 82, IV. i. 50; *Tim.*, III. vi. 94; *Lr.*, II. ii. 68; *Per.*, IV. iv. 44–5. The association goes back at least to Chaucer—'The smyler with the knyf under the cloke' (*Knight's Tale*, 1141/1999)—and may be conventional. This satiric use of *Sir* with a noun which is usually abstract is frequent: 'Sir Valour' (*Troil.*, I. iii. 176), 'Sir Prudence' (*Tp.*, II. i. 277), 'Sir Oracle' (*Mer.V.*, I. i. 93); and cf. 'Sir Knave' (*All's W.*, I. iii. 85).

comfort in't] 'I am not the first and shall not be the last.' It is proverbially comforting to have company in trouble. Tilley, C571.

197. *Whiles*] The while, as long as (*O.E.D.* 2, Schmidt 2).

201–2. *It . . . predominant*] 'The unfaithfulness of wives is like a bawdy planet which will spread ruin wherever it is in the ascendant.'

201. *strike*] Cf. *Ham.*, I. i. 162, 'The

nights are wholesome, then no planets strike.'

202. *think it*] be assured of it.

204. *Know 't*] be certain of it.

208. *they*] *F2* may be right: *they* seems more appropriate than *you*. But omission of a second *you* is a far more probable printer's error, and Leontes had himself made the comment at 134–5. He says that others had made it at 129.

213–16.] Camillo's two speeches make it clear that he has no idea of Leontes' jealousy and suspicions, and if he had none, certainly no one else would have had any. For if Camillo believed Leontes to be jealous and suspicious, these speeches would be those of an Iago, calculated to inflame Leontes still further—as is noted by Tannenbaum in *Phil.Q.*, vii, 1928, 361.

214. *still came home*] always came back, i.e. would not hold. The nautical term is still current. *O.E.D.* home *adv.*3, anchor *sb.*6e.

Leon.   Didst note it?

Cam. He would not stay at your petitions; made   215
    His business more material.

Leon.   Didst perceive it?
    [*Aside*] They're here with me already; whisp'ring,
      rounding
    'Sicilia is a so-forth': 'tis far gone,
    When I shall gust it last.—How cam 't, Camillo,
    That he did stay?

Cam.   At the good queen's entreaty.   220

Leon. At the queen's be 't: 'good' should be pertinent,
    But so it is, it is not. Was this taken
    By any understanding pate but thine?
    For thy conceit is soaking, will draw in
    More than the common blocks: not noted, is't,   225
    But of the finer natures? by some severals
    Of head-piece extraordinary? lower messes
    Perchance are to this business purblind? say!

Cam. Business, my lord? I think most understand
    Bohemia stays here longer.

Leon.   Ha?

---

217. S.D. *Aside*] *Hanmer; no S.D. in F.*

217. *They're . . . already*] 'People already appreciate my position.' The phrase probably means no more than this. Cf. 'take me with you', i.e. 'explain to me' (*1H4*, II. iv. 444; *Rom.*, III. v. 141), and modern usage 'are you with me?' = 'have you followed my meaning so far?'

rounding] whispering with an air of mystery.

218. *a so-forth*] Leontes avoids saying 'cuckold'. Cf. modern 'a so-and-so'.

far] *farre* F; possibly the comparative. Cf. IV. iv. 432n.

219. *gust*] perceive, realize. 'It must have been going on for a long time, for I shall be the last to know of it.' The cuckold is proverbially the last to be aware of his position (Tilley, C877).

222. *so it is*] as things are.

224–8. *For thy . . . purblind*] 'Your intelligence is quick and will take in more than blockheads can. It is not noted except by the cleverer people? The ordinary folk ['lower messes', inferiors; people who sat lower down the table] haven't spotted it ['purblind' here = wholly blind]?'

225. *blocks*] blockheads. 'Block' is used in this sense in *Gent.*, II. v. 22; *Per.*, III. ii. 95, and elsewhere. But the two previous lines indicate that Leontes is comparing the intelligence of the lower messes with the wooden blocks on which felt hats were shaped. Cf. *Ado*, I. i. 62; *Lr.*, IV. vi. 184.

227. *messes*] A mess was normally a group of four served at table together and still had the sense of four people in Shakespeare's day. Cf. IV. iv. 11 and *LLL.*, IV. iii. 203, 207, and Jonson, *Every Man in his Humour*, I. iii. 70–3.

230. *Ha?*] 'Do they indeed think only that?'

Cam.   Stays here longer.   230
Leon. Ay, but why?
Cam. To satisfy your highness, and the entreaties
    Of our most gracious mistress.
Leon.   Satisfy?
    Th' entreaties of your mistress? satisfy?
    Let that suffice. I have trusted thee, Camillo,   235
    With all the nearest things to my heart, as well
    My chamber-counsels, wherein, priest-like, thou
    Hast cleans'd my bosom: I from thee departed
    Thy penitent reform'd. But we have been
    Deceiv'd in thy integrity, deceiv'd   240
    In that which seems so.
Cam.   Be it forbid, my lord!
Leon. To bide upon't: thou art not honest: or,
    If thou inclin'st that way, thou art a coward,
    Which hoxes honesty behind, restraining
    From course requir'd: or else thou must be counted   245
    A servant grafted in my serious trust,
    And therein negligent; or else a fool,
    That seest a game play'd home, the rich stake drawn,
    And tak'st it all for jest.
Cam.   My gracious lord,
    I may be negligent, foolish, and fearful;   250
    In every one of these no man is free,
    But that his negligence, his folly, fear,
    Among the infinite doings of the world,

237. chamber-counsels] Chamber-Councels *F.*

237. *chamber-counsels*] private personal conversations, not Privy Council meetings. Obviously Camillo has been a close personal confidant.

238. *cleans'd my bosom*] Cf. 'Cleanse the stuff'd bosom of that perilous stuff / Which weighs upon the heart' (*Mac.*, v. iii. 44–5). Although 'bosom' is also used, as today, of any close confidant, e.g. 'I know you are of her bosom' (*Lr.*, IV. v. 26), Camillo has clearly acted as a kind of father-confessor to Leontes. Scroop had been such a bosom counsellor to Henry V (*H5*, II. ii. 96–7), Thaliard to Antio-

chus, and Helicanus to Pericles (*Per.*, I. i. 152; I. ii. 63–4), and Wolsey had been next to Henry's heart (*H8*, III. ii. 157). For 'bosom' = innermost thoughts, cf. *H8*, II. iv. 182.

242–5. *To bide . . . requir'd*] 'To dwell on it, you are not honest, or, if you have some leaning towards honesty, you lack courage [to act on it, a lack] which hamstrings honesty from the rear, preventing it from doing what is required.'

246. *grafted*] grown in, like a shoot to a tree. Cf. IV. iv. 93.

251. *free*] guiltless. Cf. II. iii. 30.

Sometime puts forth. In your affairs, my lord,
If ever I were wilful-negligent,   255
It was my folly: if industriously
I play'd the fool, it was my negligence,
Not weighing well the end: if ever fearful
To do a thing, where I the issue doubted,
Whereof the execution did cry out   260
Against the non-performance, 'twas a fear
Which oft infects the wisest: these, my lord,
Are such allow'd infirmities that honesty
Is never free of. But, beseech your Grace,
Be plainer with me; let me know my trespass   265
By its own visage: if I then deny it,
'Tis none of mine.

Leon.   Ha' not you seen, Camillo?
(But that's past doubt: you have, or your eye-glass
Is thicker than a cuckold's horn) or heard?
(For to a vision so apparent rumour   270
Cannot be mute) or thought? (for cogitation
Resides not in that man that does not think)
My wife is slippery? If thou wilt confess,
Or else be impudently negative,
To have nor eyes, nor ears, nor thought, then say   275
My wife's a hobby-horse, deserves a name

---

254. forth. In] *Theobald;* forth in *F.*   276. hobby-horse] *Rowe (3);* Holy-
Horse *F.*

254. *Sometime puts forth*] 'will come
out some time or other'. Theobald's
change in the punctuation gives sense
to the passage.

256–62. *if industriously . . . wisest*] 'If
I deliberately did not treat something
seriously it was due to lack of care and
failure to appreciate the importance of
the matter. If I was ever afraid to do
something because I was doubtful of
the outcome even though the unper-
formed task was simply crying out for
action, that was a fear of which the
wisest men are often guilty.'

263. *allow'd*] permitted, excusable.
Cf. 'allowing', 185.

267–73. *Ha' not . . . slippery?*] 'Have

you not actually seen . . . or heard
others say . . . or yourself thought . . .
that my wife is deceitful?' The situation is tense. Camillo is kept waiting
while Leontes works up to this dramatic climax.

268. *eye-glass*] lens of the eye.

270–1. *For to . . . mute*] 'for rumour
cannot be silent about something
which can be seen so clearly'.

271–2. *for cogitation . . . think*] 'for the
capacity for thought is not possessed
by any man who does not think [this]
(i.e. that my wife is slippery)'.

276. *hobby-horse*] The *holy* of *F* is
almost certainly a misprint or *hobby.*
Holy-horse is not found elsewhere, but

As rank as any flax-wench that puts to
Before her troth-plight: say't and justify 't!
Cam. I would not be a stander-by, to hear
　　　My sovereign mistress clouded so, without　　　280
　　　My present vengeance taken: 'shrew my heart,
　　　You never spoke what did become you less
　　　Than this; which to reiterate were sin
　　　As deep as that, though true.
Leon.　　　　　　　　　　Is whispering nothing?
　　　Is leaning cheek to cheek? is meeting noses?　　　285
　　　Kissing with inside lip? stopping the career
　　　Of laughter with a sigh (a note infallible
　　　Of breaking honesty)? horsing foot on foot?
　　　Skulking in corners? wishing clocks more swift?
　　　Hours, minutes? noon, midnight? and all eyes　　　290
　　　Blind with the pin and web, but theirs; theirs only.

Hobby-horse had the sense of 'loose woman' in Shakespeare's day (*O.E.D.* 3a and *Oth.*, IV. i. 151).

278. *troth-plight*] After plighting troth by present acceptance of each other as husband and wife (*sponsalia* or *verba de praesenti*) a couple were, from early times, recognized in law as married and subsequent offspring as legitimate. But the Church always held that although they might be regarded as married in law they were not married before God and they sinned if consummation took place before wedding by the Church. Nevertheless it was common in Elizabethan times, and much later among country folk where fertility is of vital importance, for troth-plighted couples to consummate their 'marriage' immediately and no church wedding took place until it was known that a child would be born or even until after birth. Shakespeare's plays apparently take the Church's view. Cf. D. P. Harding, 'Elizabethan Betrothals and "Measure for Measure"' (*J.E.G.P.* xlix, 1950, 139–58); Mary Lascelles, *Sh.'s Measure for Measure*, 1953, 38, 119–20; and *Sh. Eng.*, i. 407–8. Troth-plight or contract is mentioned again

at IV. iv. 391, 418, v. i. 203 (where, since the 'contract' is not 'celebrated' the couple are not 'married'), v. iii. 5, 151. The importance of the pre-marriage contract is emphasized throughout *All's W.* after the contract at II. iii. 176 and in *Meas.*, I. ii. 140–4, III. i. 208–11, IV. i. 70–3, v. i. 207, and *H5*, II. i. 19. In *Tp.*, IV. i. 14–18, the Church's view is strongly emphasized, and cf. 'contract . . . Confirmed . . . Attested . . . Sealed' (*Tw. N.*, v. i. 150–6) and *AYL.*, III. ii. 296. Cf. *Pandosto*, p. 212, l. 16.

281. *present*] instant, immediate.

282.] Camillo is so angry that he addresses the king bluntly as 'you' omitting the usual deferential phrase, 'my lord', or 'your highness', 'your Grace', etc.

283–4. *which . . . true*] 'which to repeat were a sin as deep as that is of which you accuse her even if that were true [which it is not]'.

286. *stopping the career*] To stop the horse in full gallop is perhaps a feat of the manage. Cf. 'Hath this brave manage, this career, been run' (*LLL.*, v. ii. 482).

291. *pin and web*] the disease of cataract. Cf. 268–9 and *Lr.*, III. iv. 115.

That would unseen be wicked? is this nothing?
Why then the world, and all that's in't, is nothing,
The covering sky is nothing, Bohemia nothing,
My wife is nothing, nor nothing have these nothings, 295
If this be nothing.

Cam.   Good my lord, be cur'd
Of this diseas'd opinion, and betimes,
For 'tis most dangerous.

Leon.   Say it be, 'tis true.

Cam. No, no, my lord.

Leon.   It is: you lie, you lie:
I say thou liest, Camillo, and I hate thee,   300
Pronounce thee a gross lout, a mindless slave,
Or else a hovering temporizer that
Canst with thine eyes at once see good and evil,
Inclining to them both: were my wife's liver
Infected, as her life, she would not live   305
The running of one glass.

Cam.   Who does infect her?

Leon. Why, he that wears her like her medal, hanging
About his neck, Bohemia; who, if I
Had servants true about me, that bare eyes
To see alike mine honour as their profits,   310
Their own particular thrifts, they would do that
Which should undo more doing: ay, and thou
His cupbearer,—whom I from meaner form
Have bench'd and rear'd to worship, who may'st see
Plainly as heaven sees earth and earth sees heaven, 315
How I am gall'd,—might'st bespice a cup,
To give mine enemy a lasting wink;

---

316. might'st] *F;* thou mightst *F2.*

292–6. *is this . . . nothing*] The mad
rising fury of this passage carries
echoes from *Oth.* and *Lr.* (cf. J. Isaacs,
Sh.'s earliest Years in the Theatre, 1953,
133–4). That nothing can come of
nothing is proverbial (Tilley, N285).

307. *wears . . . medal*] 'as if she were
her own miniature portrait pendant
about his neck'. Cf. *H8*, II. ii. 28: '. . .
loss of her / That like a jewel has hung
twenty years / About his neck,' and

Ado, v. i. 82, 'Win me and wear me';
2H4, IV. v. 222, *Sh. Eng.*, ii. 114–15,
and *Pandosto*, p. 220, ll. 10–11.

311. *thrifts*] gains.

314. *bench'd . . . worship*] given a seat
above the 'lower messes' (227), an
official position, and raised to a place
of honour.

317. *To give . . . wink*] 'to close my
enemy's eyes for ever, to kill him'.
Cf. *Tp.*, II. i. 276; 'To the perpetual

Which draught to me were cordial.

Cam.   Sir, my lord,
    I could do this, and that with no rash potion,
    But with a ling'ring dram, that should not work   320
    Maliciously, like poison: but I cannot
    Believe this crack to be in my dread mistress
    (So sovereignly being honourable).
    I have lov'd thee,—

Leon.   Make that thy question, and go rot!
    Dost think I am so muddy, so unsettled,   325
    To appoint myself in this vexation; sully
    The purity and whiteness of my sheets,
    (Which to preserve is sleep, which being spotted
    Is goads, thorns, nettles, tails of wasps)
    Give scandal to the blood o' th' prince, my son,   330
    (Who I do think is mine and love as mine)
    Without ripe moving to 't? Would I do this?
    Could man so blench?

Cam.   I must believe you, sir:

---

324. I have] *F;* T'have *N.C.Wint.;* Leo. I've *Theobald.*   thee,— / *Leo.* Make
that] *F* (*subst.*)*;* the— / *Leo.* Make that *N.C.Wint.;* thee. Make't *Theobald.*
326–7. vexation; sully / The] *As Theobald;* vexation? / Sully the *F.*

---

wink for aye might put / This ancient
morsel'.

321. *Maliciously*] violently.

323. *So . . . honourable*] 'so supremely
honourable is she'.

324. *I have . . . rot*] The chief argument against the retention of *thee* is
that nowhere else in *Wint.* (except in
the official indictment of Hermione at
III. ii. 12–21) is the 2nd pers. sing. used
by an inferior to royalty. Florizel uses
it to Perdita but not she to him. It is
found elsewhere in Shakespeare, e.g.
by Berowne to the king (*LLL.,* IV. iii.
148–9). There is nothing in the argument that the half-line must mean that
Camillo no longer loves Leontes (*N.C.
Wint.*). That obviously need not be so.
On balance it is best to keep *thee.* After
all Camillo is the king's most intimate
friend and is deeply moved (cf. 282),
and the liberty would be less than
Paulina's when she calls Leontes mad

(II. iii. 71). The spellings *thee* and *the*
are interchangeable only when *thee* is
meant. 'Make . . . question' refers to
'cannot / Believe' (321–2) and 'Make
. . . rot' means 'If you are going to
doubt that, go to blazes'. Cf. 'Go and
the rot consume thee' (Greene, *James
the Fourth,* IV. iii. 1553); 'Vengeance
rot you' (*Tit.,* v. i. 58); 'The south fog
rot him' (*Cym.,* II. iii. 131).

326. *To appoint . . . vexation*] 'to put
myself of my own wish into this
trouble'. The emphasis should be on
self. He means that it does not come
from within him, from his imagination, but has been forced on him to
designate himself a cuckold.

333. *blench*] probably 'swerve from
the path of reason' but possibly
'deceive himself'. Leontes is deluded
but, like Lysander (*MND.,* II. ii. 115),
thinks that his will is swayed by reason.

      I do; and will fetch off Bohemia for't;
      Provided, that when he's removed, your highness   335
      Will take again your queen, as yours at first,
      Even for your son's sake, and thereby for sealing
      The injury of tongues in courts and kingdoms
      Known and allied to yours.
Leon.   Thou dost advise me
      Even so as I mine own course have set down: 340
      I'll give no blemish to her honour, none.
Cam. My lord,
      Go then; and with a countenance as clear
      As friendship wears at feasts, keep with Bohemia,
      And with your queen. I am his cupbearer: 345
      If from me he have wholesome beverage,
      Account me not your servant.
Leon.   This is all:
      Do't, and thou hast the one half of my heart;
      Do't not, thou splitt'st thine own.
Cam.   I'll do't, my lord.
Leon. I will seem friendly, as thou hast advis'd me.   *Exit.*
Cam. O miserable lady! But, for me,   351
      What case stand I in? I must be the poisoner
      Of good Polixenes, and my ground to do 't
      Is the obedience to a master; one
      Who, in rebellion with himself, will have   355

---

337. *for sealing*] *F;* forestalling *N.C. Wint., conj. Kellner.*

334. *fetch off*] Here and at 347
Camillo may be equivocating. 'Fetch
off' can mean 'do away with', 'kill',
and that is the sense Camillo obviously
wishes to convey, and in fact does convey, to Leontes. But 'fetch off' can
also mean 'rescue' (*Tp.*, IV. i. 212;
All's W., III. vi. 16, 36; *Cor.*, I. iv. 63;
and cf. 'bear'st ... off', *Wint.*, I. ii. 462)
and that may already be what
Camillo intends to do. And so at 347
'Account me not your servant' may be
Camillo's way of saying to himself that
he will in fact cease to be Leontes'
servant.

337–8. *for sealing . . . tongues*]
'silencing, preventing harmful talk'.

Perhaps *for* with the sense of *fore*
should be a prefix to *sealing*. There are
several emendations, but none is
necessary: the sense, as suggested by
Sisson, is 'take your Queen as Queen
again, *for* your son's sake and *for* the
sake of silencing slander.'

347. *Account . . . servant*] See 334n.

355–6. *in rebellion . . . too*] Leontes is
in rebellion against his true, sane self
and his own true interests and would
have all who owe him obedience obey
his rebellious self, or, perhaps, would
have them also rebel against their true
selves. The picture is of perversion
throughout the ordered hierarchy
which results when the true self of the

All that are his, so too. To do this deed,
Promotion follows. If I could find example
Of thousands that had struck anointed kings
And flourish'd after, I'd not do 't: but since
Nor brass, nor stone, nor parchment bears not one,   360
Let villainy itself forswear't. I must
Forsake the court: to do't, or no, is certain
To me a break-neck. Happy star reign now!
Here comes Bohemia.

Enter POLIXENES.

Pol.   This is strange: methinks
My favour here begins to warp. Not speak?   365
Good day, Camillo.
Cam.   Hail, most royal sir!
Pol. What is the news i' th' court?
Cam.   None rare, my lord.
Pol. The king hath on him such a countenance
As he had lost some province, and a region
Lov'd as he loves himself: even now I met him   370
With customary compliment, when he,
Wafting his eyes to th' contrary, and falling
A lip of much contempt, speeds from me, and
So leaves me, to consider what is breeding
That changes thus his manners.   375
Cam. I dare not know, my lord.
Pol. How, dare not? do not? Do you know, and dare not?

man in authority is overthrown by his own rebellion against that true self. This is a breakdown of the order which was so vitally important to Shakespeare and Elizabethans generally—a rebellion in the microcosm of Leontes himself which must lead to moral chaos in him and those who erve him (Dr Brooks).

357–61. *If I . . . forswear't*] There is biblical authority for the fate of those who strike anointed kings, e.g. *2 Sam.* i. 14–15, and a contemporary example in Henri IV and Ravaillac in 1610. The comment would have been acceptable to the son of Mary, Queen

of Scots, before whom the play was given in 1611 on the anniversary of Gunpowder Plot.

362. *certain*] certainly.

372. *Wafting . . . contrary*] 'hurriedly turning his eyes in the opposite direction'.

374. *breeding*] 'what is going on, what is afoot'.

377–80. *How . . . dare not*] 'What do you mean? Dare not or do not? You know but you dare not know? Explain to *me* [what you know]: that's where the trouble is [i.e. that *I* do not know]; for as far as you yourself are concerned, if you really know something, you

Be intelligent to me: 'tis thereabouts:
For, to yourself, what you do know, you must,
And cannot say you dare not. Good Camillo,   380
Your chang'd complexions are to me a mirror
Which shows me mine chang'd too; for I must be
A party in this alteration, finding
Myself thus alter'd with 't.

Cam.   There is a sickness
Which puts some of us in distemper, but   385
I cannot name the disease, and it is caught
Of you, that yet are well.

Pol.   How caught of me?
Make me not sighted like the basilisk.
I have look'd on thousands, who have sped the better
By my regard, but kill'd none so. Camillo,—   390
As you are certainly a gentleman, thereto
Clerk-like experienc'd, which no less adorns
Our gentry than our parents' noble names,
In whose success we are gentle,—I beseech you,
If you know aught which does behove my knowledge
Thereof to be inform'd, imprison 't not   396
In ignorant concealment.

Cam.   I may not answer.

Pol. A sickness caught of me, and yet I well?

---

must know it and cannot say you dare
not it.' Cf. iv. iv. 453.

378. *intelligent*] intelligible.

381–4. *Your changed . . . with't*] 'The
changes in your face reflect mine for I
know that I have the same anxious
appearance. I sense that I must be the
cause of this alteration [in the king's
manner] since I find myself affected in
this way by it.'

388. *sighted . . . basilisk*] 'Do not
represent me as having a gaze like a
basilisk's.' The basilisk or cockatrice
was a fabulous creature said to be
hatched by a snake or toad from an egg
laid by an old cock. Its look was proverbially fatal (Tilley, B99). Cf. 'It is
a basilisk unto mine eye / Kills me to
look on it' (*Cym.*, II. iv. 107). With the
construction 'sighted like' cf. 'back'd

like a weasel' (*Ham.*, III. ii. 370).

390. *By*] for, as a result of.

391–4. *thereto . . . gentle*] 'and in addition a man of education and culture,
something which no less adorns our
nobility than the noble names held by
our parents, in succession to whom we
are noble'. Dr Brooks points out that
there is an echo here of the traditional
accounts of Nobility from Juvenal's
onwards. Here there is no questioning
of the importance of noble ancestors,
but the balancing of inheritance and
of personal attainment in addition;
and this accords with the traditional
treatment of the theme.

397. *ignorant concealment*] 'concealment that keeps one in ignorance' *or*
'concealment on pretext of ignorance'.
Cf. *Tp.*, v. i. 67.

I must be answer'd. Dost thou hear, Camillo?
I conjure thee, by all the parts of man   400
Which honour does acknowledge, whereof the least
Is not this suit of mine, that thou declare
What incidency thou dost guess of harm
Is creeping toward me; how far off, how near,
Which way to be prevented, if to be: 405
If not, how best to bear it.
Cam.   Sir, I will tell you;
Since I am charg'd in honour, and by him
That I think honourable. Therefore mark my counsel,
Which must be ev'n as swiftly follow'd as
I mean to utter it, or both yourself and me   410
Cry lost, and so good night!
Pol.   On, good Camillo.
Cam. I am appointed him to murder you.
Pol. By whom, Camillo?
Cam.   By the king.
Pol.   For what?
Cam. He thinks, nay, with all confidence he swears,
As he had seen 't, or been an instrument   415
To vice you to't, that you have touch'd his queen
Forbiddenly.
Pol.   O then, my best blood turn
To an infected jelly, and my name
Be yok'd with his that did betray the Best!
Turn then my freshest reputation to   420
A savour that may strike the dullest nostril

403. guess] ghesse *F.*

400–2. *I conjure . . . mine*] 'I urge you by all the obligations which honour imposes on a man whereof not the least is [to answer] this request of mine.'

403. *incidency*] incident, 'what harmful event *likely to happen* which you have any knowledge of'.

405. *if to be*] if that is possible.

407. *him*] Polixenes.

411. *good night*] farewell for ever. Cf. *Ant.*, III. x. 30; *Tp.*, IV. i. 54; *1H4*, I. iii. 194.

412. *him*] i.e. as the person.

416. *vice*] 'to screw or force you to it'. Cf. *Tw. N.*, v. i. 121: '. . . I partly know the instrument / That screws me from my true place in your favour, and Marston, *Antonio's Revenge*, II. ii. 41–2: '. . . I see false suspect / Is vicde; wrung hardly in a vertuous heart'. Leontes is as certain as if he himself had incited you to the crime. 'Vice' was probably used because of the association of its homonym.

419. *his . . . Best*] refers to Judas's betrayal of Jesus.

Where I arrive, and my approach be shunn'd,
Nay, hated too, worse than the great'st infection
That e'er was heard or read!
Cam.   Swear his thought over
By each particular star in heaven, and   425
By all their influences; you may as well
Forbid the sea for to obey the moon,
As or by oath remove or counsel shake
The fabric of his folly, whose foundation
Is pil'd upon his faith, and will continue   430
The standing of his body.
Pol.   How should this grow?
Cam. I know not: but I am sure 'tis safer to
Avoid what's grown than question how 'tis born.
If therefore you dare trust my honesty,
That lies enclosed in this trunk; which you   435
Shall bear along impawn'd, away to-night!
Your followers I will whisper to the business,
And will by twos and threes, at several posterns,
Clear them o' th' city. For myself, I'll put
My fortunes to your service, which are here   440
By this discovery lost. Be not uncertain,
For by the honour of my parents, I
Have utter'd truth: which if you seek to prove,
I dare not stand by; nor shall you be safer

424. *Swear . . . over*] The sense must be *repudiate, deny*, but no other example can be found. The whole phrase may echo 'swear down each particular saint' (*Meas.*, v. i. 241). There may be analogy with 'oversway' which Onions glosses as 'to prevail over, by superior authority or power'. Hence perhaps 'to swear his thought over' is 'to endeavour to prevail over his thought by the superior power of oaths'.

426. *influences*] astrological, 'the supposed flowing . . . from the stars . . . of an etherial fluid acting upon the character and destiny of men' (*O.E.D.*).

428. *As . . . shake*] F 'As (or by Oath) remoue, or (Counsaile) shake', i.e. 'as

either remove by solemn oath or change by reasoning'.

431. *The standing . . . body*] 'as long as his body lasts'.

435–6. *trunk . . . impawn'd*] 'my body which you shall take with you as a pledge'.

440–1. *which . . . uncertain*] 'By disclosing this to you my future in Sicilia is ruined. Do not doubt that what I have told you is true.'

443–6. *which . . . sworn*] 'If you try to test this I shall have to deny the facts I have told you; and as for you, you will be no safer than one whom the king has not only condemned to death but has sworn to have executed.'

Than one condemned by the king's own mouth,   445
Thereon his execution sworn.
Pol.   I do believe thee:
I saw his heart in 's face. Give me thy hand,
Be pilot to me, and thy places shall
Still neighbour mine. My ships are ready, and
My people did expect my hence departure   450
Two days ago. This jealousy
Is for a precious creature: as she's rare,
Must it be great; and, as his person's mighty,
Must it be violent; and, as he does conceive
He is dishonour'd by a man which ever   455
Profess'd to him; why, his revenges must
In that be made more bitter. Fear o'ershades me:
Good expedition be my friend, and comfort
The gracious queen, part of his theme, but nothing
Of his ill-ta'en suspicion! Come, Camillo,   460
I will respect thee as a father if
Thou bear'st my life off. Hence! let us avoid.
Cam. It is in mine authority to command
The keys of all the posterns: please your highness
To take the urgent hour. Come sir, away.   *Exeunt.*   465

---

451. jealousy] *F;* jealousy of his *Walker.*   462. off . . . avoid] off, hence: Let vs
auoid *F.*

456. *Profess'd*] professed affection.
458–60. *Good expedition . . . suspicion*]
The passage has been heavily anno-
tated and pronounced 'incomprehensible'. It may be interpreted: 'May
speed in departure save me and also be
of help to the gracious queen who must
also be an object of the king's anger
but who has done nothing to justify
his groundless suspicions.' Polixenes
knows that if he stays he will be killed,
which would be disastrous to the
queen. She would be deeply grieved
and perhaps less likely to be able to
establish her innocence. But the last
phrase may mean 'but is not an object
of his mistaken suspicion'. This is how
Pandosto could be interpreted, for
although Franion tells Egistus of 'the

whole conspiracy' (p. 188), he apparently does not tell why Pandosto wishes
to poison him (p. 189) and so Egistus
does not know that Bellaria is involved
and so does not mention her when he
leaves. But Shakespeare had departed
from *Pandosto* in this, for Polixenes
knows that Leontes believes Hermione
to have been unfaithful (I. ii. 415–17,
455); she is indeed part 'of his theme'
and 'of the cause' (II. iii. 3). But *comfort*
may = *encourage, reassure* (Schmidt 3),
giving 'encourage the queen but not
encourage his suspicion' (F. McClen-
then in *Shakespeariana*, 1888, 168), cf.
v. iv. 558.
462. *Hence!*] Away! Cf. *O.E.D.*
hence, *adv.*2, and *Wint.*, II. iii. 67, 94.
avoid] be gone. Cf. *Tp.*, IV. i. 142.

ACT II

SCENE I

Enter HERMIONE, MAMILLIUS, [*and*] *Ladies.*

Her. Take the boy to you: he so troubles me,
    'Tis past enduring.
First Lady.   Come, my gracious lord,
    Shall I be your play-fellow?
Mam.   No, I'll none of you.
First Lady. Why, my sweet lord?
Mam. You'll kiss me hard, and speak to me as if   5
    I were a baby still. I love you better.
Sec. Lady. And why so, my lord?
Mam.   Not for because
    Your brows are blacker; yet black brows, they say,
    Become some women best, so that there be not
    Too much hair there, but in a semicircle,   10
    Or a half-moon, made with a pen.
Sec. Lady.   Who taught ' this!

ACT II

Scene i

Act II] *Actus Secundus. F.*   Scene i] *Scena Prima. F.*   S.D. *Enter . . . Ladies.*]
Enter Hermione, Mamillius, Ladies: Leontes, Antigonus, Lords. F.   2. S.D. *First
Lady.*] *Rowe (1) (subst.); Lady. F.*   4. S.D. *First Lady.*] *Rowe (1) (subst.); Lady. F.*
11. taught ' this] *F;* taught you this *Rowe (1);* taught 't *Alexander.*

Scene i] In Leontes' palace.

1–32.] This passage is developed from fourteen words in *Pandosto* (p. 190, ll. 26–7). Hermione's opening words are in mock-annoyance. The episode is one of happiness.

8–11.] This reference to the eye-brow may be merely another example of a poet ridiculing feminine make-up. The eye-brow is introduced to ridicule the lover's extravagance in *ATL.*, ii. vii. 149. For eye-lids see *Wint.*, iv. iv. 121n.

11. *taught ' this*] Many edd. follow Rowe. Alexander's version, meaning *taught it,* is defended by Sisson as 'a natural piece of baby-talk', which would, however, have been more appropriate from the First Lady. In the F text of *Wint.* an apostrophe is often used for the omission of a complete word (e.g. i. i. 10; ii. i. 22; iv. iv. 273, 711; v. i. 118; v. iii. 65) as well as for the omission of a letter, or letters (cf. *N. & Q.*, May 1961, 175–6).

Mam. I learn'd it out of women's faces. Pray now,
  What colour are your eyebrows?
First Lady.   Blue, my lord.
Mam. Nay, that's a mock: I have seen a lady's nose
  That has been blue, but not her eyebrows.
First Lady.   Hark ye,   15
  The queen your mother rounds apace: we shall
  Present our services to a fine new prince
  One of these days, and then you'd wanton with us,
  If we would have you.
Sec. Lady.   She is spread of late
  Into a goodly bulk: good time encounter her!   20
Her. What wisdom stirs amongst you? Come, sir, now
  I am for you again: 'pray you, sit by us,
  And tell 's a tale.
Mam.   Merry, or sad, shall't be?
Her. As merry as you will.
Mam. A sad tale's best for winter: I have one   25
  Of sprites and goblins.
Her.   Let's have that, good sir.
  Come on, sit down, come on, and do your best
  To fright me with your sprites: you're powerful at it.
Mam. There was a man—
Her.   Nay, come sit down: then on.
Mam. Dwelt by a churchyard: I will tell it softly,   30
  Yond crickets shall not hear it.
Her.   Come on then,
  And giv't me in mine ear.

  [*Enter* LEONTES, *with* ANTIGONUS, *Lords, and others.*]

Leon. Was he met there? his train? Camillo with him?

13. S.D. *First Lady.*] *Rowe* (*1*) (*subst.*); *Lady. F.*   15. S.D. *First Lady.*] *Rowe* (*1*)
(*subst.*); *Lady. F.*   25–6. winter: I . . . one / Of] *As Dyce*; Winter: / I . . . one of F.
31–2. Come . . . ear] *As Capell; one line in F.*   32. S.D. *Enter . . . others*] *Enter Leontes
F2; no S.D. in F.*

 17. *prince*] In Elizabethan times the
sense may be masculine or feminine:
the speaker is not assuming that
Hermione will have a son.
 20. *good time . . . her*] 'Good luck to
her in the birth.' Cf. *H8*, v. i. 22.

 22. *I am for you*] 'I am ready for you.'
Abbott, §155.
 31. *Yond crickets*] As *Var.* notes, this
obviously refers to the ladies 'with
their tittering and chirping laughter'.

A Lord. Behind the tuft of pines I met them, never
          Saw I men scour so on their way: I ey'd them   35
          Even to their ships.
Leon.   How blest am I
          In my just censure! in my true opinion!
          Alack, for lesser knowledge! how accurs'd
          In being so blest! There may be in the cup
          A spider steep'd, and one may drink, depart,   40
          And yet partake no venom (for his knowledge
          Is not infected); but if one present
          Th' abhorr'd ingredient to his eye, make known
          How he hath drunk, he cracks his gorge, his sides,
          With violent hefts. I have drunk, and seen the spider. 45
          Camillo was his help in this, his pandar:
          There is a plot against my life, my crown;
          All's true that is mistrusted: that false villain,
          Whom I employ'd, was pre-employ'd by him:
          He has discover'd my design, and I   50
          Remain a pinch'd thing; yea, a very trick
          For them to play at will. How came the posterns
          So easily open?

34. S.D. *A Lord.*] *Lord.* F; *1 Lord.* Capell (*so throughout scene*).

38–9. *Alack ... blest*] 'Oh that I knew less' (ignorance would be bliss). 'How accursed that I am proved right.' The commonplace is found also in Middleton's *The Witch* (Malone Soc.), 1694–6, where Antonio suffering from a 'Kindled Ielouzie' (1745) and mistakingly thinking his wife unfaithful, exclaims: 'Oh, 'tis a paine of hell, to know ones shame, / had it byn hid, don, it' had bin don happy, / for he that's Ignorant lives long, and merry.' And cf. *Oth.*, III. iii. 342–61. Not in Tilley.

40–1. *A spider*] There was a belief that a spider in drink or food would poison the person who consumed it only if he knew the spider were there. Cf. Middleton, *No Wit like a Woman's*, II. i. 392–3: 'Even when my lip touch'd the contracting cup, / Even there to see the spider?' The belief is perhaps in *Greene's Vision* (Greene,

Grosart, XII, 146–7, 253): 'he being blinde, had eaten the flie', i.e. 'he had been made a cuckold, but not being aware of it at the time had not then suffered the torment of jealousy'.

45. *hefts*] heavings, retching.

48. *All's true . . . mistrusted*] 'All our suspicions [i.e. those things mistrusted] prove to be justified [true].'

50. *discover'd*] revealed.

51. *pinch'd*] tortured, *O.E.D.* pinch *vb.*5; subjected to physical shrinking, mental affliction or social injury, *O.E.D.* 6; reduced to straits or distress, brought into difficulties or trouble, afflicted, harassed, *O.E.D.* 7. The word here contains these senses and also the sense that Leontes feels that he has been reduced to futility. Cf. 'oft the teeming earth / Is with a kind of colic pinch'd and vex'd' (*1H4*, III. i. 28); and 'A poor vex'd thing I am' (Jonson, *Bart. Fair*, II. ii. 79).

A Lord.   By his great authority,
        Which often hath no less prevail'd than so
        On your command.
Leon.   I know't too well.   55
        Give me the boy: I am glad you did not nurse him:
        Though he does bear some signs of me, yet you
        Have too much blood in him.
Her.   What is this? sport?
Leon. Bear the boy hence, he shall not come about her,
        Away with him, and let her sport herself   60
        With that she's big with; for 'tis Polixenes
        Has made thee swell thus.   [*Exit Mamillius, with a lady.*]
Her.   But I'd say he had not;
        And I'll be sworn you would believe my saying,
        How e'er you lean to th' nay-ward.
Leon.   You, my lords,
        Look on her, mark her well: be but about   65
        To say 'she is a goodly lady,' and
        The justice of your hearts will thereto add
        ' 'Tis pity she's not honest, honourable':
        Praise her but for this her without-door form
        (Which on my faith deserves high speech) and straight
        The shrug, the hum or ha, these petty brands   71
        That calumny doth use—O, I am out,

62. S.D. *Exit . . . lady*] Capell (*subst.*) ; *no S.D. in* F.

58. *sport?*] Hermia, to whom Lysander's aberration is as serious, asks a similar question (*MND.*, III. ii. 265), and so does Lady Percy of Hotspur (*1H4*, II. iii. 96).

61. *With . . . Polixenes*] J. C. Maxwell suggests to me that the second *with* may be an interpolation. Shakespeare often omits such prepositions and the line is now a syllable too long. But there are many lines of this length; extra syllables at the end of a line are not uncommon.

62–4. *But I'd . . . nay-ward*] 'I should merely have to say he had not and I am absolutely certain you would believe my mere statement however much you are inclined to the contrary.' This is another example of the em-

phatic difference between *saying* something and *swearing* it. Hermione says that it would only be necessary for her to *say* that she is innocent. She cannot yet believe that the charge is deeply serious. The stress is on *say . . . sworn . . . saying*. *But* is used in the sense of 'merely if'. The *O.E.D.* records no other use of *nay-ward* or *nayward* in F. On analogy with *windward* it means 'the direction of saying nay, of denial'. It is not to be confused with *nayword* which means a watchword or proverb.

69. *without-door form*] external appearance. Cf. *Cym.*, I. vi. 15, 'All of her that is out of door most rich.'

72–3. *O . . . does*] 'Oh I am wrong: [I should say] these petty stigmas that mercy uses.'

That mercy does; for calumny will sear
Virtue itself—these shrugs, these hum's and ha's,
When you have said 'she's goodly', come between,   75
Ere you can say 'she's honest': but be't known,
From him that has most cause to grieve it should be,
She's an adultress!

Her.   Should a villain say so
(The most replenish'd villain in the world)
He were as much more villain: you, my lord,   80
Do but mistake.

Leon.   You have mistook, my lady,
Polixenes for Leontes. O thou thing—
Which I'll not call a creature of thy place,
Lest barbarism, making me the precedent,
Should a like language use to all degrees,   85
And mannerly distinguishment leave out
Betwixt the prince and beggar. I have said
She's an adultress; I have said with whom:
More; she's a traitor, and Camillo is
A federary with her, and one that knows,   90
What she should shame to know herself
But with her most vile principal, that she's
A bed-swerver, even as bad as those
That vulgars give bold'st titles; ay, and privy
To this their late escape.

73-4. *calumny . . . Virtue*] Cf. *Meas.*,
III. ii. 174-5: 'back-wounding calumny / The whitest virtue strikes'; and
Ham., I. iii. 38, 'Virtue itself scapes not
calumnious strokes', III. i. 136. The
sentiment is proverbial (Tilley, E175).

78. *She's an adultress!*] This plain
but vehement exclamation comes with
dramatic suddenness after the lengthy
and tortuous build-up from 64.

79. *replenish'd*] Although used in
modern sense of 'refill' in *Lucr.*, 1357,
the normal sense in Shakespeare is, as
here, 'complete', 'consummate' (*LLL.*,
IV. ii. 24; *R3*, IV. iii. 18).

81. *mistake . . . mistook*] Cf. wordplay
in II. iii. 91-2.

82-3. *O . . . place*] Leontes will not
use, for a person of Hermione's exalted

position, the harsh term he has in
mind.

86. *And . . . out*] 'and leave out fit and
proper distinction'.

90. *federary*] F *Federarie*. No other
recorded use, but *foedarie* (*Cym.*, III. ii.
21) and *fedarie* (*Meas.*, II. iv. 122).
Fedary is a form of *feudary* (lit. a feudal
tenant, and so, retainer, dependant).
Shakespeare probably had this word
in mind but with the bad sense of
confederate = accomplice (*O.E.D.* B2)
and the spelling results from the association. The metre requires pronunciation *fedary*.

94. *vulgars*] 'common people'. Nouns
formed from adjectives (Abbott §5)
are usually in the singular, e.g. 'ca-
viare to the general' (*Ham.*, II. ii. 431).

Her.   No, by my life,   95
      Privy to none of this. How will this grieve you,
      When you shall come to clearer knowledge, that
      You thus have publish'd me! Gentle my lord,
      You scarce can right me throughly, then, to say
      You did mistake.
Leon.   No: if I mistake   100
      In those foundations which I build upon,
      The centre is not big enough to bear
      A school-boy's top. Away with her, to prison!
      He who shall speak for her is afar off guilty
      But that he speaks.
Her.   There's some ill planet reigns: 105
      I must be patient till the heavens look
      With an aspect more favourable. Good my lords,
      I am not prone to weeping, as our sex
      Commonly are; the want of which vain dew
      Perchance shall dry your pities: but I have   110
      That honourable grief lodg'd here which burns

---

104. afar off] a farre-off F.

102. *centre*] The word, usually with a capital in *F*, as here, can mean the centre of the Universe, the heart of everything, the centre of the earth, and, as apparently here, the earth itself. Cf. I. ii. 138 and p. 166.

104–5. *afar . . . speaks*] 'The man who even speaks for Hermione shall, in so doing, make himself indirectly a sharer of her guilt.' Cf. *Wiv.*, I. i. 189, 'a kind of tender, made afar off' (i.e. indirectly). Katharine, similarly placed, knew that no Englishman dare even give her counsel, 'Or be a known friend 'gainst his highness' pleasure' (*H8*, III. i. 85).

105–7. *There's some . . . favourable*] There was still much popular belief in the astrology of the *Almagest* of Ptolemy (among many modern accounts of Elizabethan astrology cf. E. B. Knobel, 'Astronomy and astrology' in *Sh.Eng.*, i. 444–61, and J. Parr, *Tamburlane's Malady*, 1953): there was also much contemporary astrological

literature, e.g. 'Erra Pater', *A Prognostycacion for euer*, of which at least nine editions appeared before that of 1610. Certain planets, notably Mars and Saturn, were malefic or causes of evil, but the influence of a planet depended on its aspect. (For the five aspects of the planets see L. Spence, *An Encyclopedia of Occultism*, 1920, 46, and *O.E.D.* aspect 4.) Planets are said to reign (*O.E.D.* reign v. 3b) when situated at their zenith in the houses where they are most powerful (Spence, *loc. cit.*).

108–11. *weeping . . . burns*] Katharine also will not weep but turn her tears to 'sparks of fire' (*H8*, II. iv. 70–4). Cf. *Wint.*, III. ii. 193.

111–12. *burns . . . drown*] This is a favourite antithesis: cf. 'Thus have I shunn'd the fire for fear of burning, / And drench'd me in the sea, where I am drown'd' (*Gent.*, I. iii. 78–9); 'And these, who, often drown'd, could never die, / Transparent heretics, be

Worse than tears drown: beseech you all, my lords,
With thoughts so qualified as your charities
Shall best instruct you, measure me; and so
The king's will be perform'd.

Leon.   Shall I be heard?   115

Her. Who is't that goes with me? Beseech your highness,
My women may be with me, for you see
My plight requires it. Do not weep, good fools,
There is no cause: when you shall know your mistress
Has deserv'd prison, then abound in tears   120
As I come out: this action I now go on
Is for my better grace. Adieu, my lord:
I never wish'd to see you sorry; now
I trust I shall. My women, come; you have leave.

Leon. Go, do our bidding: hence!   125

        [Exit Queen, guarded; with Ladies.]

A Lord. Beseech your highness, call the queen again.

Ant. Be certain what you do, sir, lest your justice
Prove violence, in the which three great ones suffer,
Yourself, your queen, your son.

A Lord.   For her, my lord,
I dare my life lay down, and will do't, sir,   130
Please you t' accept it, that the queen is spotless
I' th' eyes of heaven, and to you—I mean
In this which you accuse her.

Ant.   If it prove
She's otherwise, I'll keep my stables where

---

112. beseech] 'beseech *F*.   116. Beseech] 'Beseech *F*.   125. S.D. *Exit . . .*
Ladies] Theobald; no S.D. in *F*.

---

burnt for liars!' (*Rom.*, I. ii. 90–1).

115. *heard*] obeyed. Leontes is impatient at Hermione's collected steadiness.

118. *good fools*] Hermione in thus chiding her women is clearly shown as their beloved mistress.

121–2. *this action . . . grace*] 'Action' has various meanings. Here it probably has some legal sense. 'This accusation (or trial) for which I now go to prison will ultimately redound to my honour.' It is possible that 'for my

better grace' carries also the idea of 'is sent to refine my soul through purgation' but this is unlikely since Hermione has no doubt of her own purity. The passage could mean 'this campaign on which I now set out is for my honour' since Hermione repeatedly makes it clear that she is fighting only for her good name. There is an echo of the proverbial belief that afflictions are for our own good (Tilley, A53).

134–6. *I'll keep . . . trust her*] 'I'll lock my wife up as I shut up my mares

I lodge my wife; I'll go in couples with her;   135
Than when I feel and see her no farther trust her:
For every inch of woman in the world,
Ay, every dram of woman's flesh is false,
If she be.
Leon.   Hold your peaces.
A Lord.   Good my lord,—
Ant. It is for you we speak, not for ourselves: 140
You are abus'd, and by some putter-on
That will be damn'd for 't: would I knew the villain,
I would land-damn him. Be she honour-flaw'd,
I have three daughters: the eldest is eleven;
The second and the third, nine and some five: 145
If this prove true, they'll pay for 't. By mine honour
I'll geld 'em all; fourteen they shall not see
To bring false generations: they are co-heirs,
And I had rather glib myself, than they
Should not produce fair issue.

---

143. land-damn] Land-damne *F*.   147. geld 'em] gell'd em *F*.

---

away from the stallions: I'll run
coupled to her as though we were a
pair of hounds and trust her no
farther than I can touch or see her.'
To 'keep' a stable means to 'guard'—
cf. Greene, *James the Fourth* (*Works*, ed.
Dyce, 1861, 193), 'keep his stable
when 'tis empty' (used satirically), and
Chapman, *All Fools*, IV. i. 262–5: 'But
for your wife that keeps the stable of
your honour, let her be locked in a
brazen tower, let Argus himself keep
her, yet can you never be secure of
your honour' (first published 1605).

138. *woman's*] The singular is normal
in such expressions. Cf. *LLL.*, III. i.
128.

141. *abus'd . . . putter-on*] deceived . . .
instigator, inciter (*O.E.D.* putter 8).

143. *land-damn*] This expressive
word has not been satisfactorily explained although there are many suggestions. Wright claims that it existed
in Yorks. and Glouc. dialect meaning
'to abuse with rancour' and it is also
said to be a Gloucestershire word for

punishment meted out to slanderers,
but the usages have not been sub-
stantiated. It may be an unrecorded
dialect form of *lamback* (*O.E.D.* first
record 1589) or *lambaste* (*O.E.D.* first
record 1637) meaning *thrash*. Hanmer
(Gloss.) suggested 'stop his urine'
hence 'kill' since *land* or *lant* meant
'urine'. The coarse remark would be
appropriate from the stables-minded
Antigonus but the explanation seems
far-fetched.

145. *some*] about.

148. *false generations*] 'bastard children' in contrast with 'fair issue' (150).

148–50. *they . . . issue*] Apparently
the point of this is simply to show the
extent of Antigonus' feelings; for to
geld (glib) himself can have nothing
to do with the children which his
daughters and joint heiresses may produce. But perhaps 'them' has been lost
after 'glib'. If a man only had daughters they would normally be co-heirs;
but if he had sons the eldest son would
be the heir, as in *AYL.*

Leon.   Cease; no more.   150
   You smell this business with a sense as cold
   As is a dead man's nose: but I do see 't and feel 't,
   As you feel doing thus; and see withal
   The instruments that feel.
Ant.   If it be so,
   We need no grave to bury honesty: 155
   There's not a grain of it the face to sweeten
   Of the whole dungy earth.
Leon.   What! lack I credit?
A Lord. I had rather you did lack than I, my lord,
   Upon this ground: and more it would content me
   To have her honour true than your suspicion,   160
   Be blam'd for 't how you might.
Leon.   Why, what need we
   Commune with you of this, but rather follow
   Our forceful instigation? Our prerogative
   Calls not your counsels, but our natural goodness
   Imparts this; which if you, or stupefied,   165

151. *smell*] 'To smell out a matter' is common in Shakespeare. Cf. IV. iv. 672; *1H4*, I. iii. 277; *Oth.*, v. ii. 194.

153. *As you . . . thus*] probably to be explained by stage-business, perhaps Leontes pulling Antigonus' beard—as he almost certainly does at II. iii. 161 —or nose. Such action would not surprise an Elizabethan audience. Elizabeth, in public, not infrequently boxed the ears of her ladies-in-waiting and even of her courtiers. But perhaps Leontes merely performs an action of 'feeling' something—as of grasping one hand with the other.

154. *The instruments that feel*] presumably Leontes' fingers.

157. *dungy earth*] There has been much comment on this phrase. 'Dungy' is used by Shakespeare only here and in *Ant.*, I. i. 35, 'Kingdoms are clay; our dungy earth alike / Feeds beast as man,' where Antony is declaring to Cleopatra the baseness of the world compared to the nobleness

of their love. In *Wint.* the phrase again must mean 'the base earth' which cannot be sweetened because no honesty exists to do so. It cannot mean 'the fertile earth'. There is even more bitterness in Timon's 'the earth's a thief, / That feeds and breeds by a composture stol'n / From gen'ral excrement' (*Tim.*, IV. iii. 438–40). Shakespeare uses 'dunghill' several times but 'dung' only in *Ant.* v. ii. 7. 'Dungy earth' suggests the contemptuous 'dung of the earth' of *Ps.* lxxxiii. 10 (Noble, *Biblical Knowledge*, 239).

163. *forceful instigation*] powerful impulse.

164. *Calls not*] does not call for, does not need.

165–8. *which . . . your advice*] 'in respect of which if you, either being or pretending to be so stupid in discernment, cannot or will not appreciate a truth as I can, then you can be assured I need no more of your advice.' The sense of 'seeming so' is 'cunningly pretending'.

Or seeming so, in skill, cannot or will not
Relish a truth, like us, inform yourselves
We need no more of your advice: the matter,
The loss, the gain, the ord'ring on 't, is all
Properly ours.

Ant.   And I wish, my liege,   170
You had only in your silent judgement tried it,
Without more overture.

Leon.   How could that be?
Either thou art most ignorant by age,
Or thou wert born a fool. Camillo's flight,
Added to their familiarity,   175
(Which was as gross as ever touch'd conjecture,
That lack'd sight only, nought for approbation
But only seeing, all other circumstances
Made up to th' deed) doth push on this proceeding.
Yet, for a greater confirmation   180
(For in an act of this importance, 'twere
Most piteous to be wild), I have dispatch'd in post
To sacred Delphos, to Apollo's temple,
Cleomenes and Dion, whom you know
Of stuff'd sufficiency: now from the Oracle   185
They will bring all; whose spiritual counsel had,
Shall stop or spur me. Have I done well?

A Lord. Well done, my lord.

Leon. Though I am satisfied, and need no more
Than what I know, yet shall the Oracle   190

169–70. on 't, is all / Properly] *Theobald (subst.)*; on 't. / Is all properly *F*.   184.
Cleomenes] Cleomines *F (so throughout play)*.

169–70.] Theobald's re-arrangement restores the metre if *ours* is given
two syllables.
170. *Properly ours*] by natural right
our own.
172. *overture*] opening, i.e. exposing
the matter to public view, publicity.
175–9. *Added . . . deed*] 'Added to
their public intimacy, which was as
gross as any that ever verified a suspicion which lacked nothing but the
witness of sight itself, nothing for full
proof except actually seeing [the

adultery committed]; everything else
connected with the case amounted to
[certain proof that] the deed [was
done].'
182. *wild*] rash, inconsiderate, to
act without thought. Cf. *wildly*, IV. iv.
540; v. i. 128.
183. *Delphos*] See III. i. 2n.
185. *stuff'd sufficiency*] 'more than
adequate ability'. Cf. *Rom.*, III. v. 182;
Oth., I. iii. 225.
186. *all*] the whole truth.
had] when received.

Give rest to th' minds of others; such as he
Whose ignorant credulity will not
Come up to th' truth. So have we thought it good
From our free person she should be confined,
Lest that the treachery of the two fled hence   195
Be left her to perform. Come, follow us;
We are to speak in public; for this business
Will raise us all.
Ant. [*Aside*]   To laughter, as I take it,
If the good truth were known.   *Exeunt.*

SCENE II

Enter PAULINA, *a Gentleman,* [*and Attendants*].

Paul. The keeper of the prison, call to him;
Let him have knowledge who I am. Good lady,
No court in Europe is too good for thee;
What dost thou then in prison?

[*Enter Gaoler.*]

Now good sir,
You know me, do you not?
Gaol.   For a worthy lady   5
And one who much I honour.
Paul.   Pray you then,
Conduct me to the queen.
Gaol.   I may not, madam:

Scene II

Scene II] *Scena Secunda. F.*   S.D. *Enter . . . Attendants.*] *Enter Paulina, a Gentleman,
Gaoler, Emilia. F.*   4. S.D. *Enter Gaoler*] *Rowe* (1) (*subst.*); *no S.D. in F.*

191. *he*] either 'Antigonus' or else
used indefinitely, 'anyone'.
194. *free*] openly accessible.
195. *treachery*] i.e. the plan to
murder me.
198. *raise*] rouse.

Scene II

Scene ii] A prison.
1–4. *The keeper . . . prison*] From 'The

keeper' to 'I am' is addressed to the
Gentleman who then summons the
Gaoler. From 'Good lady' to 'prison'
is soliloquy on Hermione.
2. *have knowledge*] be informed. Cf.
H8, v. iii. 4, 'Has he had knowledge of
it?'
6. *who*] for 'whom', as frequently in
Shakespeare. Cf. IV. iv. 625; v. i. 109;
and Abbott, §274.

  To the contrary I have express commandment.
Paul. Here's ado,
  To lock up honesty and honour from   10
  Th' access of gentle visitors! Is't lawful, pray you,
  To see her women? any of them? Emilia?
Gaol. So please you, madam,
  To put apart these your attendants, I
  Shall bring Emilia forth.
Paul.   I pray now, call her.   15
  Withdraw yourselves.   [*Exeunt Gentleman and Attendants.*]
Gaol.   And, madam,
  I must be present at your conference.
Paul. Well: be't so: prithee.   [*Exit Gaoler.*]
  Here's such ado to make no stain a stain
  As passes colouring.

      [*Enter Gaoler, with* EMILIA.]

       Dear gentlewoman,   20
  How fares our gracious lady?
Emil. As well as one so great and so forlorn
  May hold together: on her frights and griefs
  (Which never tender lady hath borne greater)
  She is, something before her time, deliver'd.   25
Paul. A boy?
Emil.   A daughter; and a goodly babe,
  Lusty, and like to live: the queen receives
  Much comfort in't; says, 'My poor prisoner,
  I am innocent as you.'
Paul.   I dare be sworn:
  These dangerous, unsafe lunes i' th' king, beshrew
   them!   30

9–10. Here's . . . from] *As Hanmer; one line in F.*   16. S.D. *Exeunt . . . Attendants*]
Theobald (subst.); no S.D. in F.   18. S.D. *Exit Gaoler*] *Capell (subst.); no S.D. in F.*
20. S.D. *Enter . . . Emilia*] *Enter Emilia F2; no S.D. in F.*

11–21.] Some lines have too many or too few syllables but nothing seems to be gained by re-arrangement.

19–20. *Here's . . . colouring*] 'Here's such a fuss to try to make something stainless appear to be stained, that it goes beyond all the skill of dyeing.' 'To give colour' also means 'to make plausible' so that the last three words have also the sense 'As passes all belief'. Cf. 'This stain . . . doth confirm/ Another stain' (*Cym.*, II. iv. 139).

23. *on*] following, in consequence of.
30. *lunes*] from *luna*, hence 'fits of

He must be told on't, and he shall: the office
Becomes a woman best. I'll take 't upon me:
If I prove honey-mouth'd, let my tongue blister,
And never to my red-look'd anger be
The trumpet any more. Pray you, Emilia,   35
Commend my best obedience to the queen:
If she dares trust me with her little babe,
I'll show 't the king, and undertake to be
Her advocate to th' loud'st. We do not know
How he may soften at the sight o' th' child: 40
The silence often of pure innocence
Persuades, when speaking fails.
Emil.   Most worthy madam,
Your honour and your goodness is so evident,
That your free undertaking cannot miss
A thriving issue: there is no lady living   45
So meet for this great errand. Please your ladyship
To visit the next room, I'll presently
Acquaint the queen of your most noble offer,
Who but to-day hammer'd of this design,
But durst not tempt a minister of honour,   50
Lest she should be denied.
Paul.   Tell her, Emilia,
I'll use that tongue I have: if wit flow from 't
As boldness from my bosom, let 't not be doubted
I shall do good.
Emil.   Now be you blest for it!

53. let 't] *F3;* le 't *F.*

lunacy'. Used perhaps only four times
by Shakespeare: *Wiv.,* IV. ii. 17; *Troil.,*
II. iii. 126; *Ham.,* III. iii. 7 [brows].

33. *blister*] The belief that a lie or
other evil speech blistered the tongue
is proverbial (Tilley, R84). It is mentioned in *Pandosto* (p. 192) and elsewhere in Shakespeare (e.g. *LLL.,* v. ii.
334–5—also associated with 'honey-
tongued'; *Tim.,* v. i. 130).

34–5. *to . . . trumpet*] The 'trumpet'
was the man who preceded the herald
who was usually dressed in red and
often bore an angry message.

41–2. *silence . . . fails*] Cf. '. . . in her

youth / There is a prone and speech-
less dialect / Such as move men!'
(*Meas.,* I. ii. 175–7).

44. *free*] freely-offered, generous.

49. *hammer'd of*] 'earnestly deliberated'. 'Hammered', 'hammering'
is frequently used in contemporary
literature in this sense (e.g. *Gent.,* I. iii.
18, 'that / Whereon this month I have
been hammering'; *2H6,* I. ii. 47; *R2,*
v. v. 5; *Tit.,* II. iii. 39).

50. *tempt . . . honour*] 'risk asking a
minister of rank'.

52. *wit*] appropriate words of
wisdom.

I'll to the queen: please you, come something nearer.   55
Gaol. Madam, if 't please the queen to send the babe,
     I know not what I shall incur to pass it,
     Having no warrant.
Paul.   You need not fear it, sir:
     This child was prisoner to the womb, and is
     By law and process of great nature, thence   60
     Free'd and enfranchis'd; not a party to
     The anger of the king, nor guilty of
     (If any be) the trespass of the queen.
Gaol. I do believe it.
Paul. Do not you fear: upon mine honour, I   65
     Will stand betwixt you and danger.   *Exeunt.*

SCENE III

[LEONTES *discovered.*]

Leon. Nor night, nor day, no rest: it is but weakness
     To bear the matter thus: mere weakness. If
     The cause were not in being,—part o' th' cause,

Scene III

Scene III] *Scæna Tertia.* F.   S.D. *Leontes discovered.*] *Enter Leontes, Seruants,*
Paulina, Antigonus, and Lords. F.   2. weakness. If] *Collier (1842);* weakness, if F.

55. *come . . . nearer*] Emilia is repeat-
ing her request of 46–7.
 59–61. *child . . . enfranchis'd*] Cf.
'whilst in the womb he stay'd / Attending nature's law' (*Cym.*, v. iv. 37–8).
 63. *If any be*] if there be any guilt.

Scene III

Scene iii] Leontes' palace. Tannenbaum ('Textual . . . notes on the
Winter's Tale', *Phil.Q.*, 1928, 366)
seems to be the first to note that
Leontes' opening speech must be a
soliloquy. He is on stage alone until the
servant enters at 9 and at 17 Leontes
says to him 'Leave me solely.' It also
seems that at 26 Paulina and the others
do not enter far on to the stage or else
the stage is in some way divided. They
can be seen and heard by the audience

but not by Leontes. There are of
course many examples of characters
fully on stage, who by convention are
not seen or heard by others also fully
on stage, but here Leontes has to call
at 39 to find out who is making the
noise which he has just heard from
Paulina's rising voice. She and the
others then come fully into Leontes'
view at 40.
 1–9, 18–26.] Leontes' soliloquy, his
tormented mind seeking relief in plans
for savage vengeance, makes clear that
Paulina's mission could hardly be
worse timed, and prepares for the
brutal sentence on the child and on
Antigonus.
 1–3. *but weakness . . . being*] With the
F punctuation the meaning would be
'It is weakness to take the matter in

She th' adultress: for the harlot king
Is quite beyond mine arm, out of the blank   5
And level of my brain: plot-proof: but she
I can hook to me: say that she were gone,
Given to the fire, a moiety of my rest
Might come to me again. [*Enter Servant.*] Who's there?

Serv.   My Lord!

Leon. How does the boy?

Serv.   He took good rest to-night;   10
'Tis hop'd his sickness is discharg'd.

Leon. To see his nobleness,
Conceiving the dishonour of his mother!
He straight declin'd, droop'd, took it deeply,
Fasten'd and fix'd the shame on 't in himself,   15
Threw off his spirit, his appetite, his sleep,
And downright languish'd. Leave me solely: go,
See how he fares. [*Exit Serv.*] Fie, fie! no thought of him:
The very thought of my revenges that way
Recoil upon me: in himself too mighty,   20
And in his parties, his alliance; let him be
Until a time may serve. For present vengeance,
Take it on her. Camillo and Polixenes
Laugh at me; make their pastime at my sorrow:
They should not laugh if I could reach them, nor   25
Shall she, within my power.

Enter PAULINA, [*carrying a baby, with* ANTIGONUS, *lords and
servants, who try to prevent her*].

9. S.D. *Enter Servant*] Rowe (*1*) (*subst., after there*); *no S.D. in F.*   Who's] *F3;*
Whose *F.*   10–11. to-night; / 'Tis hop'd his] *As Steevens;* to night: 'tis hop'd /
His *F.*   14. declin'd] declin'd, and *Hanmer.*   18. S.D. *Exit Serv.*] *Theobald
(subst.); no S.D. in F.*   26. S.D. *Enter . . . her.*] *Enter Paulina. F.*

this way: it were absolute weakness if
the cause of the trouble were no longer
alive.'
    4. *harlot*] lewd.
    5–6. *blank/And level*] The *blank* is the
white bull's-eye of the target in gun-
nery and the *level* is the aim, or perhaps here, the range. Cf. *Ham.,* IV. i.
42, 'As level as the cannon to his
blank'; *All's W.,* II. i. 154, 'proclaim /

Myself against the level of mine
aim'; *H8,* I. ii. 2; and *Wint.,* III. ii. 81.
    18. *See . . . him*] 'he' is Mamillius,
'him'—picking up the thought again
from 4–6—is Polixenes.
    20. *too mighty*] Cf. 'The great Antio-
chus— / 'Gainst whom I am too little
to contend, / Since he's so great' (*Per.,*
I. ii. 16).
    26. *Enter . . . her*] For the entry of

A Lord.   You must not enter.
Paul. Nay rather, good my lords, be second to me:
    Fear you his tyrannous passion more, alas,
    Than the queen's life? a gracious innocent soul,
    More free than he is jealous.
Ant.   That's enough.   30
Serv. Madam, he hath not slept to-night, commanded
    None should come at him.
Paul.   Not so hot, good sir;
    I come to bring him sleep. 'Tis such as you,
    That creep like shadows by him, and do sigh
    At each his needless heavings; such as you   35
    Nourish the cause of his awaking. I
    Do come with words as medicinal as true,
    Honest, as either, to purge him of that humour
    That presses him from sleep.
Leon.   What noise there, ho?
Paul. No noise, my lord; but needful conference   40
    About some gossips for your highness.
Leon.   How!
    Away with that audacious lady! Antigonus,
    I charg'd thee that she should not come about me.
    I knew she would.
Ant.   I told her so, my lord,
    On your displeasure's peril and on mine,   45
    She should not visit you.

---

26. *A Lord.*] *Lord. F; First Lord. Malone.*   39. What] *F2; Who F.*

characters see note at the head of this scene.

28. *tyrannous*] cruel.

30. *free*] innocent. Cf. I. ii. 251; *Ham.*, II. ii. 557, 'Make mad the guilty, and appal the free'; and *Oth.*, III. iii. 259.

35.] The realism here is noted by J. C. Bucknill, *Medical Knowledge of Shakespeare*, 1860, 129, who quotes Florence Nightingale's observation that slight noises which excite attention are more disturbing to a sick person than louder noises which are decided and undisguised.

38. *Honest, as either*] 'In honesty, as either of those two': i.e. 'my words are indeed both medicinal and true.'

humour] mental state: used as a medical and psychological term.

39. *What noise*] While this, the generally used reading from *F2* onwards, is probably correct, the *F* 'Who' may be a mistake for 'Whose'. Cf. 'Whose noise', *Oth.*, v. i. 48.

40.] For the entry of characters see note at head of this scene.

41. *gossips*] sponsors at baptism, godparents. But the word also had its modern meanings in Shakespeare's time. Cf. *MND.*, II. i. 47.

Leon.   What! canst not rule her?
Paul. From all dishonesty he can: in this—
          Unless he take the course that you have done,
          Commit me for committing honour—trust it,
          He shall not rule me.
Ant.   La you now, you hear: 50
          When she will take the rein I let her run;
          But she'll not stumble.
Paul.   Good my liege, I come,—
          And, I beseech you hear me, who professes
          Myself your loyal servant, your physician,
          Your most obedient counsellor, yet that dares   55
          Less appear so, in comforting your evils,
          Than such as most seem yours;—I say, I come
          From your good queen.
Leon.   Good queen!
Paul. Good queen, my lord, good queen: I say good queen,
          And would by combat make her good, so were I   60

58–9. Good queen! / Good queen . . . good queen,] *F (but* 'I say good queen'
appears as a separate line); From . . . lord, / Good queen . . . good queen, *Pope.*
60. good, so] *Theobald;* good so, *F.*

49. *Commit . . . honour*] 'Commit me
to prison for committing honour.'
Paulina uses 'committing' sarcastic-
ally. The normal sense is to commit a
sin, but she exclaims 'Send me to
prison for doing something honourable!'

53–5. *professes . . . dares*] Many edd.
change to *profess . . . dare* believing that
'Shakespeare could hardly have written "professes myself"' (*N.C. Wint.,*
148). But it is a confusion of construc-
tions of a kind not uncommon (Abbott
§§409–16): 'I . . . profess / Myself . . .
that dare' with 'I . . . [one] who professes / Herself . . . that dares'. Paulina
is excited. Cf. 106–7n.

56. *comforting*] encouraging, coun-
tenancing, abetting: 'I claim to be
your loyal servant, your physician,
your most obedient adviser, yet one
who dares to appear less so in this
matter of encouraging your evils
[since I do not encourage them] than

such people who appear most of all to
be your loyal servants [but who are
not because they do encourage these
evils].'

60. *by combat . . . good*] 'prove her to
be virtuous in trial by battle'. In
Pandosto the king threatens to burn his
wife and daughter but there is no
reference to trial by combat—there is
no character corresponding to Paulina. The situation is a common
romance motif and Dr Brooks points
out as examples the parallels in the
ballad *Sir Aldingar* (Child 59) and in
the story of Guinevere—e.g. Malory,
Bk xviii, Chs. iii–vii, Guinevere
appeached of high treason (treacherous murder, not adultery) and cleared
in combat by Launcelot; Bk xix, Chs.
vi–ix, Guinevere accused by Melia-
graunce and cleared in combat by
Launcelot, after being 'brought to a
fire to be burnt'; Bk xx, Chs. vii–viii,
the final exposure of Launcelot's and

A man, the worst about you.

Leon.   Force her hence.

Paul. Let him that makes but trifles of his eyes
    First hand me: on mine own accord I'll off;
    But first, I'll do my errand. The good queen
    (For she is good) hath brought you forth a daughter;   65
    Here 'tis; [*Laying down the child*] commends it to your
        blessing.

Leon.   Out!
    A mankind witch! Hence with her, out o' door:
    A most intelligencing bawd!

Paul.   Not so:
    I am as ignorant in that, as you
    In so entitling me: and no less honest   70
    Than you are mad; which is enough, I'll warrant,
    As this world goes, to pass for honest.

Leon.   Traitors!
    Will you not push her out? Give her the bastard,
    Thou dotard! thou art woman-tir'd, unroosted
    By thy dame Partlet here. Take up the bastard,   75
    Take 't up, I say; give 't to thy crone.

Paul.   For ever

66. S.D. *Laying . . . child*] Rowe (*1*) (*after* blessing); *no S.D. in* F.

Guinevere's adultery again brings her to the fire, Arthur rejecting Gawain's suggestion that he might prove her innocence by combat: 'She shall have the law.' She is rescued by Launcelot and his kin.

67. *mankind*] masculine, termagant. Cf. Beaumont and Fletcher, *Monsieur Thomas*, IV. vi. 50, ''Twas a sound knock she gave me: A plaguey mankind girl', and Udall, *Ralph Roister Doister*, IV. viii. 42, 'She is mankine' (she slew her former husband and is preparing again to fight). The word is used to describe a fierce, violent woman, a virago.

68. *intelligencing*] acting as a go-between between Hermione and Polixenes.

69. *ignorant*] uninformed, unskilled. Cf. *Cym.*, III. ii. 23.

71. *mad*] Paulina's attitude and words in this scene are reminiscent of Kent's. He calls Lear mad and speaks of himself as a physician (*Lr.*, I. i. 145, 163). Cf. Paulina here and at 37.

73. *bastard*] Leontes' horror of bastardy foreshadows Perdita's (cf. IV. iv. 88–93, pp. lxxvii, 169–70).

74. *woman-tir'd*] F *woman-tyr'd*: 'tired' is a term in falconry meaning to pull, tear (French *tirer*). Cf. *3H6*, I. i. 269, 'Tire on the flesh of me and of my son.'

75. *Partlet*] Chanticlere and Pertelote are the traditional names of the cock and the hen. Cf. *Reynard the Fox*; Chaucer, *Nuns' Priest's Tale*, and *1H4*, III. iii. 51, where Falstaff addresses the hostess as 'Dame Partlet the hen'.

Unvenerable be thy hands, if thou
Tak'st up the princess, by that forced baseness
Which he has put upon 't!

Leon.   He dreads his wife.

Paul. So I would you did; then 'twere past all doubt   80
You'd call your children yours.

Leon.   A nest of traitors!

Ant. I am none, by this good light.

Paul.   Nor I; nor any
But one that's here, and that's himself; for he,
The sacred honour of himself, his queen's,
His hopeful son's, his babe's, betrays to slander,   85
Whose sting is sharper than the sword's; and will not
(For, as the case now stands, it is a curse
He cannot be compell'd to 't) once remove
The root of his opinion, which is rotten
As ever oak or stone was sound.

Leon.   A callat   90
Of boundless tongue, who late hath beat her husband,
And now baits me! This brat is none of mine;
It is the issue of Polixenes.
Hence with it, and together with the dam
Commit them to the fire!

Paul.   It is yours;   95
And, might we lay th' old proverb to your charge,

78–9. *by . . . upon 't*] 'under that false title of bastard which he has unnaturally thrust on it' or 'accepting that description of it as bastard which he has falsely thrust upon it'. For 'force' = 'wrongfully thrust' cf. III. i. 16. Antigonus is to act like someone who refuses to answer to a name or title he repudiates—but the repudiation is to be on behalf of the child.

85–6. *slander . . . sword's*] Cf. *Cym.*, III. iv. 31, 'slander, / Whose edge is sharper than the sword', and *Wint.*, II. i. 73.

86–90. *and will . . . sound*] 'and he will never change [once remove] the source of his opinion, which is as rotten as ever oak or stone were sound because, things being as they are [i.e.,

he being a king], it is a tragedy that no one can make him change.'

90. *callat*] lewd woman.

91–2. *beat . . . baits*] 'beat' pronounced like 'bait' (Kökeritz, 94). That Leontes can pun even in his fury is typically Shakespearian. Classic examples of the grim pun include: 'a grave man' (*Rom.*, III. i. 96); 'Not on thy sole, but on thy soul, harsh Jew' (*Mer. V.*, IV. i. 123); 'I'll gild the faces of the grooms withal, / For it must seem their guilt' (*Mac.*, II. ii. 56–7); 'Is thy union here' (*Ham.*, v. ii. 318).

96. *old proverb*] Tilley, L290. Cf. Fletcher and Massinger, *Elder Brother*, II. i. p. 12: 'Your eldest Son, Sir, and your very Image, (but he's so like you, that he fares the worse for't).'

So like you, 'tis the worse. Behold, my lords,
Although the print be little, the whole matter
And copy of the father: eye, nose, lip;
The trick of's frown; his forehead; nay, the valley,   100
The pretty dimples of his chin and cheek; his smiles;
The very mould and frame of hand, nail, finger:
And thou, good goddess Nature, which hast made
So like to him that got it, if thou hast
The ordering of the mind too, 'mongst all colours   105
No yellow in 't, lest she suspect, as he does,
Her children not her husband's!

Leon.   A gross hag!
And, lozel, thou art worthy to be hang'd,
That wilt not stay her tongue.

Ant.   Hang all the husbands
That cannot do that feat, you'll leave yourself   110
Hardly one subject.

Leon.   Once more, take her hence.

98. *print*] copy.

98–9. *matter*/*And copy*] 'substance and image'. *And* may possibly be the result of mistaking manuscript *A* for ampersand. Cf. I. ii. 104. Paulina is, of course, here paying the usual flattery to a parent. Cf. *H8*, v. i. 168–74: 'as like you / As cherry is to cherry . . . / Said I for this the girl was like to him?'

100. *trick*] physical peculiarity or characteristic expression (Onions 3); cf. 'a trick of Cœur-de-lion's face' (*John*, I. i. 85).

of's frown; his forehead] Paulina is clearly indicating the baby but referring to Leontes' features.

valley] the indentation, groove, in the upper lip—the philtrum? the hollow under the lower lip? cleft in chin? Probably the first.

103. *good goddess Nature*] Cf. IV. iv. 88–96. Shakespeare is full of references to Nature the great creator. She is also Great in *Cor.*, v. iii. 33; *Cym.*, v. iv. 48; Goddess in *Lr.*, I. iv. 275; and Goddess and Divine in *Cym.*, IV. ii. 170–1.

106–7. *No yellow . . . husband's*] Yellow is the colour of jealousy. Paulina says 'Don't let this babe be

jealous lest she suspect [when she becomes a parent], just as her father does [now], that her own children are bastards.' Presumably Paulina is still being sarcastic as at 49: she is not saying that Perdita will be a faithless wife, but that Leontes' jealousy is so utterly crazy that if Perdita is infected with it she might even be crazy enough to think that her own children are bastards. But jealousy is not of oneself but of someone else and a jealous Perdita will suspect her husband's faith. This has led many to suggest that in her rage Paulina here utters the opposite of what she means—as the infuriated Hostess confuses *might* and *right* (*2H4*, v. iv. 25) and Lady Castlewood says *guests* for *hosts* (Thackeray, *Esmond*, Bk II, ch. 2)—i.e. that it is Shakespeare's deliberate expression of the kind of mistake an excited woman might easily make. But as jealousy usually means suspicion (*Lr*, v. i. 57; *Caes.*, I. ii. 162) the sense may be simply that Perdita will even suspect herself.

108. *lozel*] rogue, scoundrel.

109–11. *Hang . . . subject*] Perhaps an aside.

Paul. A most unworthy and unnatural lord
          Can do no more.
Leon.   I'll ha' thee burnt.
Paul.   I care not:
          It is an heretic that makes the fire,
          Not she which burns in 't. I'll not call you tyrant;   115
          But this most cruel usage of your queen—
          Not able to produce more accusation
          Than your own weak-hing'd fancy—something savours
          Of tyranny, and will ignoble make you,
          Yea, scandalous to the world.
Leon.   On your allegiance,   120
          Out of the chamber with her! Were I a tyrant,
          Where were her life? she durst not call me so,
          If she did know me one. Away with her!
Paul. I pray you, do not push me; I'll be gone.
          Look to your babe, my lord: 'tis yours: Jove send her
          A better guiding spirit! What needs these hands?   126
          You, that are thus so tender o'er his follies,
          Will never do him good, not one of you.
          So, so: farewell; we are gone.   *Exit.*
Leon. Thou, traitor, hast set on thy wife to this.   130
          My child? away with 't! Even thou, that hast
          A heart so tender o'er it, take it hence
          And see it instantly consum'd with fire;
          Even thou, and none but thou. Take it up straight:
          Within this hour bring me word 'tis done,   135
          And by good testimony, or I'll seize thy life,
          With what thou else call'st thine. If thou refuse
          And wilt encounter with my wrath, say so;

113–15. *I care . . . burns in 't*] 'It is the
heresy of the condemned that makes
the fire what it is—not that a woman is
burned.' Dr Brooks points out that the
further sense conveyed is 'If she is
innocent the fire becomes something
other than an instrument of justice: it
is an instrument of tyranny.' Paulina
is saying that not every execution of
a woman at the stake is what it pur-
ports to be: that depends entirely on
whether she actually is a heretic or not:

and, as for herself, Paulina is asserting
that like the martyrs so burned, she
would also be a witness to the truth
and, furthermore, that she is ready for
her fate, she will not be silenced in her
witness.

118. *weak-hing'd fancy*] Cf. *MND.*,
v. i. 25, 'fancy's images'; *Tp.*, v. i. 59,
'unsettled fancy'.

126. *What . . . hands*] 'Keep your
hands off me: you need not push me'
(cf. 124).

The bastard brains with these my proper hands
Shall I dash out. Go, take it to the fire; 140
For thou set'st on thy wife.

Ant.   I did not, sir:
These lords, my noble fellows, if they please,
Can clear me in 't.

Lords.   We can: my royal liege,
He is not guilty of her coming hither.

Leon. You're liars all. 145

A Lord. Beseech your highness, give us better credit:
We have always truly serv'd you; and beseech'
So to esteem of us: and on our knees we beg
(As recompense of our dear services
Past and to come) that you do change this purpose, 150
Which being so horrible, so bloody, must
Lead on to some foul issue. We all kneel.

Leon. I am a feather for each wind that blows:
Shall I live on to see this bastard kneel
And call me father? better burn it now 155
Than curse it then. But be it: let it live.
It shall not neither. You sir, come you hither,
You that have been so tenderly officious
With Lady Margery, your midwife there,
To save this bastard's life—for 'tis a bastard, 160
So sure as this beard's grey—what will you adventure
To save this brat's life?

Ant.   Anything, my lord,
That my ability may undergo,
And nobleness impose: at least thus much—
I'll pawn the little blood which I have left 165
To save the innocent: anything possible.

Leon. It shall be possible. Swear by this sword

---

146. *A Lord.*] *Lord. F; First Lord. Capell (subst.).*   147. beseech'] *F;* beseech *F2;*
beseech you *Rowe (1) and many edd.*

159. *Lady Margery*] used as a term of
contempt: but a 'margery-prater' was
the cant term for a hen; *Lady Margery*
is thus a variant of *Dame Partlet* (75).
    midwife] here used as term of
contempt.
    161. *this beard's grey*] The beard can

hardly be that of Leontes who is only
about thirty-three (cf. I. ii. 153–60n.).
Probably Leontes pulls Antigonus'
beard—he may have done something
similar at II. i. 153, *q.v.*
    165. *little ... left*] Antigonus is elder-
ly.

Thou wilt perform my bidding.

Ant.   I will, my lord.

Leon. Mark and perform it: seest thou? for the fail
Of any point in 't shall not only be   170
Death to thyself, but to thy lewd-tongu'd wife
(Whom for this time we pardon). We enjoin thee,
As thou art liege-man to us, that thou carry
This female bastard hence, and that thou bear it
To some remote and desert place, quite out   175
Of our dominions; and that there thou leave it
(Without more mercy) to it own protection
And favour of the climate. As by strange fortune
It came to us, I do in justice charge thee,
On thy soul's peril and thy body's torture,   180
That thou commend it strangely to some place
Where chance may nurse or end it. Take it up.

Ant. I swear to do this; though a present death
Had been more merciful. Come on, poor babe:
Some powerful spirit instruct the kites and ravens   185
To be thy nurses! Wolves and bears, they say,
Casting their savageness aside, have done
Like offices of pity. Sir, be prosperous
In more than this deed does require; and blessing
Against this cruelty, fight on thy side,   190
Poor thing, condemn'd to loss!   *Exit* [*with the child*].

191. S.D. *Exit . . . child.*] *Exit. F.*

168. *I will*] Here he touches the sword-hilt, which forms a cross.

169. *fail*] failure. *O.E.D.* first records the use of *failure* in 1641. The noun 'fail' is found also at v. i. 27; *H8*, i. ii. 145, ii. iv. 198; *Tim.*, v. i. 146; *Cym.*, iii. iv. 62.

177. *it own*] *it* is the old form of the possessive pronoun. Cf. i. ii. 151n.

178–81. *strange . . . strangely*] The sense of *strange* is *foreign, overseas*. Polixenes was a *stranger* and he, Leontes avers, brought the child. Therefore it is but justice that it be committed 'as a foreigner'; or, 'to some foreign place'.

182. *nurse or end*] To mend or end is a proverbial expression (Tilley, M874). Cf. iii. i. 18, 'clear or end'.

185. *kites and ravens*] Cf. 'kites and crows' (*2H6*, v. ii. 11 and *Cor.*, iv. v. 42, 43); 'ravens, crows and kites' (*Cæs.*, v. i. 84). Cf. also *1 Kings* xvii. 4.

186. *Wolves and bears*] Cf. *Tim.*, iii. vi. 105, iv. iii. 189, and the legend of Romulus and Remus. The hope about wild beasts here is ironically falsified in the fate of Antigonus.

189. *In . . . require*] 'to a greater extent than you deserve by this deed'.

189–91. *and . . . loss*] addressed to the babe: 'And mercy to counteract this cruelty'.

191. *loss*] destruction, ruin. Cf. iii.

Leon.   No: I'll not rear
      Another's issue.

                    Enter a Servant.

Serv.   Please your highness, posts
      From those you sent to th' Oracle, are come
      An hour since: Cleomenes and Dion,
      Being well arriv'd from Delphos, are both landed,   195
      Hasting to th' court.
A Lord.   So please you, sir, their speed
      Hath been beyond account.
Leon.   Twenty-three days
      They have been absent: 'tis good speed; foretells
      The great Apollo suddenly will have
      The truth of this appear. Prepare you, lords;   200
      Summon a session, that we may arraign
      Our most disloyal lady; for, as she hath
      Been publicly accus'd, so shall she have
      A just and open trial. While she lives
      My heart will be a burden to me. Leave me.   205
      And think upon my bidding.   *Exeunt.*

---

192. Please your] *F3;* Please' your *F.*
(*subst.*).

196. *A Lord.*] Lord. *F;* First Lord. *Capell*

iii. 51 and 'lost' III. ii. 135, 231; v. iii.
135n.; and *Pandosto*, p. 220, l. 34.
      192. *Please*] *F* Please' is probably a
misprint for '*Please.*

195. *Delphos*] See III. i. 2n.
      197. *Twenty-three days*] Cf. 'within
three weeks' (*Pandosto*, p. 196, l. 14)
for the outward journey only.

ACT III

SCENE I

Enter CLEOMENES *and* DION.

Cleo. The climate's delicate, the air most sweet,
    Fertile the isle, the temple much surpassing
    The common praise it bears.
Dion.   I shall report,
    For most it caught me, the celestial habits
    (Methinks I so should term them), and the reverence   5
    Of the grave wearers. O, the sacrifice!
    How ceremonious, solemn and unearthly
    It was i' th' offering!
Cleo.   But of all, the burst
    And the ear-deaf'ning voice o' th' Oracle,
    Kin to Jove's thunder, so surpris'd my sense,   10

ACT III

Scene 1

Act III] *Actus Tertius. F.*   Scene 1] *Scena Prima. F.*

Scene i] Sicilia: outside a village inn.

2. *the isle*] T. Spencer shows (*M.L.R.*, xlvii, 1952, 199–202) that 'in the early 17th century, the island famous in antiquity as Delos, the sacred birthplace of Apollo, *was* commonly known as Delphos'. 'Isle of Delphos' is used in *Pandosto* (p. 195); in Greene's *Menaphon*, 1598; Moraes, *Palmendos*, tr. A. Mundy, 1589; Sabie, *Fisherman's Tale*, 1595; Forde's *Parismus*, 1598; *The Thracian Wonder* (?1600–10). Shakespeare is therefore following the custom of his day in his reference to the island and oracle and Spencer shows that apologies for Shakespeare's ignor-ance or carelessness in this passage have themselves been the outcome of ignorance of contemporary practice in this matter. Spencer also considers, with reference to this scene, that it is 'hard to believe that Shakespeare had not recently glanced at' *Aeneid*, iii. 73–101 or something based on that passage since 'The germs of most of his descriptive phrases are to be found here in Virgil'.

8–9. *burst . . . ear-deaf'ning*] Thunder or thunderous noise is usual with any theophany. Jupiter 'came in thunder' (*Cym.*, v. iv. 92, 114). Ariel 'like a Harpy' comes and goes in thunder (*Tp.*, III. iii. 52, 82).

That I was nothing.

Dion.   If th' event o' th' journey
Prove as successful to the queen,—O be 't so!—
As it hath been to us, rare, pleasant, speedy,
The time is worth the use on 't.

Cleo.   Great Apollo
Turn all to th' best! These proclamations,   15
So forcing faults upon Hermione,
I little like.

Dion.   The violent carriage of it
Will clear or end the business: when the Oracle
(Thus by Apollo's great divine seal'd up)
Shall the contents discover, something rare   20
Even then will rush to knowledge. Go: fresh horses!
And gracious be the issue.   *Exeunt.*

SCENE II

Enter LEONTES, *Lords and Officers.*

Leon. This sessions (to our great grief we pronounce)
Even pushes 'gainst our heart: the party tried
The daughter of a king, our wife, and one
Of us too much belov'd. Let us be clear'd
Of being tyrannous, since we so openly   5

Scene II

Scene II] *Scœna Secunda. F.*   S.D. *Enter . . . Officers.*] *Enter Leontes, Lords, Officers:
Hermione (as to her Triall) Ladies: Cleomines, Dion. F.*

14. *The time . . . on 't*] 'The time has
been well spent on it.' Cf. 'canst use
the time well' (*Tim.*, III. i. 36).

16. *forcing*] unjustifiably thrusting.
Cf. II. iii. 78.

17. *The violent . . . it*] 'the rushed way
in which it is being carried out'.

18. *clear or end*] Cf. II. iii. 182n.

19. *divine*] priest.

20. *discover*] reveal.

21. *fresh horses*] This shows that the
messengers have travelled some distance since they landed and that the
scene is therefore inland.

Scene II

Scene ii] A court of justice, which
may be in the open air. Cf. 105.

S.D. *Enter Leontes . . . officers*] The
massed entry as in *F* is unusual only in
that it is incomplete. It does not mention Paulina or the Servant. It is the
only example, except for the omission
of reference to the babe in II. iii
of a massed entry being incomplete.
F has no other notices of entry or
exit in this scene except *Exeunt* at the
close.

5. *tyrannous*] Leontes is anxious to

Proceed in justice, which shall have due course,
Even to the guilt or the purgation.
Produce the prisoner.

Off. It is his highness' pleasure that the queen
Appear in person, here in court. Silence!   10

[*Enter* HERMIONE *guarded;* PAULINA *and Ladies attending.*]

Leon. Read the indictment.

Off. Hermione, queen to the worthy Leontes, king of
Sicilia, thou art here accused and arraigned of high
treason, in committing adultery with Polixenes, king
of Bohemia, and conspiring with Camillo to take   15
away the life of our sovereign lord the king, thy royal
husband: the pretence whereof being by circumstances partly laid open, thou, Hermione, contrary
to the faith and allegiance of a true subject, didst
counsel and aid them, for their better safety, to fly   20
away by night.

Her. Since what I am to say, must be but that
Which contradicts my accusation, and
The testimony on my part, no other
But what comes from myself, it shall scarce boot me   25
To say 'not guilty': mine integrity,
Being counted falsehood, shall, as I express it,
Be so receiv'd. But thus, if powers divine
Behold our human actions (as they do),
I doubt not then but innocence shall make   30
False accusation blush, and tyranny
Tremble at patience. You, my lord, best know
(Who least will seem to do so) my past life

---

10. Silence!] *Rowe (1)*; *Silence. F.*   S.D. *Enter . . . attending*] *Theobald (subst.)*;
no S.D. in F.   33. Who] *Rowe (1)*; Whom *F.*

stand well in public opinion and to
justify himself to himself.

7. *purgation*] acquittal.

10. *Silence!*] F prints *Silence.* towards
the right margin as if it were a S.D.
Collier supports this, believing that the
direction was to emphasize the general
suspense at Hermione's entry. But
Silence is a traditional law-court cry,

and Hermione's entrance may well
have evoked murmurs from the on-
lookers. Cf. *H8*, II. iv. 2.

17. *pretence*] design, purpose. Cf.
Gent., III. i. 47; *Mac.*, II. iii. 130; and
Pandosto, p. 194, l. 32.

30–1. *innocence . . . blush*] That a clear
conscience does not fear false accusation is proverbial (Tilley, C597).

Hath been as continent, as chaste, as true,
As I am now unhappy; which is more   35
Than history can pattern, though devis'd
And play'd to take spectators. For behold me,
A fellow of the royal bed, which owe
A moiety of the throne, a great king's daughter,
The mother to a hopeful prince, here standing   40
To prate and talk for life and honour 'fore
Who please to come and hear. For life, I prize it
As I weigh grief (which I would spare): for honour,
'Tis a derivative from me to mine,
And only that I stand for. I appeal   45
To your own conscience, sir, before Polixenes
Came to your court, how I was in your grace,
How merited to be so; since he came,
With what encounter so uncurrent I
Have strain'd t'appear thus: if one jot beyond   50
The bound of honour, or in act or will
That way inclining, harden'd be the hearts
Of all that hear me, and my near'st of kin
Cry fie upon my grave!

Leon.   I ne'er heard yet
That any of these bolder vices wanted   55
Less impudence to gainsay what they did
Than to perform it first.

Her.   That's true enough,

35. *which*] viz. 'unhappiness which'.
36. *history*] story, drama.
37. *take*] delight, charm. Cf. I. ii. 40, IV. iv. 119.
38. *owe*] own.
40. *hopeful*] Cf. 'young hopeful' (now only ironical).
41. *prate*] In *Cor.*, v. iii. 159, the word is used by Volumnia who feels that she is left to plead idly: 'here he lets me prate / Like one i' th' stocks.'
42–3. *For life . . . spare*] 'As for life, I value it as I value grief, which I would do without.' (This is substantially Johnson's explanation. For *weigh=value, care for*, see *O.E.D.* 14b; *H8*, v. i. 124, and *Mucedorus*, 1598 [Dodsley's *Select Collection of Old*

English Plays, 4th ed. W. C. Hazlitt, vii, 1874, 251, l. 5], and for *spare = give away, do without*, see *O.E.D.* 8).
43–5. *for honour . . . stand for*] 'But honour is something to be inherited from me by my children and it is only my honour I fight for.'
49–50. *With . . . thus*] 'with what intercourse so out of the ordinary I have transgressed to appear thus.' (For these senses of *encounter, uncurrent*, and *strain* see *O.E.D.* 3, 2, 11b respectively and cf. *encounters* I. i. 26). 'Uncurrent' could also carry the sense of 'base', 'false'. The corresponding passage in *Pandosto* reads 'her stale countenance should stand for no coin' (p. 195, l. 4).

Though 'tis a saying, sir, not due to me.
Leon. You will not own it.
Her.   More than mistress of
          Which comes to me in name of fault, I must not   60
          At all acknowledge. For Polixenes,
          With whom I am accus'd, I do confess
          I lov'd him as in honour he requir'd,
          With such a kind of love as might become
          A lady like me; with a love, even such,   65
          So, and no other, as yourself commanded:
          Which, not to have done, I think had been in me
          Both disobedience and ingratitude
          To you, and toward your friend, whose love had spoke,
          Even since it could speak, from an infant, freely,   70
          That it was yours. Now, for conspiracy,
          I know not how it tastes, though it be dish'd
          For me to try how: all I know of it,
          Is that Camillo was an honest man;
          And why he left your court, the gods themselves   75
          (Wotting no more than I) are ignorant.
Leon. You knew of his departure, as you know
          What you have underta'en to do in 's absence.
Her. Sir,
          You speak a language that I understand not: 80
          My life stands in the level of your dreams,
          Which I'll lay down.

70. Even] *F*; Ever *conj. Var.* (*1898*).

58. *due*] applicable.
59–61. *More ... acknowledge*] 'I must not admit being answerable for anything more than that which is now being called a fault.' She refers to her friendship with Polixenes of which she goes on to speak.
63. *in honour he requir'd*] 'as, in view of his position and mine, he had a natural right to expect'. Cf. 'your entertain shall be / As doth befit our honour and your worth' (*Per.*, I. i. 119) and *H8*, I. i. 39–40.
65–6. *a love ... commanded*] Cf. Katharine 'which of your friends / Have I not strove to love' (*H8*, II. iv. 29).

69–71. *whose love ... yours*] Cf. I. ii. 61–75.
72–3. *I know ... try how*] 'I do not know what it tastes like and should not know even if it were put before me to taste.'
76. *Wotting*] If they know.
80. *You speak ... understand not*] Cf. Desdemona, 'I understand a fury in your words, / But not the words' (*Oth.*, IV. ii. 32).
81-2. *My life ... down*] 'My life stands within the range [i.e. at the mercy] of your delusions and I will lay it down.' For 'level', cf. the metaphor in II. iii. 5–6.

Leon.   Your actions are my dreams.
    You had a bastard by Polixenes,
    And I but dream'd it! As you were past all shame
    (Those of your fact are so) so past all truth,   85
    Which to deny, concerns more than avails; for as
    Thy brat hath been cast out, like to itself,
    No father owning it (which is, indeed,
    More criminal in thee than it), so thou
    Shalt feel our justice; in whose easiest passage   90
    Look for no less than death.
Her.   Sir, spare your threats:
    The bug which you would fright me with, I seek.
    To me can life be no commodity;
    The crown and comfort of my life, your favour,
    I do give lost, for I do feel it gone,   95
    But know not how it went. My second joy,
    And first-fruits of my body, from his presence
    I am barr'd, like one infectious. My third comfort
    (Starr'd most unluckily) is from my breast
    (The innocent milk in it most innocent mouth)   100
    Hal'd out to murder; myself on every post
    Proclaim'd a strumpet, with immodest hatred
    The child-bed privilege denied, which 'longs
    To women of all fashion; lastly, hurried
    Here, to this place, i' th' open air, before   105

85. *fact*] crime. Latin *factum*, a thing
done, a deed, and, in the 16th and 17th
centuries, particularly an evil deed.
See *O.E.D.* fact 1c. Cf. *Per.*, IV. iii. 12.

86. *Which . . . avails*] 'and you are
making it a matter of more importance
to deny this than will be of any good to
you'. *Concerns* meaning 'to be of
importance' is also in *LLL.*, IV. ii. 133,
'it may concern much', and perhaps in
Cym., I. vi. 181.

87. *like to itself*] as an outcast should
be, cf. II. iii. 178–81n.

90. *in . . . passage*] This contains a
threat of torture.

92. *bug*] bugbear, bogey. Cf. *Shr.*
I. ii. 207; *Ham.*, v. ii. 22; *Cym.*, v. iii.
51; and obsolete Welsh *bwg*, ghost,
hobgoblin (mod. Welsh *bwgan*), and

L. Lavater, *Of Ghostes*, 1572, ed. 1929,
p. 184, 'If those Sprites or Bugges be
Divels'.

93. *commodity*] profit, comfort, ad-
vantage. Cf. *Mer. V.*, III. iii. 27.

99. *Starr'd . . . unluckily*] 'born under
an unlucky star'. Cf. II. i. 105.

100. *it*] On the use of *it* for *its* see
I. ii. 151n. and II. iii. 177n.

101. *post*] Public notices were fixed
to posts.

102. *immodest*] immoderate, excessive.

103. *'longs*] belongs.

104. *of all fashion*] of all sorts—
irrespective of rank. (Cf. *Per.*, IV. ii. 78,
'gentlemen of all fashions'.)

105. *open air*] Fresh air was proverbially dangerous to invalids (Tilley,

I have got strength of limit. Now, my liege,
Tell me what blessings I have here alive,
That I should fear to die? Therefore proceed.
But yet hear this: mistake me not: no life,
I prize it not a straw, but for mine honour,   110
Which I would free: if I shall be condemn'd
Upon surmises, all proofs sleeping else
But what your jealousies awake, I tell you
'Tis rigour and not law. Your honours all,
I do refer me to the Oracle: 115
Apollo be my judge!
A Lord.   This your request
Is altogether just: therefore bring forth,
And in Apollo's name, his Oracle. [*Exeunt certain Officers.*]
Her. The Emperor of Russia was my father:
O that he were alive, and here beholding   120
His daughter's trial! that he did but see

---

106. limit] *F;* limbs *F3.*   116. S.D. *A Lord.*] *Lord. F; 1 Lord. Capell (so throughout scene).*   118. S.D. *Exeunt . . . Officers*] *Capell; no S.D. in F.*

A93). Cf. *Tw. N.,* III. iv. 126; *Cæs.,* II. i. 261–7. Hermione may mean that she had to make a journey in the open air, but the phrase seems to qualify 'this place' which would mean that the actual scene was in the open air. In *Pandosto* (194, 197) the queen appears first in 'open court' and next in the 'judgment hall'. Kean placed the scene 'in the public theatre at Syracuse, the usual hall of judgement on great public occasions' (J. W. Cole, *Life . . . of Charles Kean,* 1859, ii. 170).

106. *strength of limit*] The strength which returns to a woman in a given period after childbirth. Shakespeare uses *limit* in the sense of 'prescribed period' also in *Meas.,* III. i. 211, and *R3,* III. iii. 8.

109–10. *no life . . . honour*] 'It is not life I ask for but my honour.' Cf. 42–5.

110. *straw*] Not to care a straw is proverbial (Tilley, S917).

112. *proofs*] written evidence. Cf. *Oth.,* III. iii. 327–8, 'confirmations strong / As proofs of holy writ', and *H8,* II. i. 16.

114. *rigour . . . law*] This antithesis is not common in Shakespeare although the rigour *of* the law is referred to several times (*Meas.,* I. iv. 67; *2H6,* I. iii. 194; *Rom.,* v. iii. 268). The phrase is taken directly from *Pandosto* (p. 195, l. 12).

118. *Exeunt certain officers*] It is not strictly necessary to assume that Cleomenes and Dion are off stage. They could quite well have been in the Court from the outset and be simply brought forward at 123. However, there is perhaps greater dramatic and stage effect in sending officers for them and bringing them in with some ceremonial at 123 than in having them on stage all the time.

119.] In *Pandosto* (191) the Emperor of Russia is not the father of Bellaria (= Hermione) but of the wife of Egistus (= Polixenes). But the introduction of the Emperor here gives 'a sense of majesty and pathos' (Charlton) and the old feeling of tragedy as being 'de casibus virorum illustrium' (cf. Chaucer, *Monk's Tale*).

The flatness of my misery, yet with eyes
Of pity, not revenge!

[*Enter Officers, with* CLEOMENES *and* DION.]

Off. You here shall swear upon this sword of justice,
That you, Cleomenes and Dion, have   125
Been both at Delphos, and from thence have brought
This seal'd-up Oracle, by the hand deliver'd
Of great Apollo's priest; and that since then
You have not dared to break the holy seal,
Nor read the secrets in 't.
Cleo. Dion.   All this we swear.   130
Leon. Break up the seals and read.
Off. Hermione is chaste; Polixenes blameless; Camillo
a true subject; Leontes a jealous tyrant; his in-
nocent babe truly begotten; and the king shall
live without an heir, if that which is lost be not   135
found.
Lords. Now blessed be the great Apollo!
Her.   Praised!
Leon. Hast thou read truth?
Off.   Ay, my lord, even so
As it is here set down.
Leon. There is no truth at all i' th' Oracle: 140
The sessions shall proceed: this is mere falsehood.

---

123. S.D. *Enter . . . Dion*] *Capell* (subst.) ; *Pope* (subst., *at 116*) ; *no S.D. in F. Cf. 118n.*
138–9. Ay . . . down] *As Capell ; one line in F.*

122. *flatness*] completeness (*O.E.D.* 5b). But the word also gives the sense of 'unrelieved expanse'.

130. *All . . . swear*] Here they touch the sword of justice.

132–6.] The Oracle's words follow *Pandosto* (196) almost verbatim. The edd. of 1588, 1592, 1595 read *live without an heir* as in the play, but in the edition of 1607 the reading is *die without an heir.* The next edition was apparently in 1614. This is some slight evidence for assuming that Shakespeare used an edition of before 1607. The pronounce-ment of the Oracle is criticized by

Coleridge, who is supported by Quiller-Couch (*N.C. Wint.*, xx) and others, because it does not give 'some ground for Hermione's seeming death and fifteen years . . . voluntary con-cealment' (*Shakespearean Criticism,* ed. Raysor, i. 119). Coleridge adds that this might have been done by some such sentence as 'Nor shall he ever recover an heir if he have a wife before that recovery.' But Shakespeare does not wish to hint that Hermione may be living. On the contrary he repeatedly emphasizes that she is dead (e.g. III. ii. 201; III. iii. 42; v. i. 80; v. iii. 140).

[Enter Servant.]

Serv. My lord the king, the king!
Leon.   What is the business?
Serv. O sir, I shall be hated to report it!
    The prince your son, with mere conceit and fear
    Of the queen's speed, is gone.
Leon.   How! gone?
Serv.   Is dead.   145
Leon. Apollo's angry, and the heavens themselves
    Do strike at my injustice. [*Hermione faints*] How now
      there?
Paul. This news is mortal to the queen: look down
    And see what death is doing.
Leon.   Take her hence:
    Her heart is but o'ercharg'd: she will recover.   150
    I have too much believ'd mine own suspicion:
    Beseech you, tenderly apply to her
    Some remedies for life.
             [*Exeunt Paulina and Ladies, with Hermione.*]
             Apollo, pardon
    My great profaneness 'gainst thine Oracle!
    I'll reconcile me to Polixenes,   155
    New woo my queen, recall the good Camillo,
    Whom I proclaim a man of truth, of mercy:
    For being transported by my jealousies
    To bloody thoughts and to revenge, I chose
    Camillo for the minister to poison   160
    My friend Polixenes: which had been done,
    But that the good mind of Camillo tardied
    My swift command; though I with death, and with
    Reward, did threaten and encourage him,
    Not doing it, and being done. He (most humane   165

141. S.D. *Enter Servant*] *Rowe* (*1*); *no S.D. in F.*   147. S.D. *Hermione faints*] *Rowe*
(*1*); *no S.D. in F.*   152. Beseech] 'Beseech *F.*   153. S.D. *Exeunt . . . Hermione*]
Rowe (*1*) (*at 150*); *no S.D. in F.*   156. woo] woe *F.*

144. *conceit*] thought. Cf. II. iii. 13, 'Conceiving the dishonour of his mother.' (See *O.E.D.* for the 16- and 17-cent. meanings of 'conceit'.)

145. *speed*] fate, fortune.

163-5. *with death . . . done*] a 'retrospective or respective construction'; Camillo was to receive death if he did not kill Polixenes but reward if he did kill him. Cf. IV. iv. 378-9.

And fill'd with honour) to my kingly guest
Unclasp'd my practice, quit his fortunes here
(Which you knew great) and to the certain hazard
Of all incertainties, himself commended,
No richer than his honour: how he glisters   170
Thorough my rust! and how his piety
Does my deeds make the blacker!

[Enter PAULINA.]

Paul.   Woe the while!
    O cut my lace, lest my heart, cracking it,
    Break too!
A Lord.   What fit is this, good lady?
Paul. What studied torments, tyrant, hast for me?   175
    What wheels? racks? fires? what flaying? boiling?
    In leads or oils? What old or newer torture
    Must I receive, whose every word deserves
    To taste of thy most worst? Thy tyranny,
    Together working with thy jealousies   180
    (Fancies too weak for boys, too green and idle
    For girls of nine), O think what they have done,
    And then run mad indeed: stark mad! for all
    Thy by-gone fooleries were but spices of it.
    That thou betray'dst Polixenes, 'twas nothing;   185

---

168. certain hazard] *F2;* hazard *F.*   171. Thorough my] Through my *F;*
Through my dark *F2.*   172. S.D. *Enter Paulina*] *Rowe* (*1*)*; no S.D. in F.*
176. flaying? boiling?] *F;* flaying? boyling? Burning, *F2.*   177. newer] *F;*
new *F2.*   184. of it] *F;* for it *F2.*

167. *Unclasp'd my practice*] 'disclosed my plot'. Cf. *Tw. N.,* v. i. 339,
'This practice hath most shrewdly
pass'd upon thee.'

168. *certain hazard*] Without *certain*
the line in *F* is metrically incomplete:
with it the counterbalance with *incertainties* in 169 is typically Shakespearian—cf. *Lucr.,* 1311, 'Her certain
sorrow writ uncertainly'. The guess in
F2 is probably correct. The *F2* versions at 171, 176, 177, 184 are plausible
but less convincing.

170. *No richer . . . honour*] his honour
being all that he possessed.

171. *Thorough*] The *F* spelling could
be pronounced as one or as two
syllables and was disyllabic here.

173. *cut my lace*] 'cut the lace of my
stays or I shall faint.' A common expression; cf. *Ant.,* I. iii. 71; *R3,* IV. i. 34.

176.] Although the line lacks one
syllable it has to be spoken slowly and
it has five stresses. The addition in *F2*
is unnecessary.

179. *most worst*] double superlative,
with accent on *most*.

184. *spices*] slight tastes, samples.
The words *spice* and *species* come from
the same source.

That did but show thee, of a fool, inconstant
And damnable ingrateful: nor was't much,
Thou would'st have poison'd good Camillo's honour,
To have him kill a king; poor trespasses,
More monstrous standing by: whereof I reckon   190
The casting forth to crows thy baby daughter,
To be or none or little; though a devil
Would have shed water out of fire, ere done 't:
Nor is't directly laid to thee the death
Of the young prince, whose honourable thoughts   195
(Thoughts high for one so tender) cleft the heart
That could conceive a gross and foolish sire
Blemish'd his gracious dam: this is not, no,
Laid to thy answer: but the last—O lords,
When I have said, cry 'woe!'—the queen, the queen,
The sweet'st, dear'st creature's dead: and vengeance
    for 't   201
    Not dropp'd down yet.

A Lord.   The higher powers forbid!
Paul. I say she's dead: I'll swear 't. If word nor oath
    Prevail not, go and see: if you can bring
    Tincture, or lustre in her lip, her eye,   205
    Heat outwardly or breath within, I'll serve you
    As I would do the gods. But, O thou tyrant!
    Do not repent these things, for they are heavier

186. *of a fool*] 'for a fool', as regards a fool'. Cf. *Ham.*, II.. i. 13; *H8*, IV. ii. 43; and Abbott §173. But 'for' is the normal usage in Shakespeare, e.g. 'What is he for a fool' (*Ado*, I. iii. 40) *O.E.D.* 'of' 24a cites Dryden's *Virgil*: 'Caesar . . . the greatest traveller of a prince, that has ever been.'

187. *damnable*] damnably. Adjectives are freely used as adverbs in Shakespeare (Abbott, §1).

188–9. *Thou . . . a king*] Unless Camillo had confided in her before his departure Paulina could not have known of this. It is, as *N.C. Wint.* points out, the sort of point on which Shakespeare would take no trouble. During the action of the play the audience would not remember that Paulina should be unaware of a fact which they all knew.

190. *More monstrous . . . by*] 'in the presence of [i.e. in comparison with] others more monstrous'.

193. *shed water . . . fire*] 'would have shed tears from his eyes of flame' or 'would have wept though burning with the fires of his damnation'. The tears/fire paradox is frequent in Shakespeare, e.g. II. i. 108–111; 'My drops of tears / I'll turn to sparks of fire' (*H8*, II. iv. 72); 'tears . . . / Burn out the sense and virtue of mine eye' (*Ham.*, IV. v. 151); *Tit.*, v. i. 134; *Rom.*, I. ii. 89.

200. *said*] spoken. Cf. 'I have said' = I have spoken, said my say.

Than all thy woes can stir: therefore betake thee
To nothing but despair. A thousand knees　　　210
Ten thousand years together, naked, fasting,
Upon a barren mountain, and still winter
In storm perpetual, could not move the gods
To look that way thou wert.

Leon.　　　　　　　　　　　　Go on, go on:
Thou canst not speak too much; I have deserv'd　　215
All tongues to talk their bitt'rest.

A Lord.　　　　　　　　　　　Say no more:
Howe'er the business goes, you have made fault
I' th' boldness of your speech.

Paul.　　　　　　　　　　　I am sorry for 't:
All faults I make, when I shall come to know them,
I do repent. Alas! I have show'd too much　　　220
The rashness of a woman: he is touch'd
To th' noble heart. What's gone and what's past help
Should be past grief. Do not receive affliction
At my petition; I beseech you, rather
Let me be punish'd, that have minded you　　　225
Of what you should forget. Now, good my liege,
Sir, royal sir, forgive a foolish woman:
The love I bore your queen—lo, fool again!
I'll speak of her no more, nor of your children:
I'll not remember you of my own lord　　　230
(Who is lost too): take your patience to you,
And I'll say nothing.

Leon.　　　　　　　　　Thou didst speak but well
When most the truth: which I receive much better
Than to be pitied of thee. Prithee, bring me
To the dead bodies of my queen and son:　　　235
One grave shall be for both: upon them shall
The causes of their death appear, unto

---

209. *woes can stir*] lamentations can
move. Cf. *Ado*, v. iii. 33, 'for whom we
rend'red up this woe'.

212. *still*] always, ever.

222–3. *What's gone . . . grief*] 'Never
grieve for that which you cannot help'
is proverbial (Tilley, G453). Cf. *Oth.*,
I. iii. 202; *Mac.*, III. ii. 11.

223–4. *Do not . . . petition*] 'Do not let
my petition to heaven for vengeance
(cf. 201–2) give you pain.' For this use
of *at = from* cf. v. i. 139.

228. *fool again*] All the same,
Paulina constantly *does* remind him of
those he has injured.

231. *lost*] Cf. II. iii. 191n.

Our shame perpetual. Once a day I'll visit
The chapel where they lie, and tears shed there
Shall be my recreation. So long as nature   240
Will bear up with this exercise, so long
I daily vow to use it. Come, and lead me
To these sorrows.   *Exeunt.*

SCENE III

Enter ANTIGONUS [*with the*] *Babe,* [*and*] *a Mariner.*

Ant. Thou art perfect, then, our ship hath touch'd upon
    The deserts of Bohemia?
Mar.   Ay, my lord, and fear
    We have landed in ill time: the skies look grimly,

Scene III

Scene III] *Scæna Tertia. F.*   S.D. *Enter . . . Mariner.*] *Enter Antigonus, a Marriner, Babe, Sheepeheard, and Clowne. F.*

240. *recreation*] The word contains the sense of *diversion* or *refreshment* but also that of *restoration, re-creation* of the spirit. Similarly, *exercise* in 241 has the sense both of physical and spiritual exercise.

Scene III

Scene iii] Bohemia. A desert s hore

1. *perfect*] certain.

2. *Bohemia*] The coast of Bohemia may be dismissed (as in *N.C.Wint.,* xvii) from Sterne: 'there happening throughout the whole kingdom of Bohemia, to be no sea-port . . . How the deuce should there . . . cried my Uncle Toby; for Bohemia being totally inland, it could have happened no otherwise—It might, said Trim, if it had pleased God' (*Tr. Shandy,* Bk 8, Ch. 19). But the trivial point has provoked much discussion. Shakespeare's error is usually ascribed to ignorance but there are attempts to show (1) that Bohemia had a coast, (2) that it had none and that reference to it was a stock joke of the 'Swiss Navy' or 'Horse Marines' variety. Historical atlases (e.g. Poole's, Ramsay Muir's, and Putzger's) show that Bohemia had a small foothold on the Adriatic for two short periods in the late 13th and early 16th centuries. E. Künstler in 'Böhmen am Meer' (*Sh.Jhb.,* xci, 1955, 212–16) asserts that the *Gnomologie* and *Germania* of Pius II, which say that Ottokar II's kingdom reached the Adriatic, were known in England in Shakespeare's day. But the explanation surely is that Shakespeare was simply following *Pandosto* which mentions 'the coast of Bohemia' (p. 217, l. 33). Other contemporaries, as E. Forde in *Parismus,* 1598 and 1608, refer to the Bohemian coast. Few Londoners in 1611 would know much about Bohemia. Even in 1938 a British Prime Minister, broadcasting on Czecho-Slovakia, could speak—however unjustifiably—of 'a quarrel in a far-away country between people of whom we know nothing'. Shakespeare was probably as knowledgeable as Uncle Toby, but there had to be a coast to his Bohemia and he knew it would pass in the theatre. He would have had no concern about possible criticisms on such a matter from Jonson or anyone.

And threaten present blusters. In my conscience,
The heavens with that we have in hand are angry,   5
And frown upon 's.
Ant. Their sacred wills be done! Go, get aboard:
Look to thy bark: I'll not be long before
I call upon thee.
Mar. Make your best haste, and go not   10
Too far i' th' land: 'tis like to be loud weather;
Besides, this place is famous for the creatures
Of prey that keep upon 't.
Ant.   Go thou away:
I'll follow instantly.
Mar.   I am glad at heart
To be so rid o' th' business.   *Exit.*
Ant.   Come, poor babe: 15
I have heard, but not believ'd, the spirits o' th' dead
May walk again: if such thing be, thy mother
Appear'd to me last night; for ne'er was dream
So like a waking. To me comes a creature,
Sometimes her head on one side, some another;   20
I never saw a vessel of like sorrow,
So fill'd, and so becoming: in pure white robes,
Like very sanctity, she did approach
My cabin where I lay: thrice bow'd before me,
And, gasping to begin some speech, her eyes   25

11. *loud*] windy, rough.

16. *spirits . . . dead*] Hermione is not
dead: but Antigonus and the audience think she is and the passage
strengthens that belief. Shakespeare
can therefore dramatically make her
ghost walk. He may have known such
books as those of King James, L.
Lavater, P. Le Loyer, and R. Scot,
yet he seems to have followed no
convention, but to have pleased himself and changed his views to suit his
needs, in writing of the supernatural.
Cf. pp. xxv; lix, n.4.

20. *some another*] i.e. *sometimes the
other.* Cf. IV. iv. 178.

21–2. *vessel . . . becoming*] There has
been much comment on this passage,
particularly on the words 'vessel',
'fill'd', and 'becoming'. But emendations seem unnecessary. The association of a woman in flowing white robes
with a ship under full sail was probably
traditional even by 1611—cf. *Rom.*, II.
iv. 98n. in *N.C.Rom.* The description is
of a vessel ('person' and also 'recep-
tacle') filled to overflowing (with
grief) and of great purity and beauty,
gliding with the ghostly motion and
beauty of a ship moving easily under
all sail. The term vessel is used frequently of persons (e.g. *Cæs.*, V. v. 13)
and particularly of women in the
phrase 'the weaker vessel' (*Rom.*, I. i.
16), and of persons as 'containers' (e.g.
'vessels of wrath . . . mercy', *Romans* ix.
22, 23). On the language of this speech
see p. lxxxvii.

Became two spouts; the fury spent, anon
Did this break from her: 'Good Antigonus,
Since fate, against thy better disposition,
Hath made thy person for the thrower-out
Of my poor babe, according to thine oath,   30
Places remote enough are in Bohemia,
There weep, and leave it crying: and, for the babe
Is counted lost for ever, Perdita,
I prithee, call 't. For this ungentle business,
Put on thee by my lord, thou ne'er shalt see   35
Thy wife Paulina more.' And so, with shrieks,
She melted into air. Affrighted much,
I did in time collect myself, and thought
This was so, and no slumber. Dreams are toys:
Yet for this once, yea, superstitiously,   40
I will be squar'd by this. I do believe
Hermione hath suffer'd death; and that
Apollo would, this being indeed the issue
Of King Polixenes, it should here be laid,
Either for life or death, upon the earth   45
Of its right father. Blossom, speed thee well!
There lie, and there thy character: there these,
Which may, if fortune please, both breed thee, pretty,
And still rest thine. The storm begins: poor wretch,
That for thy mother's fault art thus expos'd   50
To loss and what may follow! Weep I cannot,
But my heart bleeds; and most accurs'd am I
To be by oath enjoin'd to this. Farewell!

46. its] it's F.

33. *Perdita*] Cf. the similar naming of Marina 'for she was born at sea' (*Per.*, III. iii. 12).

40. *superstitiously*] against accepted Protestant doctrine.

41. *squar'd*] regulated, directed. Cf. v. i. 52 and *All's W.*, II. i. 149.

42–6, 50.] It is clear that Hermione's appearance to Antigonus convinces him of her guilt. Cf. p. lix, n.4.

47. *character*] the written account of the babe, the 'letters of Antigonus' of v. ii. 35.

these] the gold, jewels, etc., the 'fairy gold' which the shepherd finds in the box (120).

48–9. *both . . . thine*] 'both be enough to pay for your upbringing, pretty one, and still leave something for your future use'.

51. *loss . . . follow*] destruction (cf. II. iii. 191n.; v. iii. 135) and whatever else fate may bring [as being torn in pieces by wild beasts—cf. 12–13]'.

Weep I cannot] He cannot obey the order of Hermione's spirit in this (32).

The day frowns more and more: thou 'rt like to have
A lullaby too rough: I never saw   55
The heavens so dim by day. A savage clamour!
Well may I get aboard! This is the chase:
I am gone for ever!   *Exit, pursued by a bear.*

[*Enter a* SHEPHERD].

Shep. I would there were no age between ten and three-
and-twenty, or that youth would sleep out the rest;   60
for there is nothing in the between but getting
wenches with child, wronging the ancientry, stealing, fighting—Hark you now! Would any but these
boiled-brains of nineteen and two-and-twenty hunt

58. S.D. *Enter a Shepherd*] *F2; no S.D. in F.*

55. *lullaby too rough*] This, and
'blusters' in 4, echo the 'more bluster-
ous birth had never babe' of *Per.*, III.
i. 28.

57. *chase*] hunt. He sees the bear and
perhaps hears a hunting horn (cf.
63–5).

58. *Exit . . . bear*] A 'bear' episode
was popular at this time. *Mucedorus* as
first published in 1598 contains only a
bear's head but the version performed
at court on 3 Feb. 1610 (printed 1610)
shows the clown tumbling over a white
bear; and it is after 1610 that editions
of *Mucedorus* multiply. Jonson's *Masque
of Oberon*, first performed on 1 Jan.
1611, shows a chariot drawn by two
white bears. *N.C.Wint.* suggests that
'the Bear-Pit in Southwark, hard by
the Globe Theatre, had a tame animal
to let out'. It may have had two tame
white bears, or skins of bears may have
come into the Globe's wardrobe. J. G.
McManaway points out to me that the
idea may come from the current
knowledge of Barents' voyages on
which at least two men were 'torn to
pieces' by polar bears (cf. G. de Veer,
The true . . . Description of three Voyages,
trans. William Phillip, 1609 [Repr.
Hakluyt Soc. 1876. See p. 63]. Dutch
and German editions (1598, 1599) had
pictures (Hakluyt Soc., p. 62) showing a bear tearing at a man's shoulder

(cf. 94–5). The episode in *2 Kings* ii. 24
would also be well known. N. Coghill
believes that the 'bear' was human and
the episode intended to have a comic
effect (*Sh.Sur.* xi, 1958, 34–5). Although the 'bear' may have been a
man (for an example see Jonson, *Bart.
Fair*, ed. Horsman, 1960, III. iv. 126n.)
the dream and this episode are not
primarily comic, and the likelihood is
that the bear was real since the remark
at 128 could only be made by someone
with a knowledge of tame bears. In
many episodes which are primarily
serious a comic flavour can also be
present, as here. Coghill has expert
evidence that bears are bad-tempered
and unreliable, but Shakespeare may
have known better about a particular
bear (III. iii. 128–9) probably not from
the bear pit (cf. C. F. Reynolds,
Mucedorus, in Josephine W. Bennett,
*Studies in the English Renaissance Drama
in Honor of Karl Holzknecht*, 1956, esp.
259–64). See also 112–15n. and p. lix.

59. *ten*] Many consider this too
young for the offences mentioned. But
it is not too young for some of them and
is therefore admissible: the passage
makes no claim that all the offences
are committed at every stage of the age
group. Cf. 119–20.

64. *boiled-brains*] hot-heads, luna-
tics. Cf. *Tp.*, v. i. 60; *MND.*, v. i. 4.

this weather? They have scared away two of my best   65
sheep, which I fear the wolf will sooner find than the
master: if anywhere I have them, 'tis by the sea-side,
browzing of ivy. [*Seeing the babe*] Good luck, and 't be
thy will, what have we here? Mercy on 's, a barne!
A very pretty barne! A boy or a child, I wonder?   70
A pretty one; a very pretty one. Sure, some scape:
though I am not bookish, yet I can read waiting-
gentlewoman in the scape. This has been some
stair-work, some trunk-work, some behind-door-
work: they were warmer that got this than the poor   75
thing is here. I'll take it up for pity: yet I'll tarry till
my son come; he hallooed but even now. Whoa-ho-
hoa!

Enter CLOWN.

Clo. Hilloa, loa!

68. S.D. *Seeing the babe*] *N.C.Wint.* (*child*); *no S.D. in F.*

67. *if anywhere . . . them*] 'if I shall
find them anywhere'.

68. *ivy*] *Pandosto* specifies 'sea-ivy'
and the passage closely follows
Pandosto (p. 199). No plant called 'sea-
ivy' can be traced and even the ground
or barren ivy (*Hedera helix*) would
probably not be common on the shore.
F. G. Savage, *Flora . . . of Shakespeare*
[1923], 43, claims that sheep do
browse on ivy. According to Gerard
'the boare delighteth' in ground ivy.
Perhaps Greene meant 'sea-holly'
(*Eryngium marinum*) which grows in
sand dunes and of which Gerard says
the young leaves are 'good to be
eaten'. The candied roots, called *eryn-
goes*, were, at least from 1596, used as a
sweetmeat and regarded as an aphro-
disiac. Cf. *Wiv.*, v. v. 19, and G. Grig-
son, *The Englishman's Flora*, 1955, 208.

69. *barne*] child (O.E. bearn).
Apparently limited to northern dialect
even by Shakespeare's day (*O.E.D.*
bairn *b.*). It is used in Shakespeare
only by uneducated persons (here and
in *All's W.*, I. iii. 25) except when Beatrice uses it in a pun (*Ado*, III. iv. 42).

70. *child*] apparently used in Mid-
land and S.W. dialect for girl child.
O.E.D. (BI, 1b) has no other recorded
use before the late 18th century but
there is at least one example in
Greene, 'Whilst *Hob* your sonne, and
Sib your nutbrowne childe' (*James the
Fourth*, v. v. 2119, printed 1598),
where *childe* certainly means daughter.
Onions, 35, says that 'my child' is
always used by Shakespeare of a
daughter and cites *Tp.*, v. i. 198;
Ado, IV. i. 75; *Lr.*, IV. vii. 70.

71. *scape*] a transgression—often
applied to a breach of chastity
(*O.E.D. sb.* 2 which cites Greene:
'The old Croane . . . sayd the childe
was hers, and so saued her daughters
scape').

74–5. *stair-work . . . behind-door-work*]
a clandestine love affair in which the
lover got access to his mistress by back
or secret stairs, by concealment in a
trunk, by hiding behind doors—by
one or more of these methods. No
doubt in 'trunk-work' Shakespeare is
thinking of the Decameron source he
used for *Cym.*

Shep. What, art so near? If thou'lt see a thing to talk on   80
    when thou art dead and rotten, come hither. What
    ail'st thou man?

Clo. I have seen two such sights, by sea and by land! But
    I am not to say it is a sea, for it is now the sky: betwixt
    the firmament and it you cannot thrust a bodkin's   85
    point.

Shep. Why, boy, how is it?

Clo. I would you did but see how it chafes, how it rages,
    how it takes up the shore! But that's not to the point.
    O, the most piteous cry of the poor souls! sometimes   90
    to see 'em, and not to see 'em: now the ship boring
    the moon with her main-mast, and anon swallowed
    with yest and froth, as you 'd thrust a cork into a
    hogs-head. And then for the land-service, to see how
    the bear tore out his shoulder-bone, how he cried to   95
    me for help and said his name was Antigonus, a
    nobleman. But to make an end of the ship, to see how
    the sea flap-dragoned it: but first, how the poor souls

83–94.] Cf. with this Miranda's description of the storm and shipwreck, *Tp.*, i. ii. 2–13.

84–6. *sea . . . point*] Shakespeare seems fond of melting sea into sky as one gazes seaward. Parallels and echoes include: 'the brine and cloudy billow kiss the moon' (*Per.*, iii. i. 45–6); 'To look upon him, till the diminution / Of space had pointed him sharp as my needle' (*Cym.*, i. iii. 18–19); 'the sea, mounting to th' welkin's cheek' (*Tp.*, i. ii. 4); 'twixt the heaven and the main', 'the main and th' aerial blue / An indistinct regard' (*Oth.*, ii. i. 3, 39–40).

89. *takes up*] swallows up *or* contends with, rebukes.

90. *piteous cry . . . souls*] Cf. 'O, the cry . . . Poor souls' (*Tp.*, i. ii. 8–9).

91–2. *boring the moon*] Cf. 'cloudy billow kiss the moon' (*Per.*, iii. i. 46).

92–4. *swallowed . . . hogs-head*] This striking image helps to characterize the speaker. It is an excellent example of the decorum of the language in the play. There are no correspondingly apt images in the descriptions of the storms by Miranda or the gentlemen in *Oth.*, but the needle's point comes fittingly from Imogen (*Cym.*, i. iii. 19). Cf. 'the good ship . . . swallow'd' (*Tp.*, i. ii. 12) and 'yesty waves' (*Mac.*, iv. i. 53). Shakespeare uses 'yest' thrice (*Ham.*, v. ii. 187), always spelt 'yest'. But the word is 'yeast', here used metaphorically.

94. *land-service*] military service on land (cf. *Ant.*, ii. vi. 93) here used humorously: army matters in contrast with the naval affairs of which he has just been speaking. The phrase continued in use to distinguish army from naval service. E.g. G. Shelvocke, *A Privateer's Voyage*, 1719 (1930 ed., 45); Byron, *Don Juan*, 1819, i. 4.

98. *flap-dragoned*] swallowed. Cf. *LLL.*, v. i. 38, 'thou art easier swallowed than a flap-dragon', and *2H4*, ii. iv. 237. Johnson defines *flap-dragon* as a 'play in which they catch raisons out of burning brandy and, extinguishing them by closing the

roared, and the sea mocked them: and how the poor
gentleman roared, and the bear mocked him, both 100
roaring louder than the sea or weather.

Shep. Name of mercy, when was this, boy?

Clo. Now, now: I have not winked since I saw these
sights: the men are not yet cold under water, nor
the bear half dined on the gentleman: he's at it now. 105

Shep. Would I had been by, to have helped the old
man!

Clo. I would you had been by the ship side, to have
helped her: there your charity would have lacked
footing. 110

Shep. Heavy matters! heavy matters! But look thee
here, boy. Now bless thyself: thou met'st with things
dying, I with things new-born. Here's a sight for

mouth, eat them' (*O.E.D.* 1a). Cf.
the Christmas *snap-dragon.*

106–7. *old man*] The Shepherd
could not have known that Antigonus
was old. It was probably enough for
Shakespeare that the audience knew
(II. i. 173; II. iii. 161, 165). Theobald
emended to *the nobleman.*

108–10. *I would . . . footing*] In 106–7
the Shepherd has cast a slight on the
Clown's courage: here the Clown implies that the Shepherd is such a brag-
gart that he could no doubt have saved
the ship. It is typical yokel back-chat.

112–15. *Now bless . . . open 't*] An
example of allegorical interpretation
is that by S. L. Bethell in *Wint. ed.*
His note on this passage (197–8) considers that 'the tone changes suddenly
to extreme seriousness' and that the
episode 'would surely suggest a
Nativity scene', 'There is a triple
reference (a) on the story level, to the
renewed fortunes of Leontes; (b) to
spiritual regeneration by baptism into
the Church; (c) to the historical
events of the Incarnation and Cruci-
fixion, by which new life was won for
the world.' Surely few will see these
things in the passage. There is no
change of tone; the picture continues
the counter-boasting, showing the

Shepherd triumphantly displaying,
with some natural cupidity, what *he*
has found.

112–13. *thou met'st . . . born*] Bethell
and others attach great importance to
this statement. E.g. Traversi (*Approach,*
1938, 137): 'the central remark of the
whole scene. . . It connects Hermione's
child at once with the general theme
of "grace" and fertility born out of
passion and jealousy'. Others, while
rejecting allusions to 'grace' and all
specifically Christian interpretations,
still emphasize the importance of these
words as marking the turn in the play
from destruction to the beginning of a
new life. In such contrasts they see an
expression of Shakespeare's concep-
tion of a universal order and rhythm
in life. Whatever importance is attached to the remark it must be agreed
that it is a simple statement of fact in
language completely fitting to the occasion and to the speaker—'Now bless
'ee, thou'st found something dying, I
something new born.' It is indeed a
noteworthy contrast, and the old man,
tired of his son's boasting, now wants
to show his own find. At the same time
it is to be noted that Shakespeare often
allows his comic dialogue to carry a
serious theme. (And vice versa. Cf. 58.)

thee; look thee, a bearing-cloth for a squire's child!
look thee here; take up, take up, boy; open 't. So,   115
let's see: it was told me I should be rich by the fairies.
This is some changeling: open 't. What's within,
boy?

Clo. You're a made old man: if the sins of your youth are
forgiven you, you're well to live. Gold! all gold!   120

Shep. This is fairy gold, boy, and 'twill prove so; up
with 't, keep it close: home, home, the next way.
We are lucky, boy; and to be so still requires nothing but secrecy. Let my sheep go: come, good
boy, the next way home.   125

Clo. Go you the next way with your findings. I'll go see
if the bear be gone from the gentleman, and how
much he hath eaten; they are never curst but when
they are hungry: if there be any of him left, I'll
bury it.   130

Shep. That's a good deed. If thou mayest discern by that

---

119. made] *Theobald;* mad *F.*

114. *bearing-cloth*] The fine quality
wrap in which a child was carried to
church for baptism. Presumably the
'mantle of Queen Hermione' (v. ii.
33).

116. *told . . . fairies*] 'foretold to
me that by means of the fairies I should
be made rich'.

117. *changeling*] a child left by the
fairies in place of a human child they
have stolen.

119. *made*] Theobald's emendation
is almost certainly correct: 'mad'
could be defended in the sense of
happy, joyous, but the use of 'made for
ever' in *Pandosto* (p. 201, l. 1) probably settles the matter. For a man being 'made', i.e. his prosperity assured,
cf. *H8,* v. v. 64 (in sense of happiness);
Tp., II. ii. 34–5; and *Two Noble Kinsmen,* III. v. 155.

119–20. *sins . . . forgiven you*] Noble,
Biblical Knowledge (247), compares
'His bones are full of the sinns of his
youth' (*Job* xx. 11); 'O remember not
the sins and offences of my youth'

(*Ps.* xxv. 6). The phrase recalls 59–62
—with a little irony.

120. *well to live*] well off, well to do.
Cf. *Mer.V.,* II. ii. 47.

122. *close*] secret. It was believed
that gifts from the fairies must not be
spoken of, otherwise ill luck would
follow.   *next*] nearest.

123. *still*] always.

128. *curst*] 'bad-tempered'. This
sort of knowledge could only be held
by someone familiar with bears in
captivity. Cf. 58n.

131. *good deed*] To bury the dead is
by ancient and widespread tradition a
good deed. If the body has not been
decently buried the dead person's
spirit is restless and unhappy. Cf. the
ghost of Jack, taking service with the
impoverished Eumenides to repay his
good deed: 'are not you the man . . .
that gaue all the money you had to the
burying of a poore man, and but one
three-halfe-pence left in your pursse'
(Peele, *Old Wives' Tale,* 1595, Malone
Soc., 1908, 893–6).

which is left of him what he is, fetch me to th' sight
of him.

Clo. Marry, will I; and you shall help to put him i' th'
ground.   135

Shep. 'Tis a lucky day, boy, and we'll do good deeds
on 't.   *Exeunt.*

134. Marry] 'Marry *F*.

136. *lucky . . . deeds*] perhaps an echo of the proverb 'The better the day the
better the deed' (Tilley, D60).

ACT IV

SCENE I

Enter TIME, *the Chorus.*

Time. I that please some, try all: both joy and terror
    Of good and bad, that makes and unfolds error,
    Now take upon me, in the name of Time,
    To use my wings. Impute it not a crime
    To me, or my swift passage, that I slide   5
    O'er sixteen years, and leave the growth untried
    Of that wide gap, since it is in my power
    To o'erthrow law, and in one self-born hour
    To plant and o'erwhelm custom. Let me pass
    The same I am, ere ancient'st order was,   10
    Or what is now receiv'd. I witness to
    The times that brought them in; so shall I do

ACT IV

Scene 1

Act IV] *Actus Quartus. F.*   Scene 1] *Scena Prima. F.*   11. witness] witnesse *F ;* witness'd *Capell.*

S.D. Enter Time the Chorus] See pp. lxxxvi–lxxxvii, 167–9.

1. *try all*] That time tries all things is proverbial (Tilley, T336).

1–2. *joy . . . bad*] Cf. 'O Time, thou tutor both to good and bad' (*Lucr.*, 995).

2. *makes . . . error*] should be 'make . . . unfold' after 'I' but 'I am he that' may be understood. Cf. 'Time's office is . . . / To eat up errors . . . / Time's glory is . . . / To unmask falsehood, and bring truth to light' (*Lucr.*, 936–7, 939–40).

3. *in the name*] with the authority.

4–6. *wings . . . years*] Cf. 'Only I carry

winged time / Post on the lame feet of my rhyme' (*Per.*, IV, Prol. 47).

6. *sixteen*] IV. ii. 4 says 'fifteen'. But Forman (see p. xxii) heard 'sixteen'.

7–8. *power . . . law*] Opportunity is the servant of time (*Lucr.*, 930–2) and opportunity 'spurn'st at . . . law' (*Lucr.*, 876, 880). 'Time, whose million'd accidents / Creep in 'twixt vows and change decrees of kings' (*Sonn.* cxv).

10–12. *ancient'st . . . them in*] Cf. 'Time's glory is . . . / To stamp the seal of time in aged things' (*Lucr.*, 939–41).

75

To th' freshest things now reigning, and make stale
The glistering of this present, as my tale
Now seems to it. Your patience this allowing,   15
I turn my glass, and give my scene such growing
As you had slept between: Leontes leaving,
Th' effects of his fond jealousies so grieving
That he shuts up himself, imagine me,
Gentle spectators, that I now may be   20
In fair Bohemia, and remember well
I mentioned a son o' th' king's, which Florizel
I now name to you; and with speed so pace
To speak of Perdita, now grown in grace
Equal with wond'ring. What of her ensues   25
I list not prophesy; but let Time's news
Be known when 'tis brought forth. A shepherd's
        daughter,
And what to her adheres, which follows after,
Is th' argument of Time. Of this allow,

13–14. *make stale . . . present*] Cf. 'Time's glory is . . . To ruinate proud buildings . . . / And smear with dust their glitt'ring golden tow'rs . . . / To feed oblivion with decay of things' (*Lucr.*, 939, 944–7).

15. *seems*] seems stale.

16. *scene*] play.

17. *As*] as if.

17–19. *Leontes . . . imagine me*] 'Leaving Leontes, who so mourns the results of his foolish jealousies that he shuts himself away, imagine me.'

22. *I mentioned*] This does not imply a prologue or an earlier passage in Time's speech subsequently cancelled. Time is simply referring to the mention earlier in the play—in time just passed.

25. *Equal with wond'ring*] 'equal to the admiring amazement it excites' (Charlton).

26–7. *I list . . . forth*] Cf. 'I nill relate, action may / Conveniently the rest convey' (*Per.*, III, Prol. 55–6) and 'What shall be next, / Pardon old Gower—this longs the text' (*ibid.*, II, Prol. 39).

27–8. *daughter . . . after*] The rhyme is in *Shr.*, I. i. 237–8, and in Chapman, *Eastward Hoe*, 1605, v. i (ed. J. H. Harris, 1926, 2831–2). *Lr.*, I. iv. 318–22, rhymes *caught her, daughter, slaughter, halter, after*. Sylvester in *Bartas his Deuine Weekes*, 1605, rhymes on p. 10 *water* / *matter* and on 11 *matter* / *after* and in the same work (II, *Posthumus Bartas, The Tropheis*, 1607), p. 29 *water* / *heer-after*. The spelling *dafter* is common in the 16th to 17th centuries (notably in West Country parish registers), and in modern western dialect the *f* is silent in *after*, common pronunciations being *datter, atter*, the *au* and *a* both being short *a*. Viëtor is no doubt right in concluding that Shakespeare used some such pronunciation (*Sh.'s Pronunciation*, i. 67), and Wyld's belief that the *f* was pronounced (*Studies in English Rhymes*, 111–12) probably incorrect. Kökeritz agrees with Viëtor. Cf. the *oft* / *nought* rhyme in *Pilg.*, 18, 41–2 and E. J. Dobson, *English Pronunciation*, 1957, ii. 892, 984.

29–32. *Of this . . . never may*] 'allow' governs both 'this' and 'that Time

If ever you have spent time worse ere now;   30
If never, yet that Time himself doth say,
He wishes earnestly you never may.   *Exit.*

SCENE II

Enter POLIXENES *and* CAMILLO.

Pol. I pray thee, good Camillo, be no more importunate:
'tis a sickness denying thee anything; a death to
grant this.

Cam. It is fifteen years since I saw my country: though I
have, for the most part, been aired abroad, I desire   5
to lay my bones there. Besides, the penitent king, my
master, hath sent for me; to whose feeling sorrows I
might be some allay (or I o'erween to think so),
which is another spur to my departure.

Pol. As thou lov'st me, Camillo, wipe not out the rest of   10
thy services by leaving me now: the need I have of
thee, thine own goodness hath made; better not to
have had thee than thus to want thee. Thou, having
made me businesses, which none without thee can
sufficiently manage, must either stay to execute   15
them thyself, or take away with thee the very services thou hast done: which if I have not enough

Scene II

Scene II] *Scena Secunda. F.*

himself doth say'. 'If you have ever
spent time less agreeably than now
[or] if you have never spent time less
agreeably please admit all the same
that Time assures you he [only] wishes
with all his heart that you never
may.'

Scene II

Scene ii] Bohemia. Polixenes' Palace.

1–9.] These lines prepare us for
Camillo's motive at IV. iv. 509–14 and
his part in Florizel's and Perdita's
flight to Leontes' court and in the

pursuit by Polixenes. Cf. IV. iv. 662–
8.

4. *fifteen*] IV. i. 6 said 'sixteen' which
is supported by Forman (p. xxii).

5. *been aired abroad*] breathed foreign
air.

8. *allay*] means of diminishing,
abating.

o'erween] presume.

13–17. *Thou . . . done*] 'You, having
started affairs for me which no one but
yourself can carry out, must either stay
and see these things through yourself
or else take away with you the very
good you have done.'

considered (as too much I cannot), to be more thank-
ful to thee shall be my study; and my profit therein,
the heaping friendships. Of that fatal country,   20
Sicilia, prithee speak no more; whose very naming
punishes me with the remembrance of that penitent
(as thou call'st him) and reconciled king, my
brother; whose loss of his most precious queen and
children are even now to be afresh lamented. Say to   25
me, when sawest thou the Prince Florizel, my son?
Kings are no less unhappy, their issue not being
gracious, than they are in losing them when they
have approved their virtues.

Cam. Sir, it is three days since I saw the prince. What his   30
happier affairs may be, are to me unknown: but I
have (missingly) noted, he is of late much retired
from court, and is less frequent to his princely exer-
cises than formerly he hath appeared.

Pol. I have considered so much, Camillo, and with some   35
care; so far that I have eyes under my service which
look upon his removedness; from whom I have this
intelligence, that he is seldom from the house of a
most homely shepherd; a man, they say, that from

18. *considered*] rewarded. Cf. iv. iv.
797.

20. *the heaping friendships*] 'the heaping up of your friendly services'. Cf.
iv. iv. 517–21.

22–3. *penitent . . . him*] 'penitent, as
thou [rightly] callest him'. In his
reference to the penitent Leontes here
and in iv. i. 17–19 Shakespeare is at
pains to keep the absent not wholly
absent from our minds.

25. *are*] should be *is* after *loss*. A confusion of proximity (Abbott §412) after
'queen and children'.

28. *gracious*] good, virtuous, pleasing. But to Perdita Florizel is 'The
gracious mark o' th' land' (iv. iv. 8).
Polixenes seems to compare Florizel to
his disadvantage with the promise of
Leontes' son, the dead Mamillius.
Comparison of the two is suggested in
1(esp. ii. 164–77) and v (esp. i. 115–18,

131–3) and these comparisons are sig-
nificant since Florizel is to be heir both
to Bohemia and Sicilia, and to replace,
as far as is humanly possible, the loss of
Mamillius. Dr Brooks reminds me of
the similarities in *1H4* where the king
compares Hal to his disadvantage with
Hotspur and laments the fact that he
keeps company with those socially beneath him. Hal, when enacting his father's probable reception of him, uses
the phrase 'ungracious boy' (ii. iv. 430).

29. *approved*] proved.

32. *missingly*] 'noted from not seeing
him'; he has been conspicuous by his
absence.

36. *I have eyes*] 'I have spies watching
him'. Cf. *Mac.*, iii. iv. 132; *Ant.*, iii. vi.
62. Elizabeth used 'special agents'.
There would have been nothing
unusual to an Elizabethan audience in
this.

very nothing, and beyond the imagination of his   40
neighbours, is grown into an unspeakable estate.

Cam. I have heard, sir, of such a man, who hath a
daughter of most rare note: the report of her is extended more than can be thought to begin from such
a cottage.   45

Pol. That's likewise part of my intelligence: but, I fear,
the angle that plucks our son thither. Thou shalt
accompany us to the place, where we will (not appearing what we are) have some question with the
shepherd; from whose simplicity I think it not un-   50
easy to get the cause of my son's resort thither.
Prithee, be my present partner in this business, and
lay aside the thoughts of Sicilia.

Cam. I willingly obey your command.

Pol. My best Camillo! We must disguise ourselves.   *Exeunt.*

SCENE III

Enter AUTOLYCUS, *singing.*

When daffodils begin to peer,
With heigh! the doxy over the dale,

52. Prithee] 'Prethe *F.*   55. S.D. *Exeunt.*] *Exit. F.*

Scene III

Scene III] *Scena Tertia. F.*

41. *unspeakable*] beyond estimate, beyond description.

44. *begin*] i.e. it must originate from someone of importance.

46–7. *That's . . . thither*] 'What you say is also what I am told [viz. that the Shepherd has a remarkable daughter] but I fear [this girl to be] the baited hook which entices my son there.'

Scene III

Scene iii] A path near the Shepherd's cottage.

1. *When daffodils*] On the songs and music of the play see pp. 172–4 and

Sh.Q., Spring 1959, 161–75. No other version of *When daffodils* has been traced. The earliest known setting is that by William Boyce, *c.* 1759.

peer] 'peep above ground' but possibly meaning 'appear'.

2, 6, 10. *heigh, hey*] The spellings are as in *F.* They may represent some difference in pronunciation and meaning. In 2 and 6 the use may be only exclamatory. The country dance, or its tune, may be referred to in 10. (Cf. *LLL.*, v. i. 134, 'let them dance the hay', and Heywood, *Woman killed with Kindness*, I. i. 85, *hoigh.*) For a late

> *Why then comes in the sweet o' the year,*
>   *For the red blood reigns in the winter's pale.*
>
> *The white sheet bleaching on the hedge,*   5
>   *With hey! the sweet birds, O how they sing!*
> *Doth set my pugging tooth an edge;*
>   *For a quart of ale is a dish for a king.*
>
> *The lark, that tirra-lirra chants,*
>   *With heigh! with heigh! the thrush and the jay,*   10
> *Are summer songs for me and my aunts,*
>   *While we lie tumbling in the hay.*

4. *reigns in the*] *raigns in y* F.   9. *tirra-lirra*] *tirra-Lyra* F.

16-cent. tune for this dance see E. W. Naylor, *Sh. and Music*, 1931, 145.

2. *doxy*] rogues' slang for a female beggar or beggar's woman.

4. *pale*] cheeks made pale by winter. Perhaps the other sense of *pale* 'an enclosure' is included.

5. *white . . . hedge*] Linen set out to bleach or dry was favourite booty for the petty thief. Falstaff said that his soldiery would clothe themselves from it (*1H4*, IV. ii. 46) and clothes on a line were irresistible to Stephano and Trinculo.

7. *pugging*] The word must mean 'thieving' but it occurs nowhere else, although 'Puggard'—again a unique occurrence — apparently meaning 'thief', is in Middleton's *Roaring Girl*, v. i. 339, a scene full of 'pedlar's French'. 'Pug' = 'pull', 'offend' in Warwickshire dialect (Wright) and thus may have meant 'steal'. 'Prig', 'Priggar', 'Priggard', 'Prigging' meaning 'steal', 'thief' (particularly 'horse-thief'), 'thieving' were in common use in the 16th to 17th centuries and later (*O.E.D.*) and the word is used at 98, although not elsewhere by Shakespeare. A manuscript 'pri' in 1611–22 could easily have been misread as 'pu' but since 'prigging' was a well-known word it is unlikely that it would have been misread into one which must have been uncommon.

an] This, the F reading, gives an acceptable meaning, 'to set an edge on', 'to sharpen', hence 'to whet the appetite'. Greene says that the sight of a good horse to a horse-thief 'set the priggars teeth a water to have him' (*Second Cony-Catching*, 17). Theobald, and apparently all edd. since, change to *on*, being misled by the better known phrase 'to set on edge' even though that now gives a contrary and unacceptable sense. Cf. *O.E.D.* edge 2c. It seems that 'to set an edge' could also have the modern sense of 'set on edge,' 'grate on the nerves': cf. *1H4*, III. i. 133, and *O.E.D.* edge 4. Cf. Tilley, T431.

8.] probably inconsequent, but perhaps the ale is to be bought with money obtained for the sheet.

9. *tirra-lirra*] In later editions of *La Semaine*, including that of 1610–11, du Bartas has the lines (5th day): 'La gentile Alouette auec sone tire-lire / Tire-lire aux fachez et tire-lirant tire'. Rendered by Sylvester in 1605 (175): 'The prettie Larke, climbing the Welkin cleere, / Chaunts with a cheere, heere peere—I neere my Deere;' words which were set to music by J. Hilton in *Catch that Catch Can*, 2nd ed. 1658, 19. Malone quotes from a poem 'The Silk Worms', 1599: 'Let Philomela sing, let Progne chide, let Tyry-tyry-leerers upward flie'.

11. *aunts*] with the same meaning as *doxy* in 2.

I have served Prince Florizel, and in my time wore
three-pile, but now I am out of service.

> *But shall I go mourn for that, my dear?*   15
> *The pale moon shines by night:*
> *And when I wander here and there,*
> *I then do most go right.*

> *If tinkers may have leave to live,*
> *And bear the sow-skin budget,*   20
> *Then my account I well may give,*
> *And in the stocks avouch it.*

My traffic is sheets; when the kite builds, look to
lesser linen. My father named me Autolycus; who,

22. *avouch it*] *auouch-it F.*

14. *three-pile*] thick, costly velvet.

15. *But . . . mourn*] See pp. 172–
4 and *Sh.Q.*, Spring 1959, 162. No
other version has been traced. Apparently the earliest setting is that by
J. F. Lampe [?1745] printed on a
single folio [Brit. Mus. G. 306, piece
251].

15–18. *But shall . . . right*] 'But shall
I worry about that [i.e. having lost my
job with the prince]? On moonlight
nights when I go where I like [and
steal what I can] then I am living the
life which is the one for me.' Like the
Lincolnshire poacher it was Autolycus' 'delight on a shining night' to be
out on the prowl. For a vagabond,
since he has no specific destination, all
directions are the right direction—no
road is a wrong road. Dr Brooks cites
Cade's comment: 'But then are we in
order when we are most out of order'
(*2H6*, IV. ii. 185): anarchy is the mob's
proper principle, and to travel without
a destination is the vagabond's principle.

19–22. *If tinkers . . . it*] 'If tinkers are
allowed to trade and carry their pig-
skin bag—then I can account for
myself and if they put me in the stocks
can show my calling [i.e. that I am a
tinker and not a vagabond and therefore should be released].'

20. *budget*] a bag, usually of leather.
Here the pig-skin bag in which the
tinker carried his tools, and by which
tinkers were recognized.

23–4. *My traffic . . . linen*] 'My mer-
chandise is stolen sheets. Just as when
a kite is building it is well to watch your
smaller linen so, when I am about,
keep an eye on your sheets.' Autolycus
is the traditional tinker and petty
thief. Greene might have classified
him as a 'Lift' (whose activities
included shop-lifting) or a 'Foist' (see
Second Cony-Catching), but Shakespeare's use of 'prig', 'snapper-up' is
obviously not technical like Greene's.
Nevertheless he clearly intends to
show Autolycus as a skilled prac-
titioner. 'Snap' is used by Greene
(*Second Cony-Catching*) of the cut-
purse action of the 'Nip' (11) and of
the plunder, 'snappings', of the
'Hooker' (47–8). Moorman quotes
from J. E. Harting, *Ornithology of Sh.*,
1871, 46 a record of a kite's nest lined
with 'small pieces of linen' and other
articles. Cf. 5n.

23–31.] Dr Brooks remarks that the
style of this self-portrait is similar to
that of the 17-cent. 'Character' as
written by Overbury and Earle.

24. *Autolycus*] See pp. xxii, xxvi,
lxxix–lxxxi, 164–5.

being as I am, littered under Mercury, was likewise   25
a snapper-up of unconsidered trifles. With die and
drab I purchased this caparison, and my revenue is
the silly cheat. Gallows and knock are too powerful
on the highway: beating and hanging are terrors to
me: for the life to come, I sleep out the thought of it.   30
A prize! a prize!

Enter CLOWN.

Clo. Let me see: every 'leven wether tods; every tod

32. 'leven wether tods] *Malone;* Leauen-weather toddes *F.*

25. *Mercury*] In classical myth Autolycus was the son of Mercury and
Chione (see p. 165). Mercury (Hermes)
was the god of thieves, pickpockets,
and all dishonest persons, and was
reputed for cunning because of various
crafty thefts carried out in his infancy.
Some of his exploits are recounted in
the *Homeric Hymns* (Hymns to Hermes)
which were translated by Chapman
(Homer's *Works*, 1616).

26–8. *With die . . . cheat*] 'Through
dice and women I have come to be
dressed like this and I get my living by
petty trickery' or 'the foolish simpleton
is my source of income'.

28. *knock*] beating.

29–30. *beating . . . me*] This repeats
the sense of the previous sentence. He
is too frightened of the penalties to be a
highwayman or thief in a big way.

30. *for the life . . . it*] 'As for the future,
I don't worry about it' or 'As for the
life hereafter I don't worry about it.'
The former is supported by Autolycus' way of life which is precisely
that of one who lets tomorrow take
care of itself (cf. 15–18)—like another
tinker (*Shr.*, Ind. i. 5; ii. 140). 'Life to
come' is used in *Meas.*, v. i. 429, certainly for the future in this world, and
in *Mac.*, I. vii. 7, presumably for the
life hereafter. In *Wint.*, IV. iv. 498, 'the
time to come' certainly refers to this
world. Noble (*Biblical Knowledge*, 247)
considers the phrase to refer to the life
hereafter, equating it with the far more

precise 'life of the world to come' in
the Communion Service and Nicene
Creed. Dr Brooks agrees, believing
that as Macbeth, in the key of tragic
villainy, says he would ignore the possibility of condemnation hereafter,
'But in these cases / We still have
judgment here', so Autolycus, in the
key of comic villainy, says that the
hard knocks and gallows deter him, not
concern about the future life. Greene
(*Coosnage*, 36) says that cony-catchers
'are in religion meere atheists'. So, no
doubt, was Autolycus, perhaps so
much so that he would not have
bothered about a future life. His remark is like Feste's 'for turning away,
let summer bear it out' (*Tw.N.*, I. v.
18) and probably refers only to this
world. Even 'Hereafter, in a better
world than this' (*AYL.*, I. ii. 263) refers to this world. For 'sleep out' meaning 'be oblivious to' cf. III. iii. 60; *All's
W.*, v. iii. 66; *Lr.*, II. ii. 151; and 'That
I might sleep out this great gap of
time' (*Ant.*, I. v. 5).

32. *tods*] 'Every eleven sheep will
yield a tod (= 28 lb.) of wool.' Shakespeare's father was, among other
things, a wool-stapler and Shakespeare would have been familiar with
wool-dealing. His father started a law-
suit in 1599 for a debt incurred in 1568
of £21 for 21 tods of wool (L. Hotson,
letter in *Times*, 22 Nov. 1930, 13e
which cites this passage). It is assumed
that the Clown means that wool

yields pound and odd shilling: fifteen hundred
shorn, what comes the wool to?

Aut. [*Aside*] If the springe hold, the cock's mine.   35

Clo. I cannot do 't without counters. Let me see; what am
I to buy for our sheep-shearing feast? Three pound
of sugar, five pound of currants, rice—what will this

---

35. S.D. *Aside*] *Rowe* (*1*); *no S.D. in* F.
rants] Currence F.
36. counters] Compters F.
38. cur-

---

fetches 21s. the tod. See note to 37 *buy*.
In *History of Agriculture*, v. 408, J. E. T.
Rogers records that from 1572 to 1601
the price of wool at Eton had risen
from 20s. 9d. to 25s. 6d. the tod.

35. *cock*] Shakespeare refers elsewhere to the woodcock as being proverbially foolish, and frequently to
catching the bird by springes and gins
(Harting, *Ornithology of Sh.*, 229–32).
Cf. 'springes to catch woodcocks'
(*Ham.*, I. iii. 115 and v. ii. 298).

37. *buy*] I am indebted to Miss M. E.
Rayner, who is co-operating with
Lord Beveridge in *Prices and Wages in
England*, for the following estimates of
approximate prices in money values of
the time, in London about 1611, of
wool and the ingredients to be bought
by the Clown: wool 23s. a tod (28 lb.);
sugar 1s. 4d. a lb.; currants 5d. a lb.;
rice 6d. a lb.; saffron 2s. 6d. an oz.;
mace 16s. a lb.; nutmegs 6s. a lb.;
ginger 2s. 8d. a lb.; prunes 3d. a lb.;
raisins 10d. a lb.

sheep-shearing feast] This was an
important contemporary custom and
the description and episode here are
not of a conventional idyll but of a
popular and real festivity. Sheep-
shearing takes place late in June, but
from IV. iv. 79–81 this feast is clearly
later. There are many contemporary
references—see J. Brand, *Popular Antiquities*, ed. W. C. Hazlitt, ii, 1870, 22.
That feasts were costly is noted in
*Questions of Profitable and Pleasant Con-
cernings* (By O.B.), 1594, fo. 4a: 'If it
be a sheep-shearing feast, maister Baily
can entertaine you with his bill of
reckonings to his Maister, of three

sheapheards wages, spent on fresh
cates, besides spices and Saffron pot-
tage.' Drayton's account of the Cots-
wolds' feast in his *Ninth Eclogue* was
first printed in 1606. Shakespeare
would have seen these feasts and may
have read Drayton. The strong echo
in *Wint.* is noted by Prof. Kathleen
Tillotson in Drayton's *Works*, ed.
Hebel, 1931–41, ii. 564–70 (9th
Eclogue), v. 186–7 (Notes). In iv. 298
Drayton used some of the *Eclogue* material to describe such a feast in *Poly-
olbion*. The *Eclogue* states that shearing
takes place late in June. The shepherds
wear posies in their caps and garlands
'Baldricke-wise'. Flowers are exchanged with shepherdesses, including
lavender, rosemary, and the '*July-
Flowre*'. Bagpipes are played for the
'gay Swaynes' and a Shepherds' King
is chosen. Elaborate preparations include fair tables on a green, country
cates, new whig, plums and wildings,
cherries, fresh cheese, 'Dowsets, Curds
and clowted Creame, / Spic'd Sylli-
bubs, and Sider of the best'. Rounde-
lays are sung and 'goodly Swaynes, /
And lovely Girles attyr'd in Greene'
come 'From gathering Garlands on
the Playnes, / To crowne ... our Shep-
heards Queene'. T. Tusser, *Five
Hundred Points of Good Husbandry* [ed.
of 1610] records (98) that shearing
is in June, and gives an account on
135: 'Wife make vs a dinner, spare
flesh neither corne, / make wafers and
cakes, for our sheepe must be shorne: /
At sheepeshearing neighbours, none
other thing craue, / but good cheare,
and welcome, like neighbours to haue.'

sister of mine do with rice? But my father hath made
her mistress of the feast, and she lays it on. She hath   40
made me four-and-twenty nosegays for the shearers,
three-man song-men all, and very good ones; but
they are most of them means and basses but one
puritan amongst them, and he sings psalms to hornpipes. I must have saffron to colour the warden pies;   45
mace; dates, none—that's out of my note; nutmegs,

43. basses] bases *F*.

40. *lays it on*] does it well, thoroughly. Cf. *AYL.*, I. ii. 94; *Tp.*, III. ii. 146.
Perhaps with sense of 'she's overdoing
it'.

42. *three-man song-men*] singers of part
songs for male voices. These songs were
also often referred to as Freemen's
songs (as by Thos. Ravenscroft in
Deuteromelia, 1609). 'Freemen' is probably a corruption of 'three-man' but
the songs were not always trios: indeed
Ravenscroft refers to 'Freemen's songs
of 4 voices'. Shakespeare probably refers to the three-part form, which
Ravenscroft labels as for treble, tenor,
bass: but the upper part would be
perfectly suitable for a countertenor
(see IV. iv. 298n., p. 174).

43. *means*] the musical term used to
designate an inner part, the 'middle'
('medius') part, of a composition—'he
can sing / A mean most meanly' (*LLL.*,
v. ii. 327). By the end of the 16th century the term seems to have been used
chiefly for an alto (i.e. a countertenor)
part. Nevertheless here Shakespeare
is apparently using it for the tenor. It
would be expected that among men
singers tenors and basses would be
commoner than the altos and that
there would be no trebles. But an
Elizabethan company of players
would, of course, always have trebles
in the boy actors. There is a punning
sense in 'good ones . . . means and
bases'.

43–5. *but one puritan . . . hornpipes*]
The sense, and tone, could presumably
be interpreted: 'except for one Puritan

among them [who is an alto or treble]
and he [—would you believe it!—]
sings psalms to hornpipe music'. This
is a gentle jibe at Puritans who are freely ridiculed in contemporary drama
but only lightly by Shakespeare (e.g.
Tw.N., II. iii. 132–4). In Puritan services 'according to the stage writers . . .
psalms were delivered in a high nasal
tone' (W. P. Holden, *Anti-Puritan
Satire, 1572–1640*, 1954, 102–3). Cf.
Middleton and Rowley, *The World
tost at Tennis* [1620], 387–8: 'thou
Starch Puritan . . . whose tongue lies i'
thy nose' (cited in A. A. Myers,
*Representation . . . of the Puritan in
Elizabethan Drama*, 1931, 36). Linking
of the Puritan with hornpipes also
refers ironically to the Puritan's dis-
approval of music and dancing. The
hornpipe was a shrill instrument often
used for country dances, and the part
missing from the singing trio is the
alto or treble. Pipes 'speak i' th' nose'
in *Oth.*, III. i. 4, 19. Cf. Supp. to *Sh.Q.*,
Summer 1956, 20.

45. *warden pies*] pies of warden pears
(or apples), perhaps named after Warden Abbey, Bedfordshire (*Sh.Eng.*, i.
372). But cf. *O.E.D.* 'warden' *sb.*[2]

46. *mace*] a spice made of the outer
covering of the nutmeg.

out of my note] 'not on my list'. He
thinks of dates but, referring to his list,
sees that they are not there; or, less
probably, that they have been struck
out. The Clown, like Mopsa and
Dorcas, can read. 'Note' = 'record'.
Cf. I. ii. 2.

seven; a race or two of ginger, but that I may beg;
four pound of prunes, and as many of raisins o' th'
sun.

Aut. O that ever I was born!   [*Grovelling on the ground*]   50

Clo. I' th' name of me!

Aut. O, help me, help me! pluck but off these rags; and
then, death, death!

Clo. Alack, poor soul! thou hast need of more rags to lay
on thee, rather than have these off.   55

Aut. O sir, the loathsomeness of them offends me more
than the stripes I have received, which are mighty
ones and millions.

Clo. Alas, poor man! a million of beating may come to
a great matter.   60

Aut. I am robbed, sir, and beaten; my money and apparel ta'en from me, and these detestable things put
upon me.

Clo. What, by a horseman, or a footman?

Aut. A footman, sweet sir, a footman.   65

Clo. Indeed, he should be a footman by the garments he
has left with thee: if this be a horseman's coat, it hath
seen very hot service. Lend me thy hand, I'll help
thee: come, lend me thy hand.

---

48. prunes] Prewyns *F.*   raisins] Reysons *F.*   50. S.D. *Grovelling . . . ground*]
Rowe (*1*); *no S.D. in F.*   56. offends] *F2*; offend *F.*

---

47. *race*] root. From O.F. rais, Lat.
radicem (*O.E.D.* 'race' *sb.* 6 and
'radish'). Cf. *1H4*, II. i. 24.

48-9. *raisins . . . sun*] grapes dried
naturally in the open air. Cf. T.
Cogan, *The Haven of Health*, 1589, 96-
7. 'Among vs in Englande they bee of
two sortes, that is to say, great Raysons, and small Raysons, otherwise
called Corans [currants]. The greatest
sort are called raysons of the sunne, the
other are commonly to be had.' *Var.*
cites this and also 'the vine Scirpula,
the grapes whereof seems as if they
were Raisons of the Sunne, dried al-
readie' (Pliny, *Historie of the World*,
trans. P. Holland, 1601, 1, Bk XIV,
Cap. iii, 410).

50. *O . . . born*] For a possible source
for the trick described in the following
lines see pp. xxxiv–xxxv.

51. *I' th' name of me!*] No other
instance of this exclamation has been
traced. It has been suggested that *me* is
an incomplete *mercy*. But with Herford
and *N.C.Wint.* we may accept the
exclamation as it is. Cf. 'Body o' me!',
'For the life of me!', and 'Before me'
(*Tw.N.*, II. iii. 167).

66-8.] A horseman's coat would be
of better quality and in better condition than that of the poorer footman.
The highwayman (*O.E.D.* has no
record of this word before 1649) has
always been more aristocratic than the
footpad.

Aut. O, good sir, tenderly, O!   70
Clo. Alas, poor soul!
Aut. O, good sir, softly, good sir! I fear, sir, my shoulder-
        blade is out.
Clo. How now? canst stand?
Aut. Softly, dear sir [*Picks his pocket*]; good sir, softly. You   75
        ha' done me a charitable office.
Clo. Dost lack any money? I have a little money for thee.
Aut. No, good sweet sir; no, I beseech you, sir: I have a
        kinsman not past three-quarters of a mile hence,
        unto whom I was going: I shall there have money,   80
        or anything I want: offer me no money, I pray you;
        that kills my heart.
Clo. What manner of fellow was he that robbed you?
Aut. A fellow, sir, that I have known to go about with
        troll-my-dames: I knew him once a servant of the   85
        prince: I cannot tell, good sir, for which of his virtues
        it was, but he was certainly whipped out of the court.
Clo. His vices, you would say; there's no virtue whipped
        out of the court: they cherish it to make it stay there;
        and yet it will no more but abide.   90
Aut. Vices I would say, sir. I know this man well; he hath
        been since an ape-bearer, then a process-server (a
        bailiff), then he compassed a motion of the Prodigal

75. S.D. *picks his pocket*] Capell; no S.D. in F.

76. *charitable office*] With this false
piety cf. Greene's description of the
foist in St Paul's, who, 'as devoutly as
if he were som zealous person, standeth
soberly, with his eies elevated to
heauen, when his hand is either on the
purse or in the pocket' (*Second Cony-
Catching*, 31, 41).

82. *kills my heart*] This language of
the bogus heart-stricken is comparable
with that of Enobarbus 'This blows
my heart' when he is genuinely heart-
broken at Antony's magnanimity
(*Ant.*, IV. vi. 34).

85. *troll - my - dames*] troll - madam,
trunks, trou-madame. A game, sometimes used for illegal gambling in
which balls were rolled through arches

on a board. A similar game is still
common at fun-fairs and Autolycus
probably 'ran' one of these boards.
'Arch-board' or 'Nine-holes' was also
played by boys with marbles (*Cassell's
Complete Book of Sports*, 1888, 245).

90. *abide*] Perhaps 'stay there unwillingly, enduringly' (cf. *Pandosto*, p.
198, 'abide the pain'), or 'stay only
for a moment, pause before going on'
(H. Hulme in *Sh.Q.*, Summer 1958,
385, and *O.E.D.* abide 1 and 2).

92. *ape-bearer*] one who took a
monkey about for show.

92–3. (*a bailiff*)] The brackets are
in *F* and the sense is probably an alternative to *process-server* (see *O.E.D.*
bailiff 2).

Son, and married a tinker's wife within a mile where
my land and living lies; and, having flown over   95
many knavish professions, he settled only in rogue.
Some call him Autolycus.

Clo. Out upon him! prig, for my life, prig: he haunts
wakes, fairs, and bear-baitings.

Aut. Very true, sir; he, sir, he: that's the rogue that put   100
me into this apparel.

Clo. Not a more cowardly rogue in all Bohemia: if you
had but looked big and spit at him, he 'd have run.

Aut. I must confess to you, sir, I am no fighter: I am false
of heart that way; and that he knew, I warrant him.   105

Clo. How do you now?

Aut. Sweet sir, much better than I was: I can stand, and
walk: I will even take my leave of you, and pace
softly towards my kinsman's.

Clo. Shall I bring thee on the way?   110

Aut. No, good-faced sir; no, sweet sir.

Clo. Then fare-thee-well: I must go buy spices for our
sheep-shearing.   *Exit.*

Aut. Prosper you, sweet sir! Your purse is not hot enough
to purchase your spice. I'll be with you at your   115
sheep-shearing too: if I make not this cheat bring
out another, and the shearers prove sheep, let me

---

compassed] 'acquired' and 'went round with'. Both senses are included.

motion] puppet-show. Cf. *Gent.*, II. i. 85, 'O excellent motion! O exceeding puppet.'

95. *living*] property, estate.

98. *prig*] rogues' slang for *tinker* and *thief*. Cf. 7n.

99. *wakes*] festival, revel. *O.E.D.* wake *sb*.4b. The term is still used in the North and Midlands. In the South the equivalent is 'feast' or 'revels'. Obviously any occasion which brings a crowd together, especially if it is one for money-spending, is ideal for the activities of the pickpocket and trickster of the Autolycus type. Greene records that they haunt 'Paules, Westminster, the exchange, Plaies,

Bear-garden, running at Tilt, the L. Maiors day, any festiuall meetings, fraies, shootings, or great faires: to bee short, wheresoeuer is any extraordinary resort of people' (*Second Cony-Catching*, 30) and Autolycus himself mentions some of the occasions which yield 'a careful man work' (IV. iv. 685–6, *q.v.*). Pedlars work 'At wakes, and wassails, meetings, markets, fairs' (*LLL.*, v. ii. 318).

114–15. *purse . . . spice*] Note the word-play: 'hot' is an epithet often applicable to 'spice'. The spice to be purchased may be hot but the purse is now too cold to buy it. For 'cold' = 'empty' purse see *1H4*, II. iv. 314; *Tim.*, III. iv 15.

116–17. *cheat . . . another*] 'profitable trick pave the way for another'.

be unrolled, and my name put in the book of virtue!

> *Song.   Jog on, jog on, the foot-path way,*
> *And merrily hent the stile-a:*   120
> *A merry heart goes all the day,*
> *Your sad tires in a mile-a.*   *Exit.*

118. *unrolled*] struck off the roll of the fraternity of rogues. Cf. 'our nips and foists, who haue a kind of fraternity or brother-hood amongst them, hauing a hall or place of meeting, where they confer of waightie matters, touching their workemanship' (Greene, *Second Cony-Catching*, 35).

119. *Jog on*] See pp. 172–4. Early 17-cent. music for this song is in *Fitzwilliam* (or *Tregian's*) *Virginal Book*, ed. J. A. Fuller-Maitland and W. Barclay Squire, 2 vols., 1899. The tune, there entitled *Hanskin*, is no. 197, 494–500 of vol. 2. It is by Richard Farnaby and consists of variations on *Hanskin*. The first part of this is in John Playford's *The (English) Dancing Master*, 1651. In the reprint by Margaret Dean-Smith, 1957, the tune, called *Jog on* (without words) is on p. 45 and another version called *Halfe Hannekin* on 37. The *Fitzwilliam Virginal Book*, referred to by many, including Chappell, as *Queen Elizabeth's Virginal Book*, was apparently written by Francis Tregian between 1609 and 1619 (*Music and Letters*, July 1951, 206; Jan. 1952, 28–32; April 1952, 192). Cf. E. W. Naylor, *An Elizabethan Virginal Book*, 1905. The words of *Jog on* are reprinted, with two additional stanzas, in *The Antidote against Melan-*

choly, 1661 (repr. by J. P. Collier, ?1870, 91) and by W. Chappell, *Popular Music* [1855], i. 211–13. Stanza 1 is substantially as in *Wint.* Stanzas 2 and 3 are: 'Your paltry mony bags of gold, / What need have we to stare for, / When little or nothing soon is told, / And we have the less to care for. / Cast care away, let sorrow cease, / A fig for melancholly, / Let's laugh and sing, or, if you please, / We'l frolick with sweet Dolly.' The tune was used for a ballad on the Armada beginning 'In eighty-eight ere I was born' printed often between 1650 and 1700, and in manuscript perhaps earlier than 1650. The verses have some stylistic resemblance to *Jog on*, e.g.: 'Our Queen was then att Tilbury/ What could yow more desire-a / ffor whose sweete sake Sr. ffrancis Drake / Did sett them all on fyre-a' (B.M. Harl. MS. 791 fo. 59). In *Jog on* and Silence's song (*2H4*, v. iii. 45–7) Shakespeare was perhaps using a contemporary popular song. The *-a* ending was common (cf. *Two Noble Kinsmen*, III. v. 60). But cf. IV. iv. 298n.

120. *hent*] take hold of.

121–2.] That a merry man lives as long as a sad is proverbial (Tilley, M71).

SCENE IV

Enter FLORIZEL [*and*] PERDITA [*followed, at a little distance, by*]
SHEPHERD, CLOWN; POLIXENES, CAMILLO, [*disguised*]*;* MOPSA,
    DORCAS, *Servants,* [*Shepherds and Shepherdesses*].

Flo. These your unusual weeds, to each part of you
     Do give a life: no shepherdess, but Flora
     Peering in April's front. This your sheep-shearing
     Is as a meeting of the petty gods,
     And you the queen on 't.

Per.   Sir: my gracious lord,   5
     To chide at your extremes, it not becomes me—
     O pardon, that I name them! Your high self,
     The gracious mark o' th' land, you have obscur'd
     With a swain's wearing, and me, poor lowly maid,
     Most goddess-like prank'd up: but that our feasts   10
     In every mess have folly, and the feeders
     Digest it with a custom, I should blush

Scene IV
Scene IV] *Scena Quarta. F.*   S.D. *Enter Florizel . . . Shepherdesses.*] *Enter Florizell,
Perdita, Shepherd, Clowne, Polixenes, Camillo, Mopsa, Dorcas, Seruants, Autolicus. F.*
2. Do] Do's *F.*   12. Digest it] *F2 (subst.);* Digest *F.*

Scene iv] The Feast: outside the
Shepherd's cottage.

1. *unusual weeds*] Florizel and Perdita
are in festive garb. Perdita is undoubtedly also garlanded or bedecked with
flowers in some way (2–3). Cf.
Pandosto, p. 202: 'Fawnia . . . with a
garland of boughs and flowers,
which attire became her so gallantly as
she seemed to be the goddess Flora
herself for beauty.' Perdita considers
that Florizel's attire demeans him (9–
13, 22) and it is clearly a country
swain's clothes (30–1). Shepherd
and Clown think it is court dress (750)
but that is mere dramatic con-
venience and no more puzzling than
that they do not then recognize the
clothes or Autolycus. That the flimsi-
est disguise is always a complete
success is the most common stage
convention.

6. *extremes*] extravagances, exaggera-
tions (*O.E.D.* extreme C5).

8. *mark . . . land*] 'the person looked
up to by everyone'. Cf. *2H4,* II. iii.
31–2, 'He was the mark . . . that
fashioned others.'

9. *swain's wearing*] See 1n.

9–10. *me . . . prank'd up*] It is usually
assumed that 'you have' is to be
understood after 'maid'; i.e. that
Florizel has in some way dressed her
up—it was one of his 'extremes'. Presumably he had bedecked her with
flowers. For 'prank' = to deck oneself
out, to dress up showily, see *O.E.D.*
prank v4.

11. *mess*] Cf. I. ii. 227n.

12. *Digest . . . custom*] 'The habit acts
like a sauce to the mess, enabling them
to accept the whole business, despite
its folly.' For *digest* = to brook, endure,
put up with, cf. *O.E.D.* v6.

To see you so attir'd; swoon, I think,
To show myself a glass.

Flo.   I bless the time
When my good falcon made her flight across   15
Thy father's ground.

Per.   Now Jove afford you cause!
To me the difference forges dread (your greatness
Hath not been us'd to fear): even now I tremble
To think your father, by some accident
Should pass this way, as you did: O the Fates!   20
How would he look, to see his work, so noble,
Vilely bound up? What would he say? Or how
Should I, in these my borrowed flaunts, behold
The sternness of his presence?

Flo.   Apprehend
Nothing but jollity. The gods themselves,   25
Humbling their deities to love, have taken
The shapes of beasts upon them: Jupiter
Became a bull, and bellow'd; the green Neptune
A ram, and bleated; and the fire-rob'd god,
Golden Apollo, a poor humble swain,   30
As I seem now. Their transformations
Were never for a piece of beauty rarer,

13. swoon] *Theobald;* sworne *F.*

13. *swoon*] *sworne* would be an easy
misreading of MS. *swowne* or *swownd*—
probable spellings of *swoon* (*swooned* at
v. ii. 90 is *swownded* in *F*)—indeed,
written with a slightly splayed *r*,
sworne and *swowne* might be almost
indistinguishable. The expression
would be normal from any girl even
from one not of the swooning kind.
That Perdita could have spoken of
swooning is shown by the fact that she
can speak of trembling (18) and weeping (451) although she was not of
the trembling and weeping any more
than of the swooning kind. Perdita
dislikes the whole thing for she mistrusts all artificiality. The passage
may be paraphrased: 'Were it not
that folly holds sway on these occasions I should blush to see you

dressed up as you are and I'm sure
I'd faint if I saw myself in a glass.'
'Sworn' seems far less satisfactory,
although retained by some edd. and
by Sisson.

15. *my good falcon*] Cf. *Pandosto,* p.
204, l. 14.

17. *difference*] i.e. of our rank.

22. *bound up*] referring to Florizel's
swain's wearing. A metaphor from
book-binding (cf. *Rom.,* III. ii. 83: 'Was
ever book containing such vile
matter / So fairly bound?').

23. *flaunts*] finery.

27–30. *Jupiter . . . Neptune . . . Apollo*]
Cf. *Pandosto,* p. 210, ll. 34–5; *Wiv.,* v. v.
3; *2H4,* II. ii. 168; Greene, *Menaphon*
(Grosart), vi. 120; and Ovid, *Metam.,*
Pref. 33–4, 91, 95; vi. 127–60.

32. *piece*] Cf. 423–4n.

　　　Nor in a way so chaste, since my desires
　　　Run not before mine honour, nor my lusts
　　　Burn hotter than my faith.
Per.　　　　　　　　　　　　O, but sir,　　　　　　35
　　　Your resolution cannot hold when 'tis
　　　Oppos'd, as it must be, by th' power of the king:
　　　One of these two must be necessities,
　　　Which then will speak, that you must change this
　　　　　purpose,
　　　Or I my life.
Flo.　　　　　　　Thou dearest Perdita,　　　　　40
　　　With these forc'd thoughts, I prithee, darken not
　　　The mirth o' th' feast. Or I'll be thine, my fair,
　　　Or not my father's. For I cannot be
　　　Mine own, nor anything to any, if
　　　I be not thine. To this I am most constant,　　　45
　　　Though destiny say no. Be merry, gentle,
　　　Strangle such thoughts as these with anything
　　　That you behold the while. Your guests are coming:
　　　Lift up your countenance, as it were the day
　　　Of celebration of that nuptial which　　　　　50
　　　We two have sworn shall come.
Per.　　　　　　　　　　　O lady Fortune,
　　　Stand you auspicious!

[SHEPHERD, CLOWN, MOPSA, DORCAS, *and others come forward,
　　　with the disguised* POLIXENES *and* CAMILLO.]

Flo.　　　　　　　　　　See, your guests approach:
　　　Address yourself to entertain them sprightly,

---

35. sir] *F;* deere sir *F2.*　　　52. S.D. *Enter Shepherd . . . Camillo*] *Rowe* (*1*) *subst.,
after 54; no S.D. in F; Enter All. F2.*

33. *Nor . . . chaste*] 'nor in so chaste a
manner (as my actions are)'. Cf. IV. iv.
151 and p. lxxix, n.4.

38. *these two*] i.e. 'that you must
change this purpose, or I my life'.

40. *Or . . . life*] i.e. suffer death, or at
least some violent change such as
imprisonment. That this is probably
the meaning is indicated by Florizel's
next sentence. Dramatically, the re-

mark prepares for the exposure and
the threats of Polixenes.

dearest] *deer'st F.* But to be spoken as
two syllables, cf. *Kökeritz,* 266.

41. *forc'd*] far-fetched, unnatural.

43–5. *For . . . thine*] 'For I can be of
no good to myself or to anyone if I lose
you.'

52. *Mopsa, Dorcas*] For possible
source of names see p. 164.

And let's be red with mirth.
Shep. Fie, daughter! when my old wife liv'd, upon   55
    This day she was both pantler, butler, cook,
    Both dame and servant; welcom'd all, serv'd all;
    Would sing her song and dance her turn; now here
    At upper end o' th' table, now i' th' middle;
    On his shoulder, and his; her face o' fire   60
    With labour, and the thing she took to quench it
    She would to each one sip. You are retired,
    As if you were a feasted one, and not
    The hostess of the meeting: pray you, bid
    These unknown friends to 's welcome; for it is   65
    A way to make us better friends, more known.
    Come, quench your blushes, and present yourself
    That which you are, Mistress o' th' Feast. Come on,
    And bid us welcome to your sheep-shearing,
    As your good flock shall prosper.
Per.   [*To Pol.*] Sir, welcome: 70
    It is my father's will I should take on me
    The hostess-ship o' th' day. [*To Cam.*] You're welcome,
        sir.
    Give me those flowers there, Dorcas. Reverend sirs,
    For you, there's rosemary, and rue; these keep
    Seeming and savour all the winter long: 75
    Grace and remembrance be to you both,

70. S.D. *To Pol.*] *Malone; no S.D. in F.*   72. S.D. *To Cam.*] *Malone; no S.D. in F.*

55–70. *Fie, daughter . . . prosper*] This speech throws light on Perdita, the Shepherd and his late wife (and recalls Mopsa in *Pandosto* in so doing). It is full of strength and feeling yet very different in style from the equally striking speech beginning at 452.

56. *This day*] For a note on the sheep-shearing feast see IV. iii. 37n.

63. *feasted one*] i.e. simply one of those for whom the feast is given, one of the shepherds and shepherdesses.

65. *to 's welcome*] 'welcome these friends who are unknown to us' (cf. Abbott, §419a).

68–70. *Come on . . . prosper*] Perhaps this passage was intended for Polixenes

or Camillo rather than the Shepherd. In transcribing the *Come* of 68 the copyist may have glanced at the *Come* of 67 and so omitted the speaker's name.

75. *Seeming and savour*] appearance and scent.

76. *Grace and remembrance*] Rosemary and rue signified respectively remembrance (friendship) and grace (repentance). Rue is known as 'herb grace' (Lyte, *Herbal*, 1578, 260; Cogan, *Haven of Health*, 1589, 40). (Cf. *Ham.*, IV. v. 178 and H. N. Ellacombe, *Plantlore of Sh.*, 2nd ed., 1884, 256–62.) Meanings of some of the flowers mentioned by Perdita and Drayton (*Ninth*

And welcome to our shearing!

Pol.   Shepherdess—
A fair one are you—well you fit our ages
With flowers of winter.

Per.   Sir, the year growing ancient,
Not yet on summer's death nor on the birth   80
Of trembling winter, the fairest flowers o' th' season
Are our carnations and streak'd gillyvors,
Which some call nature's bastards: of that kind
Our rustic garden's barren; and I care not
To get slips of them.

Pol.   Wherefore, gentle maiden,   85
Do you neglect them?

Per.   For I have heard it said
There is an art which, in their piedness, shares
With great creating nature.

Pol.   Say there be;

Eclogue—see IV. iii. 37n.) are given in G. Robinson, *A handful of Pleasant Delights*, 1584 (ed. A. Arber, 1880, 3, 'A Nosegaie alwaies sweet'). Cf. 'did shew, / What every flower as countrey people hold, / Did signifie' (*Philaster*, I. ii. 133). *Remembrance* is probably to be pronounced as four syllables. In Webster, *The White Devil*, v. iv. 70, written about 1611, the mad Cornelia just before her famous dirge says, 'You're very welcome. There's Rosemarie for you, and Rue for you.' Cf. Ophelia (*Ham.*, IV. v. 172–81).

82. *gillyvors*] F *Gilly-vors*. At 98 the spelling is *Gilly'vors*. There is no other recorded use by Shakespeare. The word (*gilofre* in Chaucer, *gillofer* in Lyte's *Herbal* of 1578), sometimes thought to be a form of 'July-flower', is a corruption of *Caryophyllus* and is used for the cloves, carnations, and pinks. It was a favourite flower for garlands (carnation means the 'crowning', 'coronation' flower) and for spicing wine. Cf. Sylvester's Du Bartas, 1606 (2nd week, 3rd day, 1st book, *Vocation* 7–8): 'Some Gilly flower, or some sweet Sops-in-Wine, /

To make a Chaplet thy chaste browes to binde.' Greene associates the gillyflower with Juno and the carnation with Ceres (*Friar Bacon*, v. iii. 2085).

83. *nature's bastards*] See pp. 169–70.

88–92. *Say . . . nature makes*] This statement that any man-made means of improving nature is itself the creation of nature, since man and his powers are also natural, has come to be regarded almost as a sensational discovery. It 'is the insight of consummate genius' (*Sh.Eng.*, i. 515, quoted approvingly in *N.C.Wint.*); it is one of Shakespeare's 'keenest intellectual aperçus' (H. S. Wilson, 'Nature and art in *Winter's Tale*'— *Sh. Assoc. Bull.* xviii, July 1943, 114–20). But Wilson (119) also shows and concludes 'that Shakespeare's thought was commonplace both in antiquity and in the Renaissance, and that even the horticultural illustrations Shakespeare uses were familiar in Renaissance discussions of "nature" and "art" long before Shakespeare's time.' The truth surely is that the thought is not profound but important, especially as the fact that man and his

Yet nature is made better by no mean
But nature makes that mean: so, over that art,   90
Which you say adds to nature, is an art
That nature makes. You see, sweet maid, we marry
A gentler scion to the wildest stock,
And make conceive a bark of baser kind
By bud of nobler race. This is an art   95
Which does mend nature—change it rather—but
The art itself is nature.

Per.   So it is.

Pol. Then make your garden rich in gillyvors,
And do not call them bastards.

Per.   I'll not put
The dibble in earth to set one slip of them;   100
No more than, were I painted, I would wish
This youth should say 'twere well, and only therefore
Desire to breed by me. Here's flowers for you:

93. scion] Sien *F.*   98. your] *F2;* you *F.*

powers are a natural creation was, and is, often forgotten. Nevertheless modern critics give too much prominence and attach too much importance to what they sometimes call 'the great debate between Perdita and Polixenes' (*Sh.Sur.*, xi, 1958, 67). See also II. iii. 103n.; IV. iv. 83n. (in Appendix); and pp. lxi, lxxvi–lxxviii.

88–97.] The dramatic irony of this passage has often been noticed. The king actually upholds the practice of marrying 'A gentler scion to the wildest stock' which he is about to condemn where his son is concerned. Perdita may have Florizel and herself in mind when she answers, but much more probably, as she has no ready answer, she is merely giving a semblance of agreement where she means still to keep her own mind. The dramatic effect is no less admirable in the presentation of the persons than of the themes. Polixenes' wider and more philosophical grasp of the principles befits him: but Perdita's resolute sensitiveness and feminine refinement about anything that might savour of

sophistication or unchastity befits her. The argument does her no less honour than it does Polixenes, though, *qua* argument, he has the better of it.

96. *does mend nature*] Cf. Webster, *D. of Malfi*, II. i. 159–60: '*Bosola.* 'Tis a pretty art: this grafting. *Duch.* 'Tis so: a bettering of nature.'

98. *your*] The *F you* may possibly be *yon*, the *u* being a turned *n*.

103–80.] The beauty and charm of Perdita, which are such a powerful force in the play, are here shown at their height. The previous talk with Polixenes, showing Perdita the resolute peasant girl, leads up to this important and memorable passage where Perdita's beauty, grace, and charm of person, of movement, and of language make their profound and permanent impression. (See pp. lxi, lxxvi).

103. *you*] Perdita had given Polixenes and Camillo flowers appropriate for 'reverend sirs' at 74. She now turns from these elderly men to others of middle age (106–8). She turns to Florizel and his contemporaries at 112–14.

Hot lavender, mints, savory, marjoram,
The marigold, that goes to bed wi' th' sun   105
And with him rises, weeping: these are flowers
Of middle summer, and I think they are given
To men of middle age. Y'are very welcome.

                    [*She gives them flowers*]

Cam. I should leave grazing, were I of your flock,
And only live by gazing.
Per.   Out, alas!   110
You'd be so lean that blasts of January
Would blow you through and through. Now, my fair'st
    friend, [*To Florizel*]
I would I had some flowers o' th' spring, that might
Become your time of day; and yours, and yours,
                    [*To Mopsa and the other girls*]
That wear upon your virgin branches yet   115

---

108. S.D. *She . . . flowers*] *N.C.Wint.; no S.D. in F.*   112. S.D. *To Florizel*]
N.C.Wint.; no S.D. in F.   114. S.D. *To Mopsa . . . girls*] *N.C.Wint.; no S.D. in F.*

---

104. *Hot*] The plants have 'temperatures' (*O.E.D.* temperature 4) and lavender is described as 'hot' in William Turner, *Names of Herbes*, 1548, and later herbals such as the English version of Dodoens of 1578 where (265) its nature is given as 'hoate and dry in the second degree' and Cogan, *Haven of Health*, 1589, 56. In Gerard, *Lauander spike* is 'hot and drie' (468) whereas *French Lauander* or *Sticadoue* is apparently 'cold' (470). Perdita is therefore simply giving the common description of the plant and possibly distinguishing the variety she has. But 'hot' may refer to all the flowers in 104–5 for they are all 'hot' according to Gerard and Cogan. Bacon uses this division of herbs into 'cold' and 'hot', the former being the earlier blooming plants which 'have a quicker perception of the heat ... than the hot herbs have' and also those herbs which 'are but annual'. He lists lavender in a group which is contrasted with plants which 'are not hot' (*Sylva Sylvarum* in *Works*, Sped-

ding, ii, 1857, 519, §577; 520, §582).

105. *marigold*] Probably the *calendula officinalis* 'named ye husbandmans Dyall, for that the same so aptlye declareth the houres of mornyng and evening, by the opening and shutting of it. Also named the sunnes floure, for that after the rysing of the sunne vnto noone, this floure openeth larger and larger, but after the noone time, vnto the setting of the sun, the flour closeth and shutteth more and more so that after y⁰ setting of the sun, the floure is then wholly shutte vp togither' (T. Hill, *Profitable Art of Gardening*, 1597, 93–4). 'The flowers of Marigolds . . . doe begin to open at the rising of the Sun, at noone they are fully and wholy opened, but they are closed, or are shut when the Sun doth set. Therfore some calls it . . . *Sponsus Solis*, the Spouse of the Sunne. Because they sleepe, and are awakened with him' (T. Lupton, *A Thousand Notable Things*, 1601, Bk 6, §83, 113). Cf. Cogan, *Haven of Health*, 1589, 68.

Your maidenheads growing: O Proserpina,
For the flowers now that, frighted, thou let'st fall
From Dis's waggon! daffodils,
That come before the swallow dares, and take
The winds of March with beauty; violets, dim,   120
But sweeter than the lids of Juno's eyes
Or Cytherea's breath; pale primroses,
That die unmarried, ere they can behold
Bright Phœbus in his strength (a malady
Most incident to maids); bold oxlips and   125
The crown imperial; lilies of all kinds,
The flower-de-luce being one. O, these I lack,

116. *Proserpina*] Shakespeare here probably had in mind Ovid, *Metam.* v (see above p. xxxiv).

118. *Dis's wagon*] Pluto's chariot.

119. *take*] charm, delight, bewitch. Cf. I. ii. 40; III. ii. 37; *Ham.*, I. i. 163, 'No fairy takes, nor witch hath power to charm'; *Tp.*, v. i. 313; and Alexander xxix, 30 (Jonson's lines).

120. *violets, dim*] probably the white violet, praised by Bacon (*Of Gardens*) as the flower with the sweetest smell. 'Dim' because the hanging head is also usually concealed or partly concealed.

121. *lids*] Cf. '. . . her eyes as jewel-like, / And cas'd as richly; in pace another Juno' (*Per.*, v. i. 109-10). There are many examples of beauty attributed to the eyelids: 'When on each eyelid sweetly doe appeare / an hundred Graces as in / shade to sit' (Spenser, *Amoretti*, Sonn. 40); 'Vpon her eyelids many Graces sate, / Vnder the shadow of her euen browes' (*Faerie Queene*, II. iii. 25); 'Certainely as her eye-lids are more pleasant to behold, then two white kiddes climing up a faire tree' (Sidney, *Arcadia*, 1590, I. i, ed. Feuillerat, 1912, I. 7). There is a sense of beauty in Prospero's 'The fringed curtains of thine eye' (*Tp.*, I. ii. 408). Commentators have noted a fashion which once prevailed of kissing the eyelids, and a custom which has always been prevalent of women colouring their eye-

lids. But little comment is necessary except to agree on the beauty of the line, and, if wished, to note that eyelids can be beautiful, especially when drooping or closed in sleep. H. H. Furness notes in *Var.* the beauty of the association of love and tenderness expressed through eyes with drooping lids and the half hidden violet. Cf. v. ii. 12n.

Juno] the beautiful, Queen of the gods.

122. *Cytherea*] the surname of Venus (Aphrodite), said to have been born from the waves near the island Cythera. Elsewhere mentioned by Shakespeare only in *Cym.*, II. ii. 14, and *Shr.*, Ind. ii. 49.

122-3. *pale . . . unmarried*] See pp. 170-2.

124. *Phœbus*] Apollo, the sun god.

125. *oxlips*] larger and stronger than cowslips, they stand up boldly.

126. *crown imperial*] The plant had been newly imported from Constantinople in 1597 (Gerard, 153-4) but was then flourishing in London gardens. It is the tall yellow fritillary (E. Singleton, *The Shakespeare Garden*, 1923).

127. *flower-de-luce*] fleur-de-lis, the iris. Lyte, *Herbal*, 1578, 192, speaks of the 'Floure Deluce or Iris' and Gerard gives fifteen kinds of irises with this name. Spenser distinguishes this flower from the lily in *F.Q.*, II. 6: 'The

To make you garlands of; and my sweet friend,
To strew him o'er and o'er!

Flo.   What, like a corpse?

Per. No, like a bank, for love to lie and play on: 130
Not like a corpse; or if—not to be buried,
But quick, and in mine arms. Come, take your flowers:
Methinks I play as I have seen them do
In Whitsun pastorals: sure this robe of mine
Does change my disposition.

Flo.   What you do,   135

Lilly, lady of the flowering field, / The floure-de-luce, her lovely paramoure.'

129. *strew . . . corpse*] See 132 *quick*, n. The *F* spelling of *corpse* here and in 131 is *Coarse* but in v. i. 58 it is *Corps*.

131. *or if*] 'or if strewn with flowers like a corpse'. For similar ellipsis after *or if* see *Ant.*, IV. ii. 26; *Oth.*, III. iii. 37.

132. *quick*] 'alive'. Verbal similarity, although the idea is different, is in *Philaster*, IV. iv. 4–6, where Bellario speaks of a bank and flowers: 'I could wish / I rather were a corse strewed o'er with you / Than quick above you.' J. C. Maxwell comments that 'it looks as if *Philaster*, where the lines are much less organic, were the debtor' (*R.E.S.*, Aug. 1958, 316), but the lines seem organic in *Philaster* which is almost certainly earlier than *Wint.* There was a custom of strewing the bridal bed with flowers as well as the grave (*Ham.*, v. i. 239–40) and there is a parallel to the general sense of the passage in *Ado*, III. ii. 62. Cf. the strewing of flowers on what was thought to be the corpse of Imogen (*Cym.*, IV. ii. 219–30, 283–8), 'To strew thy green with flowers . . . / Shall as a carpet hang upon thy grave' (*Per.*, IV. i. 15 and v. iii. 43), Katharine's request in *H8*, IV. ii. 167–70, and Drayton, *Poly-Olbion*, Song xv, 138–204.

134. *Whitsun pastorals*] Whitsuntide was a time of festivities, especially of the May-games including Robin Hood plays. (Cf. Hone, *Everyday Book*, 1, 685–94; 2, 663–78; Chambers, *Book of*

Days, i, 629–39, E. K. Chambers, *Medieval Stage*, i, 160–81 and *Elizabethan Stage*—see Subject index *May games*). The festivities included morris dances—see *H5*, II. iv. 25. Cf. the Pentecost plays mentioned in *Gent.*, IV. iv. 154. Shakespeare may well have seen such plays and games at Stratford, e.g. the 'pastyme' held there in 1583 (Chambers, *Shakespeare*, i. 9).

135–46. *What you do . . . queens*] C. B. Mount (*N. & Q.*, 1893, 8.3.305) pointed out a possible source in *Arcadia*: 'The force of love . . . doth so enchaine the lovers judgment . . . that what soever she doth is ever in his eyes best. . . If she sit still, that is best . . . if she walke, no doubt that is best . . . if she be silent, that . . . is best. . . But if she speake, he will take it upon his death that is best, the quintessence of each worde being distilled downe into his affected soule' (Sidney, *Works*, ed. Feuillerat, ii, 1922, 53–4). The passage may be paraphrased (1) From *What you do* to *is done*: 'Anything you do is always yet more excellent than the last thing you did': (2) From *Each your* to *queens*: 'Everything you do [is done in a manner which] is so much your own in every little way that it gives a touch of royalty to what you are doing at present [i.e. acting as queen of the feast] because all your acts are in fact as those of a queen.' Detailed analysis is given in Bethell, *Wint. Study*, 23–6. For 'crown' = 'complete' cf. *Mac.*, IV. i. 149, 'crown my thoughts with acts'; *Tp.*, III. i. 69, 'And crown what I pro-

Still betters what is done. When you speak, sweet,
I'd have you do it ever: when you sing,
I'd have you buy and sell so, so give alms,
Pray so, and, for the ord'ring your affairs,
To sing them too: when you do dance, I wish you   140
A wave o' th' sea, that you might ever do
Nothing but that, move still, still so,
And own no other function. Each your doing,
So singular in each particular,
Crowns what you are doing, in the present deeds,   145
That all your acts are queens.

Per.   O Doricles,
Your praises are too large: but that your youth,
And the true blood which peeps fairly through 't,
Do plainly give you out an unstain'd shepherd,
With wisdom I might fear, my Doricles,   150
You woo'd me the false way.

Flo.   I think you have
As little skill to fear as I have purpose
To put you to 't. But come; our dance, I pray,
Your hand, my Perdita: so turtles pair
That never mean to part.

Per.   I'll swear for 'em.   155

Pol. This is the prettiest low-born lass that ever
Ran on the green-sward: nothing she does or seems
But smacks of something greater than herself,
Too noble for this place.

Cam.   He tells her something
That makes her blood look out: good sooth, she is   160

---

157. green-sward] greene-sord *F.*   160. out] *Theobald;* on't *F.*

fess'; and *H8*, iii. ii. 155, 'with his deed
did crown / His word.'

148. *And . . . through 't*] The sense and
emphasis of the line are perhaps best
brought out by reading it as 'And
the trúe-blood, which peeps fairly
through't.'

blood] birth and breeding.

151. *false way*] Cf. iv. iv. 33n.

152. *skill*] need, reason.

154-5. *so turtles . . . part*] Turtle
doves mate for life. Cf. v. iii. 132-5n.

155. *I'll . . . 'em*] 'I'll be sworn they
do.' Typical of Perdita's downright
country speech.

160. *out*] The main objection to
reading *out* is the apostrophe. In *F* the
n of *on't* is directly under the last letter
in 159. If the MS. were similarly
spaced, a comma placed rather below
the line after *something*—and a comma
before a relative *that* is common—
would almost certainly cause *out* to be
read *on't*. The same mistake is found in

The queen of curds and cream.

Clo. Come on, strike up!

Dor. Mopsa must be your mistress: marry, garlic to
mend her kissing with!

Mop. Now, in good time!   165

Clo. Not a word, a word; we stand upon our manners.
Come, strike up!

[*Music*]. *Here a dance of Shepherds and Shepherdesses.*

Pol. Pray, good shepherd, what fair swain is this
Which dances with your daughter?

Shep. They call him Doricles; and boasts himself   170
To have a worthy feeding: but I have it
Upon his own report and I believe it;
He looks like sooth. He says he loves my daughter:
I think so too; for never gaz'd the moon
Upon the water as he'll stand and read   175
As 'twere my daughter's eyes: and, to be plain,
I think there is not half a kiss to choose

---

167. S.D. *Music*] *Malone; not in F.*

Tw.N., III. iv. 192, and *Cym.*, II. iii. 43.
Cf. also note to II. iv. 76 in *N.C.Cym.*,
ed. J. C. Maxwell.

161. *The queen . . . cream*] *N.C.Wint.*
notes that in 'western May-games' the
queen was called 'white-pot cream'.
White-pot was a kind of cream custard
(F. Douce, *Illus. of Sh.*, 1807, ii, 457;
1839 ed., 591).

162–7. *Come . . . strike up*] This passage is printed as prose in *F* and is
almost certainly meant to be prose for
these characters do not speak in verse.
But since 161–6 can be arranged as
fairly regular blank verse most edd. so
print them. The fact that the lines can
be treated as blank verse probably
illustrates a writer's difficulty in
changing to a short passage of prose.
It is less likely that they are a verse-
fossil indicating re-writing.

163–4. *marry . . . with*] ironical: 'Give
her some garlic, it will make her kissing
more fragrant.'

165. *in good time!*] an expression of

indignation or ironical acquiescence
or question.

167. S.D. *Here a dance*] probably
some kind of morris dance. (On these
dances see Chambers, *Medieval Stage*,
i. 195–201, and Douce, *Illus. of Sh.*, ii.
431–82). In *Music and Letters*, July
1954, 197, J. P. Cutts suggests that the
music entitled *The Sheapheards Masque*
in Brit. Mus. Add. MS. 10,444 ff. 34b
and 85b (no. 66 on each folio) may
have been used in early productions of
Wint. This is pure conjecture but the
music is a contemporary setting for a
shepherds' dance. (See also pp. 172–4
and *Sh.Q.*, Spring 1959, 161–75.)

170. *and boasts*] a good example of
the nominative pronoun, when there
is no doubt about it, being omitted.
Cf. Abbott, §399.

171. *feeding*] feeding ground for
sheep or perhaps cattle, hence, as here,
'landed estate'. The term—or *feed*—is
still used in dialect for pasture lands.

175. *as*] in such a manner as.

Who loves another best.

Pol.   She dances featly.

Shep. So she does any thing, though I report it
That should be silent. If young Doricles   180
Do light upon her, she shall bring him that
Which he not dreams of.

Enter Servant.

Serv. O master! if you did but hear the pedlar at the
door, you would never dance again after a tabor
and pipe; no, the bagpipe could not move you: he   185
sings several tunes, faster than you'll tell money; he
utters them as he had eaten ballads, and all men's
ears grew to his tunes.

Clo. He could never come better: he shall come in. I love
a ballad but even too well, if it be doleful matter   190
merrily set down; or a very pleasant thing indeed,
and sung lamentably.

Serv. He hath songs for man or woman, of all sizes: no
milliner can so fit his customers with gloves: he has
the prettiest love-songs for maids, so without baw- 195

178. *another*] i.e. *the other*. Cf. III. iii. 20.

184–5. *tabor and pipe*] The small drum and the whistle-pipe or fife of some kind were the instruments used for morris dancing.

186. *several*] different.

tell] count.

187. *ballads*] i.e. the 16- and 17-cent. broadside ballads referred to elsewhere in this scene (see 190, 193, 197, 200, 220, 260nn.). They are described by Sir Charles Firth in *Sh.Eng.*, ii. 511–38.

188. *grew to*] 'were so closely attracted that they could not stop listening'. Cf. 606–20, and 'grew so', 607.

189. *better*] at a better moment.

190–1. *doleful . . . down*] Cf. *MND.*, I. ii. 11 and v. i. 57, 'very tragical mirth'.

193. *He hath songs*] The stationers who printed and sold ballads employed vagabonds of the Autolycus

type as agents to sell them up and down the country. Cf. 'a Ballad-seller, and hath a whole Armie of runnagates at his reuersion, that swarme euerie where in *England*, and with theyr ribauld songs infect the Youth of this flourishing Commonweale' (E. de Maisonneuve, *Gerileon of England . . . trans. . . . by A. M[undy]*, 1592, Sig. A4r).

sizes] lengths, kinds (*O.E.D.* 12, Schmidt 3).

193–327. *He hath . . . that have made*] These lines constitute p. 293 of *F.* They are very cramped as if the printer had misjudged the casting off, and contains more misprints than any other page. See p. xviii, n.2.

194. *milliner*] a dealer in goods from Milan; here = haberdasher.

195–6. *without bawdry*] The 'delicate burdens' which follow are all from indelicate songs.

dry (which is strange); with such delicate burdens
of dildoes and fadings, jump her and thump her;
and where some stretch-mouthed rascal would, as
it were, mean mischief and break a foul gap into
the matter, he makes the maid to answer 'Whoop,   200

197. dildoes] dildo's *F*.

197. *dildoes . . . thump her*] Dildoes and
fadings are words of obscure origin and
sense used here either to mean 'nonsense refrains' or else as the actual
refrains. Whatever meanings these
burdens may have they are certainly
not 'delicate'. *Dildo* is frequent in
refrains of 17-cent. ballads (e.g.
Choice Drollery, 1656, 31; *Bagford Ballads*, ii. 551, and Collier, *A book of
Roxburghe Ballads*, 1847, 249) and
Greene uses a form of the word in
*Francescos Fortune: or, The second part of
Greene's Never too late*, 1590: 'Dildido
dildido / Oh love, oh love / I feel thy
rage romble below and above' (*Works*,
Grosart, viii. 217, and *Plays and Poems*,
ed. J. C. Collins, ii. 303). *Fading* was
the name of a contemporary jig (*Kt
of Burning Pestle*, III. v. 138, 'I will have
him dance fading—Fading is a fine
jig') and there are songs with refrain
'With a Fading, Fading, Fading' (e.g.
Catch that Catch can, 1667, 78; Chappell,
Popular Music [1855] 1, 2, 34–6;
Rollins, *Pepys Ballads*, ii. 151, iii. 162;
Rimbault and Metcalfe, *Rounds,
Catches and Canons* [?1871], 28). In
Playford, *The (English) Dancing Master*, 1651, 54 (73 in Hilton's ed. 1658)
is a round 'Come jump at thy Cosen'
with refrain 'What jumping, jumping;
jumping, jumping call you this.' (See
also pp. 172–4 and *Sh.Q.*, Spring 1959,
161–75.)

199. *gap*] The sense appears to be
that in the ballad duet between man
and maid whenever the man seems to
stop in his part of the song, i.e. make a
gap, with the intention (which could
easily be made obvious) of inter-
polating a bawdy gag or action, the
balladist has skilfully arranged that

the girl shall check him by intervening
and putting him off with 'Whoop do
me no harm good man.' The ballad is
cleverly made to lead up to the probability of something bawdy which is
then just as cleverly diverted. But *gap*
is accepted by few editors. One emendation is *jape* which is unlikely and not
elsewhere used by Shakespeare and
rare in his day (*O.E.D.* 2) and is not
recorded in the phrase 'break a jape'.
The usual emendation is *jest* which
was in common use. 'To break' meant
'to speak', 'to utter' and 'to break a
jest' was not only a common expression but seems usually to have
referred to indecent jests (*Ado*, v. i.
180; *Shr.*, IV. v. 71; *Troil.*, I. iii. 148,
'Break scurril jests'; Webster, *D. of
Malfi*, I. i. 109; Jonson, *Bart. Fair*, v.
iii. 91, 'nor jeer, nor break jests'.
Rollins, *Pepys Ballads*, ii. 150, 'a foule
Iest doe break'). The expression is
even used in the 20th century, as by
J. L. Garvin in 'The dead hand'
(*Observer*, 25 Nov. 1923). Nevertheless
gap can be defended and I retain it,
strongly supported by Dr Brooks.

200–1. *Whoop . . . man*] Although no
more words of this song have been
found, there is a contemporary tune
with the name—with 'goodman' as
one word—by William Corkine in
*Ayres, to Sing and Play to the Lute and Basse
Viol*, 1610, fo. 11b. (Because no words
are given this is not included in the reprint by E. H. Fellowes [?1926].) This
version gives the tune with variations.
The tune may have been used for a
ballad called *Jockey and Jenny*, entered
in *Stationers' Register*, 9 Dec 1615 (iii.
579) (see Rollins, *Analytical Index to the
Ballad-Entries*, 1924, 112, item 1291),

do me no harm, good man;' puts him off, slights
him, with 'Whoop, do me no harm, good man.'

Pol. This is a brave fellow.

Clo. Believe me, thou talkest of an admirable conceited
fellow. Has he any unbraided wares?   205

Serv. He hath ribbons of all the colours i' th' rainbow;
points, more than all the lawyers in Bohemia can
learnedly handle, though they come to him by th'
gross; inkles, caddisses, cambrics, lawns: why, he
sings 'em over as they were gods or goddesses; you   210
would think a smock were a she-angel, he so chants
to the sleeve-hand and the work about the square
on 't.

Clo. Prithee bring him in; and let him approach singing.

Per. Forewarn him, that he use no scurrilous words in 's   215
tunes.   [*Exit Servant.*]

Clo. You have of these pedlars that have more in them
than you'd think, sister.

Per. Ay, good brother, or go about to think.

212. sleeve-hand] *F;* sleeve-band *Hanmer.*   216. S.D. *Exit Servant*] *Capell; no
S.D. in F.*

which presumably reappears as *Johnny
and Jinny* in *Westminster Drollery,* 1672.
Sir Frederick Bridge printed a version
of these words with a tune entitled
Whoop, etc. from a 17-cent. MS. (m.832
Vu 51, pp. 14–15, Henry Watson
Music Library, Manchester Public
Libraries) in *Shakespearian Music,* 1923,
22, 80. In *Sh. and Music,* 1931, E. W.
Naylor says that other ballads were
sung to the tune. The association of the
tune with the *Johnny and Jenny* ballads
is not firmly established. The words
were probably the refrain of a popular
song, perhaps of several—probably
ribald—songs. (See also pp. 172–4 and
Sh.Q., Spring 1959, 161–75.)

204. *admirable conceited*] wonderfully
ingenious.

205. *unbraided*] new, not shop-
soiled. Cf. *O.E.D.* 'braided' where an
obsolete meaning of *braided wares* is
given as 'goods that have changed
colour, tarnished, faded'

207. *points*] in the double sense of
(1) tagged laces, (2) legal points.

208–9. *by th' gross*] i.e. wholesale.

209. *inkles*] linen tapes.

caddisses] short for *caddis-ribbons,*
kinds of worsted tapes used for
garters, etc. (*O.E.D.*). Cf. *caddis-
garter* (*1H4,* II. iv. 68).

lawns] fine linens.

212. *sleeve-hand*] the wrist-band or
cuff for a sleeve (*O.E.D.* sleeve 8b).

square] a square piece of material
covering the bosom; the breast-piece
of a dress (*O.E.D.* 10a).

217. *You have of*] 'There are some of
these pedlars'. Cf. *Ham.,* III. ii. 40,
'there be of them that will themselves
laugh', *All's W.,* II. v. 45, 'I have kept
of them tame.'

219. *go about to*] intend to, wish to.
Cf. 701. A common idiom of the time.
Cf. *Mer.V.,* II. ix. 37. The modern
idiom would be 'have any intention of
thinking, have any desire to think'.

Enter AUTOLYCUS, *singing.*

Lawn as white as driven snow,   220
Cypress black as e'er was crow,
Gloves as sweet as damask roses,
Masks for faces and for noses:
Bugle-bracelet, necklace amber,
Perfume for a lady's chamber: 225
Golden quoifs and stomachers
For my lads to give their dears:

220. *Lawn as white*] The songs of Autolycus, particularly this and 'Will you buy' (316) are typical pedlars' songs. R. Wilson *The Pedler's Prophecy*, 1595 (Malone Soc. 1914), has several passages which recall these songs of Autolycus (e.g. on pp. 39–40) and the preparation for 'Get you hence' (*Wint.*, 293–7; Wilson, 980–90). D. Hoeniger points out to me the pedlars' song in Mundy, *Downfall of Robert Earl of Huntingdon*, 1601 (Tudor Fac. Texts, 1913), on F4v: 'What lacke ye? what lacke yee? What ist ye wil buy? / Any points, pins, or laces, any laces, points or pins? / Fine gloues, fine glasses, any buskes, or maskes? / Or any other prettie things? / Come cheape for loue, or buy for money. / Any cony cony skins, / For laces, points, or pins? faire maids come chuse or buy. / I haue prettie poting sticks, / And many other tricks, come chuse for loue, or buy for money', which may have been in Shakespeare's mind when he wrote *Lawn as white* and *Will you buy*. Cf. T. Newbery, *A booke . . . of the great Marchaunt . . . Dives Pragmaticus* 1563 (repr. 1910). There are references to the contents of pedlars' packs elsewhere, as on F3r, in Mundy's play, which Shakespeare may have used for *AYL. Lawn as white* was set to music by Dr John Wilson and printed in *Cheerful Ayres or Ballads*, 1660, 64–6, repr. in *Var.* 388–9 and elsewhere. Wilson (born 1585 or 1595) could have composed the tune in 1611 (Baldwin, *Organization*, 420–1) and in spite of E. M. Dent (Granville-Barker and G. B. Harrison, *Companion*

to Sh. Studies, 1934, 159) the setting may not be later than 1611. This Wilson may have been Jack Wilson the boy singer of *Sigh no more, ladies* (*Ado*, F text). There are echoes of *Lawn as white* and *Will you buy* in Gerrard's song in Fletcher, *Beggar's Bush*, III. i. 101–8 (after 1615) and in the round *Come pretty maidens* by John Jenkins, printed in John Hilton, *Catch that Catch can*, 1652, 87, repr. in Rimbault and Metcalfe, *Rounds, Catches and Canons* [?1871], 49. Noble, *Song*, 97, notes how appropriate the *F* punctuation is—it is followed here—to give Autolycus time to move about and display his wares. See also pp. 172–4, J. P. Cutts, *La Musique de Scène de la Troupe de Shakespeare*, 1959 and *Sh.Q.*, Spring 1959, 161–75, which repr. *Lawn as white* and *Come, pretty maidens* with music. For proverbial comparison with driven snow see Tilley, S591, and cf. IV. iv. 365.

221. *Cypress*] crape. Cf. Milton, *Il Penseroso*, 35, 'Sable stole of Cypress lawn'. Certain textiles were imported from Cyprus.

black as . . . crow] proverbial comparison (Tilley, C844).

222. *Gloves as sweet*] Gloves were commonly perfumed. Cf. 252 and *Ado*, III. iv. 55, and Jonson, *Alchemist*, IV. iv. 114.

sweet as . . . roses] proverbial comparison (Tilley, R178).

224. *Bugle-bracelet*] black glass beads threaded as bracelets. Cf. 'bugle eyeballs' (*AYL.*, III. v. 47, 129).

226. *quoifs*] coifs. Tight-fitting caps.

> *Pins, and poking-sticks of steel,*
> *What maids lack from head to heel :*
> *Come buy of me, come! come buy! come buy!*   230
> *Buy, lads, or else your lasses cry.*
> *Come buy!*

Clo. If I were not in love with Mopsa, thou shouldst take
no money of me; but being enthralled as I am, it
will also be the bondage of certain ribbons and   235
gloves.

Mop. I was promised them against the feast; but they
come not too late now.

Dor. He hath promised you more than that, or there be
liars.   240

Mop. He hath paid you all he promised you: may be he
has paid you more, which will shame you to give
him again.

Clo. Is there no manners left among maids? Will they
wear their plackets where they should bear their   245
faces? Is there not milking-time, when you are
going to bed, or kiln-hole, to whistle of these secrets,
but you must be tittle-tattling before all our guests?

241. may] 'may *F*.   247. kiln-hole] kill-hole *F*.

228. *poking-sticks*] or 'putting-stick'.
A metal rod which, when heated, was
used to stiffen the starched ruff. *F*
spelling is *poaking-stickes*; in Wilson
(see 220n.) it is *poting sticks*.

234–5. *it ... bondage*] 'My love means
that certain ribbons and gloves will
have to be parcelled up' (*O.E.D.*
bondage 2c).

237. *against*] in time for. The construction is still in dialect use. The
country peasant is usually, and
naturally, careful with his money.

245. *plackets*] aprons, petticoats, skirt-
pockets and, as probably here, the
private parts. *Wear* may have the
sense of *exhibit, display* (*O.E.D.* vb. 1,
7); *where* may be a compound relative
(*O.E.D.* 10b) a little similar to the use
in *Gent.*, v. iv. 44, 'When women cannot love where they're belov'd' and

bear may be a spelling of *bare* as at I. ii.
309. 'Will they expose their plackets in
the way that they should bare their
faces?'

247. *kiln-hole*] The *F* spelling is a dialect pronunciation (cf. *O.E.D.* kiln 2
and Sylvester, *Du Bartas*, ii. 2, *Babilon*,
1605, 416, 'busie Kil-men'). The fire-
hole of a kiln or the hovel near one 'is
still a noted gossiping place' (Harris's
note in Steevens ed. 1803). It was used
for various purposes including making
malt. It was big enough to hold Falstaff (*Wiv.*, IV. ii. 59—this is the only
other usage in Shakespeare and also
has the spelling *kill*).

whistle] to speak secretly, to whisper
(*O.E.D.* 10). Not used in this sense
elsewhere in Shakespeare. Hanmer
suggests *whistle off* = 'release', a hawking term. Cf. *Oth.*, III. iii. 266.

'Tis well they are whispering: clamor your tongues,
and not a word more.   250

Mop. I have done. Come, you promised me a tawdry-
lace and a pair of sweet gloves.

Clo. Have I not told thee how I was cozened by the way
and lost all my money?

Aut. And indeed, sir, there are cozeners abroad; there-   255
fore it behoves men to be wary.

Clo. Fear not thou, man, thou shalt lose nothing here.

Aut. I hope so, sir; for I have about me many parcels of
charge.

Clo. What hast here? ballads?   260

249. clamor] *See Comm.*

249. *clamor*] *O.E.D.* clamour V²2
gives only one other transitive use:
'Cease friendly cutting throtes, / Clamor
the Promulgation of your tongues, /
And yeeld' (J. Taylor, the Water-poet,
Sir Gregory Nonsense—in *Works*, 1630,
2nd sect., p. 1). The sense is 'to stop
noise, to silence'. The word may derive
from *clammering* or *clambering*, said to be
used for the jangling made when 'falling' bells—the sound which precedes
the silence of the bells: but this use is
not clearly authenticated. Whatever
the derivation it seems unlikely that
the word is connected with 'clamour'.
Other suggestions include 'Charm' or
'Charm a' your tongues' because 'to
charm your tongue' = 'to be silent'
was common speech (*Oth.*, v. ii. 186–7;
Shr., IV. ii. 58; *2H6*, IV. i. 64; Jonson,
Cynthia's Revels, I. i. 52, 'Charme your
skipping tongue, or I'le—'). To misread *h* as *l* would normally be unlikely
as the pronounced hook below the line
is characteristic of the Elizabethan *h*.
But if the ink had not marked this hook
or if it were obscured by the top of a
letter in the next line, then such a misreading would be easy. Sisson favours
'clam a' your tongues' = 'shut up',
which is certainly what the Clown
means.

251–2. *tawdry-lace*]   a   coloured
neckerchief, named from St Audrey
for Etheldreda, founder of Ely Cathe-
dral, who believed that a tumour in
the throat, from which she died, was a
judgment on her vanity in wearing
fine neckcloths in her youth. St
Audrey's fair, held on the saint's day
(17 Oct.) at Ely, was famous for bright
clothing and jewellery.

252. *sweet gloves*] Cf. 222.

258. *I hope so*] Modern usage would
require 'I hope not.' Cf. *Cym.*, II. iii.
149.

258–9. *parcels of charge*] 'items of
value'. In *Second Cony-Catching* Greene,
in speaking of 'Lifts' and their stealing tricks, uses the phrase 'parcels
of worth' on pp. 44, 46.

260. *ballads*] Cf. 187, 193, 197, 200,
220nn.; v. ii. 24. In the usurer's wife
and the maid turned fish, Shakespeare
is outdoing contemporary extravagances common in street ballads and
broadsides. The parody is brought out
by comparison with ballads in A.
Clark, *The Shirburn Ballads 1585–1616*,
1907; H. L. Collmann, *Ballads of the
Elizabethan Period . . . in Black-Letter*,
1912; J. Lilly, *A Collection of . . . Black-
Letter Ballads . . . printed . . . between . . .
1559 and 1597*, 1867; and references in
H. E. Rollins, *Analytical Index to the
Ballad-Entries, 1557–1709, in the Registers of the Company of Stationers*, 1924.
E.g. on monstrous births: Clark, 134;
Collmann, 40, 62; Lilly, 27, 63, 194,
201, 217, 243—all of deformed child-

Mop. Pray now, buy some: I love a ballad in print, a
life, for then we are sure they are true.

Aut. Here's one, to a very doleful tune, how a usurer's
wife was brought to bed of twenty money-bags at a
burden, and how she longed to eat adders' heads   265
and toads carbonadoed.

Mop. Is it true, think you?

Aut. Very true, and but a month old.

Dor. Bless me from marrying a usurer!

Aut. Here's the midwife's name to 't, one Mistress Tale-   270
porter, and five or six honest wives that were
present. Why should I carry lies abroad?

Mop. Pray you now, buy it.

Clo. Come on, lay it by: and let's first see moe ballads:
we'll buy the other things anon.   275

Aut. Here's another ballad of a fish that appeared upon
the coast on Wednesday the fourscore of April, forty
thousand fathom above water, and sung this ballad
against the hard hearts of maids: it was thought
she was a woman, and was turned into a cold   280

---

261. ballad] *F3;* ballet *F.*   270. Mistress] *F* (Mist.), *F2.*   273. Pray]
'Pray *F.*

ren: Shakespeare's 'money-bags' are
an extravagance in ridicule. Many
ballads show God's judgment on evil-
doers, many deal with monstrous fish,
etc., e.g. Collmann, 52, 63, 64; Lilly,
45, 145, 186 (Trinculo tells of the
popularity of monsters and calls Cali-
ban half fish, half monster—*Tp.*, II. ii.
26-38; III. ii. 28, and cf. *Mac.*, v. viii.
24-6) and many show retribution
falling on 'hard-hearted' girls, e.g.
Clark, 81, 120, 189, 297. Attestation
by witnesses is in Clark, 293, and
Collmann, 64. Rollins has entries
under *monstrous* and one of particular
interest, no. 2533, part of which was
noted by Malone. It reads (Arber's ed.
of *Registers*, 2 Apr. 1604): 'The most
true and strange report of A monstruous fishe that appeared in forme of
A woman from the wast vpward Seene
in the Sea' (probably a broadside)

and, 21 May 1604: 'a ballad of a
strange and monstruous fishe seene in
the sea on friday the 17 of february
1603' (i.e. 1604). Ballad-makers deal
in wonders (v. ii. 23-4) but Autolycus'
accounts are so openly extravagant—
'adders' heads and toads carbonadoed'
(265), 'fourscore of April', 'forty thousand fathom above water' (277-8)—
that the audience will be moved to
laughter both by the ridiculous extravagances themselves and by the ridiculous credulity of the peasants.

261-2. *a life*] on my life. More properly *o' life*, but *a* for *on* is frequent in
Shakespeare (Schmidt, *a, 3b*).

266. *carbonadoed*] cut and scored
across for broiling.

272. *Why . . . abroad?*] This typical
cheap-jack talk may still be heard.

274. *moe*] more. Cf. I. ii. 8.

276-8. *fish . . . water*] See 260n.

fish for she would not exchange flesh with one that
loved her. The ballad is very pitiful, and as true.
Dor. Is it true too, think you?
Aut. Five justices' hands at it, and witnesses more than
my pack will hold.   285
Clo. Lay it by too: another.
Aut. This is a merry ballad, but a very pretty one.
Mop. Let's have some merry ones.
Aut. Why, this is a passing merry one and goes to the
tune of 'Two maids wooing a man:' there's scarce a   290
maid westward but she sings it; 'tis in request, I can
tell you.
Mop. We can both sing it: if thou'lt bear a part, thou
shalt hear; 'tis in three parts.
Dor. We had the tune on 't a month ago.   295
Aut. I can bear my part; you must know 'tis my occupa-
tion: have at it with you:

Song.

Aut.   *Get you hence, for I must go*

297. S.D. Song] *F4*; F (*before* Get l. 298).   298. Aut.] *Rowe (1)*; Song. F.

290. *Two maids . . . man*] No tune or
ballad with this title has been traced
or anything to connect these words
with the music for *Get you hence* which
is mentioned in IV. iv. 298n. The note
in *N.C.Wint.*, p. 173, is apparently incorrect for A. T. Roffe, *Handbook of
Sh. Music*, 1878, 104, merely says that
'Of this trio . . . I know of no setting
but that . . . attributed to Dr. Boyce.'
Roffe does not mention any setting
entitled 'Two maids wooing a man'.
It must be concluded either that a
ballad of this title did exist but is lost—
at any rate under that title; or else that
Autolycus merely invented a plausible
title for the tune of *Get you hence*—a
simple invention for such a master of
persuasive talk. The title fits the words
and may be the name of the special
tune particularly associated with this
ballad. If both were a recent hit the
girls may have picked up the tune a
month ago although they had not

learned the words. There was always
a demand for new ballads. Cf. Jonson,
Bart. Fair, Ind. 127; II. ii. 41.

293.] Mopsa and Dorcas as well as
the Clown and Autolycus can read and
sing in part-songs but the text does not
justify the assumption that they could
sight-read music. It would be surprising if they could.

298. *Get you hence*] Three-part songs
are referred to in 'three-man song-
men' (IV. iii. 42). Two early versions of
'Get you hence' with music for one are
published by J. P. Cutts (*Sh.Sur.*, ix,
1956, 86–9 and Plate v and in *La
Musique de Scène de la Troupe de Shakespeare*, 1959). They are also in *Sh.Q.*,
Spring 1959, 161–75. They are from
MSS. in the Drexel collection in the
New York Public Library and one
of them contains additional verses,
printed on p. 174 below. When the
Clown says 'We'll have this song out
anon by ourselves' (IV. iv. 310) he may

> *Where it fits not you to know.*
>   D. *Whither?* M. *O whither?* D. *Whither?*   300

M.   *It becomes thy oath full well,*
    Thou to me thy secrets tell:
        D. *Me too: let me go thither.*

M.   *Or thou goest to th' grange or mill:*
D.   *If to either, thou dost ill.*   305
        A. *Neither.* D. *What neither?* A. *Neither.*

D.   *Thou hast sworn my love to be;*
M.   *Thou hast sworn it more to me:*
    Then whither goest? say whither?

Clo. We'll have this song out anon by ourselves: my   310
father and the gentlemen are in sad talk, and we'll
not trouble them. Come, bring away thy pack after
me. Wenches, I'll buy for you both. Pedlar, let's
have the first choice. Follow me, girls.

            [*Exit with Dorcas and Mopsa.*]

Aut. And you shall pay well for 'em.   315

Song.

> *Will you buy any tape,*
> *Or lace for your cape,*
> *My dainty duck, my dear-a?*
> *Any silk, any thread,*
> *Any toys for your head,*   320

299.] *As Rowe (1); Aut. Where F.*   300.] *As Capell; Dor. Whether? | Mop O whether? | Dor. Whether? | F.*   306.] *As Capell; Aut: Neither. | Dor: What neither? | Aut: Neither: | F.*   311. gentlemen] *F (Gent.); Rowe (1)* (Gentlemen). 314. S.D. *Exit . . . Mopsa*] *Rowe (1); no S.D. in F.*   316–17. *Will . . . cape,*] *One line in F.*   319–20. *Any . . . head,*] *One line in F.*

imply that there is more of it and Shakespeare may therefore be using a popular song and the audience would know that there were other verses. But lyrics and stage songs were often expanded in broadsheets in the 17th century (e.g. lyrics of Lovelace and Oldham and songs from Etherege's *She wou'd if she cou'd* and Lee's *Theodosius*) and these extra verses may be post-1611 expansions. In *F* the singers' names are printed Aut., Dor., Mop.

in roman, to distinguish them from the italic of the song.

311. *sad*] serious.

316. *Will . . . tape*] See p. 173 and *Sh.Q.*, Spring 1959, 161–75. No other version or record has been traced but one echo of the song is given in the note above on *Lawn as white* (220). The earliest known setting is that by William Boyce, written about 1769 and printed by Linley.

320. *toys*] trifles, trifling ornaments.

> *Of the new'st, and fin'st, fin'st wear-a?*
> *Come to the pedlar;*
> *Money's a meddler,*
> *That doth utter all men's ware-a.*   *Exit.*

[*Enter Servant.*]

Ser. Master, there is three carters, three shepherds,   325
three neat-herds, three swine-herds, that have
made themselves all men of hair, they call themselves Saltiers, and they have a dance which the
wenches say is a gallimaufry of gambols, because
they are not in 't: but they themselves are o' the   330
mind (if it be not too rough for some that know little
but bowling) it will please plentifully.

Shep. Away! we'll none on 't: here has been too much
homely foolery already. I know, sir, we weary you.

Pol. You weary those that refresh us: pray, let's see these   335
four threes of herdsmen.

Serv. One three of them, by their own report, sir, hath
danced before the king; and not the worst of the

---

321. *new'st . . . fin'st, fin'st*] F2; *news't . . . fins't, fins't* F.   322-3. *Come . . . meddler*]
One line in F.   324. S.D. *Enter Servant*] *Rowe (1); no S.D. in F.*

323-4. *Money's . . . ware-a*] 'Money
comes into everything and is the
power which sells all men's goods.'

325. *carters*] Theobald suggested
goatherds as an emendation in view of
336.

326. *neat-herds*] cowherds.

327-8. *men . . . Saltiers*] They were
probably dressed in skins to resemble
satyrs, indeed they may have been
adorned as were the satyrs in Jonson's
Oberon. Shakespeare probably intended *Saltiers* to suggest the dancers' two
chief attributes—they are clad as
satyrs and they are skilled *jumpers*
(339): the word *sault, salt = jump* was
in current use (*O.E.D.* sault, *sb.*²). In
Oberon the satyrs have 'tawnie wrists'
and 'shaggie thighs', they run 'leaping,
and making antique action', they perform 'an antique dance, full of gesture
and swift motion' and they 'leape, and

expresse their ioy' (Jonson, ed. Herford and Simpson, vii, 1941, *Oberon* 30,
109, 122, 282-3, 315). Cf. illus. in the
Johnson–Steevens ed. of Shakespeare,
1803, ix. 359.

329. *gallimaufry*] jumble, medley.

331-2. *if it . . . bowling*] 'if it is not too
rough for those who don't go beyond a
gentle game of bowls'. Although bowls,
then as now, could be played by the
most active of men, e.g. by Drake, it
could never have been classed with the
rough and vigorous games; and the
reference therefore makes a contrast
with the boisterous dance. Cf. 'a foolish
mild man; an honest man . . . and soon
dashed . . . and a very good bowler'
(*LLL.*, v. ii. 577). Furnivall notes that
'An honest man and a good bowler' occurs in J. Clarke, *Paroemiologia*, 1639.

338. *danced . . . king*] See p. xxii and
ll. 327-8, 343nn.

three but jumps twelve foot and a half by th'
   square.   340
Shep. Leave your prating: since these good men are
   pleased, let them come in; but quickly now.
Serv. Why, they stay at door, sir.

Here a dance of twelve Satyrs.

Pol. O, father, you'll know more of that hereafter.
   [*To Cam.*] Is it not too far gone? 'Tis time to part them.
   He's simple and tells much. [*To Flor.*] How now, fair
      shepherd!   346
   Your heart is full of something that does take
   Your mind from feasting. Sooth, when I was young
   And handed love, as you do, I was wont
   To load my she with knacks: I would have ransack'd
   The pedlar's silken treasury, and have pour'd it   351

---

340. square] squire *F.*   345. S.D. *To Cam.*] *Cambridge; no S.D. in F.*   346. S.D.
To Flor.] *N.C. Wint.; no S.D. in F.*

---

340. *square*] *squire, squier* was a common contemporary spelling of *square*.
An implement for testing the exact-
ness of an artificer's work, usually in
carpentry or joinery. A ruler of some
kind, particularly one made to measure a right angle or, when hinged, to
measure any angle (*O.E.D.* I.I). But
the phrase 'by the square' meant 'with
accuracy' or 'precisely' (*O.E.D.* I.I.b).
Cf. *LLL.*, v. ii. 474; *1H4*, II. ii. 13. In
Jonson's *Masque of Oberon* the dancing
was characterized by 'many leaps' (see
327-8n. and Devonshire MS. account
of the masque, quoted in Herford and
Simpson's Jonson, x, 1950, 522).

341. *Leave*] cease, leave off. Cf.
H8, III. i. 2, 'Leave working'.

343. *at door*] This is found at least
ten times in Shakespeare (Bartlett—
door) but normal usage is *at the door*
(e.g. *Err.*, III. i. 61, 69).

Here a dance] In *Music and Letters*,
Jan. 1922, 49-58, W. J. Lawrence
showed that the music in Brit. Mus.
Add. MS. 10,444 on ff. 31a and 82b
(No. 56 on each folio) may have been
that which was used in Jonson's

Masque of Oberon on 1 Jan. 1611. If so,
it might also have been used for the
satyrs' dance in early performances of
Wint. Cf. 327-8, 340nn., and p. xxii. In
Music and Letters, July 1954, 185-200,
and April 1955, 110-25, J. P. Cutts
shows that the music was by Robert
Johnson. (See pp. 172-4 and *Sh.Q.*,
Spring 1959, 161-75. The music is
also printed in A. J. Sabol, *Songs and
Dances for the Stuart Masque*, 1959, 130-
3). The dance was probably a brawl
or branle (see W. Sorell in *Sh.Q.*, Summer 1957, 380-1).

344. *O, father . . . hereafter*] 'seems to
be in reply to some unexpressed question from the old Shepherd' (*Var.*). He
and the king were in serious talk at
311. We must assume that they re-
sumed their talk during the satyrs'
dance. The king intended to get as
much information from the Shepherd
as he could (IV. ii. 49-51) and now
succeeds (344).

349. *handed*] handled, was engaged
in. Cf. II. iii. 63.

350. *she*] Cf. I. ii. 43-4n.

knacks] knick-knacks, trifles (358).

To her acceptance: you have let him go,
And nothing marted with him. If your lass
Interpretation should abuse, and call this
Your lack of love or bounty, you were straited   355
For a reply, at least if you make a care
Of happy holding her.

Flo.   Old sir, I know
She prizes not such trifles as these are:
The gifts she looks from me are pack'd and lock'd
Up in my heart, which I have given already,   360
But not deliver'd. O hear me breathe my life
Before this ancient sir, who, it should seem,
Hath sometime lov'd. I take thy hand, this hand,
As soft as dove's down and as white as it,
Or Ethiopian's tooth, or the fann'd snow that's bolted
By th' northern blasts twice o'er.

Pol.   What follows this? 366
How prettily the young swain seems to wash
The hand was fair before! I have put you out:
But to your protestation: let me hear
What you profess.

Flo.   Do, and be witness to 't.   370

362. who] *F2;* whom *F.*   368. hand was] hand, was *F.*

353. *nothing marted*] 'done no business', i.e. bought nothing from him.

354. *Interpretation . . . abuse*] 'should misinterpret'.

355–7. *you were . . . holding her*] 'you would be hard put to it for an answer, at least if you are concerned to keep her happy'.

359. *looks*] expects. Cf. *H8,* v. i. 117, 'I look'd / You would have given me.'

361. *breathe . . . life*] 'make vows of lifelong love'. This is addressed to Perdita. The *sir* of 357, 362 is Polixenes.

363–6. *this hand . . . twice o'er*] There are many parallels to this hyperbole. In some of the romantic passages in the last plays Shakespeare's mind seems to recollect images from the earlier romantic comedies and poems. E.g. *MND.,* III. ii. 141–3: 'That pure congealed white, high Taurus' snow, / Fann'd with the eastern wind, turns to a crow / When thou hold'st up thy hand' and 'teeth as white as whalësbone' (*LLL.,* v. ii. 332); 'Juno but an Ethiope were' (*LLL.,* IV. iii. 114); 'The dove of Paphos might with the crow / Vie feathers white' (*Per.,* IV. *Gower,* 32); 'beauty, in that white . . . / From Venus' doves doth challenge' (*Lucr.,* 57); 'white as chaste, and pure / As wind-fann'd snow' (*Two Noble Kinsmen,* v. i. 140). Cf. 220.

365. *Ethiopian*] at this time used in a general sense for *negro.*

bolted] sifted.

368. *was*] i.e. which was. Cf. Abbott, §244. The comma in *F* before *was* may be a misplaced apostrophe denoting an omission.

Pol. And this my neighbour too?

Flo.   And he, and more
Than he, and men, the earth, the heavens, and all;
That were I crown'd the most imperial monarch
Thereof most worthy, were I the fairest youth
That ever made eye swerve, had force and knowledge
More than was ever man's, I would not prize them   376
Without her love; for her, employ them all;
Commend them and condemn them to her service,
Or to their own perdition.

Pol.   Fairly offer'd.

Cam. This shows a sound affection.

Shep.   But my daughter,   380
Say you the like to him?

Per.   I cannot speak
So well, nothing so well; no, nor mean better:
By th' pattern of mine own thoughts I cut out
The purity of his.

Shep.   Take hands, a bargain!
And, friends unknown, you shall bear witness to 't.   385
I give my daughter to him, and will make
Her portion equal his.

Flo.   O, that must be
I' th' virtue of your daughter: one being dead,
I shall have more than you can dream of yet;
Enough then for your wonder. But come on,   390
Contract us 'fore these witnesses.

Shep.   Come, your hand;
And, daughter, yours.

Pol.   Soft, swain, awhile, beseech you;
Have you a father?

Flo.   I have: but what of him?

Pol. Knows he of this?

392. awhile] a-while *F.*

378–9. *Commend . . . perdition*] another example of the 'retrospective construction' noted at III. ii. 163–5. 'Commend all the good qualities to her service or condemn them to their own perdition.'

383–4. *By th' pattern . . . his*] She thinks that he must feel towards her as she does towards him. It is a woman's domestic metaphor.

389. *yet*] so far, as at present (*O.E.D.* 3).

Flo.   He neither does nor shall.
Pol. Methinks a father   395
    Is at the nuptial of his son a guest
    That best becomes the table. Pray you once more,
    Is not your father grown incapable
    Of reasonable affairs? is he not stupid
    With age and alt'ring rheums? can he speak? hear?
    Know man from man? dispute his own estate?   401
    Lies he not bed-rid? and again does nothing
    But what he did being childish?
Flo.   No, good sir;
    He has his health, and ampler strength indeed
    Than most have of his age.
Pol.   By my white beard,   405
    You offer him, if this be so, a wrong
    Something unfilial: reason my son
    Should choose himself a wife, but as good reason
    The father (all whose joy is nothing else
    But fair posterity) should hold some counsel   410
    In such a business.
Flo.   I yield all this;
    But for some other reasons, my grave sir,
    Which 'tis not fit you know, I not acquaint
    My father of this business.
Pol.   Let him know 't.
Flo. He shall not.
Pol.   Prithee, let him.
Flo.   No, he must not.   415
Shep. Let him, my son: he shall not need to grieve
    At knowing of thy choice.
Flo.   Come, come, he must not.
    Mark our contract.

---

400. *alt'ring rheums*] catarrhal de-
fluxions which change the state of
health for the worse—which act as
injurious 'alteratives'. Cf. French
altérer, and *alters* (576, 574-8n.).

406–7. *a wrong . . . unfilial*] Cf. *Tp.*,
v. i. 191: *Ferdinand* emphasizes that he
chose *Miranda* when 'I could not ask
my father for his advice.'

407. *reason my son*] 'there is reason

that my son'. This ellipsis seems common with *reason*. Cf. *John*, v. ii. 130,
and *Wiv.*, ii. ii. 13. *N.C.Wint.* records
an anon. conjecture of *the* for *my*.

413. *I not acquaint*] This is common
usage. Either an omission of *do*
(Abbott, §305) or transposition of
negative and verb.

418. *contract*] This would have been
a betrothal contract which was held to

Pol.   Mark your divorce, young sir,
                                        [*Discovering himself*]
      Whom son I dare not call; thou art too base
      To be acknowledg'd: thou a sceptre's heir,   420
      That thus affects a sheep-hook! Thou, old traitor,
      I am sorry that by hanging thee I can
      But shorten thy life one week. And thou, fresh piece
      Of excellent witchcraft, who, of force, must know
      The royal fool thou cop'st with,—
Shep.   O, my heart!   425
Pol. I'll have thy beauty scratch'd with briers and made
      More homely than thy state. For thee, fond boy,
      If I may ever know thou dost but sigh
      That thou no more shalt see this knack (as never
      I mean thou shalt), we'll bar thee from succession;   430
      Not hold thee of our blood, no, not our kin,
      Farre than Deucalion off: mark thou my words!

418. S.D. *Discovering himself*] *Rowe* (*1*); *no S.D. in F.*   420. acknowledg'd] *F2;*
acknowledge *F.*   424. who] *F2;* whom *F.*   429. shalt see] *Rowe* (*1*); shalt
neuer see *F.*

be morally and even legally as binding
as marriage although not recognized
by the Church. Cf. I. ii. 278n.; IV. iv.
391; V. i. 203 (where the 'contract'
needed only to be 'celebrated'); v. iii.
5, 151; and *Pandosto*, p. 212, l. 16.

421. *affects*] for *affect'st*. But the *F*
spelling is a not uncommon form of the
2nd pers. sing.; cf. *Ant.*, I. iii. 70,
'Has affection for'. Cf. *Tw. N.*, II.
v. 22.

423–4. *fresh . . . witchcraft*] 'young
girl excelling in witchcraft' contains
the common charge that witchcraft
has been used to obtain someone's love
(cf. *MND.*, I. i. 27; *Oth.*, I. iii. 61–4;
Per., II. v. 49; *Pandosto*, p. 223, l. 26).
For *fresh* meaning youthful cf. I. i. 39;
IV. iv. 552. *Piece* could mean a man or
woman and was not at this time normally used in a derogatory sense of a
girl (*O.E.D.* piece *sb.* 9a, b). It is 'a
favourite word for the heroines of the
last plays' (*H8*, Foakes, 1957, v. iv.
26n.). Cf. IV. iv. 32; v. i. 94; v. iii. 38;

Cym., v. iv. 140; v. v. 444; *Per.*, IV. ii.
43, 141; IV. vi. 110.

424. *of force*] 'must of course'.

425. *cop'st with*] 'hast to do with'.

427. *More homely . . . state*] 'more un-
attractive even than the lowliness of
your station'. 'Homely' meaning
'plain' is still used in this sense in the
west of England and in the U.S.A.

429. *knack*] trifle, thing of little
worth (cf. 350).

432. *Farre*] The comparative of *far*;
in M.E. *ferre* (Chaucer, *Prol.*, 47).
Other possible uses are at I. ii. 109,
218, and v. iii. 141. But *farre* is also the
normal spelling of *far* in *F* even where
the positive is certainly intended, e.g.
III. iii. 11; IV. ii. 36; IV. iv. 344, 841;
v. iii. 69, 74: *arre* is a normal spelling
for the *ar* sound (*star* is *starre* at I. ii. 1,
bar is *barre* at IV. iv. 430, *mar* is *marre* at
IV. iv. 480; v. iii. 82). Deucalion is the
classical equivalent of Noah and so
Polixenes is saying, extravagantly,
that he would utterly disclaim his son.

Follow us to the court. Thou churl, for this time,
Though full of our displeasure, yet we free thee
From the dead blow of it. And you, enchantment,—
Worthy enough a herdsman; yea, him too,　　　436
That makes himself, but for our honour therein,
Unworthy thee. If ever henceforth thou
These rural latches to his entrance open,
Or hoop his body more with thy embraces,　　　440
I will devise a death as cruel for thee
As thou art tender to 't.　　　　　　　　*Exit.*

Per.　　　　　　　　　Even here, undone,
I was not much afeard; for once or twice
I was about to speak, and tell him plainly,
The selfsame sun that shines upon his court　　　445
Hides not his visage from our cottage, but
Looks on alike. Will't please you, sir, be gone?
I told you what would come of this: beseech you,
Of your own state take care: this dream of mine—
Being now awake, I'll queen it no inch farther,　　　450
But milk my ewes, and weep.

Cam.　　　　　　　　　Why, how now, father!

---

440. hoop] *Pope;* hope *F.*

433. *Thou churl*] the Shepherd.

435. *dead*] mortal. Cf. 'So should a murderer look—so dead, so grim' (*MND.*, III. ii. 57); 'at this dead hour' (*Ham.*, I. i. 65). 'Dead' may also here have something of the sense of 'unmitigated', 'unrelieved' (*O.E.D.* VI).　　　*blow*] Cf. *Meas.*, II. ii. 30.

enchantment] Cf. 'fresh piece / Of excellent witchcraft', 423–4n. Polixenes is addressing Perdita, and the word is obviously used in both a bad sense (witch—its primary meaning in 1611) and a good sense (in appreciation of her beauty).

436–8. *yea, him . . . thee*] 'Yes, worthy (were not my royal rank and honour concerned) even of him who has lowered himself until he is not your superior but your inferior.'

445–7. *sun . . . alike*] That the sun shines upon all alike is proverbial

(Tilley, S985) and scriptural: 'The sunne that shineth, looketh vpon all things' (*Eccles.*, xlii. 16, Geneva version); 'he maketh his sun to rise on the evil and on the good' (*Matt.*, v. 45 *A.V.*); 'upon whom doth not his light arise?' (*Job*, xxv. 3, *A.V.*). Perhaps *all* or *'s* or both have dropped out after *on*. The omission of *all* would be by haplography. But the metre is against an omission and *alike* may have the sense of 'without distinction'.

449. *state*] perhaps with the double sense of 'condition' and 'royal dignity'.

450. *I'll queen it*] perhaps in the double sense of 'I'll give up any thoughts I had of ever being a queen' and 'I'll cease from being queen of this feast'. She probably removes her garlands (see IV. iv. 1n.).

451. *weep*] See IV. iv. 13n.

         Speak ere thou diest.
Shep.   I cannot speak, nor think,
      Nor dare to know that which I know. O sir!
      You have undone a man of fourscore three,
      That thought to fill his grave in quiet; yea,   455
      To die upon the bed my father died,
      To lie close by his honest bones: but now
      Some hangman must put on my shroud and lay me
      Where no priest shovels in dust. O cursed wretch,
      That knew'st this was the prince, and wouldst
         adventure   460
      To mingle faith with him! Undone! undone!
      If I might die within this hour, I have liv'd
      To die when I desire.   *Exit.*
Flo.   Why look you so upon me?
      I am but sorry, not afeard; delay'd,
      But nothing alter'd: what I was, I am;   465
      More straining on for plucking back; not following
      My leash unwillingly.
Cam.   Gracious my lord,

---

452. *Speak . . . diest*] apparently a
reminder of the sentence at 422
although this had been revoked at
434. It seems that neither Camillo nor
the Shepherd had appreciated the
reprieve.

453. *dare . . . I know*] Cf. i. ii. 376–80.
This is dramatic comparison between
the bearing of Polixenes and that of
Leontes when he also considered himself outraged. Polixenes also threatens,
but withdraws his threats. If Shakespeare had the parallel in mind,
Camillo's words at i. ii. 376 might also
have recurred to him.

459. *no priest . . . dust*] i.e. he would
be buried under the gallows with no
funeral service. *Var.* notes that in the
Catholic pre-Reformation service the
priest put earth on the body and that
it was enjoined that this should be
done by the priest also in the Protestant Liturgy of Edward VI, 1548,
but that the Review of this liturgy of

1552 (and the modern service) orders
that the earth be cast 'by some standing by'. Some priests may have continued to do this office, but attenders
at a funeral would not clearly remember who had done it. The Shepherd is
merely lamenting that he will not have
a decent Christian burial, which was
and is one of the strongest desires
and anxieties of the aged poor. Cf.
452n.

462–3. *If I . . . desire*] 'If I could die
now I should have lived as long as I
wish to live.' Cf. *Mac.*, ii. iii. 89–90.

465. *nothing alter'd*] Both his love and
his purpose are constant. He is resolute. Perdita here is not resolute in
purpose although in 577–8 she reso-
lutely denies that affliction can con-
quer the soul.

466–7. *More . . . unwillingly*] 'more
than ever eager (to wed Perdita) because of this setback and not at all
being dragged on unwillingly'.

You know your father's temper: at this time
He will allow no speech (which, I do guess,
You do not purpose to him) and as hardly   470
Will he endure your sight as yet, I fear:
Then, till the fury of his highness settle,
Come not before him.

Flo.   I not purpose it.
I think—Camillo?

Cam.   Even he, my lord.

Per. How often have I told you 'twould be thus!   475
How often said, my dignity would last
But till 'twere known!

Flo.   It cannot fail, but by
The violation of my faith; and then
Let nature crush the sides o' th' earth together,
And mar the seeds within! Lift up thy looks: 480
From my succession wipe me, father; I
Am heir to my affection.

Cam.   Be advis'd.

Flo. I am: and by my fancy. If my reason
Will thereto be obedient, I have reason;
If not, my senses, better pleas'd with madness,   485

468. your] *F2;* my *F.*   469. guess] ghesse *F.*   474. I think—Camillo?] I
think *Camillo. F.*

468. *your*] The *my* of *F* was probably
caught from the line above.

474. *I think—Camillo?*] Presumably
Florizel now recognizes Camillo who
removes his disguise.

479–80. *Let nature . . . within*] The
'seeds' are the sources of all life. To
crush the earth and destroy the seeds
would be to destroy all present life and
all possibility of future life on earth.
Cf. the cosmic image at II. i. 102 asserting Leontes' certainty—which was
illusion. This one asserts Florizel's
faith—which is unshakeable. Noble,
Biblical Knowledge, 27, 28, 68, 69, 248,
cites *Jer.*, vi. 22: 'a great nation shall
arise from the sides of the earth', and
believes that if Shakespeare was influenced by the Bible here it was by

the Genevan version. Cf. 'his seed
shall become a multitude of nations'
(*Gen.*, xlix. 19, *R.V.*). For similar use
of the images cf. 'the seeds of time',
'though the treasure / Of nature's
germens tumble all together / Even
till destruction sicken' (*Mac.*, I. iii.
58, IV. i. 58–60); 'Crack nature's
moulds, all germens spill at once' (*Lr.*,
III. ii. 8); 'The sides o' th' world may
danger' (*Ant.*, I. ii. 186); 'stretch / The
sides o' th' world' (*Cym.*, III. i. 48–9).

483–6. *I am . . . welcome*] 'I am
(advised) and by my love. If my reason
will agree with my love then I shall
keep sane. But if it will not, my senses
will prefer and welcome madness.'
'Fancy' is a fascinating word which
here seems to mean true love.

     Do bid it welcome.

Cam.   This is desperate, sir.

Flo. So call it: but it does fulfil my vow;
     I needs must think it honesty. Camillo,
     Not for Bohemia, nor the pomp that may
     Be thereat glean'd: for all the sun sees, or   490
     The close earth wombs, or the profound seas hides
     In unknown fathoms, will I break my oath
     To this my fair belov'd. Therefore, I pray you,
     As you have ever been my father's honour'd friend,
     When he shall miss me,—as, in faith, I mean not   495
     To see him any more,—cast your good counsels
     Upon his passion: let myself and fortune
     Tug for the time to come. This you may know,
     And so deliver, I am put to sea
     With her whom here I cannot hold on shore;   500
     And most opportune to our need, I have
     A vessel rides fast by, but not prepar'd
     For this design. What course I mean to hold
     Shall nothing benefit your knowledge, nor
     Concern me the reporting.

Cam.   O my lord,   505
     I would your spirit were easier for advice,
     Or stronger for your need.

Flo.   Hark, Perdita. [*Drawing her aside*]
     [*To Cam.*] I'll hear you by and by.

Cam.   He's irremoveable,
     Resolv'd for flight. Now were I happy, if
     His going I could frame to serve my turn,   510

---

491. hides] *F*; hide *F2*.   494. honour'd] *F*; *F2* omits.   500. whom] *F2*; who *F*.
501. our] *Theobald*; her *F*.   507. S.D. *Drawing her aside*] *Capell*; no S.D. in *F*.
508. S.D. *To Cam.*] *Theobald*; no S.D. in *F*.

491. *hides*] *Seas* may be treated as a collective, parallel with *earth* or else *hides* is used as an old form of the 3rd person plural.

497–8. *let . . . come*] 'As for the future let me fight it out with whatever chance may have in store.' The spirit is a little reminiscent of Autolycus (iv. iii. 30) and cf. *Mac.*, iii. i. 112.

501. *opportune*] pron. *oppórtune*.
our] If *her* is a mistake it was perhaps caught from l. 500 or arose from mishearing.

504–5. *Shall nothing . . . reporting*] 'is not for you to know or me to tell'.

506. *easier for*] more open to.

508. *by and by*] immediately (*O.E.D.* 3).

Save him from danger, do him love and honour,
Purchase the sight again of dear Sicilia
And that unhappy king, my master, whom
I so much thirst to see.

Flo.   Now good Camillo;
I am so fraught with curious business that   515
I leave out ceremony.

Cam.   Sir, I think
You have heard of my poor services, i' th' love
That I have borne your father?

Flo.   Very nobly
Have you deserv'd: it is my father's music
To speak your deeds, not little of his care   520
To have them recompens'd as thought on.

Cam.   Well, my lord,
If you may please to think I love the king,
And through him what's nearest to him, which is
Your gracious self, embrace but my direction,
If your more ponderous and settled project   525
May suffer alteration. On mine honour,
I'll point you where you shall have such receiving
As shall become your highness; where you may
Enjoy your mistress; from the whom, I see,
There's no disjunction to be made, but by—   530
As heavens forefend!—your ruin. Marry her,
And with my best endeavours in your absence
Your discontenting father strive to qualify

---

515. *curious*] requiring care, anxious.

521. *as thought on*] 'as fully as they are appreciated' or possibly 'as soon as they are thought of'.

525–6. *If your . . . alteration*] Bethell points out that this is courtier's language. Camillo knows well that Florizel has no plan. It is also a delicate emphasis of the characters of the skilled, tactful Camillo and the headstrong Florizel who needs to be handled in this way. In 'more ponderous' Camillo is tactfully and deferentially referring to Florizel's 'project' as being weightier and of greater importance than his own 'direction'.

532–4. *And with . . . liking*] 'and I will do my best in your absence to pacify your angry father and bring him round to approve of your action'.

533. *discontenting*] discontented, displeased, angry. For this use of the participle ending see Abbott, §372, and cf. 'from his all-obeying breath' (*Ant.*, III. xiii. 77), i.e. 'obeyed by all'; and 'his unrecalling crime' (*Lucr.*, 993), i.e. 'unrecalled crime'. Contrast 'grim-look'd' i.e. 'grim-looking' (*MND.*, v. i. 168).

qualify] pacify, appease. (See Onions for varied meanings.)

And bring him up to liking.

Flo.   How, Camillo,
May this, almost a miracle, be done?   535
That I may call thee something more than man
And after that trust to thee.

Cam.   Have you thought on
A place whereto you'll go?

Flo.   Not any yet:
But as th' unthought-on accident is guilty
To what we wildly do, so we profess   540
Ourselves to be the slaves of chance, and flies
Of every wind that blows.

Cam.   Then list to me:
This follows, if you will not change your purpose,
But undergo this flight; make for Sicilia,
And there present yourself and your fair princess   545
(For so I see she must be) 'fore Leontes:
She shall be habited as it becomes
The partner of your bed. Methinks I see
Leontes opening his free arms and weeping
His welcomes forth; asks thee there 'Son, forgiveness!'
As 'twere i' th' father's person; kisses the hands   551
Of your fresh princess; o'er and o'er divides him
'Twixt his unkindness and his kindness; th' one
He chides to hell, and bids the other grow

550. there 'Son, forgiveness!'] *Alexander;* there Sonne forgiuenesse, *F;* the Son forgiveness *F3.*

537. *after that*] in accordance with your superhuman quality.

539–40. *But as . . . wildly do*] 'Since the unexpected misfortune [of the king's discovery of our love for each other] is to blame for what we must now do at haphazard'.

540. *wildly*] without plan, at haphazard. Cf. v. i. 128; *wild,* II. i. 182, and 'a wild exposture to each chance' (*Cor.,* IV. i. 36). Cf. 566–9n.

549. *free*] generous, liberal.

550. *thee . . . forgiveness!*] Retention of 'there' suggests the visualizing of the scene (cf. Malvolio's 'Toby approaches; curtsies there to me', *Tw.N.,* II. v. 58), and 'Son', impossible from Ca-

millo addressing Florizel, is not out of place from Leontes. But most edd. emend to 'thee, the son, forgiveness'. This would effect a balance of 'the son . . . As 'twere i' the father's person', but is by no means an inevitable emendation.

552. *fresh*] young, lovely. Cf. 423n.

552–3. *o'er . . . kindness*] 'repeatedly alternates in his speaking of his former evil behaviour (to your father) and of his present affection (for him and for you)'. His talk is divided ('divides him') between the two subjects.

554. *chides*] consigns with sorrow and anger.

Faster than thought or time.

Flo.   Worthy Camillo,   555
    What colour for my visitation shall I
    Hold up before him?

Cam.   Sent by the king your father
    To greet him and to give him comforts. Sir,
    The manner of your bearing towards him, with
    What you (as from your father) shall deliver,   560
    Things known betwixt us three, I'll write you down:
    The which shall point you forth at every sitting
    What you must say; that he shall not perceive
    But that you have your father's bosom there
    And speak his very heart.

Flo.   I am bound to you: 565
    There is some sap in this.

Cam.   A course more promising
    Than a wild dedication of yourselves
    To unpath'd waters, undream'd shores; most certain
    To miseries enough: no hope to help you,
    But as you shake off one, to take another: 570
    Nothing so certain as your anchors, who
    Do their best office if they can but stay you
    Where you'll be loath to be. Besides, you know
    Prosperity's the very bond of love,

---

555. *Faster than thought*] proverbial
(Tilley, T240).

556. *colour*] reason, pretext. Cf.
Ant., I. iii. 32; *2H6*, III. i. 236; *H8*, I. i.
178.

558. *comforts*] reassurances of friendship.

562–3. *point . . . say*] 'indicate to you
what you are to say at every audience
(or meeting)'.

564. *bosom*] personal confidence.

566–8. *A course . . . shores*] J. C. Maxwell points out to me that this echoes
'determine on some course / More
than a wild exposture to each chance /
That starts i' th' way before thee' (*Cor.*,
IV. i. 35–7). Cf. 540, *wildly*.

571–3. *Nothing . . . to be*] 'Far from
being as satisfactory to trust to, even as
anchors (for example) which are doing

well if they can simply hold you in a
position you'll be sorry to be in [but
prefer, rather than actually to be
driven on to the rocks].' 'Nothing' has
the Elizabethan adverbial sense of 'By
no means', 'In no way' rather as
'Something' is used in the modern
sense of 'Somewhat', 'to some extent'.
'Your' has the Elizabethan sense of
'these [anchors] so well known to us
all' or '[anchors] for example'. Cf. 'As
your pearl in your foul oyster' (*AYL.*,
v. iv. 59).

574.] That prosperity gets friends is
proverbial (Tilley, P611).

574–8. *Prosperity's . . . mind*] This
echoes the main sentiment and some
of the images of *Sonn.* cxvi, particularly 'though rosy lips and cheeks /
Within his bending sickle's compass

Whose fresh complexion and whose heart together   575
Affliction alters.

Per.   One of these is true:
I think affliction may subdue the cheek,
But not take in the mind.

Cam.   Yea? say you so?
There shall not, at your father's house, these seven years
Be born another such.

Flo.   My good Camillo,   580
She is as forward of her breeding as
She is i' th' rear 'our birth.

Cam.   I cannot say 'tis pity
She lacks instructions, for she seems a mistress
To most that teach.

Per.   Your pardon, sir; for this
I'll blush you thanks.

Flo.   My prettiest Perdita!   585
But O, the thorns we stand upon! Camillo,
Preserver of my father, now of me,
The medicine of our house, how shall we do?
We are not furnish'd like Bohemia's son,
Nor shall appear in Sicilia.

Cam.   My lord,   590
Fear none of this. I think you know my fortunes
Do all lie there: it shall be so my care
To have you royally appointed, as if

---

come; / Love alters not . . . / But bears it out even to the edge of doom'. The sonnet speaks of the effects of Time but the present passage speaks of Affliction. 'Alters' means 'changes for the worse'. Cf. 400n.

576–8. *One . . . mind*] Cf. *Pandosto*, p. 221, *take in* means *subdue*, *capture*; it was the regular term for capturing a town or province. *Mind* is here used for 'the spiritual part of the human being, the soul' (*O.E.D.*, sb. III).

579. *these seven years*] proverbial expression meaning a long time (Tilley, Y25).

579–80. *There . . . such*] This passage is perhaps addressed to Florizel.

582. *'our*] Rowe (1), followed by many edd., changed this to *o'her* which could be interpreted 'She is as advanced in breeding as she is lowly in birth.' But the *F* sense 'She is, in breeding, as far ahead of her actual breeding as she is below me in birth' is less strained, and to an Elizabethan audience, a natural comment. For this use of 'in the rear' with the sense of lagging behind, cf. *Ham.*, I. iii. 34.

586. *thorns . . . upon*] proverbial for impatient anxiety (Tilley, T239).

588. *medicine*] physician. Cf. *Mac.*, v. ii. 27.

590. *appear*] 'appear as such'.

593. *royally appointed*] Camillo in

The scene you play were mine. For instance, sir,
That you may know you shall not want,—one word.

[*They talk aside*]

Enter AUTOLYCUS.

Aut. Ha, ha! what a fool Honesty is! and Trust, his   596
sworn brother, a very simple gentleman! I have
sold all my trumpery: not a counterfeit stone, not a
ribbon, glass, pomander, brooch, table-book,
ballad, knife, tape, glove, shoe-tie, bracelet, horn-   600
ring, to keep my pack from fasting: they throng
who should buy first, as if my trinkets had been
hallowed and brought a benediction to the buyer:
by which means I saw whose purse was best in pic-

595. S.D. *They talk aside*] *Rowe (1); no S.D. in F.*   601. fasting] *F;* fastning *F2.*

fact fails to get this done. It is one of
the trivial loose ends in the play.

596–620.] For other accounts of
robbing those listening to ballads
cf. Greene, *Third Cony-Catching*, 26–9
(ed. Hibbard, 1951, 49–51), and the
co-operative work of Edgworth and
Nightingale in Jonson's *Bart. Fair* (e.g.
in III. v).

599. *table-book*] tablets, note book.

600–1. *horn-ring*] Horn was often a
constituent of rings alleged to have
magic qualities. (Cf. O. M. Dalton,
*Franks Bequest. Catalogue of the Finger
Rings*, Brit. Mus., 1912, 144; Wm.
Jones, *Finger-ring lore*, 1877, 153.)

603. *hallowed*] made sacred—as by
being touched against some relic or
blessed by a church dignitary. Dr
Brooks suggests that this and the
reference to 'benediction' associates
the comic cheat Autolycus with that
other traditional comic cheat on the
pre-Shakespearian stage—the Pardoner. Cf. J. Heywood, *The Four PP;
The Pardoner and the Frere*; and Sir
David Lyndsay, *Ane Satyre of the
Thrie Estaitis* which may all have been
partly inspired by Chaucer.

604–5. *in picture*] No parallel usage
has been traced but the phrase
apparently means 'fittest for picking',

i.e. best stocked and best positioned
for the thief. Greene's Cony-Catching
pamphlets repeatedly note the nip's
or foist's concern to locate the purse
beforehand; e.g. *Second Part*, 30–1:
'when they spy a Farmer or marchant,
whome they suspect to be well monied,
they follow him hard vntill they see
him drawe his purse, then spying in
what place he puts it vp. . . . So like
wise in the markets, they note how
euery one putteth vp his purse'; 32:
'So likewise at Plaies, the nip . . . spieth
what euery man hath in his purse,
& wher in what place, and in which
sleeue or pocket he puts the boung
[purse], and according to that so hee
worketh'; *Third Part*, 27: 'The slye
mate and his fellowes, who were dis-
persed among them that stoode to
heare the songes: well noted where
euerie man that bought, put vp his
purse againe, and to such as would not
buy, counterfeit warning was . . .
giuen by the rogue . . . to beware of the
cut pursse, and looke to their pursses,
which made them often feel where
their pursses were. . . Thus the craftie
copesmates were acquainted with
what they most desired.' Cf. Jonson,
Bart. Fair, II. iii. 42–4: 'And i' your
singing, you must vse your hawks eye

ture; and what I saw, to my good use I remembered.   605
My clown (who wants but something to be a reasonable man) grew so in love with the wenches' song,
that he would not stir his pettitoes till he had both
tune and words; which so drew the rest of the herd
to me, that all their other senses stuck in ears: you   610
might have pinched a placket, it was senseless;
'twas nothing to geld a codpiece of a purse; I would
have filed keys off that hung in chains: no hearing,
no feeling, but my sir's song, and admiring the nothing of it. So that in this time of lethargy I picked   615
and cut most of their festival purses; and had not
the old man come in with a whoo-bub against his
daughter and the king's son, and scared my choughs
from the chaff, I had not left a purse alive in the
whole army.   620

[*Camillo, Florizel, and Perdita come forward.*]

Cam. Nay, but my letters, by this means being there
          So soon as you arrive, shall clear that doubt.
Flo. And those that you'll procure from King Leontes?
Cam. Shall satisfy your father.
Per.   Happy be you!
          All that you speak shows fair.

620. S.D. *Camillo . . . forward*] *Theobald; no S.D. in* F.

nimbly, and flye the purse to a marke,
still, where 'tis worne, and o' which
side'. Cf. 833.

606–20.] The appeal of the ballad
singer is also referred to in 188, 'grew
to'. Cf. 'grew so', 607.

608. *pettitoes*] trotters, but also used
of human feet.

611. *placket*] See IV. iv. 245n.

612. *geld . . . purse*] to cut a purse
from the central front pocket of trunk
hose or breeches.

614. *my sir's*] i.e. the Clown's.

614–15. *nothing*] triviality. *Nothing*
as substantive is common in Shakespeare and cf. 'Love is a pretie nothing,
(R. Jones, *Muses Garden for Delights*,
1610, ed. Squire, 1901, 2). The

secondary meaning of *nothing* = a
tune (noting) is also present as a pun.
Cf. *Ado*, II. iii. 51–3.

615–16. *picked and cut*] Autolycus
operates both as Foist (pick-pocket)
and Nip (cut-purse). The former
regarded the latter as inferiors (cf.
Greene, *Second Cony-Catching*, 30),
nevertheless 'althogh there bee some
foysts that will not vse their kniues, yet
I hold him not a perfect workeman or
maister of his Mysterie, that will not
cut a purse as well as Foyst a pocket'
(Greene, *He and She Cony-Catcher*, 14).

617. *whoo-bub*] hubbub.

618. *choughs*] The word was used or
the jackdaw as well as for the Cornish
chough or red-legged crow.

Cam. [*Seeing Autolycus*]   Who have we here?   625
    We'll make an instrument of this; omit
    Nothing may give us aid.

Aut. If they have overheard me now,—why, hanging.

Cam. How now, good fellow! why shakest thou so? Fear
    not, man; here's no harm intended to thee.   630

Aut. I am a poor fellow, sir.

Cam. Why, be so still; here's nobody will steal that from
    thee: yet for the outside of thy poverty we must
    make an exchange; therefore discase thee instantly,
    —thou must think there's a necessity in 't—and   635
    change garments with this gentleman: though the
    pennyworth on his side be the worst, yet hold thee,
    there's some boot.

Aut. I am a poor fellow, sir. [*Aside*] I know ye well
    enough.   640

Cam. Nay, prithee, dispatch: the gentleman is half
    flayed already.

Aut. Are you in earnest, sir? [*Aside*] I smell the trick on't.

Flo. Dispatch, I prithee.

Aut. Indeed, I have had earnest; but I cannot with con-   645
    science take it.

Cam. Unbuckle, unbuckle.
               [*Florizel and Autolycus exchange garments*]
    Fortunate mistress,—let my prophecy
    Come home to ye!—you must retire yourself

---

625. S.D. *Seeing Autolycus*] *Theobald; no S.D. in F.*   629–30. How . . . thee] *As Hanmer;* How . . . Fellow) / Why . . . man) / Here's . . . thee / *F.*   639. S.D. *Aside*] *Hanmer; no S.D. in F.*   643. S.D. *Aside*] *Hanmer; no S.D. in F.*   647. S.D. *Florizel . . . garments*] *Capell; no S.D. in F.*

626. *this*] this fellow.

629–30. *How . . . thee*] In spite of *F* lineation Camillo is speaking in prose to an inferior.

631. *I am . . . fellow*] Cf. Pompey's famous 'I am a poor fellow that would live' (*Meas.*, II. i. 211) and ''Tis not unknown to you, madam, I am a poor fellow' (*All's W.*, I. iii. 13).

634. *discase*] undress. Only used here and *Tp.*, v. i. 85 in this sense. Cf. 'uncasing', *Pandosto*, p. 212, l. 27.

638. *boot*] compensation, gain. (Cf.

675 and I. ii. 80 and *booties* 833.)

642. *flayed*] skinned—i.e. undressed. *F* has the old spelling *fled* for *flead* (Rowe 1). But cf. *F flayd* (785, 817), *flay'd* (806).

643. *I smell . . . on't*] He tumbles to the reason why they want his clothes —to disguise Florizel and assist his flight.

645. *earnest*] part payment in advance, the *boot* of 638.

648–9. *let . . . ye*] 'May what I have just said prove to be true.'

Into some covert: take your sweetheart's hat   650
And pluck it o'er your brows, muffle your face,
Dismantle you, and (as you can) disliken
The truth of your own seeming; that you may
(For I do fear eyes over) to shipboard
Get undescried.

Per.   I see the play so lies   655
That I must bear a part.

Cam.   No remedy.
Have you done there?

Flo.   Should I now meet my father
He would not call me son.

Cam.   Nay, you shall have no hat.
                                    [*Giving it to Perdita*]
Come, lady, come. Farewell, my friend.

Aut.   Adieu, sir.

Flo. O Perdita, what have we twain forgot?   660
     Pray you, a word.   [*They draw aside*]

---

658. S.D. *Giving . . . Perdita*] Capell; *no S.D. in F.*   661. Pray] 'Pray *F.*   S.D.
They . . . aside] *Capell (subst.) ; no S.D. in F.*

652. *disliken*] disguise.

653. *seeming*] appearance.

654. *eyes over*] overseeing eyes, viz. spies of the king. Cf. IV. ii. 36 and *LLL.*, IV. iii. 75–6, 'here sit I in the sky, / And wretched fools' secrets heedfully o'er-eye' and IV. iii. 172 'thy overview' (i.e. thy spying).

655–6. *I see . . . part*] Not an attempt to be jocular—that was not Perdita's character—but said with resignation: 'I see that we're all play-acting (dressing up) and that I have to take a part.'

660. *forgot?*] We never learn what Florizel and Perdita have forgotten or what he said to her. In *F* the question mark is often used where modern practice would use an exclamation mark and the line may mean: 'What, Perdita! Have you and I forgotten our vows, our resolution to stand by each other—that nuptial which we two have sworn shall come!' This may be another 'Lift up thy looks' to Perdita (480 and v. i. 214). Cf. 'Let our reci-

procal vows be remembered' (*Lr.*, IV. vi. 264). But the passage may merely be, in common stage convention, just another of many similar passages introduced to allow an aside. We never learn what Perdita had to listen to at 507 or Florizel at 595. We are never told Banquo's words with Ross and Angus (*Mac.*, I. iii. 126) or what Leonato had told Beatrice (*Ado*, II. i. 305) or what Mistress Quickly had in mind 'Out upon't! What have I forgot?' (*Wiv.*, I. iv. 150) or the word Sebastian has with Antonio (*Tp.*, II. i. 287). Shakespeare has hundreds of lines broken like this and we never learn the sequels. N. Coghill thinks that Florizel remembers something he had left in the clothes he has exchanged with Autolycus and that he recovers it in sight of the audience so that they do not need to be told what it is (*Sh.Sur.*, xi, 1958, 36–8). The theory is surely unnecessary and unconvincing. Eyes will be on Camillo.

Cam. What I do next, shall be to tell the king
　　Of this escape and whither they are bound;
　　Wherein my hope is I shall so prevail
　　To force him after: in whose company　　　　　665
　　I shall re-view Sicilia, for whose sight
　　I have a woman's longing.
Flo.　　　　　　　　　　　Fortune speed us!
　　Thus we set on, Camillo, to th' sea-side.
Cam. The swifter speed, the better.
　　　　　　　　　Exeunt [Florizel, Perdita, and Camillo].
Aut. I understand the business, I hear it. To have an open　670
　　ear, a quick eye, and a nimble hand, is necessary for
　　a cut-purse; a good nose is requisite also, to smell
　　out work for the other senses. I see this is the time
　　that the unjust man doth thrive. What an exchange
　　had this been without boot! What a boot is here,　675
　　with this exchange! Sure the gods do this year con-
　　nive at us, and we may do any thing extempore.
　　The prince himself is about a piece of iniquity
　　(stealing away from his father with his clog at his
　　heels): if I thought it were a piece of honesty to ac-　680
　　quaint the king withal, I would not do 't: I hold it
　　the more knavery to conceal it; and therein am I
　　constant to my profession.

　　　　　　　Enter CLOWN *and* SHEPHERD.

　　Aside, aside; here is more matter for a hot brain:

669. S.D. *Exeunt . . . Camillo.*] *Rowe (1) (subst.); Exit. F.*

670–2.] Cf. Greene, *Second Cony-Catching*, 34, 'an exquisite Foist must haue . . . An Eagles eie to spy out a purchase . . . a Lions heart . . . a Ladies hande to be little and nimble'. *F heare* possibly for *heard* from the common confusion of *d* and *e*.

673–4. *the time . . . thrive*] perhaps a biblical echo. Cf. *Job* xxi. 7; *Ps.* xxxvii. 35; lxxiii. 3; *Jer.* xii. 1.

675. *boot*] profit, extra payment. Cf. 638 and i. ii. 80.

676–7. *connive at*] look with indulgence at (*O.E.D.* +4).

extempore] 'at the moment, without

previous planning'. Cf. *MND.*, i. ii. 60; *Shr.*, ii. i. 256; *1H4*, ii. iv. 271, 307.

678. *about*] engaged in.

679. *clog*] encumbrance, i.e. Perdita. It is used in the sense of 'unwanted, encumbering wife' in *All's W.*, ii. v. 52.

680–1. *if I thought . . . do't*] It is not necessary to see an implied 'But I do not think it honest to tell the king and so I will tell him' or any other implication. The sentiment here and until 683 is a clear expression of Autolycus' comic and rascally principles.

684. *Aside*] 'Let me step to one side for a moment.'

every lane's end, every shop, church, session, hang-   685
ing, yields a careful man work.

Clo. See, see; what a man you are now! There is no other
way but to tell the king she's a changeling, and none
of your flesh and blood.

Shep. Nay, but hear me.   690

Clo. Nay, but hear me.

Shep. Go to, then.

Clo. She being none of your flesh and blood, your flesh
and blood has not offended the king; and so your
flesh and blood is not to be punished by him. Show   695
those things you found about her (those secret
things, all but what she has with her): this being
done, let the law go whistle: I warrant you.

Shep. I will tell the king all, every word, yea, and his
son's pranks too; who, I may say, is no honest man,   700
neither to his father nor to me, to go about to make
me the king's brother-in-law.

Clo. Indeed, brother-in-law was the farthest off you
could have been to him and then your blood had
been the dearer by I know how much an ounce.   705

Aut. [*Aside*] Very wisely, puppies!

Shep. Well, let us to the king: there is that in this fardel
will make him scratch his beard.

Aut. [*Aside*] I know not what impediment this com-

706. S.D. *Aside*] *Rowe* (*1*); no S.D. in F.   707. fardel] Farthell *F.*   709. S.D.
Aside] *Dyce; no S.D. in F.*

685–6. *every lane's . . . work*] Cf.
IV. iii. 99 and n. Jonson lists similar
opportunities for purse-taking, 'At
plays . . . sermons . . . sessions . . .
executions' (*Bart. Fair*, III. v. 122–
4).

688. *changeling*] Cf. III. iii. 117.

693. *flesh and blood*] proverbial
(Tilley, F366). Cf. 'collop', I. ii.
137.

698. *go whistle*] proverbial for 'any
effort will be futile' (Tilley, W313).

701. *go about to*] propose to, wish to.
Cf. IV. iv. 219.

705. *I know how*] *Var.* suggests that
this is an ironical aside, said with a

knowing wink. This is probable, because Shepherd and Clown sometimes
play the roles of clown and 'feed', they
are often twitting each other, and the
irony here would be in character.
Hanmer inserted 'not' after 'know'. It
would not be unreasonable to assume
that as the clown would believe noble
blood to be more precious than ple-
beian, he might think of it as being
more precious in terms of money. But
it is a less attractive and less likely
interpretation.

707. *fardel*] bundle. *F* prints *farthell*,
farthel throughout. *Ham.*, III. i. 76 has
fardles.

plaint may be to the flight of my master.   710

Clo. Pray heartily he be at ' palace.

Aut. [*Aside*] Though I am not naturally honest, I am so
sometimes by chance: let me pocket up my pedlar's
excrement. [*Takes off his false beard*] How now,
rustics! whither are you bound?   715

Shep. To th' palace, and it like your worship.

Aut. Your affairs there, what, with whom, the condition of that fardel, the place of your dwelling, your
names, your ages, of what having, breeding, and
any thing that is fitting to be known, discover!   720

Clo. We are but plain fellows, sir.

Aut. A lie; you are rough and hairy. Let me have no
lying: it becomes none but tradesmen, and they
often give us soldiers the lie; but we pay them for it
with stamped coin, not stabbing steel; therefore   725
they do not give us the lie.

Clo. Your worship had like to have given us one, if you
had not taken yourself with the manner.

711. Pray] 'Pray *F.*   712. S.D. *Aside*] *Dyce; no S.D. in F.*   714. S.D. *Takes
. . . beard*] *Steevens; no S.D. in F.*   718. fardel] *Farthell F.*

710. *my master*] Autolycus has been
servant to Florizel. Cf. IV. iii. 13; IV.
iv. 639, 835.

712–13. *Though I . . . chance*] He will
now do something to help the fugi-
tives (i.e. be honest) because he senses
that there is chance of further personal gain. He already has Florizel's
clothes and something to boot (638)
and his quick nose for further booty
will sense that there is something to be
got out of the rustics and maybe more
from the prince (832–7). But he is
rogue by inclination and on the whole
does good to them against his will
(v. ii. 124).

714. *excrement*] 'something which has
grown out'. Here it means his false
beard. The word usually means 'hair'
in Shakespeare. Cf. 'with my excrement, with my mustachio' (*LLL.*, v. i.
93); *Err.*, II. ii. 77 and *Mer.V.*, III.
ii. 87.

716. *and*] if. This normal contem-

porary usage is also found, for example, in 729, 742, 783, 808, v. ii. 155.

717–18. *condition*] nature, quality.

719. *having*] property, wealth.

723–4. *it becomes . . . lie*] *N.C.Wint.*,
relying on *O.E.D.* 'lie', *sb.*1c, believes
that 'to give the lie' could mean 'to
cheat' and that this passage means
'lying becomes none but tradesmen
and they often give us soldiers the lie
[i.e. cheat us by giving us short
measure or bad goods]: but we pay
them for it with good money, instead of
with stabbing steel [a soldier's retort if
'given the lie' is taken in the normal
sense—'to say a soldier lies, 'tis
stabbing' (*Oth.*, III. iv. 5)], and so they
do not really 'give' us the lie [deceit]
[because we pay them for it].'

727–8. *Your worship . . . manner*] 'Your
worship would have told us something
that was a lie had you not seen your
mistake in time.' The Clown is
referring to Autolycus' self-correction

Shep. Are you a courtier, and 't like you, sir?

Aut. Whether it like me or no, I am a courtier. Seest thou   730
not the air of the court in these enfoldings? hath not
my gait in it the measure of the court? receives not
thy nose court-odour from me? reflect I not on thy
baseness, court-contempt? Think'st thou, for that
I insinuate, or toaze from thee thy business, I am   735
therefore no courtier? I am courtier *cap-a-pe*; and
one that will either push on or pluck back thy business there: whereupon I command thee to open thy
affair.

Shep. My business, sir, is to the king.   740

Aut. What advocate hast thou to him?

Shep. I know not, and 't like you.

Clo. Advocate's the court-word for a pheasant: say you
have none.

Shep. None, sir; I have no pheasant, cock nor hen.   745

Aut. How blessed are we that are not simple men!
Yet nature might have made me as these are;

735. or] *F2*; at *F.*

'they . . . give us . . . the lie . . . they do
not give us the lie' (723–6). 'Manner'
is 'mainour', Lat. 'a manu', 'from the
hand' or 'in the act'. Cf. *LLL.*, I. i.
199, 'the manner of it is, I was taken
with the manner' (Costard with Jac-
quenetta). As one speaks of taking a
thief in the act or with the goods in his
hand so Autolycus catches himself in
his mistake in time to correct it. For a
good illustration of contemporary use
see extract from Pliny in v. ii. 101–2n.

732. *measure*] regulated and graceful
movement (lit. a stately dance).

735. *insinuate, or toaze*] For *F at*
Capell and *N.C.Wint.* read *to* and
Malone *and*. The sense is 'Thinkest
thou that because I am trying to
wheedle or tease your affairs out of you
I am therefore no courtier?' Cf. *Pro-
teus Redivivus: or the Art of Wheedling or
Insinuation* [By R. Head], 1675.

736. cap-a-pe] from top to toe
(Tilley, T436).

738. *open*] disclose.

743. *pheasant*] *F Pheazant.* Many edd.
emend to *present* and assume a mishearing by the Shepherd in 745. But
pheasant here is almost certainly correct. The only courts known to the
Clown were those of local justices.
Bribery to these by gifts of poultry was
common enough in the 17th century
for the term 'capon-justices' to be
current in 1639 (*O.E.D.* capon), and
no doubt a pheasant was a choice
bribe of this kind. Cf. the Clown taking two pigeons to court (*Tit.*, IV.
iii. 91).

746–8. *How . . . disdain*] Many edd.
print as prose, but Autolycus is a
temporary gentleman, speaking gran-
diloquently, and the *F* printing is
surely intentional. When Falstaff 'acts'
the king he opens with blank verse,
and Autolycus, here 'acting' the *grand
seigneur*, also 'doth it as like one of these
harlotry players as ever I see' (*1H4,*
II. iv. 385) and his very speech immediately impresses the Clown. Noble,

Therefore I will not disdain.

Clo. This cannot be but a great courtier.

Shep. His garments are rich, but he wears them not   750
handsomely.

Clo. He seems to be the more noble in being fantastical:
a great man, I'll warrant; I know by the picking
on's teeth.

Aut. The fardel there? What's i' th' fardel? Wherefore   755
that box?

Shep. Sir, there lies such secrets in this fardel and box,
which none must know but the king; and which he
shall know within this hour, if I may come to th'
speech of him.   760

Aut. Age, thou hast lost thy labour.

Shep. Why, sir?

Aut. The king is not at the palace; he is gone aboard a
new ship to purge melancholy and air himself: for,
if thou bee'st capable of things serious, thou must   765
know the king is full of grief.

Shep. So 'tis said, sir; about his son, that should have
married a shepherd's daughter.

Aut. If that shepherd be not in hand-fast, let him fly: the
curses he shall have, the tortures he shall feel, will   770
break the back of man, the heart of monster.

Clo. Think you so, sir?

Biblical Knowledge, remarks that the audience would recall the Pharisee's self-complacent superiority, 'God, I thanke thee, that I am not as other men are' (*Luke* xviii. 11). Cf. Touchstone's 'we that have good wits' (*AYL.*, v. i. 11). The passage is ironic in that Autolycus is soon to be seeking the favour of the rustics.

749. *be but*] Hanmer, *N.C. Wint.*, and others make an unnecessary change to *but be.* The usage *be but* was not uncommon; cf. *Pandosto*, p. 200, ll. 10–11.

750. *His . . . rich*] That the Shepherd should think this and should not recognize the garments is a piece of common stage convention (see IV. iv. 1n.).

752. *fantastical*] fanciful, capricious, odd.

753–4. *picking on's teeth*] Toothpicks were affected by travellers long before Shakespeare (cf. 'your traveller, / He and his toothpick' *John*, i. i. 189–90n. in new Arden ed.). They used to be worn in hats but that fashion had gone out by the beginning of the century (cf. *All's W.*, i. i. 152–4, 'wears her cap out of fashion . . . just like the brooch and the toothpick which wear not now' and n. in new Arden ed.). The practice of picking teeth in public was probably strange to the rustics.

761. *lost thy labour*] proverbial (Tilley, L9).

761–4. *lost . . . air himself*] Cf. *Pandosto*, p. 215, ll. 13–15. Cf. *Cym.*, i. i. 110; *Tp.*, iv. i. 70.

769. *in hand-fast*] under arrest.

Aut. Not he alone shall suffer what wit can make heavy
and vengeance bitter; but those that are germane
to him, though removed fifty times, shall all come   775
under the hangman: which, though it be great pity,
yet it is necessary. An old sheep-whistling rogue, a
ram-tender, to offer to have his daughter come into
grace! Some say he shall be stoned; but that death
is too soft for him, say I. Draw our throne into a   780
sheepcote! All deaths are too few, the sharpest too
easy.

Clo. Has the old man e'er a son, sir, do you hear, and 't
like you, sir?

Aut. He has a son, who shall be flayed alive, then 'nointed   785
over with honey, set on the head of a wasps' nest,
then stand till he be three quarters and a dram
dead; then recovered again with aqua-vitæ or some
other hot infusion; then, raw as he is, and in the
hottest day prognostication proclaims, shall he be   790
set against a brick wall, the sun looking with a
southward eye upon him, where he is to behold him,
with flies blown to death. But what talk we of these
traitorly rascals, whose miseries are to be smiled at,
their offences being so capital? Tell me (for you   795
seem to be honest plain men) what you have to the
king: being something gently considered, I'll bring
you where he is aboard, tender your persons to his

785–93. *He has . . . blown to death*]
Several edd. point out a source for this
torture in Boccaccio, *Decameron*, ii. 9
where a similar death is inflicted on
Ambrogivolo, the Iachimo of this
immediate source of *Cym.* (cf. new
Arden *Cym.*, ed. Nosworthy, 1955,
xxi). *Sh.Eng.*, i. 184–5, notes that
Shakespeare and his audience would
have knowledge of similar tortures
inflicted by the Spaniards. J. C. Maxwell brings to my notice that the
torture is mentioned in William of
Malmesbury's *Historiae Novellae* (Nel-
son's Medieval Classics), 43. The
Latin text of this was printed by Sir
Henry Savile in *Rerum Anglicarum*

Scriptores, 1596 (f. 105v, ll. 2–3), re-
issued in 1601 (p. 186, ll. 18–19). Cf.
Tp., v. i. 284.

787. *and a dram*] and a little more.

790. *prognostication*] the weather pre-
diction of the almanac. Prophesying
almanacs were popular in Shakespeare's day. Cf. II. i. 105–7n.

792. *he*] the sun.

797. *being . . . considered*] probably 'if
I am well bribed'. Cf. IV. ii. 18 and
modern 'to do something for a consideration'. But the words may also
mean 'being had somewhat in regard
as a man of noble rank' (i.e. and so
having influence).

798. *he is aboard*] To the rustics 'he'

presence, whisper him in your behalfs; and if it be
in man, besides the king, to effect your suits, here is   800
man shall do it.

Clo. He seems to be of great authority: close with him,
give him gold; and though authority be a stubborn
bear, yet he is oft led by the nose with gold: show
the inside of your purse to the outside of his hand,   805
and no more ado. Remember 'stoned', and 'flayed
alive'!

Shep. And 't please you, sir, to undertake the business for
us, here is that gold I have: I'll make it as much
more and leave this young man in pawn till I bring   810
it you.

Aut. After I have done what I promised?

Shep. Ay, sir.

Aut. Well, give me the moiety. Are you a party in this
business?   815

Clo. In some sort, sir: but though my case be a pitiful
one, I hope I shall not be flayed out of it.

Aut. O, that's the case of the shepherd's son: hang him,
he'll be made an example.

Clo. Comfort, good comfort! We must to the king and   820
show our strange sights: he must know 'tis none of
your daughter nor my sister; we are gone else. Sir,
I will give you as much as this old man does when
the business is performed, and remain, as he says,
your pawn till it be brought you.   825

Aut. I will trust you. Walk before toward the sea-side;
go on the right hand: I will but look upon the hedge
and follow you.

must mean the king. But Autolycus
refers to the prince. From this point
Autolycus begins to work out the plan
of getting them on board on the pretext that he is taking them to the king.

800. *besides*] 'who is near to' or
'other than'.

804. *led . . . nose*] 'led in docile
manner'. Cf. *Oth.*, I. iii. 395. Proverbial (Tilley, N233).

816. *case*] meaning both *condition* and
skin.

820. *We must to*] Omission of the
verb of motion is not uncommon with
must and *let* followed by an adverb or
preposition. Cf. Franz, 497, §621, and
v. iii. 146.

822. *gone*] undone.

827. *look . . . hedge*] The pretence to
want to relieve himself is merely a
dramatic device (chiefly for the
groundlings) to enable the Clown and
Shepherd to make their exits without
him.

Clo. We are blest in this man, as I may say, even blest.

Shep. Let's before, as he bids us: he was provided to do   830
    us good.   [*Exeunt Shepherd and Clown.*]

Aut. If I had a mind to be honest, I see Fortune would not
    suffer me: she drops booties in my mouth. I am
    courted now with a double occasion—gold, and a
    means to do the prince my master good; which who   835
    knows how that may turn back to my advance-
    ment? I will bring these two moles, these blind ones,
    aboard him: if he think it fit to shore them again
    and that the complaint they have to the king con-
    cerns him nothing, let him call me rogue for being   840
    so far officious; for I am proof against that title and
    what shame else belongs to 't. To him will I present
    them: there may be matter in it.   *Exit.*

831. S.D. *Exeunt . . . Clown*] *Exeunt F2; no S.D. in F.*   843. S.D. *Exit.*] *Exeunt. F.*

833. *drops . . . mouth*] Cf. Greene, *He and She Cony-Catcher*, 13–14: 'some of our Country farmers . . . are so care-lesse in a throng . . . that they shew vs the praie . . . and bequeath vs their purses, whether we will or no, for who loues wyne so ill, that hee will not eate grapes if they fall into his mouth.' 'Booties' has its normal sense of 'booty', 'plunder', and also that of 'something extra and unexpected'. Cf. i. ii. 80n. and iv. iv. 604–5n.

834. *occasion*] chance, opportunity.

836. *turn back*] recoil, turn out.

838. *to shore them*] 'to put them ashore'. Cf. Abbott, §290, for the free use of nouns and adjectives as verbs in Elizabethan English.

ACT V

SCENE I

Enter LEONTES, CLEOMENES, DION, PAULINA, [*and*] *Servants.*

Cleo. Sir, you have done enough, and have perform'd
  A saint-like sorrow: no fault could you make,
  Which you have not redeem'd; indeed, paid down
  More penitence than done trespass: at the last,
  Do as the heavens have done, forget your evil;   5
  With them, forgive yourself.

Leon.   Whilst I remember
  Her, and her virtues, I cannot forget
  My blemishes in them, and so still think of
  The wrong I did myself: which was so much,
  That heirless it hath made my kingdom, and   10
  Destroy'd the sweet'st companion that e'er man
  Bred his hopes out of.

Paul.   True, too true, my lord:
  If, one by one, you wedded all the world,
  Or from the all that are took something good,

ACT V

Scene I

Act V] *Actus Quintus. F.*   Scene I] *Scena Prima. F.*   S.D. *Enter Leontes . ..*
Servants.] *Enter Leontes, Cleomines, Dion, Paulina, Seruants: Florizel, Perdita. F.*
12. of. | *Paul.* True, too] *Theobald;* of, true. | *Paul.* Too *F.*

Scene 1] Sicilia. Leontes' Palace.
  5–6. *Do as . . . yourself*] Noble,
Biblical Knowledge, 81, 82, 248, compares with *Gent.*, v. iv. 79–81, and also
the *Common Prayer* version of *Ezek.*
xviii. 21–2, 'I wil put al his wickednes
out of my remembraunce sayeth the
Lord' and *Common Prayer* (Visitation of
the Sick) 'O most merciful God, which
. . . dost so put away the sins of those

which truly repent, that thou re-
memberest them no more.'
  8. *in them*] 'in comparison with' or
'in thinking of them'.
  14–15. *Or from . . . woman*] Cf.
AYL., III. ii. 131–142: 'Therefore
heaven Nature charg'd / That one
body should be fill'd / With all graces
wide-enlarg'd. / Nature presently distill'd / Helen's cheek, but not her

To make a perfect woman, she you kill'd   15
Would be unparallel'd.

Leon.   I think so. Kill'd!
She I kill'd! I did so: but thou strik'st me
Sorely, to say I did: it is as bitter
Upon thy tongue as in my thought. Now, good now,
Say so but seldom.

Cleo.   Not at all, good lady: 20
You might have spoken a thousand things that would
Have done the time more benefit and grac'd
Your kindness better.

Paul.   You are one of those
Would have him wed again.

Dion.   If you would not so,
You pity not the state, nor the remembrance   25
Of his most sovereign name; consider little,
What dangers, by his highness' fail of issue,
May drop upon his kingdom, and devour
Incertain lookers on. What were more holy
Than to rejoice the former queen is well?   30

---

heart, / Cleopatra's majesty, / Ata-
lanta's better part, / Sad Lucretia's
modesty. / Thus Rosalinde of many
parts / By heavenly synod was
devis'd, / Of many faces, eyes, and
hearts, / To have the touches dearest
priz'd', and 'From every one / The best
she hath, and she, of all compounded, /
Outsells them all' (*Cym.*, III. v. 73–5);
'you, O you, / So perfect and so peerless, are created / Of every creature's
best' (*Tp.*, III. i. 46–8), 'She is her selfe,
of best things the collection' (Sidney,
Arcadia, 1590, i. 1, ed. Feuillerat, i.
128). The idea is old and persistent;
see K. Clark, *The Nude . . . of Ideal Art*,
1956, 9–11, 16 and Pliny, *Historie of
the World . . . Trans. . . .* P. Holland,
1601: 'Zeuxis would needs see all the
maidens of the city, naked; and from
all that companie hee chose five of the
fairest to take out as from severall
patterns, whatsoever hee liked best in
any of them; and of all the lovely parts
of those five to make one bodie of

incomparable beautie' (ii. 534) (cf.
*The Elder Pliny's Chapters on . . . Art.
Trans. K. Jex-Blake*, 1896, lxi–lxii,
109–11). Catullus, *Carmina*, 86: 'Lesbia
formosast, quae cum pulcherrima
totast, / tum omnibus una omnis surri-
puit Veneres'—'Lesbia is beautiful:
for she possesses all the beauties, and
has stolen all the graces from all the
women alone for herself' (Loeb ed.,
F. W. Cornish, 162–3). Bacon used it
(*Of Beauty*: this passage first printed
1612, but in Harleian MS. 5106
written between 1607 and 1612):
'Apelles or Albert Durer . . . the one
would make a personage by geo-
metrical proportions; the other, by
taking the best parts out of divers
faces, to make one excellent.' Cf. also
Chateaubriand, *Mémoires d'Outre-
Tombe*, 1849, i. 234–6, 321–2.

26. *consider*] 'you consider'.

29. *Incertain*] 'those needing guidance and rule'.

30. *is well*] Cf. *Ant.*, II. v. 33, 'we use /

What holier than, for royalty's repair,
For present comfort, and for future good,
To bless the bed of majesty again
With a sweet fellow to 't?

Paul.   There is none worthy,
Respecting her that's gone. Besides, the gods   35
Will have fulfill'd their secret purposes;
For has not the divine Apollo said,
Is 't not the tenor of his Oracle,
That King Leontes shall not have an heir,
Till his lost child be found? which, that it shall,   40
Is all as monstrous to our human reason
As my Antigonus to break his grave
And come again to me; who, on my life,
Did perish with the infant. 'Tis your counsel
My lord should to the heavens be contrary,   45
Oppose against their wills. [*To Leontes*] Care not for
        issue;
The crown will find an heir. Great Alexander
Left his to th' worthiest; so his successor
Was like to be the best.

46. S.D. *To Leontes*] *Theobald (subst.); no S.D. in F.*

[i.e. it is customary] To say the dead are well'; and *2H4*, v. ii. 3; *Rom.*, IV. v. 76, v. i. 17, and the grimly ironic use in *Mac.*, IV. iii. 177 (Tilley, H437). Cf. *2 Kings* iv. 26.

35. *Respecting*] in comparison with.

36. *Will . . . purposes*] 'will see to it that their secret purposes are fulfilled'.

45. *contrary*] Cf. *Tim.*, IV. iii. 144, for similar use with accent on second syllable.

46–9. *Care not . . . best*] Perhaps here Shakespeare had in mind, and knew that he would awaken in the minds of his audiences, the fact that although many representations had been made to Elizabeth that she should marry, she cared nothing for issue and died without an heir, but that nevertheless there had been a happy succession to the throne. This particular passage

can be taken as a compliment to James. Cf. the opening of the address to the king by the translators of the *A.V.* But perhaps the passage merely echoes the sentiment in Quintus Curtius—see next note.

47–9. *Great Alexander . . . best.*] apparently not in Plutarch: probably from Quintus Curtius: *The Historie . . . conteining the Actes of . . . Alexander. Translated . . . by Iohn Brende,* ff. 295r, 300v of 1602 ed. Alexander comforts those around him: 'When I depart, you shall find a king worthy for such men as you be. . . They demanded whom he would leave his kingdome? He said: to the worthiest.' Something similar is in Arrian: *Anabasis of Alexander,* vii. 26 (Loeb ed., ii. 295). Arrian was published in Latin and in French before 1611 but not, apparently, in English.

Leon.   Good Paulina,
Who hast the memory of Hermione,   50
I know, in honour,—O, that ever I
Had squar'd me to thy counsel! Then, even now,
I might have look'd upon my queen's full eyes,
Have taken treasure from her lips,—

Paul.   And left them
More rich for what they yielded.

Leon.   . Thou speak'st truth.
No more such wives; therefore, no wife: one worse,   56
And better us'd, would make her sainted spirit
Again possess her corpse, and on this stage
(Were we offenders now) appear soul-vex'd,
And begin, 'Why to me?'

Paul.   Had she such power,   60
She had just cause.

Leon.   She had; and would incense me
To murder her I married.

Paul.   I should so:
Were I the ghost that walk'd, I'd bid you mark
Her eye, and tell me for what dull part in 't

---

59. (Were . . . appear] *Rann;* (Where we Offendors now appeare) *F;* (Where we offend Her now) appear *Theobald, etc., Alexander (subst.);* (Where we offenders now) appear *Knight, Cambridge (subst.), etc.;* (Where we offenders move) appear *Moorman (subst.), conj. Delius;* Where we offend as now, appear *Sisson.*   60. And begin, 'Why to me?'] And begin, why to me? *F.*   61. just cause] *F3;* just such cause *F.*

---

52. *squared me to*] agreed with, followed. Cf. III. iii. 41.

58. *possess her corpse*] Ballad-ghosts are usually corporeal, unlike the incorporeal ghost of the King in *Ham.*

59. *Were . . . appear*] a difficult and much debated crux for which many solutions have been offered. Rann's is adopted because it seems to arise naturally from the preceding lines and requires little alteration to the text. Leontes is saying that it would indeed be a crime to take a new wife and that if he did so (were he such an offender) it would be enough to make Hermione's spirit appear and reproach him. Alice Walker suggests to me:

'Where we offended, new-appear soulvex'd, / And begging "Why" to me.'

60. *Why to me*] 'Why [is this insult offered] to me?'

61. *just cause*] The 'such' in *F* is probably a printer's accidental interpolation caught up from the 'such' in the preceding line.

62. *To murder her*] The ghost of a first wife inciting her husband to murder his second wife sounds a likely folklore theme which might be found in ballad or play, but it has not been traced.

64–5. *for what . . . her*] Cf. 'tell me for which of my bad parts didst thou first fall in love with me? . . . But for which

You chose her: then I'd shriek, that even your ears   65
　　Should rift to hear me; and the words that follow'd
　　Should be 'Remember mine.'
Leon.　　　　　　　　Stars, stars,
　　And all eyes else, dead coals! Fear thou no wife;
　　I'll have no wife, Paulina.
Paul.　　　　　　　Will you swear
　　Never to marry, but by my free leave?   70
Leon. Never, Paulina; so be blest my spirit!
Paul. Then, good my lords, bear witness to his oath.
Cleo. You tempt him over-much.
Paul.　　　　　　　Unless another,
　　As like Hermione as is her picture,
　　Affront his eye.
Cleo.　　　　Good madam,—
Paul.　　　　　　　I have done.   75
　　Yet, if my lord will marry,—if you will, sir;
　　No remedy but you will,—give me the office
　　To choose you a queen: she shall not be so young
　　As was your former, but she shall be such
　　As, walk'd your first queen's ghost, it should take joy   80
　　To see her in your arms.
Leon.　　　　　　　My true Paulina,
　　We shall not marry till thou bid'st us.
Paul.　　　　　　　That
　　Shall be when your first queen's again in breath:
　　Never till then.

Enter a Servant.

75. *Cleo.* Good . . . done] *As Capell; Cleo.* Good Madame, I haue done. *F; Cleo.* Good Madam, pray have done. *Rowe (I), Theobald, etc.*

---

of my good parts did you first suffer love for me?' (*Ado,* v. ii. 51–7). The implication in *Wint.* is different but the phrasing is parallel.

67. *Remember mine*] This recalls the Ghost's exit words 'Remember me' in *Ham.* (I. v. 91) and Dr Brooks points out that with this clue one can see that Paulina's comparison of the first wife with any second has resemblance with Hamlet's indignant comparison of

Gertrude's first husband with her second ('Hyperion to a satyr', *Ham.,* I. ii. 140).

75. *Affront*] confront, meet.

84. Enter a Servant] The king's servant here would be a gentleman. Theobald and most edd. since have substituted *Gentleman* for *Servant* in the text here and for his speeches. The character is sometimes referred to as the Gentleman-poet in view of 98–

Ser. One that gives out himself Prince Florizel,   85
         Son of Polixenes, with his princess (she
         The fairest I have yet beheld) desires access
         To your high presence.
Leon.   What with him? he comes not
         Like to his father's greatness: his approach
         (So out of circumstance, and sudden) tells us   90
         'Tis not a visitation fram'd, but forc'd
         By need and accident. What train?
Ser.   But few,
         And those but mean.
Leon.   His princess, say you, with him?
Ser. Ay, the most peerless piece of earth, I think,
         That e'er the sun shone bright on.
Paul.   O Hermione,   95
         As every present time doth boast itself
         Above a better gone, so must thy grave
         Give way to what's seen now! Sir, you yourself
         Have said, and writ so; but your writing now
         Is colder than that theme: 'She had not been,   100
         Nor was not to be equall'd';—thus your verse
         Flow'd with her beauty once: 'tis shrewdly ebb'd,
         To say you have seen a better.
Ser.   Pardon, madam:
         The one I have almost forgot,—your pardon,—
         The other, when she has obtain'd your eye,   105
         Will have your tongue too. This is a creature,
         Would she begin a sect, might quench the zeal
         Of all professors else; make proselytes
         Of who she but bid follow.
Paul.   How! not women?

103. Some official is intended, lower in status than the courtier-Gentlemen of v. ii or the Lord of v. i. 177.

85. *gives out*] announces, professes. Cf. *Tp.*, v. i. 223.

90. *out of circumstance*] without ceremony.

94. *piece*] Cf. iv. iv. 423–4n.

97. *thy grave*] 'you now in your grave'.

100–1. *She . . . equall'd*] Hanmer

pointed out that this was an extract from the gentleman-poet's verse, and should be in inverted commas.

107–9. *Would . . . follow*] 'If she should begin a new sect, she would cause all who professed other forms of Christianity to change their views and make converts of all that she merely told to follow.' For 'professor' = professor of Christianity, cf. *H8*, iii. i. 115.

Ser. Women will love her, that she is a woman   110
        More worth than any man; men, that she is
        The rarest of all women.
Leon.   Go, Cleomenes;
        Yourself, assisted with your honour'd friends,
        Bring them to our embracement.

                          Exeunt [*Cleomenes and others*].
                              Still, 'tis strange
        He thus should steal upon us.
Paul.   Had our prince   115
        (Jewel of children) seen this hour, he had pair'd
        Well with this lord: there was not full a month
        Between their births.
Leon.   Prithee, no more; cease; thou know'st
        He dies to me again, when talk'd of: sure,
        When I shall see this gentleman, thy speeches   120
        Will bring me to consider that which may
        Unfurnish me of reason. They are come.

        Enter FLORIZEL, PERDITA, CLEOMENES *and others*.

        Your mother was most true to wedlock, prince;
        For she did print your royal father off,
        Conceiving you. Were I but twenty-one,   125
        Your father's image is so hit in you,
        His very air, that I should call you brother,
        As I did him, and speak of something wildly
        By us perform'd before. Most dearly welcome!
        And your fair princess,—goddess!—O, alas!   130
        I lost a couple, that 'twixt heaven and earth
        Might thus have stood, begetting wonder, as
        You, gracious couple, do: and then I lost—
        All mine own folly—the society,
        Amity too, of your brave father, whom   135

---

114. S.D. *Exeunt . . . others.*] *Exit. F* (*after* upon us. *115*).   118. Prithee] 'Prethee *F*.

115–16. *our prince . . . pair'd*] Shakespeare clearly wishes us to match Florizel with Mamillius.

119. *dies to me again*] Proverbially the revealing of griefs is a renewing of sorrow (Tilley, R89).

130. *princess, — goddess! — O,*] *F Princesse (Goddesse) oh: N.C. Wint.* puts S.D. 'she unveils' after *princess* and 'he gazes at her' after *O*.

135–7. *your brave . . . on him*] 'your brave father, whom, although my life

(Though bearing misery) I desire my life
Once more to look on him.

Flo.   By his command
Have I here touch'd Sicilia, and from him
Give you all greetings that a king (at friend)
Can send his brother: and, but infirmity   140
(Which waits upon worn times) hath something seiz'd
His wish'd ability, he had himself
The lands and waters 'twixt your throne and his
Measur'd, to look upon you; whom he loves
(He bade me say so) more than all the sceptres   145
And those that bear them living.

Leon.   O my brother,—
Good gentleman!—the wrongs I have done thee stir
Afresh within me; and these thy offices,
So rarely kind, are as interpreters
Of my behind-hand slackness! Welcome hither,   150
As is the spring to th' earth. And hath he too
Expos'd this paragon to th' fearful usage
(At least ungentle) of the dreadful Neptune,
To greet a man not worth her pains, much less
Th' adventure of her person?

Flo.   Good my lord,   155
She came from Libya.

Leon.   Where the warlike Smalus,

---

139. at friend] *F*; as friend *F2*.

is full of misery, I want to go on living
in order to see once again'. The final
'him' is redundant.

139. *at friend*] *at* is probably used in
the sense of *a* or *as* (Abbott, §§140,
143–4). Some usages of *at* in Shakespeare may derive from dialect. A
parallel to *at friend* is *the wind at help*
(*Ham.*, IV. iii. 44). Others for addition
to Abbott's lists are the common *at
full* (*All's W.*, II. i. 131; *2H6*, II. ii. 6;
Ham., IV. iii. 63), *at each* (*Lr.*, IV. vi.
53), *at foot*, *at aught* (*Ham.*, IV. iii. 54,
58), *at fall* (*Tim.*, II. ii. 205), and *at
Bohemia* (*Wint.*, I. ii. 39). Cf. also 'well
to friend' (*Cæs.*, III. i. 144) and 'at
other' (*Pandosto*, p. 204, l. 11).

140. *but*] but that.

141–2. *Which . . . ability*] 'which
comes with old age has somewhat
reduced the strength he would like to
have'.

148. *offices*] friendly greetings.

149–50. *interpreters . . . slackness*]
'remind me of my laggard remiss-
ness [in marks of friendship to Polix-
enes]'.

155. *adventure*] venturing, hazard.

156. *Smalus*] Perhaps from the Biblical Ishmael (J. Perin, *Onomasticon
totius latinitatis*, 1913, 'Ismaelus . . .
olim . . . Smaelus', and F. G. Stokes,
Dict. of Sh., 1924). In the life of Dion,
Plutarch speaks of sailing from Libya

That noble honour'd lord, is fear'd and lov'd?
Flo. Most royal sir, from thence; from him, whose daughter
His tears proclaim'd his, parting with her: thence,
A prosperous south-wind friendly, we have cross'd,   160
To execute the charge my father gave me
For visiting your highness: my best train
I have from your Sicilian shores dismiss'd;
Who for Bohemia bend, to signify
Not only my success in Libya, sir,   165
But my arrival, and my wife's, in safety
Here, where we are.
Leon.   The blessed gods
Purge all infection from our air whilst you
Do climate here! You have a holy father,
A graceful gentleman; against whose person   170
(So sacred as it is) I have done sin,
For which, the heavens (taking angry note)
Have left me issueless: and your father's blest
(As he from heaven merits it) with you,
Worthy his goodness. What might I have been,   175
Might I a son and daughter now have look'd on,
Such goodly things as you!

Enter a Lord.

Lord.   Most noble sir,
That which I shall report will bear no credit,

158. Most . . . daughter] Most . . . Sir, / From . . . Daughter *F.*

to a Sicilian village governed by a
Carthagian captain *Synalus* (Nonesuch
ed. of North, iv. 410). Misreading *yn*
as tailed *m*, or an *i* for *y* spelling,
would lead to *Smalus*. Hence *Synalus*
may be the name Shakespeare intended, having taken it, with most
of the others, from Plutarch. (See pp.
163–5.)

169. *climate*] O.E.D. cites as a verbal
use meaning 'to live in particular dis-
trict' from *climate*: 'a region of the
earth'. It has here no reference to
climatic conditions.

holy father] Cf. *Tp.*, v. i. 62, 'Holy
Gonzalo, honourable man.'

170. *graceful*] full of grace, virtuous.

173. *and*] 'on the other hand'. The
word is not essential and, as the line is
a syllable too long, may be an accidental insertion [Tannenbaum]. But
an extra syllable at the caesura is
common enough.

176. *son and daughter*] Since in Elizabethan English 'son' is normal also for
'son-in-law' Leontes is in fact looking
on his son-to-be, as well as on his
daughter. Cf. 207–8n.

Were not the proof so nigh. Please you, great sir,
Bohemia greets you from himself, by me;   180
Desires you to attach his son, who has—
His dignity and duty both cast off—
Fled from his father, from his hopes, and with
A shepherd's daughter.
Leon.   Where's Bohemia? speak.
Lord. Here in your city; I now came from him.   185
  I speak amazedly, and it becomes
  My marvel and my message. To your court
  Whiles he was hast'ning—in the chase, it seems,
  Of this fair couple—meets he on the way
  The father of this seeming lady and   190
  Her brother, having both their country quitted
  With this young prince.
Flo.   Camillo has betray'd me;
  Whose honour and whose honesty till now
  Endur'd all weathers.
Lord.   Lay 't so to his charge:
  He's with the king your father.
Leon.   Who? Camillo?   195
Lord. Camillo, sir; I spake with him; who now
  Has these poor men in question. Never saw I
  Wretches so quake: they kneel, they kiss the earth;
  Forswear themselves as often as they speak.
  Bohemia stops his ears, and threatens them   200
  With divers deaths in death.
Per.   O my poor father!
  The heaven sets spies upon us, will not have
  Our contract celebrated.
Leon.   You are married?
Flo. We are not, sir, nor are we like to be:

---

181. *attach*] arrest.

186–7. *it becomes . . . marvel*] 'My excited way of speaking befits my
astonishment.'

188. *Whiles*] While.

198. *kiss the earth*] a form of 'lick the
dust' (Tilley, D651).

202. *heaven sets spies*] heaven = the

gods; spies = informers. *Wint.* like
Lr. is set in heathen times. T. M.
Parrott (*Sh.Q.*, iv, 1953, 431) argues
that a Christian God needs no spies
but that the heathen gods did use
human informers. It is, however, unlikely that Shakespeare had in mind
any distinction of this kind.

The stars, I see, will kiss the valley's first: 205
    The odds for high and low's alike.
Leon.   My lord.
    Is this the daughter of a king?
Flo.   She is,
    When once she is my wife.
Leon. That 'once', I see, by your good father's speed,
    Will come on very slowly. I am sorry,   210
    Most sorry, you have broken from his liking,
    Where you were tied in duty; and as sorry
    Your choice is not so rich in worth as beauty,
    That you might well enjoy her.
Flo.   Dear, look up:
    Though Fortune, visible an enemy,
    Should chase us, with my father, power no jot
    Hath she to change our loves. Beseech you, sir,
    Remember since you ow'd no more to time
    Than I do now: with thought of such affections,
    Step forth mine advocate: at your request,   220
    My father will grant precious things as trifles.
Leon. Would he do so, I'd beg your precious mistress,
    Which he counts but a trifle.
Paul.   Sir, my liege,
    Your eye hath too much youth in 't; not a month
    'Fore your queen died, she was more worth such gazes
    Than what you look on now.
Leon.   I thought of her,   226

206. *The odds . . . alike*] 'Chance is the same for rich (prince) and poor (shepherdess),' or 'Privilege of rank is gone' (cf. *Ant.*, IV. xv. 66). Douce suggested that there might be a reference to the false dice called 'high and low'. *N.C.Wint.* adopts this and, citing 'And high and low beguiles the rich and poor' (*Wiv.*, I. iii. 83), interprets the line: 'Fortune is a cheater who beguiles princes and shepherds alike with his false dice.' Bethell disputes this, but such a sense could be extracted from the words.

207–8. *daughter . . . wife*] play on the Elizabethan 'daughter' and 'daughter' = 'daughter-in-law'. Cf. 176n.

212. *tied*] bound. Cf. *H8*, IV. ii. 36; *Cym.*, I. vi. 23.

213. *worth*] rank.

214. *look up*] Cf. IV. iv. 41, 480.

215–17. *Though Fortune . . . loves*] 'Even though Fortune could actually be seen as an enemy accompanying my father in pursuit of us she has not the slightest power to change our loves.'

218–19. *Remember . . . now*] 'Remember the time when (since) you were as young as I am now.'

Even as these looks I made. [*To Florizel*] But your
    petition
Is yet unanswer'd. I will to your father:
Your honour not o'erthrown by your desires,
I am friend to them and you: upon which errand   230
I now go toward him; therefore follow me
And mark what way I make. Come, good my lord.

                                            Exeunt.

SCENE II

Enter AUTOLYCUS *and a Gentleman.*

Aut. Beseech you, sir, were you present at this relation?
First Gent. I was by at the opening of the fardel, heard the
    old shepherd deliver the manner how he found it:
    whereupon, after a little amazedness, we were all
    commanded out of the chamber; only this, me-   5
    thought I heard the shepherd say he found the
    child.
Aut. I would most gladly know the issue of it.
First Gent. I make a broken delivery of the business; but
    the changes I perceived in the king and Camillo were   10
    very notes of admiration: they seemed almost, with
    staring on one another, to tear the cases of their eyes:
    there was speech in their dumbness, language in

227. S.D. *To Florizel*] *Theobald; no S.D. in* F.

Scene II

Scene II] *Scæna Secunda.* F.   2. *First Gent.*] *Gent.1.* F (*and throughout scene*).

229. *Your honour . . . desires*] 'Provided your wishes prove not to be in-
compatible with your honour'. It is
probable too that there is a reference
here to honourable love, just as
Prospero was concerned about Ferdinand's possible behaviour after
betrothal (*Tp.*, IV. i. 15–23). At IV. iv.
33–5 Florizel has declared that his love
is honourable.

Scene II

Scene ii] Before Leontes' palace.

4. *after . . . amazedness*] 'when they
had got over their astonishment'.

11. *very . . . admiration*] 'veritable
exclamations of wonder'.

12. *cases . . . eyes*] eye-lids. 'Her eye-
lids, cases to those heavenly jewels',
'her eyes as jewel-like, / And cas'd as
richly' (*Per.*, III. ii. 104; v. i. 109–10).
The parts containing the eye proper.
Cf. *Lr.*, IV. vi. 144; *Cym.*, I. iii. 17. The
sense here is like the modern 'Their
eyes were almost starting out of their
heads.'

their very gesture; they looked as they had heard of
a world ransomed, or one destroyed: a notable pas-   15
sion of wonder appeared in them; but the wisest be-
holder, that knew no more but seeing, could not say
if th' importance were joy or sorrow; but in the extremity of the one it must needs be.

Enter another Gentleman.

Here comes a gentleman that haply knows more.   20
The news, Rogero?
Sec. Gent. Nothing but bonfires: the Oracle is fulfilled;
the king's daughter is found: such a deal of wonder
is broken out within this hour, that ballad-makers
cannot be able to express it.   25

Enter [a third] Gentleman.

Here comes the Lady Paulina's steward: he can deliver you more. How goes it now, sir? This news,
which is called true, is so like an old tale that the
verity of it is in strong suspicion. Has the king found
his heir?   30
Third Gent. Most true, if ever truth were pregnant by
circumstance: that which you hear you'll swear you
see, there is such unity in the proofs. The mantle of
Queen Hermione's, her jewel about the neck of it,

20. haply] happily *F.*   22. *Sec. Gent.*] *Gent.2. F (and throughout scene).*
25. S.D. *a third*] *Capell; another F.*   31. *Third Gent.*] *Gent.3. F (and throughout*
scene).

17. *seeing*] what he saw.
17–19. *could . . . be*] 'could not say
whether it all signified joy or sorrow
but it was certainly the height (or
depth) of one or the other'.
18. *importance*] import, meaning.
20. *haply*] The spellings 'haply' and
'happily' were interchangeable.
21. *Rogero*] This is unlike the Plu-
tarchian names of the other male
characters. It was the name of a popular tune (H. E. Rollins, *A Pepysian
Garland*, 1922, 176), and another called
'New Rogero' existed in 1589 (H. L.
Collmann, *Ballads . . . of the Elizabethan*

Period, 1912, nos. 10, 43), and is in the
Orlando Furioso.
22. *bonfires*] Cf. 'threw their hats . . .
some to make bonfires, some to drinke'
(*Philaster*, i. i. 48) and *Pandosto*, pp.
184, l. 33; 224, l. 34.
24. *ballad-makers*] The ballads were
the sensational press of the age. Cf.
iv. iv. 260n.
31–2. *pregnant by circumstance*] 'made
convincing by evidence'.
33. *mantle*] Arviragus is also identified by a 'mantle, wrought by . . . / . . .
his queen mother' (*Cym.*, v. v. 361–2).
34. *jewel*] Thaisa 'resurrected' from

the letters of Antigonus found with it, which they   35
know to be his character; the majesty of the creature
in resemblance of the mother, the affection of nobleness which nature shows above her breeding, and
many other evidences proclaim her, with all certainty, to be the king's daughter. Did you see the   40
meeting of the two kings?

Sec. Gent. No.

Third Gent. Then have you lost a sight which was to be
seen, cannot be spoken of. There might you have be-
held one joy crown another, so and in such manner   45
that it seemed sorrow wept to take leave of them, for
their joy waded in tears. There was casting up of
eyes, holding up of hands, with countenance of such
distraction, that they were to be known by garment,
not by favour. Our king, being ready to leap out of   50
himself for joy of his found daughter, as if that joy
were now become a loss, cries 'O, thy mother, thy
mother!' then asks Bohemia forgiveness; then embraces his son-in-law; then again worries he his
daughter with clipping her; now he thanks the old   55
shepherd, which stands by, like a weather-bitten
conduit of many kings' reigns. I never heard of such
another encounter, which lames report to follow it,
and undoes description to do it.

56. weather-bitten] *F*; weather-beaten *F3*.

the sea is identified partly by a ring
(*Per.*, v. iii. 40).

36. *character*] handwriting.

37. *affection*] quality.

48. *countenance*] demeanour, appearance.

49. *distraction*] distortion. Cf. 'a mere
distraction' (*H8*, III. i. 112).

50. *favour*] features, appearance.

50–1. *leap out of himself*] a form of
'jump out of his skin' (Tilley, S507).

55. *clipping*] embracing.

56–7. *weather-bitten . . . reigns*] 'an
old weather-beaten (or weather-
corroded) water-spout in the form of
a human figure which has seen the
reigns of many kings'. 'Conduit' could

mean not only the pipe through which
water ran but also the structure from
which it issued and this was often in
the shape of a human figure or head
(*O.E.D.* conduit *sb*.2 and Onions, and
cf. *Tit.*, II. iv. 30; *Rom.*, III. v. 129).
Well-known conduits of this kind
would be the gargoyles on churches
and other large buildings, and these
were frequently in the form of an old
man's head. The image is of the old
shepherd weeping. Cf. 'in rime
doggrell (like thy Winter bitten
Epitaph)' (E. de Maisonneuve, *Geri-
leon of England . . . trans. . . . . A. M[undy*],
1592, Sig. A4v).

59. *do*] express, do justice to.

Sec. Gent. What, pray you, became of Antigonus, that   60
    carried hence the child?

Third Gent. Like an old tale still, which will have matter
    to rehearse, though credit be asleep and not an ear
    open. He was torn to pieces with a bear: this avouches
    the shepherd's son; who has not only his innocence,   65
    which seems much, to justify him, but a handker-
    chief and rings of his that Paulina knows.

First Gent. What became of his bark and his followers?

Third Gent. Wrecked the same instant of their master's
    death, and in the view of the shepherd: so that all   70
    the instruments which aided to expose the child were
    even then lost when it was found. But O, the noble
    combat that 'twixt joy and sorrow was fought in
    Paulina! She had one eye declined for the loss of her
    husband, another elevated that the Oracle was ful-   75
    filled: she lifted the princess from the earth, and so
    locks her in embracing as if she would pin her to her
    heart, that she might no more be in danger of losing.

First Gent. The dignity of this act was worth the audience
    of kings and princes; for by such was it acted.   80

Third Gent. One of the prettiest touches of all, and that
    which angled for mine eyes (caught the water though
    not the fish) was, when at the relation of the queen's
    death (with the manner how she came to 't bravely
    confessed and lamented by the king) how attentive-   85

60. pray] 'pray *F.*   78. losing] loosing *F.*

63. *credit*] belief.

64–5. *this avouches . . . son*] 'This the
shepherd's son avouches.'

74–5. *one eye . . . elevated*] another
version of Claudius's 'an auspicious,
and a dropping eye' (*Ham.*, I. ii. 11)
meaning 'with a mixture of happiness
and grief'. Beatrice White (*Anglia*,
lxxvii, 1959, 204–7) holds that in
Ham. the expression indicates that
Claudius was a hypocrite (cf. Chaucer,
Book of the Duchess, i. 633). In *Wint.* the
expression certainly indicates nothing
of the kind concerning Paulina. 'To
cry (look down) with one eye and

laugh (look up) with the other' is in
proverbial use at least since 1520
(Tilley, E248). It is apparently widespread and was used in the 19th century: e.g. 'en pleurant d'un œil pour
le passé et en riant de l'autre pour le
présent' (E. Souvestre, *Le foyer Breton*,
1864, i. 178). See p. lxxxviii.

78. *losing*] being lost. But 'loosing',
carrying on the sense of 'pin', may be
right: 'that she might no longer be in
danger of being physically separated
from her'. Probably both senses are
present.

85–6. *attentiveness*] listening to this.

ness wounded his daughter; till, from one sign of
dolour to another, she did, with an 'Alas,' I would
fain say, bleed tears, for I am sure my heart wept
blood. Who was most marble, there changed colour;
some swooned, all sorrowed: if all the world could   90
have seen 't, the woe had been universal.

First Gent. Are they returned to the court?

Third Gent. No: the princess hearing of her mother's
statue, which is in the keeping of Paulina,—a piece
many years in doing and now newly performed by   95
that rare Italian master, Julio Romano, who, had
he himself eternity and could put breath into his
work, would beguile Nature of her custom, so perfectly he is her ape: he so near to Hermione hath
done Hermione, that they say one would speak to   100

---

90. swooned] swownded *F.*

87–8. *Alas . . . tears*] perhaps suggested by the belief that sighs did cost
the heart blood.

89. *Who . . . marble*] 'Whoever was
most insusceptible and incapable of
changing colour, did change colour.'

96. *Julio Romano*] The introduction
of this Italian painter (d. 1546) is a
well-known anachronism. Elze (*Essays
on Sh.*, 284–9) points out that Vasari
shows that Julio was also a sculptor
from the lines on his tomb: *Videbat
Iuppiter corpora sculpta pictaque | Spirare,
et ædes mortalium æquarier Cælo | Iulii
virtute Romani.* (*Lives of . . . Painters*,
trans. Mrs J. Foster, 1911, iv. 58n.)
and he was also an architect. Shakespeare may have seen some of Julio's
paintings, and Vasari's *Lives* in Italian.
Elze notes the similarity between 97–
100 and the epitaph: 'Jupiter saw
sculptured and painted statues breathe
and earthly buildings made equal to
[*æquarier* for *æquari*] those in heaven by
the skill of Julio Romano.' (The epitaph goes on to say that Jupiter carried
Julio off because he could not tolerate
being surpassed in artistic work by
a mortal.) S. C. Chew, *The Virtues
Reconciled*, 1947, 11, suggests that as

performed means 'completed by painting' (cf. *O.E.D.*+2b, last recorded use
1612) the Third Gent. is saying that
Julio merely painted the statue, showing that Shakespeare believed that he
was only a painter. But the passage
indicates that the whole statue, in form
and colouring, was a speaking likeness. That 'performed' had this meaning is confirmed by 174, for the Clown,
having no other information but
this, there refers to 'the queen's picture', and cf. v. iii. 47, 81. It might be
possible to trace works by Giulio which
Shakespeare could have seen in England through F. Hartt, *Giulio Romano*,
2 vols., 1958.

98. *beguile . . . custom*] 'deprive
Nature of her trade—do Nature's
work for her in peopling the earth with
creatures of his manufacture'. The
strife of art with nature is frequently
referred to: cf. v. iii. 19, 68; *Cym.*, II.
iv. 72–85; *Ant.*, II. ii. 204; *Shr.*, Ind. II.
50–60; *Ven.*, 289–32; *Lucr.*, 1366–1568,
and *To the Reader* verse in *F.* It is related
to the grafting talk of Perdita |
Polixenes, IV. iv. 85–103.

100–1. *one . . . answer*] The widespread view that eye-deceiving veri-

her and stand in hope of answer. Thither with all
greediness of affection are they gone, and there
they intend to sup.

Sec. Gent. I thought she had some great matter there in
hand; for she hath privately twice or thrice a day,   105
ever since the death of Hermione, visited that removed house. Shall we thither, and with our company piece the rejoicing?

First Gent. Who would be thence that has the benefit of
access? Every wink of an eye, some new grace will   110
be born: our absence makes us unthrifty to our
knowledge. Let's along.   *Exeunt [Gentlemen].*

Aut. Now, had I not the dash of my former life in me,
would preferment drop on my head. I brought the
old man and his son aboard the prince; told him I   115
heard them talk of a fardel and I know not what:
but he at that time overfond of the shepherd's
daughter (so he then took her to be), who began to
be much sea-sick, and himself little better, extremity of weather continuing, this mystery re-   120

---

112. S.D. *Exeunt Gentlemen] Exit F.*

similitude was great merit in the
painter's art is shown in the oft-
repeated story found in Pliny, *Historie
of the World . . . Trans. . . . P. Holland*,
1601, ii. 535: '*Zeuxis* for proofe of his
cunning, brought . . . a table [i.e.
picture] wherein were clustres of
grapes so lively painted, that the very
birds of the aire flew flocking thither
for to bee pecking at the grapes.
Parasius . . . came with another picture, wherein he had painted a linnen
sheet, so like unto a sheet indeed, that
Zeuxis . . . came unto *Parasius* with
these words by way of a scorne and
frumpe, Come on sir, away with your
sheet once, that we may see your
goodly picture: But taking himselfe
with the manner, and perceiving his
owne error, hee was mightily abashed,
& like an honest minded man yeelded
the victory unto his adversary, saying
withall, *Zeuxis* hath beguiled poore

birds, but *Parrhasius* hath deceived
Zeuxis.' (Cf. also *The Elder Pliny's
Chapters on the History of Art, trans. K.
Jex-Blake*, 1896, lxi–lxii, 109–11.) The
story is referred to in *Pandosto*, p. 211,
l. 15.

102. *greediness of affection*] 'eagerness
of natural love'.

106–7. *removed*] withdrawn, seques-
tered.

108. *piece*] augment, help to complete, join. Cf. v. iii. 56.

111. *unthrifty to*] 'wasting opportunity to increase'.

113. *dash*] stain.

118. *so*] as.

119. *sea-sick*] There is the same touch
of realism in Lyly, *Euphues and his England*, where Philautus is unable to pay
full attention to Euphues' story because he is 'Sea-sicke' and has 'a quesie
stomacke' (ed. R. W. Bond, 1902, ii.
29, 33).

mained undiscovered. But 'tis all one to me; for had
I been the finder out of this secret, it would not have
relished among my other discredits.

Enter SHEPHERD *and* CLOWN.

Here come those I have done good to against my
will, and already appearing in the blossoms of their   125
fortune.

Shep. Come, boy; I am past moe children, but thy sons
and daughters will be all gentlemen born.

Clo. You are well met, sir. You denied to fight with me
this other day, because I was no gentleman born.   130
See you these clothes? say you see them not and
think me still no gentleman born: you were best say
these robes are not gentleman born: give me the lie;
do; and try whether I am not now a gentleman
born.   135

Aut. I know you are now, sir, a gentleman born.

Clo. Ay, and have been so any time these four hours.

Shep. And so have I, boy.

Clo. So you have: but I was a gentleman born before my
father; for the king's son took me by the hand, and   140
called me brother; and then the two kings called
my father brother; and then the prince, my
brother, and the princess, my sister, called my
father father; and so we wept; and there was the
first gentleman-like tears that ever we shed.   145

Shep. We may live, son, to shed many more.

127. moe] *F;* more *F2.*

123. *relished*] pleased. 'It would not
have done me any good because of my
other discredits'. Dr Brooks notes that
Autolycus seems to have, to admiration, that discreet estimate of himself
and his place in life which Parolles so
signally lacked, and, without Parolles'
catastrophe to chasten him, he too is
resolved that 'Simply the thing I am /
Shall make me live' (*All's W.,* IV. iii.
310–11).

127. *moe*] more (cf. I. ii. 8).

128. *gentlemen born*] 'It takes three

generations to make a gentleman' is
still a current saying, and *The Booke of
Honour and Armes* (1590) says that 'a
gentleman borne' must be descended
from three degrees of gentry on both
sides. However, many 16–17-cent.
'gentry' had arrived almost as quickly
as the Clown.

131–3.] That clothes make the man
is proverbial (Tilley, A283) and cf.
'apparel oft proclaims the man' (*Ham.,*
I. iii. 72). Cf. *Cym.,* IV. ii. 82–4, and
Pandosto, p. 211, l. 14.

Clo. Ay; or else 'twere hard luck, being in so preposterous estate as we are.

Aut. I humbly beseech you, sir, to pardon me all the faults I have committed to your worship, and to   150
give me your good report to the prince my master.

Shep. Prithee, son, do; for we must be gentle, now we are gentlemen.

Clo. Thou wilt amend thy life?

Aut. Ay, and it like your good worship.   155

Clo. Give me thy hand: I will swear to the prince thou art as honest a true fellow as any is in Bohemia.

Shep. You may say it, but not swear it.

Clo. Not swear it, now I am a gentleman? Let boors and franklins say it, I'll swear it.   160

Shep. How if it be false, son?

Clo. If it be ne'er so false, a true gentleman may swear it in the behalf of his friend: and I'll swear to the prince thou art a tall fellow of thy hands and that thou wilt not be drunk; but I know thou art no tall   165
fellow of thy hands and that thou wilt be drunk: but I'll swear it, and I would thou would'st be a tall fellow of thy hands.

Aut. I will prove so, sir, to my power.

Clo. Ay, by any means prove a tall fellow: if I do not   170
wonder how thou dar'st venture to be drunk, not

152. Prithee] 'Prethee *F.*

147–8. *preposterous*] the Clown's apt mistake for 'prosperous'.

152. *gentle*] 'act with dignity, as befitting someone who is well born'. The shepherd is quick to accept the doctrine of *noblesse oblige*.

154. *amend thy life*] Cf. *1H4*, 'I'll amend my life' (III. iii. 24); 'a good amendment of life in thee' (I. ii. 99).

155. *and*] if. Cf. IV. iv. 716.

158. *You . . . swear it*] Cf. Johnson's support of the dictum that 'A man will *say* what he will not *swear*' (Boswell, *Journal of a Tour to the Hebrides*, 1785–10 Nov. 1773). The distinction is also emphasized at I. ii. 34–7, II. i. 62–4. Cf. *Cym.*, II. iii. 90–1; II. iv. 122, 143.

159. *boors*] peasants. That swearing is the prerogative of gentlemen is also asserted by Cloten (*Cym.*, II. i. 10).

160. *franklins*] yeomen: not, like Chaucer's franklin, a country gentleman.

164. *tall . . . hands*] 'a doughty man'. The use of 'a tall man' in this sense was new in the 1590s. It is in *R3* (I. iv. 149), *Shr.* (IV. iv. 17), *Rom.* (II. iv. 30, where it is described as new), and *Tw.N.* (I. iii. 18, where it is not understood). Cf. R. Cotgrave, *Dictionarie of the French and English Tongues*, 1611, '*Homme à la main*, a man of execution or valour, a man of his hands', and Tilley, M163.

being a tall fellow, trust me not. Hark! the kings
and the princes, our kindred, are going to see the
queen's picture. Come, follow us: we'll be thy good
masters.   *Exeunt.*   175

SCENE III

Enter LEONTES, POLIXENES, FLORIZEL, PERDITA, CAMILLO,
PAULINA, *Lords,* [*and Attendants*].

Leon. O grave and good Paulina, the great comfort
    That I have had of thee!
Paul.   What, sovereign sir,
    I did not well, I meant well. All my services
    You have paid home: but that you have vouchsaf'd,
    With your crown'd brother and these your contracted   5
    Heirs of your kingdoms, my poor house to visit,
    It is a surplus of your grace, which never
    My life may last to answer.
Leon.   O Paulina,
    We honour you with trouble: but we came
    To see the statue of our queen: your gallery   10
    Have we pass'd through, not without much content
    In many singularities; but we saw not
    That which my daughter came to look upon,
    The statue of her mother.
Paul.   As she liv'd peerless,
    So her dead likeness, I do well believe,   15
    Excels whatever yet you look'd upon,

Scene III

Scene III] *Scæna Tertia. F.*   S.D. *Enter Leontes . . . Attendants.*] *Enter Leontes,
Polixenes, Florizell, Perdita, Camillo, Paulina: Hermione (like a Statue:) Lords, &c. F.*

174. *picture*] here meaning 'painted
statue'. Cf. 96n.

Scene III

Scene iii] A room in Paulina's house·
    5. *these your contracted*] Staunton, *N.C.
Wint.*, and others believe this *your* to be
a compositor's addition, and delete it.
Alexander retains, but its authenticity
is doubtful.

9. *We . . . trouble*] i.e. 'I fear that this
honour you speak of is merely giving
you trouble.' Cf. *Mac.*, I. vi. 11; *Ado*,
I. i. 81, 83. In *Cym.*, II. iii. 88, the sense is
different but may be worth noting as
the antithesis of 'swear' and 'say'
occurs in 90, 91. Cf. *Wint.*, v. ii.
158n.
    12. *In many singularities*] 'at its many
rarities'.

Or hand of man hath done; therefore I keep it
Lonely, apart. But here it is: prepare
To see the life as lively mock'd as ever
Still sleep mock'd death: behold, and say 'tis well.   20

               [Paulina draws a curtain, and discovers
                          Hermione standing like a statue]

I like your silence, it the more shows off
Your wonder: but yet speak; first you, my liege.
Comes it not something near?

Leon.   Her natural posture!
Chide me, dear stone, that I may say indeed
Thou art Hermione; or rather, thou art she   25
In thy not chiding; for she was as tender
As infancy and grace. But yet, Paulina,
Hermione was not so much wrinkled, nothing
So aged as this seems.

Pol.   O, not by much.

Paul. So much the more our carver's excellence,   30
Which lets go by some sixteen years and makes her
As she liv'd now.

Leon.   As now she might have done,
So much to my good comfort as it is
Now piercing to my soul. O, thus she stood,
Even with such life of majesty, warm life,   35
As now it coldly stands, when first I woo'd her!
I am asham'd: does not the stone rebuke me

---

18. Lonely] *Hanmer and many edd.;* Louely F.   21. S.D. *Paulina . . . statue]*
Rowe (1); no S.D. in F.

18. *Lonely*] *Lonely* has a normal contemporary sense of 'isolated' (*O.E.D.* 2). Leontes has just asked why they have not yet seen the statue, and Paulina tells him—because the statue, being peerless, is kept apart and by itself. *Lovely* is possible, referring back to the excelling merit of the work and to Hermione's mature beauty, but its use would be strained here and Hanmer almost certainly only corrects a printer's error.

19–20. *life . . . death*] 'life imitated as closely as ever sleep imitated death'. That sleep is the image of death is proverbial (Tilley, S527). Cf. 'sleep, thou ape of death' (*Cym.*, II. iii. 31) and *Wint.*, v. ii. 98, 100–1nn., *Shr.*, Ind. i. 34, and word-echo 'dull sleep / Did mock sad fools' (*Per.*, v. i. 160).

20. *say 'tis well*] The audience do not know that Hermione is alive. For them as well as for everyone else on the stage except Paulina the statue can be nothing but a statue.

37. *stone rebuke me*] Noble, *Biblical Knowledge*, 248, draws attention to 'Thou hast consulted shame to thine owne house, by destroying many people, and hast sinned against thine

For being more stone than it? O royal piece!
There's magic in thy majesty, which has
My evils conjur'd to remembrance, and   40
From thy admiring daughter took the spirits,
Standing like stone with thee.

Per.   And give me leave,
And do not say 'tis superstition, that
I kneel, and then implore her blessing. Lady,
Dear queen, that ended when I but began,   45
Give me that hand of yours to kiss.

Paul.   O patience!
The statue is but newly fix'd, the colour's
Not dry.

Cam. My lord, your sorrow was too sore laid on,
Which sixteen winters cannot blow away,   50
So many summers dry: scarce any joy
Did ever so long live; no sorrow
But kill'd itself much sooner.

Pol.   Dear my brother,
Let him that was the cause of this have power
To take off so much grief from you as he   55

owne soule. For the stone shall crie out of the wall' (*Habakkuk*, ii. 10–11).

38. *piece*] work of art. Cf. IV. iv. 423.

41. *admiring*] wondering, filled with awe.

47. *fix'd*] here means 'painted'. Cf. V. ii. 96n.

52.] The line is a syllable short. Perhaps the *But* of 53 should have been printed at the end of 52 where *F* has 'sorrow'. Other suggestions are 'sorrow sir' (Capell), 'sorrow ever' (Knightley), 'nor ever sorrow' (anon. Cambridge).

54. *Let him . . . this*] Polixenes takes blame upon himself and his magnanimity is typical of ideal friendship of the day found frequently in Shakespeare. The heavens are continuing the love between the two friends (I. i. 23, 31). The emotional profundity of Tudor friendship is described by L. J. Mills in *One Soul in Bodies Twain. Friendship in Tudor Literature and Stuart*

Drama, 1937. Cf. Valentine's magnanimity in forgiving Proteus: 'And, that my love may appear plain and free, / All that was mine in Silvia I give thee' (*Gent.*, v. iv. 82). In the light of the friendship tradition that particular scene is really emotional. And so here Polixenes, in deep emotional friendship which would be well understood by the audience, exaggerates his responsibility for Hermione's 'death' and, in sympathy for the overpowering remorse in which Leontes is lost, further exaggerates it in order to help his friend. Cf. *Cæs.*, IV. iii. 85, 'A friend should bear his friend's infirmities', and 'Such is my love, to thee I so belong, / That for thy right myself will bear all wrong' (*Sonn.* lxxxviii. Cf. also *Sonn.* xxxv, lxxxix) and *The Two Noble Kinsmen*: 'an endless mine to one another / . . . am not I / Part of your blood, part of your soul?' (II. ii. 79, 178–9).

Will piece up in himself.

Paul.   Indeed, my lord,
    If I had thought the sight of my poor image
    Would thus have wrought you—for the stone is mine—
    I'd not have show'd it.

Leon.   Do not draw the curtain.

Paul. No longer shall you gaze on 't, lest your fancy   60
    May think anon it moves.

Leon.   Let be, let be!
    Would I were dead, but that methinks already—
    What was he that did make it?—See, my lord,
    Would you not deem it breath'd? and that those veins
    Did verily bear blood?

Pol.   Masterly done: 65
    The very life seems warm upon her lip.

Leon. The fixure of her eye has motion in 't,
    As we are mock'd with art.

Paul.   I'll draw the curtain:
    My lord's almost so far transported that
    He'll think anon it lives.

Leon.   O sweet Paulina,   70
    Make me to think so twenty years together!
    No settled senses of the world can match
    The pleasure of that madness. Let 't alone.

Paul. I am sorry, sir, I have thus far stirr'd you: but
    I could afflict you farther.

Leon.   Do, Paulina;   75

---

65. Masterly] 'Masterly *F*.   67. fixture] *F*; fixture *F4*.

56. *piece up*] add to, parcel up. Cf. v. ii. 108. 'Allow the person (i.e. Polixenes) who was the cause of all this trouble to relieve you of some of your grief which he will bear himself.'

62. *Would . . . already*] Staunton's interpretation 'May I die, if I do not think [it moves] already' seems right. Some edd. have conjectured a line missing. But the language, as it is, is typical of Leontes' broken speech under emotion.

67. *fixure*] 'The very colouring and setting of her eye suggests that it could move.' *Fixure* is an earlier form of *fixture*. The sense is both of colour, painting (cf. 47), and also of fixture since that yields the paradox 'the fixture . . . has motion in it.'

68. *As*] so, in such a way (Abbott, §110).

72–3. *No settled . . . madness*] Dr Brooks points out the parallel with Florizel in IV. iv. 483–6. Florizel in his love of Perdita and Leontes in his love of Hermione each recognizes something stronger than the rational.

For this affliction has a taste as sweet
As any cordial comfort. Still methinks
There is an air comes from her. What fine chisel
Could ever yet cut breath? Let no man mock me,
For I will kiss her.
Paul.   Good my lord, forbear: 80
The ruddiness upon her lip is wet;
You'll mar it if you kiss it, stain your own
With oily painting. Shall I draw the curtain?
Leon. No: not these twenty years.
Per.   So long could I
Stand by, a looker on.
Paul.   Either forbear,   85
Quit presently the chapel, or resolve you
For more amazement. If you can behold it,
I'll make the statue move indeed; descend,
And take you by the hand: but then you'll think
(Which I protest against) I am assisted   90
By wicked powers.
Leon.   What you can make her do,
I am content to look on: what to speak,
I am content to hear; for 'tis as easy
To make her speak as move.
Paul.   It is requir'd
You do awake your faith. Then all stand still: 95
Or—those that think it is unlawful business
I am about, let them depart.
Leon.   Proceed:
No foot shall stir.

96. Or] *Hanmer;* On: *F.*

86. *presently*] immediately.
88. *indeed*] in very truth, actually.
91. *wicked powers*] Shakespeare is careful to emphasize that black magic is not being used, as also in 110–11. Cf. C. J. Sisson, 'The magic of Prospero' (*Sh.Sur.*, xi, esp. 70, 74).
96. *Or—those*] Hanmer's emendation gives to Paulina's injunction that all should stand still the alternative which seems to be required: 'stand still, or [rather as an afterthought as she changes her mind] those who have any doubts, let them go'. In manuscript *n* and *r* could be similar, and a broken flourish at the end of either could be like a colon. It must however be recorded that *On* is often used with the sense of 'Let us proceed', 'Come on' (e.g. i. ii. 411; ii. i. 29; *Ant.*, i. ii. 93; *H8*, i. ii. 192), but a three-fold shift 'Stand still: Proceed: Depart' would surely leave an audience puzzled as to what such instructions intended.

Paul.   Music, awake her; strike!   [*Music*]
  'Tis time; descend; be stone no more; approach;
  Strike all that look upon with marvel. Come!   100
  I'll fill your grave up: stir, nay, come away:
  Bequeath to death your numbness; for from him
  Dear life redeems you. You perceive she stirs:
                              [*Hermione comes down*]
  Start not; her actions shall be holy as
  You hear my spell is lawful. [*To Leontes*] Do not shun her
  Until you see her die again; for then   106
  You kill her double. Nay, present your hand:
  When she was young you woo'd her; now, in age,
  Is she become the suitor?
Leon.   O, she's warm!
  If this be magic, let it be an art   110
  Lawful as eating.
Pol.   She embraces him!
Cam. She hangs about his neck!
  If she pertain to life, let her speak too!
Pol. Ay, and make it manifest where she has liv'd,
  Or how stolen from the dead!
Paul.   That she is living,   115
  Were it but told you, should be hooted at
  Like an old tale: but it appears she lives,

98. S.D. *Music*] *Rowe* (*1*) ; *no S.D. in F.*   103. S.D. *Hermione comes down*] *Rowe*
(*1*) ; *no S.D. in F.*   105. S.D. *To Leontes*] *This ed.* ; *no S.D. in F.*

98. *Music . . . strike*] As in the
awakening of Thaisa from her trance
(*Per.*, III. ii. 93–101) and, in mysterious
way, at the recovery of Pericles (v. i.
222–33), there may also be here an
underlying idea that music has the
power of restoring the dead to life (cf.
G. H. Cowling, *Music on the Shakespearian Stage*, 1913, 72–3). Certainly
here 'it functions as the specifically
releasing agent' (G. Wilson Knight,
The Crown of Life, 1947, 124).

100. *upon*] on.

101. *I'll fill . . . up*] Paulina emphasizes that Hermione has returned as
from the grave to actual life. When it
comes to be learnt what Paulina has

done and that Hermione never has
died then the very thought of Hermione's 'grave' will be obliterated
from men's minds.

105. To Leontes] Paulina has been
addressing the whole assembly with
Leontes as her chief auditor, but here
she addresses him particularly.

107. *double*] 'for the second time'.
Even at this stage Paulina reminds
Leontes of his crime.

117. *an old tale*] Cf. p. liii. Dr
Brooks points out that on one level
this contributes to the sense of
actuality: 'this is like an old tale,
therefore it is not one'; but on a deeper
level to the sense of various planes of

Though yet she speak not. Mark a little while.
[*To Perdita*] Please you to interpose, fair madam, kneel
And pray your mother's blessing. [*To Hermione*] Turn,
    good lady,   120
Our Perdita is found.

Her.   You gods, look down,
And from your sacred vials pour your graces
Upon my daughter's head! Tell me, mine own,
Where hast thou been preserv'd? where liv'd? how
    found
Thy father's court? for thou shalt hear that I,   125
Knowing by Paulina that the Oracle
Gave hope thou wast in being, have preserv'd
Myself to see the issue.

Paul.   There's time enough for that;
Lest they desire (upon this push) to trouble
Your joys with like relation. Go together,   130
You precious winners all; your exultation
Partake to every one. I, an old turtle,
Will wing me to some wither'd bough, and there
My mate (that's never to be found again)
Lament, till I am lost.

---

119. S.D. *To Perdita*] *This ed.; no S.D. in F.*   120. S.D. *To Hermione*] *This ed.; no
S.D. in F.*   122. vials] *Pope;* Viols *F.*

reality as so often suggested in Shakespeare by a comment that reminds us that the action is itself enacted story. E.g. IV. iv. 133–4; 'the quick comedians / Extemporally will stage us . . . / Some squeaking Cleopatra boy my greatness' (*Ant.*, v. ii. 215–19); 'If this were played upon a stage now, I could condemn it as an improbable fiction' (*Tw.N.*, III. iv. 121); 'he doth it as like one of these harlotry players as ever I see' (*1H4*, II. iv. 384); 'Shall's have a play of this' (*Cym.*, v. v. 228).

121–3. *You gods . . . head*] Cf. *Tp.*, v. i. 201–2.

126. *Knowing by Paulina*] In fact, Hermione herself heard the Oracle read (III. ii. 137).

129–30. *upon . . . relation*] 'at this

critical moment to disturb your happiness with their stories'.

132. *Partake to*] 'share with'.

132–5. *I . . . lost*] Paulina's lament carries an echo in sentiment and word of that of Thaisa in *Per.*, III. iv. 8–11, and, as noted by Moorman, of Lodge's *Rosalynde* (Montanus Sonnet, p. 132 of Caxton Series edn, 1902): 'A turtle sate upon a leavelesse tree, / Mourning her absent pheare, / With sad and sorry cheare'. The turtle dove is symbolic of constancy. 'As true as a turtle to her mate' is proverbial (Tilley, T624). The turtle pairs for life. Cf. IV. iv. 154–5.

135. *lost*] 'broken with grief' or 'dead'. For this sense of 'lost' meaning 'destroyed', 'ruined' cf. Katharine's 'A woman lost among ye' (*H8*, III. i.

Leon.   O, peace, Paulina!   135
Thou shouldst a husband take by my consent,
As I by thine a wife: this is a match,
And made between 's by vows. Thou hast found mine;
But how, is to be question'd; for I saw her,
As I thought, dead; and have in vain said many   140
A prayer upon her grave. I'll not seek far—
For him, I partly know his mind—to find thee
An honourable husband. Come, Camillo,
And take her by the hand; whose worth and honesty
Is richly noted; and here justified   145
By us, a pair of kings. Let's from this place.
[*To Hermione*] What! look upon my brother: both your
        pardons,
That e'er I put between your holy looks
My ill suspicion. This your son-in-law,
And son unto the king, whom, heavens directing,   150
Is troth-plight to your daughter. Good Paulina,
Lead us from hence, where we may leisurely
Each one demand, and answer to his part
Perform'd in this wide gap of time, since first
We were dissever'd: hastily lead away.   *Exeunt.*   155

---

147. S.D. *To Hermione*] *This ed.; no S.D. in F.*

107) and the 'loss' of *Wint.*, II. iii. 191n.; III. iii. 51.

139–40. *for I saw . . . dead*] Cf. 'But we saw him dead' (*Cym.*, v. v. 126).

141. *far*] *farre* F. Perhaps the comparative. Cf. IV. iv. 432n.

142. *For*] As for.

144. *by the*] These words overweight the line but would be slurred in speech.

144–6. *whose worth . . . kings*] Mason and *N.C. Wint.* believe these words refer to Camillo since Polixenes hardly knew Paulina. But he did know her and they are spoken by Leontes who knew her well. There is little doubt that they refer to Paulina.

145. *Is . . . justified*] 'are well known and are here vouched for'. For *justify* cf. I. ii. 278 and *O.E.D.* 5, Schmidt 2.

146. *Let's from*] Omission of the verb of motion is common with *let* and *must* followed by a preposition or adverb. There are 19 other examples under *let* in Bartlett. Cf. IV. iv. 820 and Franz, 497, §621.

149. *This*] Often so printed for 'this is', as here.

151. *troth-plight*] Cf. I. ii. 278n. and IV. iv. 418n.

153. *demand, and answer*] Retirement for exchange of experiences is common at the close of Shakespeare's plays, particularly of those which end happily.

154. *gap of time*] The phrase is also in *Ant.*, I. v. 5, and cf. *Cym.*, III. ii. 61–2. Its use here reminds us of Time and his promise to present what we have now seen completed.

APPENDIX I

MISCELLANEOUS LONGER NOTES

I. NAMES OF THE CHARACTERS

Shakespeare took most of the characters' names from Plutarch, from North's translation, probably from an edition of 1603.[1] This contains the names *Leontes, Camillus, Antigonus, Cleomenes, Dion, Polyxemus, Archidamus, Autolycus, Hermione,* and *Aemylia,* and although *Paulina* is not there, Paulinus is. *Leontes* is in Plutarch only as a name of a tribe (Themistocles, 203; Aristides, 153) but there are several names based on Leo-, e.g. Leonidas (in Agis, a king who is hated by the citizens since he has caused the murder of three people), Leonatus (used in *Cymbeline*), Leontidas, and Leontini. All these names in Plutarch, except Autolycus, the female names, and perhaps Leontes, were probably the direct sources of the names in the play, and even the exceptions may have been seen by Shakespeare in Plutarch and have influenced him to choose those names although the immediate source was elsewhere. Antigonus, besides being in Plutarch, is also in Josephus, *Antiquities of the Jews.*[2] Neither *Florizel* nor his pseudonym *Doricles* (IV. iv. 170) is in Plutarch: but Plutarch has Doricus, Doris, and Doreo.[3] In Plutarch the names occur chiefly in the lives of Camillus and of Agis and Cleomenes; and Shakespeare was possibly indebted to the Lives for rather more than the names: Camillus, for example, is a kind and noble man in Plutarch as Camillo is in the play, where he is mainly Shakespeare's creation.[4] Apart from the Roman plays,

1. Repr. by the Nonesuch Press, 5 vol., 1929–30. References are to that reprint. The handiest name index to the *Lives* seems to be that, in Latinized form, to the Teubner ed. of the Greek text.

2. There were editions in English of Josephus' *Works* in 1602 and 1609.

3. Polyxenes is in *Troil.* and Dionyza in *Per.,* Florizel is Dorastus in *Pandosto.* For Smalus see v. i. 156n.

4. Although Shakespeare probably took Camillo from Plutarch, the name was well known in Shakespeare's day. The Patrician name continued as a sur-name and Christian name in Italy and several books by authors named Camillus were printed before 1611. Camillo is the name of a character in Webster's *The White Devil,* probably written in 1611. A well-known contemporary Camillo is St Camillus de Lellis who established the order of 'Fathers of a Good Death' in

Shakespeare's debt to Plutarch has not been fully explored.[1] The few Leo- names in Shakespeare are not of heroic characters. Leonato (*Ado*) is light-hearted, fierce at times, but weak in believing the slander on his daughter; Leonardo (*Mer.V.*) is a servant; Leonine (*Per.*) is a servant and murderer. There is, however, striking similarity between Leontes and Posthumus Leonatus (*Cym.*). In each the Leo- character behaves weakly and foolishly; each is overcome by jealousy, each wills the death of his wife and actually thinks that he has caused it, each is shown his criminal folly, becomes remorseful, and is reunited to and reconciled with his wife. Leon, Leonatus, Leontius are in the *Arcadia*.

Of the other names *Mamillius* may be taken from Greene's two romances entitled *Mamillia* (1583, 1593). *Florizel* probably comes from *Amadis de Grecia*, one of Feliciano de Silva's continuations of *Amadis de Gaule*.[2] Greene used this but did not take the name Florizel from it although he took Garinter. Florizel's pseudonym *Doricles* (IV. iv. 170) is in the *Iliad* and *Aeneid*, Dorcus in *Troilus*, Dorastus in *Pandosto*, Dorus, Dorilaus in the *Arcadia*.[3] *Hermione* is in Plutarch and Homer and is the name of a male character in *The Rare Triumphs of Love and Fortune* acted at Court in 1581–2 and printed in 1589.[4] Perdita derives from the Oracle in *Pandosto* (p. 196)—'that which is lost'—and the reason for the name is specifically given (III. iii. 33). There may be an added hint for the formation of the name in *Pericles*, III. iii. 13; Perdita parallels Marina and will be paralleled by Miranda. *Mopsa* is the name of the shepherd's wife in *Pandosto* and is also in Sidney's *Arcadia*. *Dorcas* is Biblical (*Acts* ix. 36, 39).

1584. Camillus resigned the headship in 1607 being succeeded by an Englishman named Roger—a name also used in *Wint.* (see v. ii. 21n.). [*Catholic Encyclopaedia*, under 'Camillus'.]

  1. C. F. T. Brooke, *Sh.'s Plutarch*, 2 vols., 1909 and M. W. MacCallum, *Sh.'s Roman Plays and Their Background*, 1910 do not mention *Wint.*; W. W. Skeat, *Sh.'s Plutarch*, 1904, merely notes, concerning *Wint.*, that the names Cleomenes, Dion, Camillo, and Antigonus may have been taken from North, and M. H. Shackford, *Plutarch in Renaissance England*, 1929, does not add to this. Shakespeare certainly used North for some details of Theseus' part in *MND*. See also J. K. Thomson, *Sh. and the Classics*, 1952, and W. Oakeshott, 'Sh. and Plutarch' (*Talking of Sh.*, ed. J. Garrett, 1954, 111–25).

  2. See H. Thomas, *Sh. and Spain*, 1922, 21–5; E. A. J. Honigmann, 'Secondary Sources of *The Winter's Tale*' (*Phil.Q.*, Jan. 1955, 27–38); S. Guttmann, *The Foreign Sources of Sh.'s Works*, 1947.   3. Doricles may be a nonce-word from *Doric*.

  4. Repr. in Dodsley's *Old English Plays*, ed. W. C. Hazlitt, 1874, vi, and Malone Soc., ed. W. W. Greg, 1930. A quick reading of l. 360 of the 1589 ed. might well give the impression that Hermione was a woman's name. J. M. Nosworthy (New Arden *Cym.*, xxiv–xxvi) argues that Shakespeare probably made some use of *The Rare Triumphs* for *Cym.* and even for *Wint.*

Although the name *Autolycus* is in Plutarch, Shakespeare probably took it, with one idea for the character, from Ovid's *Meta-
morphoses*, from the Latin or Golding's translation. Ovid tells how
Chione was visited by Apollo coming from Delphos and by
Hermes (Mercury); and Golding's version then runs:

Now when shee full her tyme had gon, shee bare by *Mercurye*
A sonne that hyght *Awtolychus*, who provde a wyly pye,
And such a fellow as in theft and filching had no peere.
He was his fathers owne sonne right: he could mennes eyes
  so bleere,
As for too make ye black things whyght, and whyght things
  black appeere.[1]

In the *Odyssey* there is, among other references, one to 'Autolycus . . . who excelled all men in thievery and in oaths'.[2] Although
Chapman's translation was apparently not published until 1615
Shakespeare may have seen it in manuscript before 1611.[3] The
relevant passage[4] runs:

With his grand Sire, *Autolycus*: who, th'Art
Of Theft and swearing (not out of the hart,
But by equivocation) first adorn'd
Your witty man withall; and was suborn'd
By *Ioues* descent (ingenious *Mercurie*).

II. AFFECTION (I. ii. 137–46)
The text in *F* is:

Most dear'st, my Collop: Can thy Dam, may't be
Affection? thy Intention stabs the Center.
Thou do'st make possible things not so held,
Communicat'st with Dreames (how can this be?)
With what's vnreall: thou coactiue art,
And fellow'st nothing. Then 'tis very credent,
Thou may'st co-ioyne with something, and thou do'st,
(And that beyond Commission) and I find it,
(And that to the infection of my Braines,
And hardning of my Browes.)

'This is the obscurest passage in Shakespeare, and it is no wonder
that Polixenes puts in: "What means Sicilia?". Leontes means in
general that the impossible has become all too possible, but the

1. *Ovid* (1904), Bk XI, ll. 359–63, p. 226.   2. *Odyssey* xix. 294–6 (Loeb).
3. *S.T.C.* 13637 was entered at Stationer's Hall, 2 Nov. 1614. The dedicatory
verses to Prince Henry are reprinted from *The Iliads* (*S.T.C.* 13634) and must
have been written before the prince died on 2 Nov. 1612. *S.T.C.* 13637 was bound
up with a reprint of *S.T.C.* 13634 and issued as *The Whole Works of Homer*, 1616
(*S.T.C.* 13624).   4. *S.T.C.* 13637 or 13624, *Odyssey*, xix, p. 300.

particulars of his meaning are his own'.[1] It has been described as
the 'passage which no one has been able to read'.[2] The speech is
meant to be incoherent, as is shown by Polixenes' question.[3] But
Leontes is tortured in mind and in speech and this clouded, bitter
language also effectively illustrates his condition. The speech might
be paraphrased: Can your mother (be faithless)? Is it possible?
Lustful passions: your intensity penetrates to the very heart and
soul of man.[4] You make possible things normally held to be impossible just as dreams do [communicate = partake of the nature
of. *O.E.D.* 5]. How can this be? Lust causes one to associate in the
mind with persons who are purely imaginary, who do not exist at
all, therefore it is very credible that the most unthinkable lustful
association can take place between real people: and lust, you have
brought it about in this case, going beyond what is lawful—and I
am the sufferer to such an extent that I am losing my senses and
grow cuckold's horns.[5]

H. G. Goddard[6] considers that Leontes diagnoses his own case
in this passage: 'emotion, he declares, brings within the realm of
possibility things non-existent. But, continuing, he hopelessly confuses cause and effect. Since emotion can give reality to "nothing",
he argues, it is very credible that "nothing" should join on to
"something" in the external world (that the idea of a faithless
Hermione should fit Hermione herself). And that thought, he
confesses, infects his brain. But the truth of course is the other way
around: it is the infection of the brain that has fitted the fantasy to
the present instance'.

Whatever interpretation is adopted, 'affection' is a key word.
In the essay 'Our affections are transported beyond our selues',[7]
Montaigne says, 'We are never in our selves, but beyond. Fear,
desire and hope draw vs ever towards that which is to come'. '*Affection* meant burning or passionate love . . . Ben Jonson describes
"Affection . . . in her hand a flaming heart"'.[8] Jonson also speaks
of 'blinde Affection, which doth ne're aduance / The truth, but
gropes, and vrgeth all by chance' (Alexander, xxviii, 9–10). The
word had many shades of meaning of which 'lustful passion' was

1. M. van Doren, *Shakespeare*, 1939, 316.
2. C. D. Stewart, *Some Textual Difficulties in Sh.*, 1914, 96–109.
3. Just as Desdemona cannot understand Othello (*Oth.*, iv. ii. 33).
4. *Centre*. This word can mean the centre of the Universe—the heart of everything. 'I will find / Where truth is hid, though it were hid indeed / Within the
centre' (*Ham.*, ii. ii. 157). Cf. *MND.*, iii. ii. 54; *Wint.*, ii. i. 102n.
5. For the relationship of dream and fact cf. *Oth.*, iii. iii. 421–31.
6. *The Meaning of Sh.*, 1951, 651.
7. *Essayes . . . done into English by J. Florio*, 1603, Bk i, p. 5.
8. L. Hotson, *The First Night of Twelfth Night*, 1954, 105.

one.[1] It is used only five or six times in the Bible and at least three times it has this sense: *Col.* iii. 5, *unnaturall lust (Great Bible,* 1539), *inordinate affection (A.V.* 1611), *passion (R.V.* 1881); *Romans* i. 26 *shamefull lustes* (1539), *vile affections* (1611), *vile passions* (1881); *Gal.* v. 24 *affections and lustes* (1539 and 1611), *passions and lustes* (1881). A contemporary Bible dictionary[2] gives the meaning 'Passions which affect the mind with some griefe or paine, especially when they are strong and vehement. *Romans* vii. 5. *The affections of sin wrought in us*'.[3] In Shakespeare the sense is exemplified in *Lucr.* 271, where Tarquin silences his conscience, 'Affection is my captain, and he leadeth', and *Mer. V.*, iv. i. 50–2, 'for affection, / Mistress of passion, sways it to the mood / Of what it likes or loathes'. For intention = intensity, intensification, see *O.E.D.* 1.8 and i, 1 and 7.

III. TIME, THE CHORUS (IV. i)

The importance of 'Truth the Daughter of Time' is discussed on pp. xxvii, lxviii–lxx, lxxxvi–lxxxvii. It is Greene's favourite motto and *Pandosto* is specifically described as *The Triumph of Time.* This may have suggested to Shakespeare the idea of using a personification of *Time* to explain the gap. But it is an obvious device to give necessary information and emblematically to emphasize the passage of time. Shakespeare would often have seen emblematic representations of Time—some of which are discussed in Fritz Saxl, *Veritas Filia Temporis* (R. Klibansky and H. J. Paton, *Philosophy and History. Essays presented to Ernst Cassirer,* 1936, 197–222) and Rosemary Freeman, *English Emblem Books,* 1948. A contemporary account of common pictorial representations of Time is in Henry Peacham's *The Gentlemans Exercise . . . in Lymning, Painting, etc.,* 1612 (also issued in 1612 with the title *Graphice, etc.*) (the Second Book of Drawing, pp. 115–16):

I haue seene time drawne by a painter standing vpon an old ruine, winged, and with Iron teeth.

But I rather allow his deuise that drew him an old man in a garment of starres, vpon his head a Garland of Roses, eares of Corne and dry stickes, standing vpŏ the Zodiack (for he hath his strength from heauen) holding a looking glasse in his hand, as beholding onely the present time, two children at his feete, one fat, and well liking, the other leane, writing both in one booke[;] vpon the heade of one, the sunne[;] vpon the other, the Moone.

1. Frequently in Shakespeare it also means 'troubles, concerns, heavy matters which are on one's mind' (e.g. *Rom.*, I. i. 124, 145; *John*, v. ii. 41).

2. T. Wilson, *A Christian Dictionarie,* 1612, 6.

3. Wilson was not using the 1539 or 1611 versions. They read here respectively *lustes of sinne* and *motions of sins,* which become *sinful passions* in 1881.

Hee is commonly drawne vpon tombes in Gardens, and other places an olde man bald, winged with a Sith and an hower glasse.[1]

Since the common representation of Time in Peacham's day was apparently as described in his last paragraph, this is probably how Time appeared in *Wint.* Certainly he had wings (l. 4), was old (l. 10), and carried a glass, presumably an hour glass (l. 16) since by turning it and letting the sands run he can give his play such development as if his audience had slept in the meantime. There is no mention of the scythe, and as many emblematic figures of Time do not carry a scythe Shakespeare's Time may not have had one, although elsewhere Shakespeare refers to Time's scythe (e.g. *Sonn.* 123). Time is bald in *Err.*, II. ii. 69, 105; *John*, III. i. 324.

B. Spivack, in *Shakespeare and the Allegory of Evil*, 1958, 310–11, contends that *Time* here and *Rumour* in *2H4* are choric figures deriving from the Moralities. These surviving personifications are meant to be, and to be seen to be, abstract. They are outside the play and do not need to conform in behaviour, appearance, or language to the world of living people. Indeed the contrary is the case; 'they and their special function need to be as clearly distinguished as a frame is from its picture'. So, as *Rumour* enters 'painted full of tongues' in *2H4*, Time in *Wint.* presumably is a bald old man with wings and an hour glass.

Time's speech is not an interpolation but an integral part of the play. It is in the conventional language used in contemporary Lord Mayors' pageants, and entirely befits the character of Time and the purpose of the speech. It acts as a bridge, gives information, and distinguishes Time from other characters.

Whereas it is surely wrong to assume that Shakespeare makes Time speak as the author, he is certainly making Time speak as the controller of events, the father of truth: this, however, is merely conventional expression of Time's function: 'Time's the king of men / . . . And gives them what he will, not what they crave' (*Per.*, II. iii. 45, 47). Personified Time controls events in the contemporary Goldsmiths' pageant *Chruso-thriambos*, 1611, by A. Mundy. But Shakespeare is not saying that Time actually does control events.[2] It is only natural that *Time* should arrogate to himself power to which he is proverbially entitled. He would be out of character if he did not do so. It is quite another matter to say that author or audience subscribe to this. They are free to hold that human char-

---

1. Punctuation in square brackets is from ed. of 1661, pp. 400–1.

2. But there is the sense that in time right will triumph. Cf. Elizabeth's 'Time hath brought us hither' (*Passage of our most drad Soueraigne*, 1558).

acter, chance, and the gods shape events, although all must agree
that events are shaped in time. Even when Time speaks of the past
in the play he is not speaking as the author; so l. 22 may be interpreted, 'In time past a son of the king's was mentioned'. 'Shakespeare allows one to laugh with Time but not at him ... Old Father
Time is allowed his power, but his senile humour lightens the discourse and leads naturally into the rustic comedy scenes that follow'
(F. Williams, *Mr. Shakespeare of the Globe*, 1941, 280).

IV. NATURE'S BASTARDS (IV. iv. 83)

Perdita's side of her talk with Polixenes on art and nature, which
has been given such extraordinary prominence in modern criticism, may derive immediately from Montaigne although it was a
common topic of the time. F. Kermode in the New Arden *Tp.*,
1954, xxxv, holds that the 'dispute is central to *The Winter's Tale*'
and refers to the literature. The relevant passage in Montaigne's
essay 'Of the Caniballes' occurs in Bk I of Florio's translation of
1603, pp. 101–2 (Saintsbury's ed. of 1892, i. 221).

> They [American Indians] are even savage, as we call those
> fruites wilde, which nature of hir selfe, and of hir ordinarie pro-
> gresse hath produced: whereas indeede, they are those which our
> selves have altered by our artificiall devises, and diverted from
> their common order, we should rather terme savage. In those
> are the true and most profitable vertues, and naturall proprie-
> ties most livelie and vigorous, which in these we have bastard-
> ized, applying them to the pleasure of our corrupted taste. And
> if notwithstanding, in divers fruites of those countries that were
> never tilled, we shall finde, that in respect of ours they are most
> excellent, and as delicate vnto our taste; there is no reason, arte
> should gaine the point of honour of our great and puissant
> mother Nature. We have so much by our inventions, sur-
> charged the beauties and riches of hir workes, that we have al-
> together over-choaked hir: yet where-ever hir puritie shineth, she
> makes our vaine, and frivolus enterprises wonderfully ashamed.

Puttenham, in *The Arte of English Poesie*, 1598, pp. 253–7 (ed. Willcock and Walker, 1936, 303–7), has a lengthy discourse on art and
nature which puts Polixenes' case rather than Perdita's:

> In some cases we say arte is an ayde and coadiutor to nature, or
> peradventure a meane to supply her wants... In another respect
> arte is not only an aide and coadiutor to nature in all her actions,
> but an alterer of them, and in some sort a surmounter of her
> skill, so as by means of it her owne effects shall appeare more
> beautifull or straunge and miraculous ... the Gardiner by his
> arte will ... embellish [a flower or fruit] in vertue, shape, odour

and taste, that nature of her selfe woulde never haue done: as to make the single gillifloure, or marigold, or daisie, double: and the white rose, redde, yellow, or carnation . . . the cunning gardiner . . . vsing nature as a coadiutor, furders her conclusions & many times makes her effectes more absolute and straunge.

There was much interest in cross-breeding of plants and grafting in Shakespeare's day—the image is used at I. ii. 246—but the gilly-flower was also thought to produce cross-breeds without human aid (see Helen Gardner, 'The argument about "The Ecstasy" ' in *Elizabethan Studies presented to F. P. Wilson*, 1959, 299–300) and to be the flower which above all others showed variety. So for his miscellany of 1580 Humfrey Gifford chose the title *A Posie of Gillo-flowers, eche differing from other*. There were many treatises on graft-ing, and their popularity is shown by the fact that L. Mascall's *A Booke of . . . how to Plant and Graffe, etc.* went through at least six editions between 1572 and 1596. The *Georgics* (especially Bk ii) would also be well known. Bacon speaks much of such experiments in *Sylva Sylvarum* (published 1626, written after 1620), e.g. 'Take Gilly-Flower Seed of one kinde of Gilly-Flower . . . And sow it; and there will come up Gilly-Flowers, some of one Colour, and some of another . . . As Purple, Carnation of severall Stripes' (*Works*, ed. Spedding, ii, 1857, p. 504). In other words they are 'nature's bast-ards'. (Cf. *Shakespeare's England*, i. 513–15.) Yet Perdita feels that they are still bastards and that there is some unnatural art in their creation (87–8). Furthermore the *gillyflower* was associated with unchastity (see *O.E.D.*). Perhaps, as suggested by Bethell (note in *Wint. ed.*, 207), the streaks suggested painting, and 'painted women' were traditionally unchaste. Cf. IV. iv. 101; *Meas.*, IV. ii. 34; and Spenser, *Shepherd's Calendar*, April, l. 136:

> Bring hether the Pincke and purple Cullambine,
>   With Gelliflowres:
> Bring Coronations, and Sops in wine, worne of
>   Paramoures.

See also II. iii. 73n., 103n., IV. iv. 88–92n., and p. lxxvii. The taunt 'bastard slips' is also used for illegitimate children (cf. p. lxxvii, n.2, and Crabbe, *The Borough, xx : Ellen Orford*, 247).

v. PALE PRIMROSES (IV. iv. 122–5)
The *F* text is:

>   . . . pale Prime-roses,
> That dye vnmarried, ere they can behold
> Bright Phœbus in his strength (a Maladie
> Most incident to Maids:) . . .

The reference here is to chlorosis—the green sickness, the maiden's malady (Jonson, *The Magnetick Lady*, II. ii. 22)—a malady most incident to maids which is still common and was often fatal until the late nineteenth century. There was a legend that young unmarried girls who died from this anaemia—of which one sign is a yellowy-green complexion—were turned to primroses. Cf. Herrick, *Poems*, ed. L. C. Martin, 64:

How Primroses came green.

Virgins, time-past, known were these,
Troubled with Green-sicknesses,
Turn'd to flowers: stil the hieu,
Sickly Girles, they beare of you.

Herrick also refers to it in *The Primrose* and in *To Anthea*. This proves that the legend was long established by 1648. The same anaemia is behind the phrase *maid-pale* (*R2*, III. iii. 98) and *pale-visaged maids* (*John*, V. ii. 154) and is in the angry Capulet's outburst to his weeping, despairing daughter, 'Out, you green-sickness carrion . . . / You tallow-face!' (*Rom.*, III. v. 156–7). Cf. *Ant.*, III. ii. 6; *2H4*, IV. iii. 94; *Cym.*, IV. ii. 222; and *Per.*, IV. vi. 14 for a metaphorical use. References to the primrose associated with the death of maidens are fairly common in literature (cf. V. Rendall, *Wild Flowers in Literature*, 1934): a good example is in Milton's first draft of *Lycidas*, where the idea may even have been taken from *Wint.*:

Bring the rathe primrose that unwedded dies
colouring the pale cheeke of uninjoyd love.
(Columbia ed. Vol. 1, Pt 2, 470)

Green-sickness is often mentioned in contemporary literature: e.g. 'his daughter . . . would . . . fall into the greene sicknes for want of a husband' (Greene, *Mamillia*, ed. Grosart, ii. 36); and cf. Jonson, *Alchemist*, IV. vi. 53.

Late in the nineteenth century a classical myth seems to have been invented to explain the 'unmarried' primrose, which had puzzled commentators. In various modern books on flower-lore[1] a legend is cited to the effect that a youth Paralisos, son of Priapus and Flora, broken-hearted at the death of his betrothed, died, and was by the gods turned into a primrose. This seems to be without authority: Paralisos cannot be traced, although Gerard (p. 637) says that the common primrose (the flower of which Shakespeare almost certainly speaks) is called *herba paralysis* because it is good

1. E.g. L. Deas, *Flower Favourites*, 1898, 43; E. Singleton, *The Sh. Garden*, 1923, 97.

for stiff joints.[1] There is probably no significance in the fact that Shakespeare's only reference to Flora is in *Wint.* (IV. iv. 2). The name is used in *Pandosto* and by Sabie and was well known. Shakespeare's only reference to Priapus is in *Per.* (IV. vi. 4).

The yellowy-green complexion of girls afflicted with this complaint, some of whom would die unmarried, was a common sight in Shakespeare's day and although the comparison with the primrose seems to have been already in literary tradition, it is likely that the memory of these girls brought this vivid piece of imagery to Shakespeare's mind and made him speak in this way of the early spring flower with anaemic appearance[2] which dies before the coming of the full summer sun.[3]

APPENDIX II

MUSIC AND THE SONGS[4]

For a more detailed treatment of this subject reference may be made to 'Music and its Function in the Romances of Shakespeare' by J. M. Nosworthy,[5] to writings of J. P. Cutts,[6] and to 'Music, and the Songs in *The Winter's Tale*'.[7] The two main collections including early music for *The Winter's Tale* are those by William Linley and John Caulfield.[8]

Although not prominent, music is important in the play. It is required for the shepherd's dance at IV. iv. 167 and presumably for the satyrs' dance at IV. iv. 343 and briefly for the awakening of Hermione at v. iii. 98. But it is the singing voice in IV. iii and the first part of IV. iv which is the chief musical element in *The Winter's Tale*. There is also talk of songs and ballads in IV. iv. 183–202—a

1. In the 1571 English version of the *Herbal* of Dodoens it is said (p. 132) that primroses are called 'in shoppes *Primulæ veris*, and *Herbæ paralysis*, and of some Artheticæ'.

2. Cf. 'faint primrose beds' (*MND.*, I. i. 215); 'Look pale as primrose' (*2H6*, III. ii. 63).

3. There is a reference to the rose dying unmarried in 'But earthlier happy is the rose distill'd / Than that which withering on the virgin thorn / Grows, lives, and dies, in single blessedness' (*MND.*, I. i. 76–8).

4. See Comm. to IV. iii. 1–20, 119; IV. iv. 167, 185, 195, 199, 220, 289, 292, 297–323, 341; V. iii. 98.

5. *Sh.Sur.*, xi, 1958, 60–9.   6. See Comm. to IV. iv. 220, 297.

7. *Sh.Q.* x, Spring 1959, 161–75. I am obliged to the editor for permission to make use of this article.

8. W. Linley, *Dramatic Songs of Sh.*, 1816; J. Caulfield, *Collection of the Vocal Music in Sh.'s Plays*, ii, 1864. (The latter—originally compiled c. 1800—was reprinted by Messrs French, though without Caulfield's name, in 1922–5.)

passage which is described by E. W. Naylor as one which 'contains a large quantity of the history of songs in the sixteenth century, and is one of the most important to be found in Shakespeare'.[1]

There are six songs, five sung by Autolycus alone and the other by a trio in which he leads. They are: 1. *When daffodils* (IV. iii. 1–12); 2. *But shall I go mourn* (IV. iii. 15–22); 3. *Jog on* (IV. iii. 119–22); 4. *Lawn as white* (IV. iv. 220–32); 5. *Get you hence* (IV. iv. 298–309); 6. *Will you buy* (IV. iv. 316–24). Notes on the early music of these songs are given in the Commentary on the text.

It will thus be seen that the musical element in the play is practically confined to IV. iii and to the first 343 lines of IV. iv: it all comes within some 450 consecutive lines in a play of 3,074 lines, with an additional brief use at Hermione's awakening at v. iii. 98. The singing voice is of great importance to the spirit of the play and it also expresses something in Autolycus: his singing and his love of singing soften his vices and add to the attractiveness of his character. Richmond Noble notes this[2] and also points out that the songs are in the latest manner of Shakespeare's songs and in themselves provide evidence that the play belongs to Shakespeare's last group. It has been said that the secret of Shakespeare's success in his songs lies in 'a fusion of the natural with the artificial',[3] but in these songs there is much more of the natural than of the artificial, much more of the traditional and unaffected singing 'of tavern and field' and much less of 'delicate artifice and charming affectation' than is the case with most of Shakespeare's earlier songs. This is not to say that the songs of *The Winter's Tale* are without artifice; but they are strongly realistic and the view which holds that *When Daffodils* 'is *not* an Elizabethan "nature" lyric but a product of Jacobean wit which incidentally parodies the Elizabethan simplicities'[4] surely sees a subtlety which is not there. The first part of the comment is true enough: the song is certainly not simple pastoral. It hardly could be to be in character with its singer. It has the straightforward insolent merry roguishness which a song from Autolycus should have.

It is known that Shakespeare, like other Elizabethan dramatists, used popular songs in his plays,[5] and in these songs, or in some of them, he may be using or adapting songs current at the time. He may have done this particularly with *Jog on, Lawn as white, Get you*

1. *Sh. and Music,* new ed., 1931, 77.   2. *Sh.'s Use of Song,* 1923.

3. G. Rylands, 'Sh. the Poet' (in *A Companion to Sh. Studies,* ed. H. Granville Barker and G. B. Harrison, 1934, 112).

4. Bethell, *Wint. ed.,* 201.

5. F. W. Sternfeld, 'Sh.'s use of Popular Song' (in *Elizabethan Studies Presented to F. P. Wilson,* 1959, 150–66).

hence, and *Will you buy*: but, whether entirely original or not, all the
songs were appropriate, and as with Shakespeare's songs generally,
but especially his later songs, they do indeed help to 'localize or
enrich the scene, or depict a character'.[1]

There are two early versions of *Get you hence* in MSS. in the Drexel
collection of the New York Public Library (see IV. iv. 298n.). The
first, in MS. Dx.4175 on f. 23, may be by Robert Johnson. The MS.
dates from about 1620 and its text could therefore be a few months
earlier than that used for printing *The Winter's Tale*. J. P. Cutts
gives the music. The second is in MS. Dx.4041 on ff. 127–9 and is
dated about 1640. The former gives, with slight variations, only
the lines as in *The Winter's Tale*, the latter has these and extra verses.
The words in the two MSS. are:

Dx.4175:

Get yee hence for I must goe	if thou goest to Grange or Mill
Where it fitts not you to know	If to either, thou dost ill,
Whether O whether, whether	Neither what neither neither,
it befitts thine oath full well,	thou hast vow'de thy loue to mee,
thou to mee thy secrets tell	thou hast sworne my loue to bee:
And mee to let mee goe thether,	then whether goest say whither,
	whither?

Dx.4041:

Gett you hence for I must goe	never more forr lasses sake
where it fitts not you to know	will I dance at fare or wake
whether, o whether	15 Ah mee A Ah me Ah mee
itt becomes thy oath full well	Who shall then were a raced shooe
5 thou to me thy secrets tell	or what shall yᵉ bagpipe doe
and me to lett me goe theither	recant or elce you slay mee
if thou goest to grange or mill	if thou leaue our Andorne greene
if to either thou doest ill	20 where shall fill or frize be seene
neither what neither neither	sleeping what sleeping sleeping
10 thou hast sworne my loue to bee	no Ile warrant the sitting sadly
thou hast sworne itt more to mee	or Idely walking madly
then whether whether goest thou	in some darke darke Corner
whether	weeping.

1. you] *altered from* ye.   3. *A repeat mark at the end of the line.*   12. *Occurs at the
top of the page. At the foot of the previous page* then whether *is written on the line without
notation and again as catchwords*   15. A] *perhaps* O. *The mark is like two musical flat
signs placed back to back and not joined.*   16. raced shooe] *A fancy shoe, a shoe cut or
slashed in an ornamental fashion* (O.E.D. race *v3, 1b*); *cf.* 'two Provincial roses on my
razed shoes', *Ham.*, III. II. 271.   19. Andorne] *Perhaps a copying error for* Arboure.
20. fill or frize] *perhaps countrywomen's names:* 'fill' *short for Phillis, Phillida, and 'frize'
occurring in The Two Noble Kinsmen*, III. V. 27 [*Cutts*].   24. *At top of page.* In some
darke *is at foot of previous page also. The earliest known printed setting seems to be that by
William Boyce, written c. 1759, which is given by Linley and by Caulfield* (*see p. 172*).

1. J. R. Moore, 'The Function of the Songs in Sh.'s Plays' (in *Sh. Studies by
Members of the Dept. of English of the Univ. of Wisconsin*, 1916, 78–102. The work
contains only one brief reference to *Wint.*).

APPENDIX III

STAGE HISTORY

The best general accounts are those by Joseph Knight[1] and Harold Child[2] but invaluable work has been done since, notably by A. C. Sprague,[3] C. B. Hogan,[4] W. M. Merchant,[5] and E. L. Avery.[6] Reference to these works, to the surveys by H. Krause[7] and G. C. D. Odell,[8] and to the entries 'London Playbills' and 'Notable Productions and important Revivals on the London Stage' in *Who's Who in the Theatre*, as well as to accounts of productions in periodical literature, will show that *The Winter's Tale* has been fairly popular whenever Shakespeare's comedies have had any popularity at all.

Greg[9] and Child note that the play was popular until 1640.[10] There are no other recorded performances in the seventeenth century and no editions apart from the Folios until Rowe's of 1709. But other interest in *The Winter's Tale* may be noted in the ballad, which is apparently a direct summary of the text, made by Thomas Jordan and published in 1664 in a volume containing similar poor ballad summaries of other plays by Shakespeare.[11] It is possible too —chiefly because of some of the names—that Richard Brathwait used *The Winter's Tale*, and no doubt Greene as well, for his prose romance published in 1640.[12] Shakespeare's comedies were not

1. *The Henry Irving Sh.*, ed. by H. Irving and F. A. Marshall, vii, 1890, 312–18.

2. *N.C. Wint.*, 185–93.

3. *Sh. and the Actors*, 1945; *Shakespearian Players and Performances*, 1954.

4. *Sh. in the Theatre 1701–1800* i and ii (performances in London), 1952, 1957. (Volumes on British provincial and American performances are to follow.)

5. *Sh. and the Artist*, 1959. (Surveys illustrations chiefly from printed editions and of actual productions, and discusses productions.)

6. *The London Stage, 1660–1800*. Part 2: 1700–29, 2 vols., 1960. (Other parts, by other editors, to follow.)

7. *Umarbeitungen und Bühneneinrichtungen von Shakespeares The Winter's Tale* (thesis, Univ. of Rostock, published at Bern, 1913).

8. *Sh. from Betterton to Irving*, 2 vols., 1921.   9. *First Folio*, 415.

10. But of the eight recorded performances, seven are at Court. This proves popularity with a sophisticated audience and probably indicates general popularity.

11. *A Royal Arbor of Loyal Poesie*, pp. 123–7, 'The jealous Duke, and the injur'd Dutchess; a story. Tune, The Dream'. Repr. by J. P. Collier in *Illustrations of Old English Literature* iii, 1866. The ballad is also in Collier's ed. of Shakespeare, 2nd ed., 1858 (cf. *Var.* 389). A summary of Jordan's poem, and of an early 18th-century version, are in J. O. Halliwell's ed. of Shakespeare, viii, 1859, 6–7.

12. *The two Lancashire lovers or the excellent history of Philocles and Doriclea. Expressing the faithful constancy and mutuall fidelity of two loyal lovers. By Mucaeus Palatinus.* [i.e. R.B.], 1660. (Doriclea is the heroine. One lover, Camillus, is rejected. Another,

popular after the re-opening of the theatres at the Restoration
and the next recorded performance is at Goodman's Fields on
15 January 1741, which was probably justified in its claim that the
play had not been acted for a hundred years.[1] There were eight
performances, followed by three at Covent Garden beginning on
11 November 1741 and another there on 21 January 1742. In the
period 1701–50 Hogan shows that out of the thirty-four plays of
Shakespeare of which records of performances survive, *The
Winter's Tale* comes twenty-seventh in order of popularity, if that
is judged by the number of performances. In the second half of the
century, however, there were twenty-nine plays acted and *The
Winter's Tale* comes seventh in popularity with 112 recorded performances as against fourteen in the first half of the century. For the
whole century it occupies twenty-third place out of thirty-six plays
recorded as having been acted.[2]

'The history of *The Winter's Tale* during the eighteenth century
and the first half of the nineteenth provides one of the clearest
examples of the shift in critical taste shown in painting and en-
graving'.[3] In the early eighteenth century and in the mid-nine-
teenth, interest was centred on Hermione, particularly in the
statue scene,[4] but between these two periods 'the play had been
seen as a sheep-shearing feast'.[5] This between-period was pre-
eminently one of altered versions, particularly much shortened
stage adaptations.[6] No acting version was apparently published

---

Philocles her tutor, is accepted by Doriclea but not by her parents. Philocles flees
overseas and enters a religious retreat. Doriclea goes into a decline and her
parents recall Philocles, who is discovered to be of gentlemanly blood; and the
lovers marry.) Brathwait perhaps shows interest in *Wint.* themes in his prose–
poetical fantasy translation of M. Silesio, *The Arcadian Princesse; or, the Triumph
of Justice*, 1635.

1. The play attracted little interest of any kind in the period 1700–40: the
periodical literature of that period can show only one brief reference to it (*Sh.Q.*
ii, 1951, 228).

2. Among the comedies and last plays it was less popular than *Mer.V.*, *Shr.*,
AYL., *Cym.*, *Tp.*, *Ado*, *Wiv.*, *H8*, *Tw.N.*

3. W. M. Merchant, *Sh. and the Artist*, 1959, 208.

4. Rowe chose this scene for the single illustration in his ed. of 1709.

5. Merchant, *op. cit.*

6. The very existence of these versions indicates that the stage itself did not
regard the play as suitable for production in its entirety. In her preface to
Kemble's version Mrs Inchbald says: 'The "Winter's Tale" was very successful
at Drury Lane . . . yet, it seems to class among those dramas that charm more in
perusal than in representation. The long absence from the scene of the two most
important characters . . . and the introduction of various other persons . . . divert
. . . the attention of an audience; and they do not so feelingly unite all they see
and . . . hear into a single story, as he who, with the book in his hand . . . combines,
and enjoys the whole grand variety . . . some of the poetry is less calculated for

before 1750 but afterwards there are many. Details of these versions, which are usually entitled 'Florizel and Perdita' or 'The Sheep Shearing', are given by Hogan; the chief adapters, with dates of the first editions, are M. Morgan, 1755, in whose version Leontes and Hermione do not appear; Garrick, 1756; T. Hull, 1773; and G. Colman, the elder, 1777. Hogan also gives a synopsis of the new plots, indicating the chief omissions and additions.

Garrick's three-act version was much approved in his day. On 12 June 1758 Warburton wrote to Garrick[1]: 'As you know me to be less an idolizer of Shakespeare than yourself, you will less suspect me of compliment when I tell you, that besides your giving an elegant form to a monstrous composition, you have in your own additions written up to the best scenes in this play, so that you will easily imagine I read the "Reformed Winter's Tale" with great pleasure.' Thomas Davies,[2] however, understood the wholeness of *Wint.* and notes 'that it cannot be changed without maiming or defacing the whole structure'. Yet 'mutilated as Mr. Garrick's revived play was, it had considerable merit as well as success'. Davies also records that 'Mr. Garrick's Leontes, though he gave but half of that finished character, was masterly; his action and whole behaviour, during the supposed disenchanting of Hermione, was extremely affecting. Mrs. Cibber's Perdita, Mrs. Pritchard's Hermione, Woodward's Clown, Berry's Old Shepherd, John Beard's Peasant, and, above all, Yates's Autolicus, were such portraits of nature, as we must almost despair of seeing again in one piece'. In 1761 Covent Garden converted the sheep-shearing into a little opera. In 1771 it put on a nearly complete version of the play (claimed as not acted for thirty years), the chief omission being of Autolycus, Shepherd, and Clown from v. ii. This was published in Bell's edition in 1773. Next year Covent Garden reverted to Garrick's version. With the turn of the century the play seems to

---

that energetic delivery which the stage requires, than for the quiet contemplation of one who reads'. Mrs Inchbald feels that the love-making of Florizel and Perdita is tender rather than fervent and more 'properly adapted to steal upon the heart of an individual' than to affect an audience. She adds that 'the unfounded suspicion of Leontes . . . is a much greater fault, and one with which imagination can less accord, than with the hasty strides of time. . . It is easier for fancy to over leap whole ages, than to overlook one powerful demonstration of insanity in that mind which is reputed sane' (Inchbald's *British Theatre. The Winter's Tale* [?1808], 3–4).

1. D. Garrick, *Private Correspondence*, 1831, i. 88–9 (in *Var.* xii, the word *no* has mistakenly been inserted between *be* and *less* in the first line of Warburton's letter).

2. *Memoirs of the Life of David Garrick.* [First published 1780.] 2 vols. 1781, i. 286–7 (1808, i. 313–14).

have come back to the stage in a form a little closer to the original
text. In 1802 Kemble produced it at Drury Lane with a text something like Bell's edition of 1773, omitting, *inter alia*, Time, the
Oracle scene, and the grafting debate, and using Garrick's ending
which brings Leontes, Hermione, and Paulina to Bohemia but
retains the statue scene. Hazlitt was deeply impressed with this
production; he eulogizes Kemble[1]: 'In Leontes ... (a character he
at one time played often), the growing jealousy of the King, and
the exclusive possession which this passion gradually obtains over
his mind, were marked by him in the finest manner, particularly
where he exclaims:

> "—Is whispering nothing? ...
> My wife is nothing, if this be nothing!"   [I. ii. 284–96]

In the course of this enumeration, every proof told stronger, and
followed with quicker and harder strokes; his conversation became
more rivetted at every step of his progress; and at the end, his mind
and "every corporal agent", appeared wound up to a frenzy of
despair'. Hazlitt also commended Mrs Siddons, who 'acted the
painted statue to the life', and Bannister's performance of Autolycus, and was convinced that 'we shall never see these parts so
acted again'.[2] Kemble produced the play at Covent Garden at
intervals from 1807 to 1812,[3] and Coleridge imitated it in *Zapolya*
(1814–16).[4] Macready played Leontes in a series of productions of
which the first was at Bath in 1815; others were at Drury Lane in
1823, Covent Garden in 1837–9, and Drury Lane in 1842–3. Macready had Helena Faucit (Lady Martin) as Hermione when he
chose the play to open his management of Covent Garden in 1837,
and she pays a striking tribute to Macready's acting in the statue
scene.[5] Contemporary press-notices show that her own performance must have been of remarkable quality.[6] It is difficult to find
anything about Macready's own interpretation of Leontes. He
acted Leontes first in 1815, 'in which character I produced in later
years a strong impression'.[7] He was fond of the play but it would
seem from Helena Faucit's comment and from the only one of his

---

1. *Works*, ed. P. P. Howe, v, 376–7; cf. for almost the same words xviii. 198–9.

2. *Op. cit.*, iv. 325–6. Boaden, *Life of Kemble*, 1825, ii. 314 (quoted in *Var.* 389),
also speaks of the great success of the 1802 revival and of the impressiveness of the
statue scene. T. Campbell's eulogy of Mrs Siddons as Hermione in the statue
scene (*Life of Mrs Siddons*, 1834) is also cited in *Var.* 390.

3. *The Times*, 29 Nov. 1811, did not share Hazlitt's enthusiasm: 'We think the
theatre might have bestowed its splendid trappings upon a more vivifying play
than the Winter's Tale.'

4. See above, pp. xxxix, n.1; lii, n.2.

5. *Var.* 391.   6. *Var.* 392–5.   7. *Reminiscences*, 1876, 85.

own that has been traced,[1] that he regarded the statue scene as that which gave him most scope for his powers.

Samuel Phelps put the play on forty-five times in the season 1845–6 at Sadler's Wells, and *The Times* of 28 November 1845 praises the production, especially the statue scene. In 1847–8 Mrs Warner managed and acted in *The Winter's Tale* at the Theatre Royal, Marylebone; but the next great production is that of Charles Kean, who put the play on at the Princess's Theatre on 28 April 1856, when it ran for 102 consecutive nights. This production was a stupendous spectacle, with classical Greek costumes and scenery, and the account of it by Merchant, giving many reproductions of scenes, should be read.[2] The production included an allegorical representation of Time, with Luna in her car and Phoebus in his chariot.[3] 'The effect baffles description. The entire allegory may be pronounced the greatest triumph of art ever exhibited on the stage'.[4] The statue scene was again praised and a picture of it is reproduced by Odell and by Merchant from the *Illus. London News* of 10 May 1856, p. 504. In 1878 Chatterton revived the play at Drury Lane and Odell[5] quotes Dutton Cook's review of a lavish performance. In 1881 the Saxe-Meiningen Company played *The Winter's Tale* at Drury Lane and Odell records that the trial scene had special praise.

If Kean's was the most striking production of the century, one with even greater beauty and charm was undoubtedly that of Mary Anderson which ran throughout most of the 1887–8 season. She herself doubled Perdita and Hermione and great praise was given to her in both parts, particularly for her dancing as Perdita and her

1. *Ibid.*, 432. Diaries, ed. Toynbee, i. 412, 30 Sept. 1837: 'Acted Leontes artist-like, but not until the last act, very effectively.' See also J. C. Trewin, *Mr Macready*, 1955, 134.

2. *Sh. and the Artist*, 1959, 208–20.

3. The many contemporary accounts reveal that interest was largely in the play as a spectacle and that the text was of secondary importance. Kean was in difficulties about the time gap, but 'Fortunately . . . the text of Shakespeare came to the assistance of the stage-conductor' since it was actually found that '*Time*, as *Chorus*, usually omitted, appears in the book for the purpose of rendering some account of the interval' (*Illus. Lond. News*, 17 May 1856, 534). It is not said who had this novel idea of referring to the complete text, but Kean, his problem solved, improved on Shakespeare's simple use of Father Time.

4. J. W. Cole, *Life . . . of Charles Kean*, 2 vols., 2nd ed., 1859, ii. 172. The production is described in detail on pp. 167–80. Cole recognizes the unity of the play, although it is 'a *bilogy*; a story related in two distinct sections . . . there is something so clear, comprehensive, and identical in all Shakespeare's designs, that any material alteration mars them entirely' (ii. 168). Cole is quoted in Odell, ii. 291, 339–43, 367.

5. *Op. cit.*, ii. 259, 308, 367.

superb Hermione in the trial and statue scenes.[1] A sidelight on the contemporary attitude to the play is given in her preface to the acting edition of 1887: 'Of the larger excisions it is unnecessary to speak, they are unavoidable; no audience of these days would desire to have the *Winter's Tale* produced in its entirety... A literal adhesion to the text as it has been handed down to us would in any case savour of superstition'. This is quoted by Odell,[2] who adds that 'the critics as well firmly believed in this doctrine'.[3] Odell also analyses her version: she ended the play with a couplet from *All's Well*, considering that it gave a better climax than the original.

Wint. was played at Stratford-upon-Avon in 1895 with Irving as Leontes. In 1906 Beerbohm Tree produced it at His Majesty's Theatre and it has been played in many provincial theatres. In September 1912 Granville Barker put the play on at the Savoy. He used an apron stage, 'renaissance-classic' costume, no scenery, but decoration. He published an acting edition in 1912 which has illustrations of some costumes. The production excited great interest, being greatly praised and bitterly attacked.[4] Details of the production, including the original account books, can be seen in the Library of the British Drama League, London. The *Times* commented that it was 'very startling and provocative and audacious, and on the whole we like it' and found it 'amusing'.[5] It subsequently printed a letter from John Masefield,[6] who wished 'to protest against the abuse with which Mr. Granville Barker's production... has been received by some English critics' and spoke of 'the vitality, the newness, and the excellence of Mr. Barker's effort. He has presented the whole play directly (but for the one necessary interval) as Shakespeare meant it to be presented, as a continuous stream of human fate, and this with a colour and vivacity as new as they are delightful; and the performance... gave me (for the first time in any English theatre) a sense of Shakespeare's power and art, of his mind at work shaping and directing, and of his dramatic intention. The performance seemed to me to be a riper and juster piece of Shakespearian criticism, a clearer perception and grasping of the Shakespearian idea, than I have seen hitherto in print or on the stage'.

1. G. R. Foss, *What the Author Meant*, 1932, 136.

2. *Op. cit.*, ii. 382, 396, 403, 407–8, 437–8.

3. Quite apart from the 'sheep-shearing' versions the play always seems to have been cut.

4. *Athenaeum*, 28 Sept. 1912, 351. It failed to attract audiences (W. Macqueen-Pope, *Carriages at Eleven*, 1947, 196).

5. 23 Sept. 1912. 7d.   6. 27 Sept. 1912. 7f.

In March 1926 M. MacOwen produced the play at the Old Vic and in August 1937 Robert Atkins included it in his productions at the Open Air Theatre, Regent's Park, where it was played again, produced by S. Thomas, in May 1944 and also, produced by Atkins, in May 1950. The most important production in recent years was that by Peter Brook at the Phoenix in June 1951 and at the Edinburgh festival in the same year. Leontes was played by Sir John Gielgud, Hermione by Diana Wynyard, Paulina by Flora Robson, Perdita by Virginia McKenna, and Autolycus by George Rose. It was perhaps the first production in which Leontes was interpreted as being jealous from his first appearance—an interpretation criticized by G. Rylands who believes that had Sir John Gielgud followed Shakespeare and shown the jealousy coming as a sudden attack 'The whole play would have gained in intensity and passion'.[1] In November 1955 M. Benthall produced the play at the Old Vic and in the 1960 season it was produced by Mr Peter Wood at Stratford-upon-Avon.

APPENDIX IV

GREENE'S PANDOSTO. TEXT[2]

The following text is that of the edition of 1595, in modernized spelling and punctuation, collated with the editions of 1588 and 1592. There are only minor differences between all three. Material in italics is *not* in the 1588 or 1592 editions; material in square brackets is in one or both of those editions but not in that of 1595. References to corresponding parts of the play are placed within angled brackets ⟨ ⟩ in the appropriate places in the text.

There is only one known copy of each edition: that of 1588 is in the British Museum and is imperfect, lacking all four leaves of sig. B, the passage from and including 'men that causeless' on p. 187, l. 17 of the present reprint to the passage 'to the king, who quite' on p. 194, l. 10. It is therefore not possible to collate other editions with that part. In 'The Shakespeare Library' edition by P. G. Thomas, Chatto and Windus, 1907, the 1588 edition was used and completed from the edition of 1607, and Thomas's version of the 1607 edition for the missing passage has been collated with the

1. *Sh.Sur.* vi, 1953, 143–5. Cf. pp. xxv–xxvi, lvi–lviii.
2. For the title, and the significance of the editions with relation to the play, see pp. xxvii–xxviii.

1595 edition. The only known copy of the 1592 edition is in the Folger Library, Washington, and of the 1595 edition is in the Huntington Library, California.[1]

PANDOSTO.

The Triumph
of Time.

TO THE GENTLEMEN READERS,
HEALTH.

THE paltering Poet Aphranius, being blamed for troubling the Emperor Trajan with so many doting poems, adventured notwithstanding still to present him with rude and homely verses, excusing himself with the courtesy of the Emperor, which did as friendly accept, as he fondly offered. So, Gentlemen, if any condemn my rashness for troubling your ears with so many unlearned pamphlets, I will straight shroud myself under the shadow of your courtesies, and with Aphranius lay the blame on you, as well for friendly reading them, as on myself for fondly penning them. Hoping, though fond, curious, or rather currish backbiters breathe out slanderous speeches, yet the courteous Readers (whom I fear to offend) will requite my travail at the least with silence: and in this hope I rest, wishing you health and happiness.

ROBERT GREENE.

TO THE

RIGHT HONOURABLE GEORGE CLIFFORD,
EARL OF CUMBERLAND,

ROBERT GREENE
WISHETH INCREASE OF HONOUR AND VIRTUE.

THE Rascians (right honourable), when by long gazing against the sun they become half blind, recover their sights by looking on the black load-stone. Unicorns, being glutted with browsing on roots of liquorice, sharpen their stomachs with crushing bitter grass.

---

1. I have used photographic copies of the 1588 and 1592 editions. To the Huntington Library I am indebted not only for a photographic copy of the 1595 edition but also for permission to use it for the text in the present edition. I am obliged also to Messrs Chatto and Windus for permission to use the text of the 1907 edition as basic copy for printing the following text, and I have largely accepted the modernizations of spelling and punctuation made by P. G. Thomas.

Alexander vouchsafed as well to smile at the crooked picture of Vulcan, as to wonder at the curious counterfeit of Venus. The mind is sometimes delighted as much with small trifles as with sumptuous triumphs; and as well pleased with hearing of Pan's homely fancies, as of Hercules' renowned labours.

Silly Baucis could not serve Jupiter in a silver plate, but in a wooden dish. All that honour Esculapius deck not his shrine with jewels. Apollo gives oracles as well to the poor man for his mite, as to the rich man for his treasure. The stone *Hebites* [Echites] is not so much liked for the colour, as for virtue, and *pitts* [gifts] are not to be measured by the worth, but by the will. Mison, that unskilful painter of Greece, adventured to give unto Darius the shield of Pallas, so roughly shadowed, as he smiled more at the folly of the man, than at the imperfection of his art. So I present unto your honour the triumph of time, so rudely finished, as I fear your honour will rather frown at my impudence, than laugh at my ignorance: but I hope my willing mind shall excuse my slender skill, and your honour's courtesy shadow my rashness.

They which fear the biting of vipers do carry in their hands the plumes of a Phœnix. Phidias drew Vulcan sitting in a chair of ivory. Cæsar's crow durst never cry, Ave, but when she was pearked on the Capitol. And I seek to shroud this imperfect pamphlet under your honour's patronage, doubting the dint of such invenomed vipers, as seek with their slanderous reproaches to carp at all, being oftentimes most unlearned of all; and assure myself, that your honour's renowned valour and virtuous disposition shall be a sufficient defence to protect me from the poisoned tongues of such scorning sycophants; hoping that as Jupiter vouchsafed to lodge in Philemon's thatched cottage, and Philip of Macedon to take a bunch of grapes of a country peasant, so I hope your honour, measuring my work by my will, and weighing more the mind than the matter, will, when you have cast a glance at this toy, with Minerva, under your golden target cover a deformed owl. And in this hope I rest, wishing unto you, and the virtuous Countess your wife, such happy success as your honours can desire or [I] imagine.

Your Lordship's most dutifully to command,

ROBERT GREENE.

THE HISTORY

OF

DORASTUS AND FAWNIA

Among all the passions wherewith human minds are perplexed, there is none that so galleth with restless despite as *that* [the] infectious sore of jealousy; for all other griefs are either to be appeased with sensible persuasions, to be cured with wholesome counsel, to be relieved in want, or by tract of time to be worn out, jealousy only excepted which is [so] sauced with suspicious doubts and pinching mistrust, that whoso seeks by friendly counsel to rase out this hellish passion, it forthwith suspecteth that he giveth this advice to cover his own guiltiness. Yea, whoso is pained with this restless torment doubteth all, distrusteth himself, is always frozen with fear and *fixed* [fired] with suspicion, having that wherein *consists* [consisteth] all his joy to be the breeder of his misery. Yea, it is such a heavy enemy to that holy estate of matrimony, sowing between the married couples such deadly seeds of secret hatred, as, love being once rased out by spiteful distrust, there oft ensueth bloody revenge, as this ensuing history manifestly proveth: wherein Pandosto, furiously incensed by causeless jealousy, procured the death of his most loving and loyal wife and his own endless sorrow and misery.

In the country of Bohemia, there reigned a king called Pandosto, whose fortunate success in wars against his foes, and bountiful courtesy towards his friends in peace, made him to be greatly feared and loved of all men. This Pandosto had to wife a lady called Bellaria, by birth royal, learned by education, fair by nature, by virtues famous, so that it was hard to judge whether her beauty, fortune, or virtue won the greatest commendations. These two, linked together in perfect love, led their lives with such fortunate content that their subjects greatly rejoiced to see their quiet disposition. They had not been married long, but Fortune, willing to increase their happiness, lent them a son, so adorned with the gifts of nature, as the perfection of the child ⟨I. i. 34–45; v. i. 116⟩ greatly augmented the love of the parents and the joy of their commons; in so much that the Bohemians, to show their inward joys by outward actions, made bonfires ⟨v. ii. 22⟩ and triumphs throughout all the kingdom, appointing jousts and tourneys for the honour of their young prince: whither resorted not only his nobles, but also divers kings and princes which were his neighbours, willing to shew their friendship they ought to Pandosto, and to win fame and glory by their prowess and valour. Pandosto, whose mind was fraught with princely liberality, entertained the kings, princes, and noblemen with such submiss courtesy and magnifical bounty, that they all saw how willing he was to gratify their good wills, making a general feast for his subjects, which continued by the space of twenty days; all which time the jousts and tourneys were kept to the great content both of the lords and ladies there present. This solemn triumph being once ended, the assembly, taking their leave of Pandosto and Bellaria, the young son (who was called Garinter) was nursed up in the house to the great joy and content of the parents.

Fortune envious of such happy success, willing to shew some sign of her inconstancy, turned her wheel, and darkened their bright sun of prosperity with the misty clouds of mishap and misery. For it so happened that Egistus, king of Sicilia, who in his youth had been brought up with Pandosto ⟨I. i. 22⟩, desirous to shew that neither tract of time nor distance of place could diminish their former friendship ⟨I. i. 25–32⟩, provided a navy of ships and sailed into Bohemia to visit his old friend and companion; who, hearing of his arrival, went himself in person and his wife Bellaria, accompanied with a great train of lords and ladies, to meet Egistus; and espying him, alighted from his horse, embraced him very lovingly, protesting that nothing in the world could have happened more acceptable to him than his coming, wishing his wife to welcome his old friend and acquaintance: who, to shew how she liked him whom her husband loved, entertained him with such familiar courtesy ⟨III. ii. 61–6⟩ as Egistus perceived himself to be very well welcome. After they had thus saluted and embraced each other, they mounted again on horseback and rode toward the city, devising and recounting how being children they had passed their youth in friendly pastimes: where, by the means of the citizens, Egistus was received with triumphs and shows, in such sort that he marvelled how on so small a warning they could make such preparation.

Passing the streets, thus, with such rare sights, they rode on to the palace, where Pandosto entertained Egistus and his Sicilians with such banqueting and sumptuous cheer, so royally as they all had cause to commend his princely liberality; yea, the very basest slave that was known to come from Sicilia was used with such courtesy that Egistus might easily perceive how both he and his were honoured for his friend's sake. Bellaria, who in her time was the flower of courtesy, willing to shew how unfeignedly she loved her husband by his friend's entertainment, used him likewise so familiarly that her countenance bewrayed how her mind was affected towards him, oftentimes coming herself into his bed chamber to see that nothing should be amiss to mislike him. This honest familiarity increased daily more and more betwixt them; for Bellaria, noting in Egistus a princely and bountiful mind, adorned with sundry and excellent qualities, and Egistus, finding in her a virtuous and courteous disposition, there grew such a secret uniting of their affections, that the one could not well be without the company of the other: in so much, that when Pandosto was busied with such urgent affairs that he could not be present with his friend Egistus, Bellaria would walk with him into the garden ⟨I. ii. 178⟩, where they two in private and pleasant devices would pass away the time to both their contents. This custom still continuing betwixt them, a certain melancholy passion entering the mind of Pandosto drave him into sundry and doubtful thoughts ⟨I. ii. 108 ff.⟩. First, he called to mind the beauty of his wife Bellaria, the comeliness and bravery of his friend Egistus, thinking that love was above all laws and, therefore, to be stayed with no law; that it was hard to put fire and flax together without burning; that their open pleasures might breed his secret displeasures. He considered with himself that Egistus was a man and must needs love, that his wife was a woman, and therefore, subject unto love, and that where fancy forced, friendship was of no force.

These and such like doubtful thoughts, a long time smothering in his stomach, began at last to kindle in his mind a secret mistrust, which, increased by suspicion, grew at last to a flaming jealousy that so tormented him as he could take no rest ⟨II. iii. 1⟩. He then began to measure all their actions, and [to] misconstrue of their too private familiarity, judging that it was not for honest affection, but for disordinate fancy, so *as* [that] he began to watch them more narrowly to see if he could get any true or certain proof to confirm his doubtful suspicion. While thus he noted their looks and gestures and suspected their thoughts and meanings, they two silly souls, who doubted nothing of this his treacherous intent, frequented daily each other's company, which drave him into such a frantic passion, that he began to bear a secret hate to Egistus and a louring countenance to Bellaria ⟨I. ii. 148–50, 365⟩; who marvelling at such unaccustomed frowns, began to cast beyond the moon, and to enter into a thousand sundry thoughts, which way she should offend her husband: but finding in herself a clear conscience ceased to muse, until such time as she might find fit opportunity to demand the cause of his dumps. In the meantime Pandosto's mind was so far charged with jealousy, that he [did] no longer doubt*ed*, but was assured ⟨I. ii. 180 ff.⟩, as he thought, that his friend Egistus had entered a wrong point in his tables, and so had played him false play: whereupon, desirous to revenge so great an injury, he thought best to dissemble the grudge with a fair and friendly countenance ⟨I. ii. 150, 350⟩, and so under the shape of a friend to shew him the trick of a foe. Devising with himself a long time how he might best put away Egistus without suspicion of treacherous murder, [he] concluded at last to poison him ⟨I. ii. 316⟩; which opinion pleasing his humour he became resolute in his determination, and the better to bring the matter to pass he called [un]to him his cup-bearer ⟨I. ii. 345⟩, with whom in secret he brake the matter, promising to him for [the] performance thereof to give him a thousand crowns of yearly revenues.

His cupbearer, either being of a good conscience or willing for fashion sake to deny such a bloody request, began with great reasons to persuade Pandosto from his determinate mischief ⟨I. ii. 321–4⟩, shewing him what an offence murder was to the Gods: how such unnatural actions did more displease the heavens than men, *and* that causeless cruelty did seldom or never escape without revenge: he laid before his face that Egistus was his friend, a king, and one that was come into his kingdom to confirm a league of perpetual amity betwixt them; that he had and did shew him a most friendly countenance; how Egistus was not only honoured of his own people by obedience, but also loved of the Bohemians for his courtesy, and that if he now should without any just or manifest cause poison him, it would not only be a great dishonour to his majesty, and a means to sow perpetual enmity between the Sicilians and the Bohemians, but also his own subjects would repine at such treacherous cruelty ⟨I. ii. 335–9⟩. These and such like persuasions of Franion—for so was his cupbearer called—could no whit prevail to dissuade him from his devilish enterprise, but, remaining resolute in his determination (his fury so fired with rage as it could not be appeased with reason), he began with bitter taunts to take up his man, and to lay before him two baits, preferment and death; saying that if he should poison Egistus, he would advance him to high dignities; if he refused to do it of an obstinate mind, no torture should be too great to requite his disobedience ⟨I. ii. 242–9, 299–304, 324, 348, 355; III. ii. 162–5⟩. Franion, seeing that to persuade Pandosto any more was but to strive against the stream, consented, as soon as opportunity would give him leave, to dispatch Egistus ⟨I. ii. 334⟩: wherewith Pandosto remained somewhat satisfied, hoping now he should be fully revenged of such mistrusted injuries, intending also as soon as Egistus was dead to give his wife a sop of the same sauce, and so be rid of those which were the cause of his restless sorrow ⟨II. iii. 7–9⟩. While thus he lived in this hope, Franion being secret in his chamber began to meditate with himself in these terms:

'Ah, Franion, treason is loved of many, but the traitor hated of all: unjust offences may for a time escape without danger, but never without revenge. Thou art servant to a king and must obey at command; yet, Franion, against law and conscience it is not good to resist a tyrant with arms, nor to please an unjust king with obedience. What shalt thou do? Folly refused gold, and frenzy preferment: wisdom seeketh after dignity, and counsel looketh for gain. Egistus is a stranger to thee, and Pandosto thy sovereign: thou hast little cause to respect the one, and oughtest to have great care to obey the other. Think this, Franion, that a pound of gold is worth a ton of lead: great gifts are little Gods; and preferment to a mean man is a whetstone to courage: there is nothing sweeter than promotion, nor lighter than report. Care not then though most count thee a traitor, so all call thee rich. Dignity, Franion, advanceth thy posterity, and evil report can hurt but thyself. Know this, where eagles build, falcons may prey; where lions haunt, foxes may steal. Kings are known to command, servants are blameless to consent: fear not thou then to lift at Egistus; Pandosto shall bear the burthen. Yea but, Franion, conscience is a worm that ever biteth, but never ceaseth: that which is rubbed with the stone Galactites will never be hot. Flesh dipped in the sea Ægeum will never be sweet: the herb Trigion being once bit with an aspis never groweth, and conscience once stained with innocent blood is always tied to a guilty remorse. Prefer thy content before riches, and a clear mind before dignity; so being poor thou shalt have rich peace, or else rich, thou shalt enjoy disquiet.'

Franion having muttered out these or such like words, seeing either he must die with a clear mind, or live with a spotted conscience, he was so cumbered with divers cogitations that he could take no rest, until at least he determined to break the matter to Egistus; but, fearing that the king should either suspect or hear of such matters, he concealed the device till opportunity would permit him to reveal it ⟨I. ii. 351–64⟩. Lingering thus in doubtful fear, in an evening he went to Egistus' lodging, and desirous to break with him of certain affairs that touched the king, after all were commanded out of the chamber, Franion made manifest the whole conspiracy which Pandosto had devised against him, desiring Egistus not to account him a traitor for bewraying his master's counsel, but to think that he did it for conscience: hoping that although his master, inflamed with rage or incensed by some sinister reports or slanderous speeches, had imagined such causeless mischief, yet when time should pacify his anger, and try those talebearers but flattering parasites, then he would count him as a faithful servant that with such care had kept his master's credit. Egistus had not fully heard Franion tell forth his tale, but a quaking fear possessed all his limbs ⟨I. ii. 457⟩, thinking that there was some treason wrought, and that Franion did but shadow his craft with these false colours: wherefore he began to wax in choler, and said that he doubted not Pandosto, sith he was his friend, and there had never as yet been any breach of amity. He had not sought to invade his lands, to conspire with his enemies, to dissuade his subjects from their allegiance; but in word and thought he rested his at all times: he knew not, therefore, any cause that should move Pandosto to seek his death, but suspected it to be a compacted knavery of the Bohemians to bring the king and him at odds.

Franion, staying him in the midst of his talk, told him that to dally with princes was with the swans to sing against their death ⟨I. ii. 424–31⟩, and that, if the Bohemians had intended any such *secret* mischief, it might have been better brought to pass than by revealing the conspiracy: therefore his Majesty did ill to misconstrue of his good meaning, sith his intent was to hinder treason, not to become a traitor; and to confirm his *premises* [promises], if it pleased his Majesty to *flee* [fly] into Sicilia for the safeguard of his life, he would go with him, and if then he found not such a practice to be pretended, let his imagined treachery be repaid with most monstrous torments. Egistus, hearing the solemn protestation of Franion, began to consider that in love and kingdoms neither faith nor law is to be respected, doubting that Pandosto thought by his death to destroy his men, and with speedy war to invade Sicilia. These and such doubts throughly weighed, he gave great thanks to Franion, promising if he might with life return to Syracusa, that he would create him a duke in Sicilia, craving his counsel how he might escape out of the country ⟨I. ii. 460–2⟩. Franion, who having some small skill in navigation was well acquainted with the ports and havens, and knew every danger in the sea, joining in counsel with the master of Egistus' navy, rigged all their ships, and, setting them afloat, let them lie at anchor to be in the more readiness when time and wind should serve ⟨I. ii. 449⟩.

Fortune, although blind, yet by chance favouring this just cause, sent them within six days a good gale of wind; which Franion seeing fit for their purpose, to put Pandosto out of suspicion, the night before they should sail he went to him, and promised that the next day he would put the device in practice, for he had got such a forcible poison, as the very smell thereof *should* [would] procure sudden death. Pandosto was joyful to hear this good news, and thought every hour a day till he might be glutted with bloody revenge; but his suit had but ill success. For Egistus, fearing that delay might breed danger, and willing that the grass should not be cut from under his feet, taking bag and baggage ⟨I. ii. 206⟩, *with* [by] the help of Franion conveyed himself and his men out *of* [at] a postern gate ⟨I. ii. 464; II. i. 52⟩ of the city, so secretly and speedily that without any suspicion they got to the sea shore; where, with many a bitter curse taking their leave of Bohemia, they went aboard. Weighing their anchors and hoisting sail, they passed as fast as wind and sea would permit towards Sicilia, Egistus being a joyful man that he had safely passed such treacherous perils. But as they were quietly floating on the sea, so Pandosto and his citizens were in an uproar; for, seeing that the Sicilians without taking their leave were fled away by night, the Bohemians feared some treason, and the king thought that without question his suspicion was true ⟨II. i. 37⟩, seeing his cupbearer had bewrayed the sum of his secret pretence. Whereupon he began to imagine that Franion and his wife Bellaria had conspired with Egistus ⟨III. ii. 15; II. i. 47⟩, and that the fervent affection she bare him was the only means of his secret departure; in so much that, incensed with rage, he *commanded* [commands] that his wife should be carried to straight prison ⟨II. i. 103⟩ until they heard further of his pleasure. The guard, unwilling to lay their hands on such a virtuous princess and yet fearing the king's fury, went very sorrowful*ly* to fulfil their charge. Coming to the queen's lodging they found her playing with her young son Garinter ⟨II. i. 1–32⟩, unto whom with tears doing the message, Bellaria, astonished at such a hard censure and finding her clear conscience a sure advocate to plead in her case, went to the prison most willingly ⟨II. i. 121–2⟩, where with sighs and tears she passed away the time till she might come to her trial.

But Pandosto, whose reason was suppressed with rage and whose unbridled folly was incensed with fury, seeing Franion had bewrayed his secrets, and that Egistus might well be railed on, but not revenged ⟨II. iii. 5⟩, determined to wreak all his wrath on poor Bellaria ⟨II. iii. 6–7⟩. He, therefore, caused a general proclamation to be made through all his realm that the queen and Egistus had, by the help of Franion, not only committed most incestuous adultery, but also had conspired the king's death ⟨III. ii. 13–17, 101–2; II. i. 47⟩; whereupon the traitor Franion was fled away with Egistus, and Bellaria was most justly imprisoned. This proclamation being once blazed through the country ⟨III. ii. 101⟩, although the virtuous disposition of the queen did half discredit the contents,

yet the sudden and speedy passage of Egistus and the secret departure of Franion induced them, the circumstances throughly considered, to think that both the proclamation was true, and the king
greatly injured: yet they pitied her case, as sorrowful that so good
a lady should be crossed with such adverse fortune. But the king,
whose restless rage would admit no pity, thought that although he
might sufficiently requite his wife's falsehood with the bitter plague
of pinching penury, yet his mind should never be glutted with revenge till he might have fit time and opportunity to repay the
treachery of Egistus with a fatal injury. But a curst cow hath oft-
times short horns, and a willing mind but a weak arm; for Pandosto, although he felt that revenge was a spur to war, and that
envy always proffereth steel, yet he saw that Egistus was not only
of great puissance and prowess to withstand him, but had also
many kings of his alliance to aid him, if need should serve ⟨II. iii.
4–6, 20–1⟩, for he married *to* the Emperor's daughter of Russia
⟨III. ii. 119⟩. These and the like considerations something daunted
Pandosto his courage, so that he was content rather to put up a
manifest injury with peace, than hunt after revenge, dishonour and
loss; determining, since Egistus had escaped scot-free, that Bellaria
should pay ⟨II. iii. 6–8⟩ for all at an unreasonable price.

Remaining thus resolute in his determination, Bellaria continuing still in prison and hearing the contents of the proclamation,
knowing that her mind was never touched with such affection, nor
that Egistus had ever offered her such discourtesy, would gladly
have come to her answer, that both she might have known her *un-*
just accusers, and cleared herself of that guiltless crime.

But Pandosto was so inflamed with rage and infected with jealousy, as he would not vouchsafe to hear her, nor admit any just
excuse; so that she was fain to make a virtue of her need and with
patience to bear *these* [those] heavy injuries. As thus she lay crossed
with calamities, a great cause to increase her grief, she found herself quick with child, which as soon as she felt stir in her body she
burst forth into bitter tears, exclaiming against fortune in these
terms:

'Alas, Bellaria, how unfortunate art thou, because fortunate!
Better *hadst thou* [thou hadst] been born a beggar than a prince, so
shouldest thou have bridled fortune with want, where now she
sporteth herself with thy plenty. Ah, happy life, where poor
thoughts and mean desires live in secure content, not fearing fortune because too low for fortune! Thou seest now, Bellaria, that
care is a companion to honour, not to poverty; that high cedars
are crushed with tempests, when low shrubs are not touched with

the wind; precious diamonds are cut with the file, when despised pebbles lie safe in the sand. Delphos is sought to by princes, not beggars, and Fortune's altars smoke with kings' presents, not with poor men's gifts. Happy are such, Bellaria, that curse fortune for contempt, not fear, and may wish they were, not sorrow they have been. Thou art a princess, Bellaria, and yet a prisoner; born to the one by descent, assigned to the other by despite; accused without cause, and therefore oughtest to die without care, for patience is a shield against fortune, and a guiltless mind yieldeth *not* to sorrow. Ah, but infamy galleth unto death, and liveth after death: report is plumed with Time's feathers, and envy oftentimes soundeth Fame's trumpet: thy suspected adultery shall fly in the air, and thy known virtues shall lie hid in the earth; one mole staineth *a* [the] whole face, and what is once spotted with infamy can hardly be worn out with time. Die then, Bellaria; Bellaria, die; for if the Gods should say thou art guiltless, yet envy would hear the Gods, but never believe the Gods. Ah, hapless wretch, cease these terms: desperate thoughts are fit for them that fear shame, not for such as hope for credit. Pandosto hath darkened thy fame, but shall never discredit thy virtues. Suspicion may enter a false action, but proof shall never put in his plea: care not then for envy, sith report hath a blister on her tongue ⟨ii. ii. 33⟩, and let sorrow bite them which offend, not touch thee that art faultless. But alas, poor soul, how canst thou not sorrow? Thou art with child, and by him that in stead of kind pity pincheth thee in cold prison.' And with that, such gasping sighs so stopping her breath that she could not utter any mo[re] words, but wringing her hands, and gushing forth streams of tears, she passed away the time with bitter complaints.

The jailor, pitying those her heavy passions, thinking that if the king knew she were with child he would somewhat appease his fury ⟨ii. ii. 40⟩ and release her from prison, went in all haste and certified Pandosto what the effect of Bellaria's complaint was; who no sooner heard the jailor say she was with child, but as one possessed with a frenzy he rose up in a rage, swearing that she and the bastard brat she was [big] withal should die if the Gods themselves said no ⟨ii. iii. 94–5; iii. ii. 140⟩; thinking that surely by computation of time ⟨i. ii. 1⟩ that Egistus and not he was [the] father to the child. This suspicious thought galled afresh this half healed sore, insomuch as he could take no rest ⟨ii. iii. 1⟩ until he might mitigate his choler with a just revenge, which happened presently after. For Bellaria was brought to bed of a fair and beautiful daughter, which no sooner Pandosto heard, but he determined that both Bellaria and the young infant should be burnt with fire ⟨ii. iii. 95, 133⟩. His nobles hearing of the king's cruel sentence sought by persuasions to divert him from his bloody determination, laying before his face the innocency of the child, and *the* virtuous disposition of his wife, how she had continually loved and honoured him so tenderly that without due proof he could not, nor ought not to appeach her of that crime ⟨II. i. 126–72⟩. And if she had faulted, yet it were more honourable to pardon with mercy than to punish with extremity, and more kingly to be commended of pity than accused of rigour. And as for the child, if he should punish it for the mother's offence, it were to strive against nature and justice; and that unnatural actions do more offend the Gods than men; how causeless cruelty nor innocent blood never scapes without revenge. These and such like reasons could not appease his rage, but he rested resolute in this, that Bellaria being an adultress the child was a bastard, and he would not suffer that such an infamous brat should call him father ⟨II. iii. 154–5⟩. Yet at last, seeing his noblemen were importunate upon him, he was content to spare the child's life, and yet to put it to a worse*r* death ⟨II. iii. 156–7⟩. For he found out this device, that seeing, as he thought, it came by fortune, so he would commit it to the charge of fortune ⟨II. iii. 178–82⟩; and, therefore, he caused a little cock-boat to be provided, wherein he meant to put the babe, and then send it to the mercy of the seas and the destinies ⟨II. iii. 174–82⟩. From this his peers in no wise could persuade him, but that he sent presently two of his guard to fetch the child: who being come to the prison, and with weeping tears recounting their master's message, Bellaria no sooner heard the rigorous resolution of her merciless husband, but she fell down in a swound, so that all thought she had been dead: yet at last being come to herself, she cried and scritched out in this wise:

'Alas, sweet unfortunate babe, scarce born before envied by fortune! Would the day of thy birth had been the term of thy life; then shouldest thou have made an end to care and prevented thy father's rigour. Thy faults cannot yet deserve such hateful revenge; thy days are too short for so sharp a doom; but thy untimely death must pay thy mother's debts, and her guiltless crime must be thy ghastly curse. And shalt thou, sweet babe, be committed to fortune, when thou art already spited by fortune? Shall the seas be thy harbour and the hard boat thy cradle? Shall thy tender mouth, instead of sweet kisses, be nipped with bitter storms? Shalt thou have the whistling winds for thy lullaby ⟨III. iii. 55⟩, and the salt sea foam instead of sweet milk? Alas, what destinies would assign such hard hap? What father would be so cruel, or what gods will not revenge such rigour? Let me kiss thy lips, sweet infant, and wet thy tender

cheeks with my tears, and put this chain about thy little neck, that
if fortune save thee, it may help to succour thee. Thus, since thou
must go to surge in the ghastful seas, with a sorrowful kiss I bid thee
farewell, and I pray the gods thou mayest fare well.'

Such and so great was her grief, that her vital spirits being suppressed with sorrow, she fell again down into a trance, having her
senses so sotted with care that after she was revived yet she lost her
memory, and lay for a great time without moving, as one in a
trance. The guard left her in this perplexity, and carried the child
to the king, who, quite devoid of pity, commanded that without
delay it should be put in*to* the boat, having neither sail nor *other*
[rudder] to guide it, and so to be carried into the midst of the sea,
and there left to the wind and wave as the destinies please to appoint. The very shipmen, seeing the sweet countenance of the
young babe, began to accuse the king of rigour, and to pity the
child's hard fortune; but fear constrained them to that which their
nature did abhor, so that they placed it in one of the ends of the
boat, and with a few green boughs made a homely cabin to shroud
it as they could from wind and weather. Having thus trimmed the
boat they tied it to a ship and so haled it into the main sea, and then
cut in sunder the cord; which they had no sooner done, but there
arose a mighty tempest, which tossed the little boat so vehemently
in the waves that the shipmen thought it could not continue long
without sinking; yea, the storm grew so great that with much labour
and peril they got to the shore.

But leaving the child to her fortunes, again to Pandosto, who not
yet glutted with sufficient revenge devised which way he should
best increase his wife's calamity. But first assembling his nobles and
counsellors, he called her for the more reproach into open court,
where it was objected against her that she had committed adultery
with Egistus, and conspired with Franion to poison Pandosto her
husband, but their pretence being partly spied, she counselled them
to fly away by night for their better safety ⟨III. ii. 12–21⟩. Bellaria,
who standing like a prisoner at the bar, feeling in herself a clear
conscience to withstand her false accusers, seeing that no less than
death could pacify her husband's wrath, waxed bold and desired
that she might have law and justice, for mercy she neither craved
nor hoped [for]; and that those perjured wretches which had falsely
accused her to the king might be brought before her face to give in
evidence. But Pandosto, whose rage and jealousy was such as no
reason nor equity could appease, told her that, for her accusers,
they were of such credit as their words were sufficient witness, and
that the sudden and secret flight of Egistus and Franion confirmed

that which they had confessed; and as for her, it was her part to deny such a monstrous crime, and to be impudent in forswearing the fact, since she had passed all shame in committing the fault ⟨III. ii. 54–7⟩: but her stale countenance should stand for no coin, for as the bastard which she bare was served, so she should with some cruel death be requited. Bellaria, no whit dismayed with this rough reply, told her husband Pandosto that he spake upon choler and not conscience, for her virtuous life had been ever such as no spot of suspicion could ever stain ⟨III. ii. 33–5⟩. And if she had borne a friendly countenance to Egistus, it was in respect he was his friend ⟨III. ii. 61–71⟩, and not for any lusting affection; therefore, if she were condemned without any further proof it was rigour and not law ⟨III. ii. 109–14⟩.

The noblemen, which sate in judgment, said that Bellaria spake reason ⟨III. ii. 116–17⟩, and intreated the king that the accusers might be openly examined and sworn, [and] if then the evidence were such as the jury might find her guilty (for seeing she was a prince she ought to be tried by her peers), then let her have such punishment as the extremity of the law will assign to such malefactors. The king presently made answer that in this case he might and would dispense with the law, and that the jury being once panelled they should take his word for sufficient evidence; otherwise he would make the proudest of them repent it. The noblemen seeing the king in choler were all whist; but Bellaria, whose life then hung in the balance, fearing more perpetual infamy than momentary death ⟨III. ii. 109–11⟩, told the king if his fury might stand for a law that it were vain to have the jury yield their verdict; and, therefore, she fell down upon her knees, and desired the king that for the love he bare to his young son Garinter, whom she brought into the world, that he would grant her a request; *the* which was this, that it would please his majesty to send six of his noblemen whom he best trusted to the Isle of Delphos, there to inquire of the oracle of Apollo ⟨II. i. 183; III. i. 2; III. ii. 114–16⟩ whether she had committed adultery with Egistus, or conspired to poison him with Franion? and if the god Apollo, who by his divine essence knew all secrets, gave answer that she was guilty, she were content to suffer any torment were it never so terrible. The request was so reasonable that Pandosto could not for shame deny it, unless he would be counted of all his subjects more wilful than wise: he, therefore, agreed that with as much speed as might be there should be certain ambassadors dispatched to the Isle of Delphos, and in the mean season he commanded that his wife should be kept in close prison ⟨II. i. 194⟩.

Bellaria, having obtained this grant, was now more careful for her little babe that floated on the seas than sorrowful for her own mishap; for of that she doubted, of herself she was assured; knowing if Apollo should give oracle according to the thoughts of the heart, yet the sentence should go on her side, such was the clearness of her mind in this case. But Pandosto, whose suspicious head still remained in one song, chose out six of his nobility whom he knew were scarce indifferent men in the queen's behalf, and providing all things fit for their journey sent them to Delphos: they willing to fulfil the king's command, and desirous to see the situation and custom of the island, dispatched their affairs with as much speed as might be, and embarked themselves to *the* [this] voyage, which, the wind and weather serving fit for their purpose, was soon ended. For within three weeks ⟨II. iii. 197⟩ they arrived at Delphos, where they were no sooner set on land but with great devotion they went to the temple of Apollo, and there offering sacrifice to the God and gifts to the priest, as the custom was, they humbly craved an answer of their demand. They had not long kneeled at the altar, but Apollo with a loud voice said: 'Bohemians, what you find behind the altar take, and depart.' They forthwith obeying the oracle found a scroll of parchment ⟨III. i. 19⟩, wherein was written these words in letters of gold—

THE ORACLE

SUSPICION IS NO PROOF: JEALOUSY IS AN UNEQUAL JUDGE: BELLARIA IS CHASTE: EGISTUS BLAMELESS: FRANION A TRUE SUBJECT: PANDOSTO TREACHEROUS: HIS BABE AN INNOCENT; AND THE KING SHALL LIVE WITHOUT AN HEIR, IF THAT WHICH IS LOST BE NOT FOUND ⟨III. ii. 132–6⟩.

As soon as they had taken out this scroll the priest of the God commanded them that they should not presume to read it before they came in the presence of Pandosto ⟨III. i. 8–11; III. ii. 126–30⟩, unless they would incur the displeasure of Apollo. The Bohemian lords carefully obeying his command, taking their leave of the priest with great reverence, departed out of the temple, and went to their ships, and as soon as wind would permit them sailed toward Bohemia, whither in short time they safely arrived; and with great triumph issuing out of their ships went to the king's palace, whom they found in his chamber accompanied with other noblemen. Pandosto no sooner saw them but with a merry countenance he welcomed them home, asking what news? they told his majesty that they had received an answer of the God written in a scroll, but with this charge, that they should not read the contents before they came in the presence of the king, and with that they delivered him the parchment: but his noblemen entreated him that, sith therein was contained either the safety of his wife's life and honesty or her death and perpetual infamy, that he would have his nobles and commons assembled in the judgment hall, where the queen, brought in as prisoner ⟨III. ii. 9–10⟩, should hear the contents. If she were found guilty by the oracle of the God, then all should have cause to think his rigour proceeded of due desert: if her grace were found faultless, then she should be cleared before all, sith she had been accused openly ⟨III. ii. 4–7⟩. This pleased the king so, that he appointed the day, and assembled all his lords and commons, and caused the queen to be brought in before the judgment seat, commanding than the indictment should be read wherein she was accused of adultery with Egistus and of conspiracy with Franion. Bellaria hearing the contents was no whit astonished, but made this cheerful answer—

'If the divine powers be privy to human actions—as no doubt they are—I hope my patience shall make fortune blush, and my unspotted life shall stain spiteful*ly* discredit. For although lying report hath sought to appeach mine honour, and suspicion hath intended to soil my credit with infamy, yet where virtue keepeth the fort, report and suspicion may assail, but never sack: how I have led my life before Egistus' coming, I appeal, Pandosto, to the gods and to thy conscience. What hath passed betwixt him and me, the gods only know, and I hope will presently reveal: that I loved Egistus I cannot deny; that I honoured him I shame not to confess: to the one I was forced by his virtues, to the other for his dignities. But as touching lascivious lust, I say Egistus is honest, and hope myself to be found without spot: for Franion, I can neither accuse him nor excuse him, for I was not privy to his departure; and that this is true which I have here rehearsed I refer myself to the divine oracle.' ⟨III. ii. 28–33, 45–8, 73–6, 115.⟩

Bellaria had no sooner said but the king commanded that one of his dukes should read the contents of the scroll, which after the commons had heard they gave a great shout, rejoicing and clapping their hands that the queen was clear of that false accusation ⟨III. ii. 137⟩. But the king, whose conscience was a witness against him of his witless fury and false suspected jealousy, was so ashamed of his rash folly that he entreated his nobles to persuade Bellaria to forgive and forget these injuries; promising not only to shew himself a loyal and loving husband, but also to reconcile himself to Egistus and Franion; revealing then before them all the cause of their secret flight, and how treacherously he thought to have practised death, if the good mind of his cupbearer had not prevented his purpose. As thus he was relating the whole matter, there was word brought him that his young son Garinter was suddenly dead ⟨III. ii. 145⟩, which news so soon as Bellaria heard, surcharged before with extreme joy and now suppressed with heavy sorrow, her vital spirits were so stopped that she fell down presently dead, and could be never revived ⟨III. ii. 148–9, 201⟩. This sudden sight so appalled the king's senses, that he sank from his seat in a swound, so as he was fain to be carried by his nobles to his palace, where he lay by the space of three days without speech. His commons were, as men in despair, *so* diversely distressed: there was nothing but mourning and lamentation to be heard throughout all Bohemia: their young prince dead, their virtuous queen bereaved of her life, and their king and sovereign in great hazard. This tragical discourse of fortune so daunted them, as they went like shadows, not men; yet somewhat to comfort their heavy hearts, they heard that Pandosto was come to himself, and had recovered his speech, who as in a fury brayed out these bitter speeches:

'O miserable Pandosto! what surer witness than conscience! what thoughts more sour than suspicion! what plague more bad than jealousy! unnatural actions offend the gods more than men, and causeless cruelty never scapes without revenge. I have committed such a bloody fact, as repent I may, but recall I cannot. Ah, jealousy! a hell to the mind, and a horror to the conscience, suppressing reason, and inciting rage; a worse passion than frenzy, a greater plague than madness. Are the gods just? then let them revenge such brutish cruelty. My innocent babe I have drowned in the seas; my loving wife I have slain with slanderous suspicion; my trusty friend I have sought to betray, and yet the gods are slack to plague such offences. Ah, unjust Apollo! Pandosto is the man that hath committed the fault; why should Garinter, silly child, abide the pain? Well, sith the gods mean to prolong my days to increase my dolour, I will offer my guilty blood a sacrifice to those sackless souls whose lives are lost by my rigorous folly.'

And with that he reached at a rapier to have murdered himself, but his peers being present stayed him from such a bloody act, persuading him to think that the commonwealth consisted on his safety, and that those sheep could not but perish that wanted a shepherd; wishing that if he would not live for himself, yet he should have care of his subjects, and to put such fancies out of his mind, sith in sores past help salves do not heal but hurt, and in things past cure, care is a corrosive. With these and such like persuasions the king was overcome, and began somewhat to quiet his mind; so that as soon as he could go abroad he caused his wife to be embalmed, and wrapt in lead with her young son Garinter; erecting a rich and famous sepulchre wherein he entombed them both ⟨III. ii. 236–40⟩, making such solemn obsequies at her funeral as all Bohemia might perceive he did greatly repent him of his fore-passed folly; causing this epitaph to be engraven on her tomb in letters of gold—

¶ THE EPITAPH

HERE LIES ENTOMBED BELLARIA FAIR,
FALSELY ACCUSED TO BE UNCHASTE:
CLEARED BY APOLLO'S SACRED DOOM,
YET SLAIN BY JEALOUSY AT LAST.
WHAT ERE THOU BE THAT PASSEST BY,
CURSE HIM THAT CAUSED THIS QUEEN TO DIE.

This epitaph being engraven, Pandosto would once a day repair to the tomb ⟨III. ii. 242⟩, and there with watery plaints bewail his misfortune, coveting no other companion but sorrow, nor no other harmony but repentance. But leaving him to his dolorous passions, at last let us come to shew the tragical discourse of the young infant.

Who being tossed with wind and wave floated two whole days without succour, ready at every puff to be drowned in the sea, till at last the tempest ⟨III. iii. 65⟩ ceased and the little boat was driven with the tide into the coast of Sicilia ⟨III. iii. 2⟩, where sticking upon the sands it rested. Fortune minding to be wanton, willing to shew that as she hath wrinkles on her brows so she hath dimples in her cheeks, thought after so many sour looks to lend a feigned smile, and after a puffing storm to bring a pretty calm, she began thus to dally. It fortuned a poor mercenary shepherd that dwelled in Sicilia, who got his living by other men's flocks, missed one of his sheep, and, thinking it had strayed into the covert that was hard by, sought very diligently to find that which he could not see, fearing either that the wolves or eagles had undone him (for he was so poor as a sheep was half his substance), wandered down toward the sea cliffs to see if perchance the sheep was browsing on the sea ivy ⟨III. iii. 65–8⟩, whereon they greatly do feed; but not finding her there, as he was ready to return to his flock he heard a child cry, but knowing there was no house near, he thought he had mistaken the sound and that it was the bleating of his sheep. Wherefore, looking more narrowly, as he cast his eye to the sea he spied a little boat, from whence, as he attentively listened, he might hear the cry to come. Standing a good while in a maze, at last he went to the shore, and wading to the boat, as he looked in he saw the little babe lying all alone ready to die for hunger and cold, wrapped in a mantle of scarlet richly embroidered with gold, and having a chain about the neck ⟨III. iii. 69–70, 113–24; v. ii. 33–4⟩.

The shepherd, who before had never seen so fair a babe nor so rich jewels, thought assuredly that it was some little god, and began with great devotion to knock on his breast. The babe, who writhed with the head to seek for the pap, began again to cry afresh, whereby the poor man knew that it was a child, which by some sinister means was driven thither by distress of weather; marvelling how such a silly infant, which by the mantle and the chain could not be but born of noble parentage, should be so hardly crossed with deadly mishap. The poor shepherd, perplexed thus with divers thoughts, took pity of the child, and determined with himself to carry it to the king, that there it might be brought up according to the worthiness of birth, for his ability could not afford to foster it, though his [good] mind was willing to further it. Taking therefore the child in his arms, as he folded the mantle together the better to defend it from cold there fell down at his foot a very fair and rich purse, wherein he found a great sum of gold; which sight so revived the shepherd's spirits, as he was greatly ravished with joy and daunted with fear; joyful to see such a sum in his power, and fearful, if it should be known, that it might breed his further danger ⟨III. iii. 119–24⟩. Necessity wished him at the least to retain the gold, though he would not keep the child: the simplicity *if* [of] his conscience feared him from such deceitful bribery. Thus was the poor man perplexed with a doubtful dilemma until at last the covetousness of the coin overcame him; for what will not the greedy desire of gold cause a man to do? So that he was resolved in himself to foster the child, and with the sum to relieve his want. Resting thus resolute in this point he left seeking of his sheep, and, as covertly and secretly as he could, went by a by-way to his house, lest any of his neighbours should perceive his carriage. As soon as he was got home, entering in at the door, the child began to cry, which his wife hearing, and seeing her husband with a young babe in his arms, began to be somewhat jealous, yet marvelling that her husband should be so wanton abroad sith he was so quiet at home: but as women are naturally given to believe the worst, so his wife, thinking it was some bastard, began to crow against her goodman, and taking up a cudgel (for the most master went breechless) swore solemnly that she would make clubs trumps if he brought any bastard brat within her doors. The goodman, seeing his wife in her majesty with her mace in her hand, thought it was time to bow for fear of blows, and desired her to be quiet, for there was none such

matter; but if she could hold her peace they were made for ever
⟨III. iii. 119⟩: and with that he told her the whole matter, how he
had found the child in a little boat, without any succour, wrapped
in that costly mantle ⟨v. ii. 33–4⟩, and having that rich chain about
the neck. But at last, when he shewed her the purse full of gold, she
began to simper something sweetly, and, taking her husband about
the neck kissed him after her homely fashion, saying that she hoped
God had seen their want and now meant to relieve their poverty,
and, seeing they could get no children, had sent them this little
babe to be their heir. 'Take heed, in any case,' quoth the shepherd,
'that you be secret ⟨III. iii. 124⟩, and blab it not out when you meet
with your gossips, for, if you do, we are like not only to lose the
gold and jewels, but our other goods and lives.' 'Tush,' quoth his
wife, 'profit is a good hatch before the door: fear not, I have other
things to talk of than this; but I pray you let us lay up the money
surely and the jewels, lest by any mishap it be spied.'

After that they had set all things in order, the shepherd went to
his sheep with a merry note, and the good wife learned to sing
lullaby at home with her young babe, wrapping it in a homely
blanket instead of a rich mantle; nourishing it so cleanly and carefully as it began to be a jolly girl, insomuch that they began both
of them to be very fond of it, seeing as it waxed in age so it increased
in beauty. The shepherd every night at his coming home would
sing and dance it on his knee and prattle, that in a short time it
began to speak and call him Dad and her Mam: at last when grew it
to ripe years that it was about seven years old, the shepherd left
keeping of other men's sheep, and with the money he found in the
purse he bought him the lease of a pretty farm, and got a small flock
of sheep, which, when Fawnia (for so they named the child) came
to the age of ten years, he set her to keep, and she with such diligence performed her charge as the sheep prospered marvellously
under her hands. Fawnia thought Porrus had been her father and
Mopsa her mother (for so was the shepherd and his wife called),
honoured and obeyed them with such reverence that all the neighbours praised the dutiful obedience of the child. Porrus grew in
short time to be a man of some wealth and credit ⟨IV. ii. 39–41⟩,
for fortune so favoured him in having no charge but Fawnia, that
he began to purchase land, intending after his death to give it to
his daughter, so that divers rich farmers' sons came as wooers to his
house. For Fawnia was something cleanly attired, being of such
singular beauty and excellent wit, that whoso saw her would have
thought she had been some heavenly nymph and not a mortal
creature, insomuch that, when she came to the age of sixteen years

⟨IV. i. 6⟩, she so increased with exquisite perfection both of body and mind ⟨IV. i. 24–5⟩, as her natural disposition did bewray that she was born of some high parentage ⟨IV. iv. 156–9⟩; but the people thinking she was daughter to the shepherd Porrus rested only amazed at her beauty and wit; yea, she won such favour and commendations in every man's eye, as her beauty was not only praised in the country, but also spoken of in the court ⟨IV. ii. 42–6⟩; yet such was her submiss modesty, that although her praise daily increased, her mind was no whit puffed up with pride, but humbled herself as became a country maid and the daughter of a poor shepherd. Every day she went forth with her sheep to the field, keeping them with such care and diligence as all men thought she was very painful, defending her face from the heat of the sun with no other veil but with a garland made of boughs and flowers, which attire became her so gallantly as she seemed to be the goddess Flora herself for beauty ⟨IV. iv. 1–3⟩.

Fortune, who all this while had shewed a friendly face, began now to turn her back and to shew a louring countenance, intending as she had given Fawnia a slender check, so she would give her a harder mate; to bring which to pass, she laid her train on this wise. Egistus had but one only son, called Dorastus, about the age of twenty years; a prince so decked and adorned with the gifts of nature, so fraught with beauty and virtuous qualities, as not only his father joyed to have so good a son, *and* [but] all his commons rejoiced that God had lent them such a noble prince to succeed in the kingdom ⟨IV. iv. 7–8; I. i. 34–6⟩. Egistus placing all his joy in the perfection of his son, seeing that he was now marriageable, sent ambassadors to the king of Denmark to entreat a marriage between him and his daughter, who willingly consenting made answer that the next spring, if it please Egistus with his son to come into Denmark, he doubted not but they should agree upon reasonable conditions. Egistus, resting satisfied with this friendly answer, thought convenient in the meantime to break with his son: finding therefore on a day fit opportunity, he spake to him in these fatherly terms:

'Dorastus, thy youth warneth me to prevent the worst, and mine age to provide the best. Opportunities neglected are signs of folly: actions measured by time are seldom bitten with repentance. Thou art young, and I old; age hath taught me that which thy youth cannot yet conceive. I, therefore, will counsel thee as a father, hoping thou wilt obey as a child. Thou seest my white hairs are blossoms for the grave, and thy fresh colour fruit for time and fortune, so that it behoveth me to think how to die, and for thee to care how to live. My crown I must leave by death, and thou enjoy my kingdom by succession, wherein I hope thy virtue and prowess shall be such, as though my subjects want my person, yet they shall see in thee my perfection. That nothing either may fail to satisfy thy mind or increase thy dignities, the only care I have is to see thee well married, before I die and thou become old.'

Dorastus, who from his infancy delighted rather to die with Mars in the field than to dally with Venus in the chamber, fearing to displease his father, and yet not willing to be wed, made him this reverent answer:

'Sir, there is no greater bond than duty, nor no straiter law than nature: disobedience in youth is often galled with despite in age. The command of the father ought to be a constraint to the child: so parents' wills are laws, so they pass not all laws. May it please your Grace, therefore, to appoint whom I shall love, rather than by denial I should be appeached of disobedience. I rest content to love, though it be the only thing I hate.'

Egistus, hearing his son to fly far from the mark, began to be somewhat choleric, and, therefore, made him this hasty answer:

'What, Dorastus, canst thou not love? Cometh this cynical passion of prone desires or peevish frowardness? What, dost thou think thyself too good for all, or none good enough for thee? I tell thee, Dorastus, there is nothing sweeter than youth, nor swifter decreasing while it is increasing. Time passed with folly may be repented, but not recalled. If thou marry in age, thy wife's fresh colours will breed in thee dead thoughts and suspicion, and thy white hairs her loathsomeness and sorrow; for Venus' affections are not fed with kingdoms, or treasures, but with youthful conceits and sweet amours. Vulcan was allotted to shake the tree, but Mars allowed to reap the fruit. Yield, Dorastus, to thy father's persuasions, which may prevent thy perils. I have chosen thee a wife, fair by nature, royal by birth, by virtues famous, learned by education and rich by possessions, so that it is hard to judge whether her bounty or fortune, her beauty or virtue be of greater force. I mean, Dorastus, Euphania, daughter and heir to the king of Denmark.'

Egistus pausing here awhile, looking when his son should make him answer, and seeing that he stood still as one in a trance, he shook him up thus sharply:

'Well, Dorastus, take heed; the tree Alpya wasteth not with fire, but withereth with the dew: that which love nourisheth not, perisheth with hate. If thou like Euphania, thou breedest my content, and in loving her thou shalt have my love; otherwise'—— and with that he flung from his son in a rage, leaving him a sorrowful man, in that he had by denial displeased his father, and half angry with himself that he could not yield to that passion whereto both reason and his father persuaded him. But see how fortune is plumed with time's feathers, and how she can minister strange causes to breed strange effects.

It happened not long after this that there was a meeting of all the farmers' daughters in Sicilia, whither Fawnia was also bidden as the mistress of the feast ⟨IV. iv. 68⟩, who, having attired herself in her best garments, went among the rest of her companions to the merry meeting, there spending the day in such homely pastimes as shepherds use ⟨IV. iv. 10–12⟩. As the evening grew on and their sports ceased, each taking their leave at other, Fawnia, desiring one of her companions to bear her company, went home by the flock to see if they were well folded, and, as they returned, it fortuned that Dorastus, who all that day had been hawking ⟨IV. iv. 14–16⟩, and killed store of game, encountered by the way these two maids, and, casting his eye suddenly on Fawnia, he was half afraid, fearing that with Actæon he had seen Diana; for he thought such exquisite perfection could not be found in any mortal creature. As thus he stood in a maze, one of his pages told him that the maid with the garland on her head was Fawnia ⟨IV. iv. 1, 10⟩, the fair shepherd whose beauty was so much talked of in the court ⟨IV. ii. 42–6⟩. Dorastus, desirous to see if nature had adorned her mind with any inward qualities, as she had decked her body with outward shape, began to question with her whose daughter she was, of what age, and how she had been trained up? who answered him with such modest reverence and sharpness of wit that Dorastus thought her outward beauty was but a counterfeit to darken her inward qualities ⟨IV. iv. 579–82⟩, wondering how so courtly behaviour could be found in so simple a cottage, and cursing fortune that had shadowed wit and beauty with such hard fortune. *And* [As] thus he held her a long while with chat, beauty seeing him at discovert thought not to lose the vantage, but struck him so deeply with an envenomed shaft, as he wholly lost his liberty and became a slave to love, which before contemned love, glad now to gaze on a poor shepherd, who before refused the offer of a rich princess; for the perfection of Fawnia had so *fixed* [fired] his fancy as he felt his mind greatly changed and his affections altered, cursing love that had wrought such a change, and blaming the baseness of his mind that would make such a choice; but, thinking that these were but passionate toys that might be thrust out at pleasure, to avoid the siren that enchanted him he put spurs to his horse, and bade this fair shepherd farewell.

Fawnia, who all this while had marked the princely gesture of Dorastus, seeing his face so well featured, and each limb so perfectly framed, began greatly to praise his perfection, commending him so long till she found herself faulty, and perceived that, if she waded but a little further, she might slip over *the* [her] shoes: she, therefore, seeking to quench that fire which never was put out, went home and feigning herself not well at ease, got her to bed; where, casting a thousand thoughts in her head, she could take no rest: for, if she waked, she began to call to mind his beauty, and, thinking to beguile such thoughts with sleep, she then dreamed of his perfection. Pestered thus with these unacquainted passions, she passed the night as she could in short slumbers.

Dorastus, who all this while rode with a flea in his ear, could not by any means forget the sweet favour of Fawnia, but rested so bewitched with her wit and beauty, as he could take no rest. He felt fancy to give the assault and his wounded mind ready to yield as vanquished: yet he began with divers considerations to suppress *his* [this] frantic affection, calling to mind that Fawnia was a shepherd, one not worthy to be looked at of a prince, much less to be loved of such a potentate; thinking what a discredit it were to himself, and what a grief it would be to his father, blaming fortune and accusing his own folly that should be so fond as but once to cast a glance at such a country slut. As thus he was raging against himself, Love, fearing if she *dally* [dallied] long to lose her champion, stept more nigh and gave him such a fresh wound as it pierced him at the heart, that he was fain to yield, maugre his face, and to forsake the company and get him to his chamber, where being solemnly set he burst into these passionate terms:

'Ah, Dorastus, art thou alone? No, not alone, while thou art tried with these unacquainted passions. Yield to fancy thou canst not by thy father's counsel, but in a frenzy thou art by just destinies. Thy father were content if thou couldst love, and thou, therefore, discontent because thou dost love. O, divine love! feared of men because honoured of the Gods, not to be suppressed by wisdom, because not to be comprehended by reason; without law, and, therefore, above all law. How now, Dorastus! why dost thou blaze that with praises, which thou hast cause to blaspheme with curses? yet why should they curse love *which* [that] are in love? Blush, Dorastus, at thy fortune, thy choice, thy love: thy thoughts cannot be uttered without shame, nor thy affections without discredit. Ah, Fawnia, sweet Fawnia, thy beauty, Fawnia! Shamest not thou, Dorastus, to name one unfit for thy birth, thy dignities, thy kingdoms? Die, Dorastus; Dorastus, die. Better hadst thou perish with high desires than live in base thoughts. Yea, but beauty must be obeyed because it is beauty, yet framed of the Gods to feed the eye, not to fetter the heart. Ah, but he that striveth against love shooteth with them of Scyrum against the wind, and with the cockatrice pecketh against the steel. I will, therefore, obey, because I must obey. Fawnia, yea Fawnia shall be my fortune in spite of fortune. The Gods above disdain not to love women beneath. Phœbus liked Sibylla, Jupiter Io, and why not I then Fawnia? one something inferior to these in birth, but far superior to them in beauty, born to be a shepherd, but worthy to be a goddess. Ah, Dorastus, wilt thou so forget thyself as to suffer affection to suppress wisdom, and love to violate thine honour? How sour will thy choice be to thy father, sorrowful to thy subjects, to thy friends a grief, most gladsome to thy foes! Subdue then thy affection[s], and cease to love her whom thou couldst not love, unless blinded with too much love. Tush, I talk to the wind, and in seeking to prevent the causes I further the effects. I will yet praise Fawnia; honour, yea, and love Fawnia, and at this day follow content, not counsel. Do, Dorastus: thou canst but repent.' And, with that, his page came into the chamber, whereupon he ceased from [his] complaints, hoping that time would wear out that which fortune had wrought. As thus he was pained, so poor Fawnia was diversely perplexed; for the next morning getting up very early she went to her sheep, thinking with hard labours to pass away her new conceived amours, beginning very busily to drive them to the field, and then to shift the folds. At last, wearied with toil, she sat her down, where (poor soul) she was more tried with fond affections; for love began to assault her, in so much that, as she sate upon the side of a hill, she began to accuse her own folly in these terms:

'Unfortunate Fawnia, and therefore unfortunate because Fawnia! thy shepherd's hook sheweth thy poor state, thy proud desires an aspiring mind: the one declareth thy want, the other thy pride. No bastard hawk must soar so high as the hobby, no fowl gaze against the sun but the eagle: actions wrought against nature reap despite, and thoughts above fortune disdain. Fawnia, thou art a shepherd, daughter to poor Porrus: if thou rest content with this thou art like to stand; if thou climb thou art sure to fall. The herb Anita, growing higher than six inches, becometh a weed. Nylus, flowing more than twelve cubits, procureth a dearth. Daring affections that pass measure are cut short by time or fortune: suppress then, Fawnia, those thoughts which thou mayest shame to express. But ah, Fawnia, love is a lord who will command by power, and constrain by force. Dorastus, ah, Dorastus is the man I love! the worse is thy hap, and the less cause hast thou to hope. Will eagles catch at flies? will cedars stoop to brambles, or mighty princes look at such homely trulls? No, no; think this: Dorastus' disdain is greater than thy desire; he is a prince respecting his honour, thou a beggar's brat forgetting thy calling. Cease then not only to say, but to think to love Dorastus, and dissemble thy love, Fawnia; for better it were to die with grief, than to live with shame. Yet, in despite of love, I will sigh to see if I can sigh out love.'

Fawnia, somewhat appeasing her griefs with these pithy persuasions, began, after her wonted manner, to walk about her sheep, and to keep them from straying into the corn, suppressing her affection with the due consideration of her base estate, and with the impossibilities of her love; thinking it were frenzy, not fancy, to covet that which the very destinies [did] deny her to obtain.

But Dorastus was more impatient in his passions, for love so fiercely assailed him, that neither company nor music could mitigate his martyrdom, but did rather far the more increase his malady: shame would not let him crave counsel in this case, nor fear of his father's displeasure reveal it to any secret friend; but he was fain to make a secretary of himself, and to participate his thoughts with his own troubled mind. Lingering thus awhile in doubtful suspense, at *lost* [last], stealing secretly from the court without either men or page, he went to see if he could espy Fawnia walking abroad in the field; but, as one having a great deal more skill to retrieve the partridge with his spaniels than to hunt after such a strange prey, he sought, but was little the better; which cross luck drave him into a great choler, that he began both to accuse love and fortune. But, as he was ready to retire, he saw Fawnia sitting all alone under the side of a hill, making a garland of such homely flowers as the fields did afford. This sight so revived his spirits that he drew nigh, with more judgment to take a view of her singular perfection, which he found to be such as, in that country attire, she stained all the courtly dames of Sicilia. While thus he stood gazing with piercing looks on her surpassing beauty, Fawnia cast her eye aside and spied Dorastus, *with* [which] sudden sight made the poor girl to blush, and to dye her crystal cheeks with a vermilion red, which gave her such a grace as she seemed *far* more beautiful. And with that she rose up, saluting the prince with such modest curtesies as he wondered how a country maid could afford such courtly behaviour. Dorastus, repaying her curtesy with a smiling countenance, began to parley with her on this manner:

'Fair maid,' quoth he, 'either your want is great, or a shepherd's life very sweet, that your delight is in such country labours. I cannot conceive what pleasure you should take, unless you mean to imitate the nymphs, being yourself so like a nymph. To put me out of this doubt, shew me what is to be commended in a shepherd's life, and what pleasures you have to countervail these drudging labours.'

Fawnia, with blushing face, made him this ready answer: 'Sir, what richer state than content, or what sweeter life than quiet? We shepherds are not born to honour, nor beholding unto beauty, the less care we have to fear fame or fortune. We count our attire brave enough if warm enough, and our food dainty if to suffice nature: our greatest enemy is the wolf, our only care in safe keeping our flock: instead of courtly ditties we spend the days with country songs: our amorous conceits are homely thoughts: delighting as much to talk of Pan and his country pranks, as ladies to tell of Venus and her wanton toys. Our toil is in shifting the folds and looking to the lambs, easy labours: oft singing and telling tales, homely pleasures: our greatest wealth not to covet, our honour not to climb, our quiet not to care. Envy looketh not so low as shepherds: shepherds gaze not so high as ambition. We are rich in that we are poor with content, and proud only in this, that we have no cause to be proud.'

This witty answer of Fawnia so inflamed Dorastus' fancy, as he commended himself for making so good a choice, thinking if her birth were answerable to her wit and beauty, that she were a fit mate for the most famous prince in the world ⟨IV. iv. 576–82⟩. He, therefore, began to sift her more narrowly on this manner:

'Fawnia, I see thou art content with country labours, because thou knowest not courtly pleasures. I commend thy wit, and pity thy want; but wilt thou leave thy father's cottage and serve a courtly mistress?'

'Sir,' quoth she, 'beggars ought not to strive against fortune, nor to gaze after honour, lest either their fall be greater, or they become blind. I am born to toil for the court, not in the court, my nature unfit for their nurture: better live, then, in mean degree than in high disdain.'

'Well said, Fawnia,' quoth Dorastus: 'I guess at thy thoughts; thou art in love with some country shepherd.'

'No, sir,' quoth she: 'shepherds cannot love that are so simple, and maids may not love that are so young.'

'Nay, therefore,' quoth Dorastus, 'maids must love because they are young; for Cupid is a child, and Venus, though old, is painted with fresh colours.'

'I grant,' *said* [quoth] she, 'age may be painted with new shadows, and youth may have imperfect affections; but what art concealeth in one ignorance revealeth in the other.' Dorastus, seeing Fawnia held him so hard, thought it was vain so long to beat about the bush; therefore he thought to have given her a fresh charge, but he was so prevented by certain of his men, who, missing their master, came *posting* [puffing] to seek him, seeing that he was gone forth all alone: yet, before they drew so nigh that they might hear their talk, he used these speeches:

'Why, Fawnia, perhaps I love thee, and then thou must needs yield, for thou knowest I can command and constrain.' 'Truth, sir,' quoth she, 'but not to love; for constrained love is force, not love: and know this, sir, mine honesty is such, as I had rather die than be a concubine, even *un*to a king, and my birth is so base as I am unfit to be a wife to a poor farmer.' 'Why then,' quoth he, 'thou canst not love Dorastus.' 'Yes,' said Fawnia, 'when Dorastus becomes a shepherd.' And with that the presence of his men broke off their parle, so that he went with them to the palace and left Fawnia sitting still on the hill side, who, seeing that the night drew on, shifted her folds, and busied herself about other work to drive away such fond fancies as began to trouble her brain. But all this could not prevail; for the beauty of Dorastus had made such a deep impression in her heart, as it could not be worn out without cracking, so that she was forced to blame her own folly in this wise:

'Ah, Fawnia, why dost thou gaze against the sun, or catch at the wind? stars are to be looked at with the eye, not reached at with the hand: thoughts are to be measured by fortunes, not by desires; falls come not by sitting low, but by climbing too high. What then, shall all fear to fall because some hap to fall? No, luck cometh by lot, and fortune windeth those threads which the destinies spin. Thou art favoured, Fawnia, of a prince, and yet thou art so fond to reject desired favours: thou hast denial at thy tongue's end, and desire at thy heart's bottom; a woman's fault to spurn at that with her foot, which she greedily catcheth at with her hand. Thou lovest Dorastus, Fawnia, and yet seemest to lour. Take heed: if he retire thou wilt repent; for unless he love, thou canst but die. Die then, Fawnia, for Dorastus doth but jest: the lion never preyeth on the mouse, nor falcons stoop not to dead stales. Sit down then in sorrow, cease to love and content thyself that Dorastus will vouchsafe *for* to flatter Fawnia, though not to fancy Fawnia. Heigh ho! ah fool, it were seemlier for thee to whistle, as a shepherd, than to sigh as a lover.' And with that she ceased from these perplexed passions, tolding her sheep and hieing home to her poor cottage.

But such was the incessant sorrow of Dorastus to think on the wit and beauty of Fawnia, and to see how fond he was being a prince, and how froward she was being a beggar, *then* [that] he began to lose his wonted appetite, to look pale and wan; instead of mirth, to feed on melancholy, for courtly dances to use cold dumps: insomuch that not only his own men, but his father and all the court began to marvel at his sudden change, thinking that some lingering sickness had brought him into this state. Wherefore he caused physicians to come, but Dorastus neither would let them minister, nor so much as suffer them to see his urine; but remained still so oppressed with these passions, as he feared in himself a farther inconvenience. His honour wished him to cease from such folly, but love forced him to follow fancy. Yea, and in despite of honour, love won the conquest, so that his hot desires caused him to find new devices; for he presently made himself a shepherd's coat, that he might go unknown and with the less suspicion to prattle with Fawnia, and conveyed it secretly into a thick grove hard joining to the palace, whither, finding fit time and opportunity, he went all alone, and, putting off his princely apparel, got on those shepherd's robes, and, taking a great hook in his hand, which he had also gotten, he went very anciently to find out the mistress of his affection. But, as he went by the way, seeing himself clad in such unseemly rags, he began to smile at his own folly and to reprove his fondness in these terms.

'Well,' said Dorastus, 'thou keepest a right decorum—base desires and homely attires; thy thoughts are fit for none but a shepherd, and thy apparel such as only become[s] a shepherd. A strange change from a prince to a peasant! what, is it thy wretched fortune or thy wilful folly? Is it thy cursed destinies, or thy crooked desires, that appointeth thee this penance? Ah, Dorastus, thou canst but love; and, unless thou love, thou art like to perish for love. Yet, fond fool, choose flowers, not weeds; diamonds, not pebbles; ladies which may honour thee, not shepherds which may disgrace thee. Venus is painted in silks, not in rags; and Cupid treadeth on disdain when he reacheth at dignity. And yet, Dorastus, shame not at thy shepherd's weed. The heavenly gods have sometime earthly thoughts. Neptune became a ram, Jupiter a bull, Apollo a shepherd ⟨IV. iv. 25–30⟩: they gods, and yet in love; and thou a man appointed to love.'

Devising thus with himself, he drew nigh to the place where Fawnia was keeping her sheep, who casting her eye aside and seeing such a mannerly shepherd, perfectly *limmed* [limbed] and coming with so good a pace, she began half to forget Dorastus and to favour this pretty shepherd, whom she thought she might both love and obtain. But as she was in these thoughts, she perceived then it was the young prince Dorastus, wherefore she rose up and reverently saluted him. Dorastus, taking her by the hand, repaid her courtesy with a sweet kiss, and, praying her to sit down by him, he began thus to lay the battery:

'If thou marvel, Fawnia, at my strange attire, thou wouldest more muse at my unaccustomed thoughts: the one disgraceth but my outward shape, the other disturbeth my inward senses. I love, Fawnia, and, therefore, what love liketh I cannot mislike. Fawnia, thou hast promised to love, and I hope thou wilt perform no less. I have fulfilled thy request, and now thou canst but grant my desire. Thou wert content to love Dorastus, when he ceased to be a prince and to become a shepherd, and see I have made the change, and, therefore, not to miss of my choice.'

'Truth,' quoth Fawnia, 'but all that wear cowls are not monks: painted eagles are pictures, not eagles. Zeuxis' grapes were like grapes, yet shadows: rich clothing make not princes, nor homely attire beggars ⟨v. ii. 131–5⟩: shepherds are not called shepherds because they wear hooks and bags, but [that] they are born poor and live to keep sheep; so this attire hath not made Dorastus a shepherd, but to seem like a shepherd.'

'Well, Fawnia,' answered Dorastus, 'were I a shepherd, I could not but like thee, and, being a prince, I am forced to love thee. Take heed, Fawnia: be not proud of beauty's painting, for it is a flower that fadeth in the blossom. Those, which disdain in youth, are despised in age. Beauty's shadows are tricked up with time's colours, which, being set to dry in the sun, are stained with the sun, scarce pleasing the sight ere they begin not to be worth the sight; not much unlike the herb Ephemeron, which flourisheth in the morning and is withered before the sun setting. If my desire were against law, thou mightest justly deny me by reason; but I love thee, Fawnia, not to misuse thee as a concubine, but to use thee as my wife. I can promise no more, and mean to perform no less.'

Fawnia, hearing this solemn protestation of Dorastus, could no longer withstand the assault, but yielded up the fort in these friendly terms:

'Ah, Dorastus, I shame to express that thou forcest me with thy sugared speech to confess: my base birth causeth the one, and thy high dignities the other. Beggars' thoughts ought not to reach so far as kings, and yet my desires reach as high as princes. I dare not say, Dorastus, I love thee, because I am a shepherd; but the Gods know I have honoured Dorastus (pardon if I say amiss), yea, and loved Dorastus with such dutiful affection as Fawnia can perform, or Dorastus desire. I yield, not overcome with prayers but with love, resting Dorastus' handmaid, ready to obey his will, if no prejudice at all to his honour, nor to my credit.'

Dorastus, hearing this friendly conclusion of Fawnia, embraced her in his arms, swearing that neither distance, time, nor adverse fortune, should diminish his affection; but that, in despite of the destinies, he would remain loyal unto death. Having thus plight[ed] their troth each to other, seeing they could not have the full fruition of their love in Sicilia, for that Egistus' consent would never be granted to so mean a match, Dorastus determined, as soon as time and opportunity would give them leave, to provide a great mass of money and many rich and costly jewels for the easier carriage, and then to transport themselves and their treasure into Italy, where they should lead a contented life, until such time as either he could be reconciled to his father, or else by succession come to the kingdom. This device was greatly praised of Fawnia, for she feared if the king his father should but hear of the contract, that his fury would be such as no less than death would stand for payment. She, therefore, told him that delay bred danger; that many mishaps did fall out between the cup and the lip; and that, to avoid [d]anger, it were best with as much speed as might be to pass out of Sicilia, lest fortune might prevent their pretence with some new despite. Dorastus, whom love pricked forward with desire, promised to dispatch his affairs with as great haste as either time or opportunity would give him leave, and so, resting upon this point, after many embracings and sweet kisses, they departed.

Dorastus, having taken his leave of his best beloved Fawnia, went to the grove where he had his rich apparel, and there, uncasing himself as secretly as might be, hiding up his shepherd's attire till occasion should serve again to use it, he went to the palace, shewing by his merry countenance that either the state of his body was amended, or the case of his mind greatly redressed. Fawnia, poor soul, was no less joyful, that, being a shepherd, fortune had favoured her so as to reward her with the love of a prince, hoping in time to be advanced from the daughter of a poor farmer to be the wife of a rich king; so that she thought every hour a year, till by their departure they might prevent danger, not ceasing still to go every day to her sheep, not so much for the care of her flock, as for the desire she had to see her love and lord, Dorastus, who oftentimes, when opportunity would serve, repaired thither to feed his fancy with the sweet content of Fawnia's presence. And although he never went to visit her but in his shepherd's rags, yet his oft repair made him not only suspected, but known to divers of their neighbours; who, for the good will they bare to old Porrus, told him secretly of the matter, wishing him to keep his daughter at home, lest she went so oft to the field that she brought him home a young son, for they feared that Fawnia, being so beautiful, the young prince would allure her to folly. Porrus was stricken into a dump at these news, so that, thanking his neighbours for their good will, he hied him home to his wife, and calling her aside, wringing his hands and shedding forth tears, he brake the matter to her in these terms:

'I am afraid, wife, that my daughter hath made herself so fine, that she will buy repentance too dear. I hear news, which, if they be true, some will wish they had not proved true. It is told me by my neighbours that Dorastus, the king's son, begins to look at our daughter Fawnia; which, if it be so, I will not give her a halfpenny for her honesty at the year's end. I tell thee, wife, nowadays beauty is a great stale to trap young men, and fair words and sweet promises are two great enemies to a maiden's honesty; and thou knowest, where poor men entreat and cannot obtain, there princes may command and will obtain. Though kings' sons dance in nets, they may not be seen; but poor men's faults are spied at a little hole. Well, it is a hard case where kings' lusts are laws, and that they should bind poor men to that which they themselves wilfully break.'

'Peace, husband,' quoth his wife, 'take heed what you say: speak no more than you should, lest you hear what you would not: great streams are to be stopped by sleight, not by force, and princes to be persuaded by submission, not by rigour. Do what you can, but no more than you may, lest in saving Fawnia's maidenhead you lose your own head. Take heed, I say: it is ill jesting with edged tools, and bad sporting with kings. The wolf had his skin pulled over his ears for but looking into the lion's den.' 'Tush, wife,' quoth he, 'thou speakest like a fool: if the king should know that Dorastus had begotten our daughter with child, as I fear it will fall out little better, the king's fury would be such as, no doubt, we should both lose our goods and lives. Necessity, therefore, hath no law, and I will prevent this mischief with a new device that is come in my head, which shall neither offend the king nor displease Dorastus. I mean to take the chain and the jewels that I found with Fawnia, and carry them to the king, letting him then to understand how she is none of my daughter, but that I found her beaten up with the water, alone in a little boat, wrapped in a rich mantle ⟨v. ii. 33⟩, wherein was inclosed this treasure. By this means, I hope the king will take Fawnia into his service, and we, whatsoever chanceth, shall be blameless.' This device pleased the good wife very well, so that they determined, as soon as they might know the king at leisure, to make him privy to this case.

In the meantime, Dorastus was not slack in his affairs, but applied his matters with such diligence that he provided all things fit for their journey. Treasure and jewels he had gotten great store, thinking there was no better friend than money in a strange country: rich attire he had provided for Fawnia, and, because he could not bring the matter to pass without the help and advice of some one, he made an old servant of his, called Capnio, who had served him from his childhood, privy to his affairs; who, seeing no persuasions could prevail to divert him from his settled determination, gave his consent, and dealt so secretly in the cause that within short space he had gotten a ship ready for their passage. The mariners, seeing a fit gale of wind for their purpose, wished Capnio to make no delays, lest, if they pretermitted this good weather, they might stay long ere they had such a fair wind. Capnio, fearing that his negligence should hinder the journey, in the night time conveyed the trunks full of treasure into the ship, and by secret means let Fawnia understand that the next morning they meant to depart. She, upon this news, slept very little that night, but got *her* up very early, and went to her sheep, looking every minute when she should see Dorastus, who tarried not long for fear delay might breed danger ⟨IV. iv. 669⟩, but came as fast as he could gallop, and without any great circumstance took Fawnia up behind him, and rode to the haven where the ship lay, which was not three quarters of a mile distant from that place. He no sooner came there, but the mariners were ready with their cock-boat to set them aboard, where, being couched together in a cabin, they passed away the time in recounting their old loves, till their man Capnio *could* [should] come. Porrus, who had heard that this morning the king would go abroad to take the air, called in haste to his wife to bring him his holiday hose and his best jacket, that he might go, like an honest substantial man, to tell his tale. His wife, a good cleanly wench, brought him all things fit, and sponged him up very handsomely, giving him the chains and *the* jewels in a little box, which Porrus, for the more safety, put in his bosom. Having thus all his trinkets in a readiness, taking his staff in his hand he bade his wife kiss him for good luck, and so he went towards the palace. But, as he was going, fortune, who meant to shew him a little false play, prevented his purpose in this wise.

He met by chance in his way Capnio, who, trudging as fast as he could with a little coffer under his arm to the ship, and spying Porrus, whom he knew to be Fawnia's father, going towards the

palace, being a wily fellow, began to doubt the worst ⟨IV. iv.
670–86⟩, and, therefore, crossed him [by] the way, and asked him
whither he was going so early this morning? Porrus, who knew by
his face that he was one of the court, meaning simply, told him that
the king's son Dorastus dealt hardly with him, for he had but one
daughter who was a little beautiful, and that *his* [the] neighbours
told him the young prince had allured her to folly: he went, therefore, now to complain to the king how greatly he was abused.

Capnio, who straightway smelt the whole matter ⟨IV. iv. 642,
672⟩, began to soothe him in his talk, and said that Dorastus dealt
not like a prince to spoil any poor man's daughter in that sort: he,
therefore, would do the best for him he could, because he knew he
was an honest man. 'But,' quoth Capnio, 'you lose your labour in
going to the palace, for the king means this day to take the air of
the sea, and to go aboard of a ship that lies in the haven ⟨IV. iv.
761–4⟩. I am going before, you see, to provide all things in a readiness, and, if you will follow my counsel, turn back with me to the
haven, where I will set you in such a fit place as you may speak to
the king at your pleasure ⟨IV. iv. 797–9⟩.' Porrus, giving credit to
Capnio's smooth tale, gave him a thousand thanks for his friendly
advice and went with him to the haven, making all the way his
complaints of Dorastus, yet concealing secretly the chain and the
jewels. As soon as they were come to the sea side, the mariners, seeing Capnio, came a land with their cock-boat, who, still dissembling the matter, demanded of Porrus if he would go see the ship,
who, unwilling and fearing the worst, because he was not well acquainted with Capnio, made his excuse that he could not brook the
sea, therefore would not trouble him.

Capnio, seeing that by fair means he could not get him aboard,
commanded the mariners that by violence they should carry him
into the ship; who, like sturdy knaves, hoisted the poor shepherd
on their backs, and bearing him to the boat launched from the land
⟨V. ii. 115–16⟩.

Porrus, seeing himself so cunningly betrayed, durst not cry out,
for he saw it would not prevail, but began to entreat Capnio and
the mariners to be good to him, and to pity his estate: he was but
a poor man that lived by his labour. They, laughing to see the
shepherd so afraid, made as much haste as they could, and set him
aboard. Porrus was no sooner in the ship but he saw Dorastus walking with Fawnia; yet he scarce knew her, for she had attired herself
in rich apparel, which so increased her beauty that she resembled
rather an angel than a mortal creature.

Dorastus and Fawnia were half astonished to see the old shepherd, marvelling greatly what wind had brought him thither, till Capnio told *them* [him] all the whole discourse; how Porrus was going to make his complaint to the king ⟨v. ii. 115–16⟩, if by policy he had not prevented him ⟨iv. iv. 761–4⟩, and therefore now, sith he was aboard, for the avoiding of further danger it were best to carry him into Italy.

Dorastus praised greatly his man's device, and allowed of his counsel; but Fawnia, who still feared Porrus as her father, began to blush for shame, that by her means he should either incur danger or displeasure.

The old shepherd, hearing this hard sentence, that he should on such a sudden be carried from his wife, his country, and kinsfolk, into a foreign land amongst strangers, began with bitter tears to make his complaint, and on his knees to entreat Dorastus, that, pardoning his unadvised folly, he would give him leave to go home; swearing that he would keep all things as secret as they could wish. But these protestations could not prevail, although Fawnia entreated Dorastus very earnestly; but the mariners hoisting their mainsails weighed anchors and haled into the deep, where we leave them to the favour of the wind and seas, and return to Egistus.

Who, having appointed this day to hunt in one of his forests, called for his son Dorastus to go sport himself, because he saw that of late he began to lour; but his men made answer that he was gone abroad, none knew whither, except he were gone to the grove to walk all alone, as his custom was to do every day.

The king, willing to waken him out of his dumps, sent one of his men to go seek him, but in vain, for at last he returned, but find him he could not, so that the king went himself to go see the sport; where, passing away the day, returning at night from hunting, he asked for his son, but he could not be heard of, which drave the king into a great choler: whereupon most of his noblemen and other courtiers posted abroad to seek him, but they could not hear of him through all Sicilia, only they missed Capnio his man, which again made the king suspect that he was not gone far.

Two or three days being past and no news heard of Dorastus, Egistus began to fear that he was devoured with some wild beasts, and upon that made out a great troop of men to go seek him; who coasted through all the country, and searched in every dangerous and secret place, until at last they met with a fisherman that was sitting in a little covert hard by the sea side mending his nets, when Dorastus and Fawnia took shipping; who, being examined if he either knew or heard where the king's son was, without any secrecy at all revealed the whole matter, how he was sailed two days past, and had in his company his man Capnio, Porrus and his fair daughter Fawnia. This heavy news was presently carried to the king, who, half dead for sorrow, commanded Porrus' wife be to sent for. She, being come to the palace, after due examination, confessed that her neighbours had oft told her that the king's son was too familiar with Fawnia, her daughter; whereupon, her husband, fearing the worst, about two days past, hearing the king should go an hunting, rose early in the morning and went to make his complaint; but since she neither heard of him, nor saw him. Egistus, perceiving the woman's unfeigned simplicity, let her depart without incurring further displeasure, conceiving such secret grief for his son's reckless folly, that he had so forgotten his honour and parentage by so base a choice to dishonour his father and discredit himself, that with very care and thought he fell into a quartan fever, which was so unfit for his aged years and complexion, that he became so weak as the physicians would grant him no life.

But his son Dorastus little regarded either father, country, or kingdom in respect of his lady Fawnia; for fortune, smiling on [t]his young novice, *let* [lent] him so lucky a gale of wind for the space of a day and a night, that the mariners lay and slept upon the hatches; but, on the next morning, about the break of *the* day the air began to overcast, the winds to rise, the seas to swell, yea, presently there arose such a fearful tempest ⟨v. ii. 119–21⟩, as the ship was in danger to be swallowed up with every sea, the mainmast with the violence of the wind was thrown overboard, the sails were torn, the tackling[s] went in sunder, the storm raging still so furiously that poor Fawnia was almost dead for fear, but that she was greatly comforted with the presence of Dorastus. The tempest continued three days, all which time the mariners every minute looked for death, and the air was so darkened with clouds that the master could not tell by his compass in what coast they were. But upon the fourth day, about ten of the clock, the wind began to cease, the sea to wax calm, and the sky to be clear, and the mariners descried the coast of Bohemia, shooting of [f] their ordnance for joy that they had escaped such a fearful tempest.

Dorastus, hearing that they were arrived at some harbour, sweetly kissed Fawnia, and bade her be of good cheer: when they told him that the port belonged unto the chief city of Bohemia, where Pandosto kept his court, Dorastus began to be sad, knowing that his father hated no man so much as Pandosto, and that the king himself had sought secretly to betray Egistus: this considered, he was half afraid to go on land, but that Capnio counselled him to change his name and his country, until such time as they could get

some other bark to transport them into Italy. Dorastus, liking this
device, made his case privy to the mariners, rewarding them boun-
tifully for their pains, and charging them to say that he was a gentleman of Trapolonia called Meleagrus. The shipmen, willing to shew
what friendship they could to Dorastus, promised to be as secret as
they could, or he might wish; and upon this they landed in a little
village a mile distant from the city, where, after they had rested a
day, thinking to make provision for their marriage, the fame of
Fawnia's beauty was spread throughout all the city, so that [it]
came to the ear[s] of Pandosto ⟨v. i. 94–5⟩; who, then being about
the age of fifty, had, notwithstanding, young and fresh affections
⟨v. i. 222–4⟩, so that he desired greatly to see Fawnia; and, to bring
this matter the better to pass, hearing they had but one man, and
how they rested at a very homely house, he caused them to be ap-
prehended as spies, and sent a dozen of his guard to take them:
who, being come to their lodging, told them the king's message.
Dorastus, no whit dismayed, accompanied with Fawnia and Capnio, went to the court (for they left Porrus to keep the stuff), who,
being admitted to the king's presence, Dorastus and Fawnia with
humble obeisance saluted his majesty.

Pandosto, amazed at the singular perfection of Fawnia, stood
half astonished, viewing her beauty, so that he had almost forgot
himself what he had to do: at last, with stern countenance he demanded their names, and of what country they were, and what
caused them to land in Bohemia. 'Sir,' quoth Dorastus, 'know that
my name Meleagrus is, a knight born and brought up in Trapolonia, and this gentlewoman, whom I mean to take to my wife, is
an Italian, born in Padua, from whence I have now brought her
⟨v. i. 156–60⟩. The cause I have so small a train ⟨v. i. 162–3⟩
with me is for that, her friends unwilling to consent, I intended
secretly to convey her into Trapolonia; whither, as I was sailing,
by distress of weather I was driven into these coasts: thus, have
you heard my name, my country, and the cause of my voyage.'
Pandosto, starting from his seat as one in choler, made this rough
reply:

'Meleagrus, I fear this smooth tale hath but small truth, and that
thou coverest a foul skin with fair paintings. No doubt, this lady by
her grace and beauty is of *hier* (=higher) [her] degree more meet
for a mighty prince than for a simple knight, and thou, like a perjured traitor, hath bereft her of her parents, to their present grief
and her ensuing sorrow. Till, therefore, I hear more of her parentage and of thy calling I will stay you both here in Bohemia.'

Dorastus, in whom rested nothing but kingly valour, was not

able to suffer the reproaches of Pandosto, but that he made him this answer:

'It is not meet for a king, without due proof, to appeach any man of ill behaviour, nor, upon suspicion, to infer belief: strangers ought to be entertained with courtesy, not to be entreated with cruelty, lest, being forced by want to put up injuries, the gods revenge their cause with rigour.'

Pandosto, hearing Dorastus utter these words, commanded that he should straight be committed to prison, until such time as they heard further of his pleasure; but, as for Fawnia, he charged that she should be entertained in the court with such courtesy as belonged to a stranger and her calling. The rest of the shipmen he put into the dungeon.

Having, thus, hardly handled the supposed Trapolonians, Pandosto, contrary to his aged years, began to be somewhat tickled with the beauty of Fawnia ⟨v. i. 222–4⟩, insomuch that he could take no rest, but cast in his old head a thousand new devices: at last, he fell into these thoughts:

'How art thou pestered, Pandosto, with fresh affections, and unfit fancies, wishing to possess with an unwilling mind and a hot desire, troubled with a cold disdain! shall thy mind yield in age to that thou hast resisted in youth? Peace, Pandosto: blab not out that which thou mayest be ashamed to reveal to thyself. Ah, Fawnia is beautiful, and it is [not] for thine honour, fond fool, to name her that is thy captive, and another man's concubine. Alas, I reach at that with my hand which my heart would fain refuse; playing like the bird Ibis in Egypt, which hateth serpents, yet feedeth on *her* [their] eggs. Tush, hot desires turn oftentimes to cold disdain: love is brittle, where appetite, not reason, bears the sway: king's thoughts ought not to climb so high as the heavens, but to look no lower than honour: better it is to peck at the stars with the young eagles, than to prey on dead carcasses with the vulture: tis more honourable for Pandosto to die by concealing love, than to enjoy such unfit love. Doth Pandosto then love? Yea! Whom? A maid unknown, yea, and perhaps immodest, straggled out of her own country: beautiful, but not therefore chaste; comely in body, but perhaps crooked in mind. Cease then, Pandosto, to look at Fawnia, much less to love her: be not overtaken with a woman's beauty, whose eyes are framed by art to enamour, whose heart is framed by nature to enchant, whose false tears know their true times, and whose sweet words pierce deeper than sharp swords.'

Here Pandosto [ceased] from his talk, but not from his love: for, although he sought by reason and wisdom to suppress this frantic

affection, yet he could take no rest, the beauty of Fawnia had made
such a deep impression in his heart. But, on a day, walking abroad
into a park which was hard adjoining to his house, he sent by one
of his servants for Fawnia, unto whom he uttered these words:

'Fawnia, I commend thy beauty and wit, and now pity thy distress and want; but, if thou wilt forsake Sir Meleagrus, whose
poverty, though a knight, is not able to maintain an estate answerable to thy beauty, and yield thy consent to Pandosto, I will both
increase thee with dignities and riches.' 'No, sir,' answered Fawnia;
'Meleagrus is a knight that hath won me by love, and none but he
shall wear me ⟨I. ii. 307⟩: his sinister mischance shall not diminish
my affection, but rather increase my good will: think not, though
your grace hath imprisoned him without cause, that fear shall make
me yield my consent: I had rather be Meleagrus' wife and a beggar
than live in plenty and be Pandosto's concubine.' Pandosto, hearing the assured answer of Fawnia, would, notwithstanding, prose-
cute his suit to the uttermost, seeking with fair words and great
promises to scale the fort of her chastity, swearing that if she would
grant to his desire Meleagrus should not only be set at liberty, but
honoured in his court amongst his nobles. But these alluring baits
could not entice her mind from the love of her new betrothed mate
Meleagrus; which Pandosto seeing, he left her alone for that time
to consider more of the demand. Fawnia, being alone by herself,
began to enter into these solitary meditations:

'Ah, unfortunate Fawnia! thou seest to desire above fortune is to
strive against the gods and fortune. Who gazeth at the sun weaken-
eth his sight: they, which stare at the sky, fall oft into deep pits:
haddest thou rested content to have been a shepherd, thou needest
not to have feared mischance: better had it been for thee by sitting
low to have had quiet, than by climbing high to have fallen into
misery ⟨IV. iv. 446–9; v. i. 206⟩. But alas, I fear not mine own
danger, but Dorastus' displeasure. Ah, sweet Dorastus, thou art a
prince, but now a prisoner, by too much love procuring thine own
loss: haddest thou not loved Fawnia thou hadst been fortunate:
shall I then be false to him that hath forsaken kingdoms for my
cause? no: would my death might deliver him, so mine honour
might be preserved!' With that, fetching a deep sigh, she ceased
from her complaints, and went again to the palace, enjoying a
liberty without content, and proffered pleasure with small joy. But
poor Dorastus lay all this while in close prison, being pinched with
a hard restraint, and pained with the burden of cold and heavy
irons, sorrowing sometimes that his fond affection had procured
him this mishap, that by the disobedience of his parents he had

wrought his own despite: another while cursing the gods and fortune that they should cross him with such sinister chance, uttering
at last his passions in these words:

'Ah, unfortunate wretch! born to mishap, now thy folly hath his
desert: art thou not worthy for thy base mind to have bad fortune?
could the destinies favour thee, which hast forgot thine honour and
dignities? will not the gods plague him *with* [in] despite, that pain-
eth his father with disobedience? Oh, gods! if any favour or justice
be left, plague me, but favour poor Fawnia, and shroud her from
the tyrannies of wretched Pandosto; but let my death free her from
mishap, and then welcome death.' Dorastus, pained with these
heavy passions, sorrowed and sighed, but in vain, for which he used
the more patience. But again to Pandosto, who, broiling at the heat
of unlawful lust, could take no rest, but still felt his mind disquieted
with his new love, so that his nobles and subjects marvelled greatly
at this sudden alteration, not being able to conjecture the cause of
this his continued care. Pandosto, thinking every hour a year till
he had talked once again with Fawnia, sent for her secretly into his
chamber, whither though Fawnia unwillingly coming, Pandosto
entertained her very courteously, using these familiar speeches,
which Fawnia answered as shortly in this wise.

Pandosto.

'Fawnia, are you become less wilful and more wise to prefer
the love of a king before the liking of a poor knight? I think, ere
this, you think it is better to be favoured of a king than of a subject.'

Fawnia.

'Pandosto, the body is subject to victories, but the mind not to
be subdued by conquest ⟨IV. iv. 576–8⟩: honesty is to be preferred
before honour; and a dram of faith weigheth down a ton of gold.
I have promised to Meleagrus to love, and will perform no less.'

Pandosto.

'Fawnia, I know thou art not so unwise in thy choice as to refuse
the offer of a king, nor so ungrateful as to despise a good turn. Thou
art now in that place where I may command, and yet thou seest I
entreat: my power is such as I may compel by force, and yet I sue
by prayers. Yield, Fawnia, thy love to him which burneth in thy
love: Meleagrus shall be set free, thy countrymen discharged, and
thou both loved and honoured.'

Fawnia.

'I see, Pandosto, where lust ruleth it is a miserable thing to be a virgin; but know this, that I will always prefer fame before life, and rather choose death than dishonour ⟨III. ii. 42–5⟩.'

Pandosto, seeing that there was in Fawnia a determinate courage to love Meleagrus, and a resolution without fear to hate him, *fleeing* [flung] away from her in a rage, swearing, if in short time she would not be won *by* [with] reason, he would forget all courtesy, and compel her to grant by rigour: but these threatening words no whit dismayed Fawnia, but that she still both despited and despised Pandosto.

While thus these two lovers strove, the one to win love, the other to live in hate, Egistus heard certain news by merchants of Bohemia, that his son Dorastus was imprisoned by Pandosto, which made him fear greatly that his son should be but hardly entreated: yet, considering that Bellaria and he was cleared by the Oracle of Apollo from that crime wherewith Pandosto had unjustly charged them, he thought best to send with all speed to Pandosto, that he should set free his son Dorastus, and put to death Fawnia and her father Porrus. Finding this by the advice of counsel the speediest remedy to release his son, he caused presently two of his ships to be rigged, and thoroughly furnished with provision of men and victuals, and sent divers of his nobles ambassadors into Bohemia; who, willing to obey their king and receive their young prince, made no delays for fear of danger, but with as much speed as might be, sailed towards Bohemia. The wind and seas favoured them greatly, which made them hope of some good hap, for within three days they were landed; which Pandosto no sooner heard of their arrival, but he in person went to meet them ⟨V. i. 231⟩, entreating them with such sumptuous and familiar courtesy, that they might well perceive how sorry he was for the former injuries he had offered to their king, and how willing, if it might be, to make amends.

As Pandosto made report to them, how one Meleagrus, a knight of Trapolonia, was lately arrived with a lady, called Fawnia, in his land, coming very suspiciously, accompanied only with one servant and an old shepherd, the ambassadors perceived by the half, what the whole tale meant, and began to conjecture that it was Dorastus, who, for fear to be known, had changed his name; but, dissembling the matter, they shortly arrived at the court, where, after they had been very solemnly and sumptuously feasted, the noblemen of Sicilia being gathered together, they made report of their embassage, where they certified Pandosto that Meleagrus was son and heir to the king Egistus, and that his name was Dorastus; how, contrary to the king's mind, he had privily conveyed away that Fawnia, intending to marry her, being but daughter to that poor shepherd

Porrus: whereupon, the king's request was that Capnio, Fawnia, and Porrus might be murdered and put to death, and that his son Dorastus might be sent home in safety. Pandosto, having attentively and with great marvel heard their embassage, willing to reconcile himself to Egistus and to shew him how greatly he esteemed his *labour* [favour], although love and fancy forbade him to hurt Fawnia, yet in despite of love he determined to execute Egistus' will without mercy; and, therefore, he presently sent for Dorastus out of prison, who, marvelling at this unlooked-for courtesy, found at his coming to the king's presence that which he least doubted of, his father's ambassadors; who no sooner saw him, but with great reverence they honoured him, and Pandosto embracing Dorastus set him by him very lovingly in a chair of estate. Dorastus, ashamed that his folly was bewrayed, sate a long time as one in a muse, till Pandosto told him the sum of his father's embassage; which he had no sooner heard, but he was touched at the quick, for the cruel sentence that was pronounced against Fawnia. But neither could his sorrow nor [his] persuasions prevail, for Pandosto commanded that Fawnia, Porrus, and Capnio should be brought to his presence; who were no sooner come, but Pandosto, having his former love turned to a disdainful hate, began to rage against Fawnia in these terms:

'Thou disdainful vassal, thou currish kite ⟨iv. iii. 23⟩, assigned by the destinies to base fortune, and yet with an aspiring mind gazing after honour, how durst thou presume, being a beggar, to match with a prince? by thy alluring looks to enchant the son of a king ⟨iv. iv. 423–4, 435⟩ to leave his own country to fulfil thy disordinate lusts? O despiteful mind! a proud heart in a beggar is not unlike to a great fire in a small cottage, which warmeth not the house, but burneth it: assure thyself [that] thou shalt die. And thou, old doting fool, whose folly hath been such as to suffer thy daughter to reach above thy fortune, look for no other meed but the like punishment ⟨iv. iv. 421–3, 433⟩. But Capnio, thou which hast betrayed the king, and hast consented to the unlawful lust of thy lord and master, I know not how justly I may plague thee: death is too easy a punishment for thy falsehood, and to live (if not in extreme misery) were not to shew thee equity. I, therefore, award that thou shalt have thine eyes put out, and continually *till* [while] thou diest, grind in a mill like a brute beast.' The fear of death brought a sorrowful silence upon Fawnia and Capnio, but Porrus seeing no hope of life burst forth into these speeches:

'Pandosto, and ye noble ambassadors of Sicilia, seeing without cause I am condemned to die, I am yet glad I have opportunity to disburden my conscience before my death. I will tell you as much as I know, and yet no more than is true. Whereas I am accused that I have been a supporter of Fawnia's pride, and she disdained as a vile beggar, so it is, that I am neither father unto her, nor she daughter unto me. For so it happened, that I being a poor shepherd in Sicilia, living by keeping other men's flocks, one of my sheep straying down to the sea side, as I went to seek her, I saw a little boat driven upon the shore, wherein I found a babe of six days old, wrapped in a mantle of scarlet, having about the neck this chain ⟨III. iii. 119–21; v. ii. 33–4⟩. I, pitying the child and desirous of the treasure, carried it home ⟨III. iii. 122⟩ to my wife, who with great care nursed it up and set it to keep sheep. Here is the chain and the jewels, and this Fawnia is the child whom I found in the boat. What she is or of what parentage I know not, but this I am assured, that she is none of mine.'

Pandosto would scarce suffer him to tell out his tale but that he inquired the time of the year, the manner of the boat, and other circumstances; which when he found agreeing to his count, he suddenly leapt from his seat and kissed Fawnia, wetting her tender cheeks with his tears ⟨v. ii. 46–55⟩, and crying, 'My daughter Fawnia! ah sweet Fawnia! I am thy father, Fawnia.' This sudden passion of the king drave them all into a maze, especially Fawnia and Dorastus. But, when the king had breathed himself a while in this new joy, he rehearsed before the ambassadors the whole matter, how he had entreated his wife Bellaria for jealousy, and that this was the child, whom he [had] sent to float in the seas.

Fawnia was not more joyful that she had found such a father, than Dorastus was glad he should get such a wife. The ambassadors rejoiced that their young prince had made such a choice, that those kingdoms, which through enmity had long time been dissevered, should now through perpetual amity be united and reconciled. The citizens and subjects of Bohemia, hearing that the king had found again his daughter, which was supposed dead, joyful that there was an heir apparent to his kingdom, made bonfires ⟨v. ii. 22⟩ and shows throughout the city. The courtiers and knights appointed jousts and tourneys to signify their willing minds in gratifying the king's hap.

Eighteen days being past in these princely sports, Pandosto, willing to recompense old Porrus, of a shepherd made him a knight; which done, providing a sufficient navy to receive him and his retinue, accompanied with Dorastus, Fawnia, and the Sicilian ambassadors, he sailed towards Sicilia, where he was most princely entertained by Egistus; who, hearing this [most] comical event, rejoiced greatly at his son's good hap, and without delay (to the perpetual joy of the two young lovers) celebrated the marriage: which was no sooner ended, but Pandosto, calling to mind how first he betrayed his friend Egistus, how his jealousy was the cause of Bellaria's death, that contrary to the law of nature he had lusted after his own daughter, moved with these desperate thoughts, he fell into a melancholy fit, and, to close up the comedy with a tragical stratagem, he slew himself; whose death being many days bewailed of Fawnia, Dorastus, and his dear friend Egistus, Dorastus, taking his leave of his father, went with his wife and the dead corpse into Bohemia, where, after they were sumptuously entombed, Dorastus ended his days in contented quiet.

FINIS.